Diana Barsham is a cultural historian and biographer with a special interest in lives that combine the secular and the spiritual. She has published several books in this field including a ground-breaking study of Sir Arthur Conan Doyle and another on the Victorian women's movement and alternative spiritualities. Her interest in Mary Magdalene derives from her work at the University of New York in London where she taught courses on ancient culture and early Christianity. She currently lives in Provence where *The Touch of the Magdalene* is set and in Somerset where there are many churches dedicated to the saint.

This book is dedicated to my husband, Peter Hoye.

Diana Barsham

THE TOUCH OF
THE MAGDALENE

In the Writing of the Fourth Gospel

AUSTIN MACAULEY PUBLISHERS™

LONDON * CAMBRIDGE * NEW YORK * SHARJAH

A CIP catalogue record for this title is available from the British Library.

ISBN 9781788780728 (Paperback)
ISBN 9781788782395 (Hardback)
ISBN 9781788787505 (ePub e-book)

www.austinmacauley.com

First Published (2021)
Austin Macauley Publishers Ltd
25 Canada Square
Canary Wharf
London
E14 5LQ

Many incidents and individuals have contributed to the writing of this book. To five people, in particular, those who read and commented on the first version of it, I owe a special debt of gratitude. These are the novelists: Maggie Power who assured me it was readable, Revd Canon Graham Hendy who commented on the theology, Prof James Booth whose review of the first draft helped me to see the book as I should have written it and Prof Alec Ryrie whose understanding of Mary Magdalene's role in the incarnation has informed my own. Finally, thanks are due to Peter Hoye for the hours he has spent discussing with me both the Gospels and the formation of the early Christian church.

"Jesus saith unto her, Touch me not; for I am not yet ascended to my Father."

—The Gospel according to John[i], King James' Version

"...this is what defines our faith, the resurrection of the Lord Jesus Christ."

—St Augustine, Sermons[ii]

*

Preface

The resurrection of Jesus Christ on Easter Sunday, the third day after his crucifixion, is the founding event of the Christian religion and yet the event itself is, and always has been, a problematic one. Many who consider themselves Christians have difficulty knowing what to make of this last, great miracle in the earthly life of Jesus of Nazareth. Many of his disciples in 1st century Judea felt exactly the same.

Part at least of this difficulty can be traced to Mary Magdalene, the mysterious woman who, according to all four Gospels, was the first witness of the Resurrection, the *apostola apostalorum* who proclaimed the Risen Christ to the eleven remaining male disciples. According to three of these Gospels, the message she had been commissioned by Christ to deliver was not believed. No one considered her a reliable witness. It is only in the Gospel of John, the last of the four to be written, that her words are accepted without contradiction and confirmed by the appearance of Christ himself.

Like the message she brought, Mary Magdalene herself remains difficult to decipher. Her representation in the Gospels is fractured and partial. We are never allowed to see her clearly. We construct her instead from a series of hints and innuendos that reveal a woman who is both unconventional and controversial, defended by Christ but a cause of disagreement among his disciples and evangelists. Luke is especially disparaging, describing her as a woman from whom seven demons had to be exorcised, a number that suggests either mental instability or a personality a little larger than life.

Luke consistently underplays her significance and seeks to invalidate her testimony, substituting for her vision of the risen Christ one experienced by two men instead. His gospel prompts a number of awkward questions for which there is no straightforward answer. Is the demon-ridden Magdalene the same woman who, in a significantly late addition to John's Gospel, was taken in adultery and condemned to death by stoning? Was she also the sinful woman who, according to Luke, interrupted a respectable supper party to make an exhibition of herself by pouring expensive ointment over Christ's feet, before washing them with her tears and wiping them with her erotically luxuriant hair?

A further confusion of identity exists between Mary Magdalene and her opposite number, the quiet and scholarly Mary of Bethany, a woman also to be found at Christ's feet, but in this instance listening to his teaching rather than mopping up spillage on the floor. Clearly, neither of these versions of Mary found discipleship easy! This second, more self-possessed Mary also performs an act of anointing, but hers is no better received than the first. Her sinful waste of an expensive perfume serves as the immediate trigger for Judas' betrayal of his master, and Mary carries a share of responsibility for the tragedy about to unfold. The Gospel of John reiterates this point when Jesus, at Mary's entreaty, raises her brother Lazarus from the dead, a loving gesture that will cost Jesus his life.

John's Gospel is not the only one to include this incident. It is also mentioned in a fragment from a manuscript now known as *The Secret Gospel of Mark,* one of two fragments that, if genuine, testify to the existence of an earlier version of Mark's Gospel. This version apparently refers to esoteric initiation rituals for new disciples, a passage which led to the gospel's suppression as an incitement to heresy, not to mention other forms of deviancy.

There has been considerable debate about the validity of these fragments; some scholars regard them as a forgery. Either way, they provide a useful pointer to the distinctive and interesting relationship that exists between the Gospel of Mark, to which the apostle Peter is believed to have contributed, and the Gospel of John, the so-called 'Beloved disciple'. This relationship between the two gospels is one I have explored in the current book and made central to the identity of its chief male character, the scribe who, at different stages in his life, was employed to work on both of these texts.

The centuries-old controversy surrounding Mary Magdalene received a new lease of life with the accidental discovery in 1945 of the now famous 'Gnostic Gospels' at Nag Hammadi in Egypt. Her sensational representation in these Gospels as the intimate companion of Christ and his star pupil have helped to transform Mary Magdalene into a heroine of late 20th century Christianity, a transformation which reached a peak in *The Da Vinci Code.* In Dan Brown's best-selling novel, Mary Magdalene is revealed not just as the bride of Christ, but the mother of his bloodline too. As the supposed mother of Christ's child, Mary Magdalene's name remains one around which conspiracy theories continue to circulate. The suggestion is, of course, an appealing one, though it is a based on a fundamental misreading of John's Gospel. As *The Touch of the Magdalene* aims to make clear, the opening chapter of John's gospel proclaims itself concerned with an altogether different kind of birth, with "*children born not of natural descent, nor of human decision or a husband's will, but born of God.*"

While contemporary feminist and post-feminist scholarship and creative work has been at pains to rehabilitate the Magdalene and address the bias of negative representation that the early church seemed to encourage, we should, nonetheless, recognise Browne's narrative for what it is: just another stage in the development of a 2000-year-old legend. The history of this legend is itself a remarkable one as the image of the Magdalene changes dramatically – from prostitute to penitent, rich girl to recluse, and from sinner to scholar – depending on the different interest groups who, like the Dominican Friars, made use of her as their figurehead.

She eventually emerges in the twentieth century as a woman of strength and agency determined to fight the discrimination and self-interest of a blinkered and patriarchal church. After such a demanding career, the respectable marriage and motherhood finally awarded her in the twenty-first century must have come as something of a relief! Compelled to appear in the costume of each age, the Magdalene remains a complex and composite figure. We encounter her through conflicting images and representations: a historical figure according to all known gospels, but one who carries the accretions of two thousand years of scholarship and creative interpretation via sermons, songs, fiction, film, artworks and commercialised fantasy.

In my own view, we should neither minimise the controversy that has always surrounded the Magdalene; nor should we fail to recognise Christ's unfailing ability to incorporate and affirm the difference of perspective, action and understanding that she brought to his movement. These controversies contain vital issues for the formation of our own cultural understanding of the role of women and their relation to questions of spirituality and the divine. The Magdalene's relative exclusion from the formal liturgy of the church and from its liturgical practice has left congregations without a mediator more able than most to explain that combination of miracle and historicity that lie at the heart of Christianity. If the Virgin Mary is the pure silence at the inception of the Christian story, then Mary Magdalene is the voice that marks its culmination.

There is no need to apologise for a new book on the Magdalene. Though the facts of her life are few, one thing remains clear: in proclaiming the Risen Christ, she assumed, for as long as the gospel is preached, the task of keeping Christ alive. It is a task she continues to fulfil through the many books, films and artefacts devoted to her memory.

In *The Touch of the Magdalene*, I have tried to draw on as many of the legends associated with her as possible. Most important of these is the time-honoured belief that, after the Resurrection, she journeyed to Provence and spent the remainder of her life there. Creatively evolved, these legends help to constitute the identity of Magdalene; they are what she has become. An 'Everywoman' who encounters and embodies many forms of Christian experience, she is the essential representative of female spirituality and its dilemmas to the world.

In this book, we meet the Magdalene during the last phase of her life, a woman no longer young but still trying to process and understand the tumultuous events of her youth. The arrival of a stranger, who calls himself Marcus, alerts her to what has happened to the new church since she lost contact with it. After so long in the wilderness, Marcus finally offers her the chance to tell her own story and to break the self-imposed silence of nearly forty years. Hers is not an easy story to tell; it is fraught with trauma, guilt and self-mistrust. She is eventually persuaded that the Gospel of John will offer fresh insight into the life of Christ and a new interpretation of his resurrection, including her own contribution to it.

This is a book about the composition of that gospel, and the issues and incidents that make it so different from the other three. What interests me particularly here is the way in which oral testimony is transformed as it becomes incorporated and integrated into a written narrative. John's Gospel is full of dramatic moments and I have tried where possible to 'read back' from these to the Magdalene herself as she relives the story of her early life. Each of these incidents in John, retain, I believe, at least a touch of the Magdalene. The reader, meanwhile, is invited to take a journey in the opposite direction and to travel back from her story, as told here, to the Gospel of John with a fresh perspective on what is to be found there.

Mary Magdalene was simultaneously a real woman, a great spiritual identity and a legendary figure around whom centuries of fiction have accumulated. In choosing to write about her, I came to the conclusion that the writing itself needed to reflect these diverse traditions. What follows is a work of scholarship, one that adheres closely to the gospels, both canonical and gnostic, but wears, as a mark of the Magdalene's continuing independence from them, a carefully woven fictional dress. It is the often-neglected themes and scholarly puzzles surrounding her that have inspired this work and it should not be read primarily as a historical novel. I see it rather as 'a teaching story', one intended to help Christians and interested non-Christians alike to understand a little more about its chief subject, that of Christ's mysterious and apparently miraculous Resurrection.

I acknowledge a huge debt of gratitude to scholars of all kinds, whose work has informed and challenged my own thinking, and also to the many creative writers whose novels and pseudo-autobiographies on this subject I have read with such pleasure and stimulation. I have tried where possible to indicate these debts in footnotes, aimed at informing interested readers of the immense variety of scholarship that surrounds what still remains, even in this age of rampant secularism, one of the most meaningful stories in the history of the world. Mary Magdalene, who has worn so many different costumes, will, I hope, find herself at home in this diversity of discourses and in its combination of secular irreverence and unswerving faith.

The genesis of this book was a course I taught at NYU in London on early Christianity and the ancient world. The students came from across the globe and from a wide variety of cultural and religious backgrounds. Despite my enthusiasm for the subject, I was never able to persuade myself that I had done it full justice. One young woman in the class asked me once in genuine bewilderment: "Gee, Professor, how is it you got interested in all this old stuff?"

This book is my answer to that question.

Diana Barsham
Nether Stowey
Somerset
January 2021

*

13

"The true light that gives light to everyone was coming into the world…He came to that which was his own, but his own did not receive him. Yet to all who did receive him, to those who believed in his name, he gave the right to become children of God – children born not of natural descent, nor of human decision or a husband's will, but born of God."

—John 1: 9 – 13

*

Part 1
Angel from the Past

According to medieval legend, Mary Magdalene left Judea after the resurrection of Christ and travelled across the northern Mediterranean to Provence. There are many different versions of this legend. In some, she is described as sailing with members of her own family; in others, she travels with a small group of women or a mixed party of named apostles.

In one version only, the English version followed here, Mary Magdalene makes her journey alone.

Did she come to Provence to teach and evangelise the people of Southern Gaul, or to hide away from a treacherous, injurious and confusing world?

*

"Treasures are hidden in inconspicuous pots."[iii]

—The Gospel of Philip

*

AD 73, Méthamis, Provence

1.1   "Forgive Us Our Trespasses..."

"Aboon dabashmaya
nethkadash shamak..."[iv]

I remember the prayer that Yeshua taught us in the old tongue, the Aramaic we spoke with each other: but that life is over now. I have not spoken it to anyone for years. I say the words slowly to myself in the new tongue, the language I had to learn when I came here as a complete stranger, a woman from the boat, hardly knowing who I was anymore.

I tried to speak to them of who He was, I tried to teach my fellow travellers some of the things I had seen and known, miraculous things, but the words wouldn't come properly. They seemed as strange and out of place as I was. I found myself crying before I'd hardly said a word. What we shared with each other most was a terrible hunger and, at the same time, a terrible sickness: the sea's tossing overwhelmed us, turned us into little more than water ourselves.

15

Those were the times there was hardly anything left of us. We were empty. So, instead of teaching, I said the prayer. Daily bread was easy to ask for:

"Dona-nos mei nostre pan de cada jorn…"[v]

I got through a few lines, *"Give us this day our daily…"* And then I stumbled. My voice broke; my throat a snapped reed. I don't cry any longer. The tears have dried up now. But still, even at this distance in time, I stumble and falter. It is not the giving but the forgiving that takes away my words. It is still too much; too much to ask. Every day I try:

"Forgive us our…" Our what? *Nostres deutes*! Our debts, the things we take or borrow from other people? Our sinfulness then; our wrongdoing? Our trespass against the rights and boundaries of others?

Or is it against ourselves that we sin the most?

"Forgive us our sins, as we forgive those who…those who…"

But my heart fails me. Each day I repeat it to myself, though the stone is cold and hard on my knees and I never quite achieve what I pray for. At best, my concentration goes and I lose for a while my sense of other, older injuries. I pick up the thread and continue:

"Forgive us our sins…as we forgive those who…"

A sound like an echo, like the vibration of a bell. Someone is calling me. I am startled out of my meditation, the prayer words flying off into the shadows at the back of my cave, into the darkness where everything I value is kept.

There is a disturbance outside, a knock I do not recognise. I hear a man's voice raised in what sounds like a warning: my neighbour, Pons, a good man but melancholy, like all of us cave dwellers. He is shouting my name, banging on the wooden partition that separates our lives.

"Midons! Midons Marianne!"

"Qu'est-ce qui se passe?"

I stand up too quickly and in the clumsiness of so many of my movements these days, a half-empty cup clatters to the floor at my feet. *Age*! I think wearily, this dropping of things, this increased unwillingness to bend down and pick them up.

"Il y a un homme ici, midons, un étranger. Il vous cherche."
"A quelle nom?"
"Au nom de Marcus."

And so, it starts: A stranger asking questions in the village. An unfamiliar voice making me forget all over again the very things I have been trying to remember.

Beginnings bring their moment. We sense their angel. I peep through the slatted fence and see a face, tired and with the strained eyes of a traveller, but dark, strong-featured; attractively Jewish but with an unmistakably Greek sheen to his expression and posture. I recognise something, know at once what he had come for: this is not quarry business. He has come here to find me; come from a different world, a different life.

How do I know this? How do I know it for sure this time?

It is the resemblance in his face, as if another, internal one is inscribed beneath his features. A different identity is at work in him, one I have never forgotten. I know this for certain. My mind spins. Great currents of time go rushing and pulsing through me until I am back where I was, nearly forty years before.

Beginnings pin us to their moment. Endings release us; they bring their difficult, unwelcome freedom. I came from an ending I have spent the rest of my life trying to understand. Whatever it was that I was part of then, in that other life, this man was part of it too.

I move back into the shadows and stand there, hidden.

"Tell him to wait!"

I know a lot about endings, endings that empty you out like a bucket of water tossed across the flagstones. Life is a well, they say, filling and emptying. I was the water first, then the broom, endlessly sweeping the flagstones clean. Cleaning up after the ruptures in my life, mopping up the spillage.

This cave, this mountain village, is my well now. It is bone dry and empty most of the year. I have known safety in this. I have been contained.

The images form slowly as I try to assemble myself. They are the images I cherish, my closest companions. They give me the power to keep him waiting, to keep the world waiting if I chose! It is the weight in the scale of my life, this power I have now, to hold back, withhold myself. I, who was once so quick, so impulsive, so recklessly precipitate.

Pons will speak for me.

"You will have to wait!" I hear him say. *"She won't come at once."*

That particular ending, the one that has brought him here, was unlike all the other endings in my life. This one threw the baby out with the bathwater. It threw all the babies. The spillage spread everywhere. The water carried me away from everything I had known. Rivers and lakes and seas, a floodgate of dispersals, I crossed them all on that journey.

A traveller in tears: I see myself as I was then, nameless, bearing the joy of the world in the emptiness of my luggage.

There had been no goodbyes or ritual of farewell to ease the parting. No chance to plead, to protest, to argue or make a scene: just the rush, the multi-directional hurry, the lethal currents of fast running water. Something had begun happening. There was no saying then what it really was or where it would lead us.

When it started happening, that deathly event I dreaded, I had only one thought outside myself.

Felix! If only I could get in touch with Felix. Surely, he with his great power, for he was a legate then, soon to be a procurator, out across the lands into Syria, surely, he could put a stop to it all!

Old habits die hard. Judaea and Galilee had been Roman lands for longer than anyone could remember, for two hundred years or more. If you wanted something doing, you had to ask a Roman.

I was literally beside myself all of that day, aware of someone shouting, crying, running, someone I was attached to; the woman at my side I hardly recognised as myself. And then the darkness, the death in the air, the terrible black cloud of dirt and dust that suddenly engulfed us all and made breathing seem unnatural. The earth shook. It would not stop shaking.[vi] Someone told me the veil of the temple had been torn down, ripped in half. Ghosts wearing nothing stood in the street, wringing their hands, unable to remember who or where they were.

When it started happening, that ending, it brought nothing to a stand but was so full of pushing and pummelling, as one senseless necessity jostled against another. On and on it swept, that unstoppable darkness, out across the desert sands, out across the seas, out across the sun and beyond the stars. And then suddenly, the other thing, its opposite, a resistance, something that was there, standing against it, the Christ himself, alive again, as if one man alone could do that, hold up his hand and say to the breaking heart of time, *Stop! Arretez!* Against every chance, the panting and heaving stilled into silence, and we could hear his voice again.

"Peace! Peace! Shalom! Shalom! You do not understand. You do not understand at all. This is not the end; it is the beginning; the calm after the storm, the new birth I promised you!"

What manner of man was he? A man who spoke of birth in the midst of such carnage and betrayal! And I was to stay calm through everything, above all to keep breathing, to breathe deep and steady just as he had taught me. This was the real thing now; it wasn't a rehearsal.

Was it joy we experienced, a figure suddenly taking shape out of the darkness, moulding into his own features the swirling atoms of desert sand? Was it joy we were supposed to feel, was it recognition and deliverance, so soon after the annihilation of everything we had worked for? Had we misunderstood completely; the whole tragedy transformed in an instant into some harlequin masquerade? Speed, a mad speed, fiercer and faster than sirocco; suddenly switching course, become a different season, the dance of light on a spring morning, the sound of birdsong.

But by then, by the time it could settle in our minds, I had already gone. Everything was already behind me.

There was, after all, only a few minutes, a few hours, a few days to take it in, to grasp what was happening. I put out my hand to touch it, this new order, I felt its light on my face, but then it eluded me. My heart had burst open. Something – someone – stood inside it, taking a new shape, saying this is what you have cherished there for so long. It is gone now! Something came out of me! It was palpable, the sudden sliding out of me of a curious bundle of grief. A kind of birth pang!

Then I was in motion again, went as directed, met the other women standing in a huddle at the gate. I had got there earlier than they had; they were there waiting for me. They all knew by then that the tomb was empty, but they just stood rooted to the spot, terrified and shaking, clutching at my clothes, tugging my sleeve like the hands of the dead. "*No,*" they were saying, "*no, Magdalene, don't speak of it! We don't understand this. We don't know what is happening. It's safer not to. Someone else must…one of the men must…*"

The women understood enough to know that what we had seen would bring some unimaginable change, beyond our power to accommodate. Their instinct was fear: fear that what had happened was demonic, against nature, some spirit of evil that haunted places of damnation such as this. They knew it would cause trouble and bring danger in its wake.

Then Mary S spoke up. "Go!" She said. "Don't listen to them, Magdalene. Do as he told you. It's your task; he chose you to do this for him."

She knew a lot, the other Mary. More than I had thought.

I ran on ahead of them, aware I hadn't told them everything I'd seen, everything I'd been half prepared for. I was running for my life, like some Greek athlete bursting his heart to come pouring through the sunlight and into the mad elation of the victory roar. *I had seen him! He had spoken to me. Commissioned me! All would be well!* I burst in on the men where they were hiding, their faces sullen with anxiety. For a moment I stood on the threshold, gasping and laughing like a thing possessed, but I spoke as calmly and clearly as I could. "*The tomb is empty,*" I said. "*He's alive! I have seen him. He spoke to me. He told me to tell you…*"

Then felt the sudden sting of someone's palm against my face, as if I were hysterical and needed a sharp reality check. My cheek swelled and reddened. My tongue locked dry. I could have stayed silent then. I remember thinking, *So I have this choice!* and held back the spurt of tears. Standing as tall as I could, I glared at little Simon, then put my hand on his chest and pushed him out of my way, surprised at my own strength. James said, "What is all this, Magda?" So I turned to him instead and delivered my message. They all recoiled and started talking at once, a barrage of disbelief and hostility. "Don't listen to her. She's delusional. You know how she is! Remember how she—"

Then Mary S appeared at the door. She was his sister; they always treated her with respect. She put her arm round my shoulder, pulled the hair from my face. "Magda is speaking the truth. What she has told you is true."

Another pause. A shudder ran through all of us, like a great shock. That extraordinary lull, time switching its tracks as a camel will sometimes dig in its feet, halt, then lurch off unstoppably in some different direction. They pushed past me. When I caught up with them again, John was whistling between his teeth, Peter breathless and sweating, the others falling over themselves to get out of the way of this new juggernaut. I felt as if I had been seized by the shoulders and shaken with such force that my teeth chattered, but it was not joy I was feeling, it was not exaltation. It was more like wild panic, uncontrollable anxiety, intolerable suspense. We hardly knew ourselves.

"So what do we do now?"

They all thought he had been whistling in the dark, hopelessly out matched by the strength of his enemies. No one had believed him. What we had seen him suffer in those last hours had put it beyond all possibility. He was almost unrecognisable in his pain, his flesh torn and bleeding, his body twisted, his face a contorted mask.

John spoke first as if, as so often, he alone had some special insight. "I knew something like this was going to happen." He put his arms round me, whispered something comforting. He stroked my hair and gathered it back into its clasp again.

Thomas spun round on him. "What are you talking about, you fool?" he said. "There *is* nothing like this!"

And then I had, and ever after found it hard to forgive myself for having, a sudden crisis of confidence: all my strength, everything that had held me up over the past few days, suddenly collapsed inside me. I had been with him, I had watched it all, been with him through it all, given them his message but my mouth went desert dry. I trembled and shook, my body cold as ice. I felt as if I would never speak again. I sat down on the bench someone steered me towards. I was jittering and moaning like an idiot.

That moment of weakness decided my fate. Later that day, as soon as it got dark, I was hurried away to begin a journey I had never even thought of, let alone prepared for. I had a young man at my side, Joses, who had the directions; also a house servant who carried an old goatskin bag with a few of my clothes and hastily assembled belongings inside it. A cloak was round my face and they pressed it closer, to protect me, they said, against our enemies, those determined to quash the rumours, suppress the truth, the great good news that first morning had brought us.

"You must leave us for a while, Magda," James told me with his most serious expression. "We must get you to safety, immediately. It's too dangerous for you to stay. Dangerous for you, for all of us but most of all for him! News like this travels fast. After what you have said, they will arrest you, question you; break you down with torture. They will force you to say whatever they want, admit you were lying, that you are a crazy woman, deranged by grief. You must go into hiding, as far from here as possible."

Philip and Andrew, men I trusted, were at his shoulder, nodding seriously.

Then Peter stepped forward, his eyes narrow under swollen lids. "You must go, Magda. After what you've...seen. After what you've told us, there's no choice. And it is what he wanted, isn't it, John? He made us promise we would look after you; make sure you didn't get caught up in...the aftermath. I personally gave him my word. If what you say is true, and of course we believe you, you must be kept safe, hidden somewhere...until he..."

I looked from him to John. I remember both of their faces, John's still with its boyish beauty, Peter red-eyed and unpredictable. I saw the sense of what they were saying, of course I did. But I couldn't help noticing that they had seen it first, had seen it before I had, agreed it amongst themselves, decided what should happen. I was no longer Magda with my own part to play, I was no longer a woman with her own agency, but someone to be 'taken care of', kept out of harm's way. Perhaps I was touched by their concern; it had not always been like that. Something had taken over now; it lifted me clean out of time, like a fish hooked from the water.

"Leave it to us, Magda. We'll take it forward from here."

"But I..."

"We'll be in touch," they said. Peter pressed me to him for a moment, strong and warm as an ox and with that distinctive smell his body always had strangely intensified. "All's well, Magda. But remember: you've got to keep silent from now on. A wrong word could spell disaster. Everything you've told us, yes, we believe you, we know it for a...but you must keep calm; you must trust us from here. Just do what we tell you for once, hey!" He gives me a mock squeeze, as if we were friends.

"But who..."

"It's all been arranged, yes, Joseph had the instructions. He surely warned you, didn't he? He's not a man to trifle with, Magda. He has power and wealth and holdings across the empire, and above all, he's keen to help us now. Who knows how long that'll last? So do as he says, Magda. Joses will see you to the boat; he'll see you on board, you'll be ready to sail by nightfall tomorrow. The captain will take over from there. So make haste. No time to lose!"

It had all been arranged. I hadn't seen that before. I hadn't seen that I, too, would become part of the arrangements. As usual, nothing had been left to chance. Only this time I didn't know about it, I hadn't been told. I hadn't been consulted at all.

*

1.2   The Stranger Called Marcus

I stand back behind the sack curtain hung across the opening and look again at the stranger.

I am not mistaken. I see it in his face. He has come from that land across the Great Sea, and before I can speak with him, there is one other abyss that has to be crossed. I must summon up the ghost of the woman I used to be: young, beautiful perhaps, in the way men like, intelligent, erratic and with a subtle sense of her own power. I remember myself as a woman full of warmth and misgiving, living in the light of something far beyond her own understanding. A woman whose early past had been cancelled out, whose sins had been forgiven, a woman, as it turned out, with no shadow at all to cast into the future.

I was bound to him, strange and often distant as I knew him to be, by ties I never once thought of untying. I had known other men, far too many to remember with pleasure, but nothing I had learned from them explained why it was he had chosen me. I knew what they wanted but with Yeshua it was different. I did not know. I only knew he wanted me to be different, to be remade in some new image that he had of me, an image that came from his own mind. He wanted qualities I wasn't even aware that I possessed. And my money came in handy too.

Whatever the reason, he had chosen me to be his close companion, to love the ground he walked on, to study as best I could the ecstatic power in his spirit, the strict compulsion of his destiny. He had chosen me to watch him suffer a death of humiliating agony, to be plunged into a black pit of despair and then, as if nothing much out of the ordinary had happened, to meet him on the rebound, I heart-stricken, he reenergised by my grief, light-footing it out of the tomb.

He gave me a message to deliver; a message like myself that no one quite knew what to make of; a parcel with a hard core of controversy at its centre, a mystery impossible to decipher. A crucial stone had gone missing. In its place, there was pure golden fire.

"Set the world alight for me, Magda! But keep the stone. It is all I have to leave you."

He trusted me with a truth that no one wanted to hear from my lips, a message as dubious as I was myself. My hands clenched tight over a mystery. Two yellow butterflies flew upwards when I opened them.

He trusted me with that message. And so of course I believed it. His resurrection was my burial ground.

*

Still the stranger stands outside, patiently waiting. And still, I do not move. Now it is my time to be the one inside, the one about to emerge from the darkness, the one having to learn all over again what it is to breathe. I am waiting for the breath to return before I step forward into time again. Part of me is reluctant; part of me does not want to move at all. And yet it is not a matter of choice. It is a circle that must be closed.

I watch him as he waits, this man Marcus, drinking the spring water Pons has given him. My heart twists inside me. That is not how I waited. For months afterwards, for weeks and months and years, I waited, waited to hear something, some message that would give me back a little of myself. But nothing came. The waiting became a sickness, gnawing inside me. I tugged and wrestled and pulled against it as if it were – because it was – my own inner being I was struggling against, its strength and weakness equally matched, the contest unwinnable.

Will she come to me again, that young woman who believed she knew a man so intensely lovable he must have come, just as he told her he did, straight from God? He said it laughing sometimes, but mostly he was serious. He was a serious man. I wonder now that I dared speak to him at all, so unlike was he to the other men I had known, the powerful ones included. He had few of the trappings that power usually brings but you felt it nonetheless: that concentrated presence, the peculiar magnetism of his eyes and voice, the way he could draw people to himself, command attention.

There was something around him too, not just a retinue of people but something, a force, a power he could summon up when he needed to, something he could step back from as well, becoming almost invisible when he did. Many sensed this about him, but I have tried so often to define it that I have come to fear I am inventing the very thing I am trying to describe.

It was a space charged with some deep attraction; step inside it and it would pull you to him. His body, there at the centre, was only a small part of him. Sometimes he would suddenly be there, without your noticing, as if time itself was a veil that he could step through. When he became visible like that, fully visible, something would occur, one of his miracles; then he would step back, become for a time almost ordinary again.

I understood only a little of this at first. He was an enigma, that much was obvious but it never occurred to me to question what I was doing, caught up as I was in living the life of a woman, quick and clever but always at odds with herself, daring and damaged with only a brittle carapace, a mirror brass image, to protect her. I took risks with myself, went everywhere, belonged nowhere, felt only myself with him. He healed me of that brittle self, made himself part of me, showed me for the first time a love I wanted and could trust, it fixed itself inside me like a star. I learned how to sit still.

And so it is that we are taking our time now, she and I. There are three strangers here on this threshold and she, my younger self, is one of them. Soon enough I must step into the open; undergo this small drama of recognition.

If he wants to know what I remember most of that time, the answer is: I remember the absence, white, unending, thick as a wall and absolutely impenetrable. I remember the beginning that brought me here, the aloneness of it, my head bent down, staring into the dark waters as the boat tossed and scudded forward. I remember the churning depth below and my terror of being drowned in it.

"Look higher, Magda," Yeshua said to me once. *"Look into the stillness. Nail your eyes to the stars. See the light there, how it cries out in pain! That is the pain of its own brilliance."*

I didn't know what he was talking about then. I didn't understand how the stars could be hurt. I only knew his words had spun me into a whole new identity, not the self I knew but something more than that. Someone different.

"Look at me, Magda. Look right into my eyes. Who is it that you see there?"

Then he would laugh, his short, heart-stopping laugh that would break off so abruptly. Laugh at my astonished expression and the absurdity of our words. 'Lovers talk', you might call it, but it was not that. He was telling me, I think, not to take it too personally.

*

I move out of the cool shadows of my cave now, fixing my eyes on the place where this new stranger is standing, looking directly at his face. I want him to understand right from the start that I too have eyes that can pierce, eyes that can see through him, can see his place in the pattern, even if I have never met him before.

He is younger than I am, perhaps, but only a little. We belong to the same generation. We have experience in common.

Neither of us moves for a moment. I take a step forward, then stand completely still. He pushes himself lightly away from the tree he is leaning against and moves towards me, his shoulders and head ducked slightly, a supplicant but somehow quite at his ease.

"Marianne?" he says. "Midons Marianne? I am looking for someone who once had a name very like yours. It is so important that I find her. I have come a long way."

I bow my head slightly, to avoid recognition but also, if he wants to take it that way, to give assent.

"I am Marcus," he says. "If you are who I think you may be, we have much to speak of, many things in common. We once inhabited the same part of the world, a place you will not have forgotten, though it is many years ago and a long way from here. When you know what it is that we have shared, you will not fear me, Madame Marianne. You will trust me instead. I have looked for you a long time. I have come from Judea, from Alexandria, from Ephesus; places you will have heard of, no doubt, important places, Rome itself, I should add, though I do not say that to frighten you. I should have sent you a letter, shouldn't I, explaining who I am and why I have come? But I wasn't sure if you could even…whether a letter, if it found you, would be the best way of explaining all the things you need to know."

Still I do not speak. The years have eaten away my voice. I feel myself swaying slightly and put up a hand against the wooden doorpost to stay still.

He moves a step closer. "I must know if you are the one I've been looking for, the one who…"

"Yes," I say. We speak and move as if performing some secret ritual.

He scuffs the dirt beneath his feet, draws a sign with the toe of his sandal.

I nod and he erases it at once.

"Secrecy is still necessary, more necessary than ever," he says. "Even in these remote villages. You will understand that. You have made such a secret of yourself. I want to talk to you, Madame Marianne, but I should have found some way to let you know I was coming, I should have sent you some warning, but I didn't know how I would find you or if you would even see me. I wasn't even sure you were still alive; let alone what kind of welcome to expect. Forgive me for taking you by surprise like this. I have many things to tell you. Things I am sure you will want to hear."

"It is no surprise." I tear a blister off my tongue to get these words spoken. "I too have waited many years."

I feel the woman inside me start weeping at this, but I am her angel, stronger than she is, and I do not give way. *Why has he come?* I am asking myself. *Why now? What has happened? What does he want of me?*

"And," I cannot stop my angel from adding, "you need not have worried. I can read and write in three languages."[vii]

He laughs, unashamed of his mistake. "You have not been idle then! I heard you had many skills. But time has changed all of us in ways we could never have imagined. We live in a new age, Madame Marianne! Or Miriam, should I say? We are no longer the people we were. You no doubt remember us as we were back then, so broken and disorganised. But events have changed all that. Prophecies have been fulfilled. History has been on our side.

"Do you, I wonder, get any news of us, hidden away up here in these mountains? News travels everywhere across the empire and the Way we follow is undoubtedly news. The Romans like this province, don't they? *The Province*, I've heard it's called. They have their villas here by choice, so word must reach you occasionally, a whisper at least of what happened in—"

But it is too soon to go there. I cut him off before he can name the city.

"There are no Roman villas here, Marcus, but yes, I have heard things. There are quarries nearby, big stone and plaster works, and the quarries are full of slaves; renegades, prisoners of war, unlucky ones of every sort. They come from all over the empire and they have their own network, their own type of news. There's river transport in the valley here and a town not far away, Veisoun, an important place, with theatres and baths and shops and a large market near the forum. News of every kind travels there. I go and I listen, sometimes, maybe twice a year, when I have things for the market."

"You are a working woman then, Madame Marianne. You handle the clay?"

"That, and other things too: brooms and baskets occasionally, but mostly jars, boxes, small containers of different kinds. As for the perfumes themselves, the herbs that grow here are better, lighter and sweeter than those in Judea and Samaria. The Veisoun ladies like them."

"I heard a rumour on my way; someone said the woman I was looking for had connections in the cloth trade."

I look at him warily. Cloth workers have a special reputation in these parts, not bad exactly but the kind the authorities like to keep an eye on. "I do occasional work of that sort, but it is private work. I do not advertise."

Shrouds, winding sheets, burial clothes.

I stand squarely across the entrance to my cave. I want him to know he is not to be invited inside.

"Forgive me," he says, his whole frame sagging suddenly as if something had defeated him. "I've come all this way and I still don't know what to say to you. I am not here to pry into your livelihood or how you chose to live."

We are both aware of Pons watching us from a not too discreet distance. The stranger sighs, letting me hear his weariness.

"I should go back to the village. I'm in need of food, rest, and a few hours' sleep. I hope you'll let me come back so we can talk further, when the shock of our meeting has worn off. Please believe me: I mean no harm to you, only good."

I watch him walk away; his broad shoulders do not suggest a man easily deflected. As for the shock, it is all my own. I stand at my door composed enough but trembling violently inside.

Shock is a shelter I am familiar with. It gathers around you for a while, protective, slightly deafening, as if all the noises of the world have been muted. My cave lodged above the river here is another form of shelter. I sense neither will be adequate much longer. I don't know what this man knows of my past, how much he has been told. Only the great mountain at my back still stands its ground, its silence unbreakable, the equal of anything.

As I watch him head to the village, I unclench my hand and study it closely. There, in the middle of the palm, a declivity, a sudden break in the lifeline, a white void stretching across it.

Another of my skills, my secret livelihood: I can see illness in the hand; I can see where the knots and tensions cause difficulty. And I understand better than most the twisted paths that life can take, and how those errors trace their histories into the palm.

Before he comes back, before I speak to him again, I must summon her up once again, that girl, that woman who took the catastrophic path I see in mine. Even though she does not live here now, even though she has never lived here, even though she vanished like a ghost, I must recall her before he returns, recall who she was at the start and who she became afterwards when she too was part of the Way and Yeshua's close companion.

I have to remind myself of the secrets she had, things never to be spoken of to anyone. This secrecy has bound me tight for years. If I peel off those layers of silence, yellow with time, what will I find inside? A shrivelled corpse, collapsing into dust as the sunlight touches it, or is it a still-living thing, kept close and magically alive in its beautiful robes? Is that far-off time still alive in me somewhere or has it decomposed, rotted into nothingness and disillusion?

To hear myself speak again of the secrets that were his as well as mine, will that prove a healing miracle or a plunge back into suffering, the embrace of some ultimate folly?

*

1.3 Galilee, AD 27: Magda's Story

Magda was my name. It was what he and the others always called me, the name I came to know myself by. I was one of the lucky ones. Most of the women in the group simply got called 'Mary'. *A safety precaution*, they said, *to protect us*, but I think it was mainly to save the men the trouble of having to remember each of us individually. They saw us as men tend to, as a category, a collective, a group of not-men. But I gave them money at the start, nearly everything I had, and that made the difference. My wealth gave me identity.

Joanna was the same. She gave more than I did; wherever it came from, she gave more and for longer. Someone was funding her to do so but no one questioned her too closely about it. "My husband," she used to say vaguely, "so busy with other affairs! He likes me to be…well informed about the region, the needs of the people. Obviously, I am here to learn, to learn and to follow."[viii]

Money. That was the unspoken thing. I have learned at last to respect it: that godlike power that was his greatest rival. Hard coin. Towards the end, things got very difficult. The money started to run out. *"But what will we live on?"* the new disciples used to ask. *"If we give up all our goods, as you tell us to, what will we eat, Master?"* When he told them in one of his strange voices that, if all else failed, they would have to start eating him, they stopped liking what they heard. People fell away. A kind of desperation took hold of us. The stakes got higher. He decided to return to Jerusalem.

I have a memory of that second return, a mixed memory, one I don't want to recall. It was winter, just after the reconciliation with my sister. I had returned to her house after years of estrangement, and knew I was there under sufferance. The very first time he broke bread for us in that special way, and gave us the cup of wine, he told us it was his own blood we were drinking. I was so shocked that I burst out laughing. My sister was furious. She sent me out of the room, saying I was too giddy to be allowed to join in the ceremony again. I sat by myself in the back room, still rocking with laughing, great snorts of it still seizing me for a while, and then my mood changed. I got a hold of myself; saw that my laughter, though caused by the shock of his words, had been altogether out of place. I had been rude and wrong.

He came out soon afterwards and when he appeared in the doorway and stood there looking at me, I said, "I'm so sorry, that was wrong of me, wasn't it, to laugh when I did?" He said nothing, his expression serious, puzzled. I hurried on, "It's just that…what you said, about yourself, about eating…it sounded so…funny!" My lips started twitching again so I bit the bottom one hard, then had a curious sensation: part of me wanted to fill with laughter again but another part was wrung with tears.

To my astonishment, he came towards me, not angry like my sister: almost pitying instead.

"You have a gift for laughter, Magda," he said, his grey eyes intent as an eagle's. *"Not an easy thing to have the dead always with you like that. It is a gift you will need. One day it will take you laughing into heaven."*[ix]

I thought of my little brother when he said that. He had died so young, before my first marriage, but he still came to me sometimes. He was not entirely gone. Perhaps he nudged me now.

"I do like you, Rabboni. Honestly, I do! I don't understand my own laughter. But I like you so very much."

'*That too*,' he said. And kissed me as his pupil for the first time.

*

We had a whole string of beginnings. They came and went. There would be long periods in between while we were something else to each other. Then it would start up again. The kisses were where we met; a line of little crosses that marked our journey together.

*

I came to understand the ceremony of the bread and wine after that and I never laughed again. I came to see, after that incident, how we could live on the extraordinary hope and happiness that Yeshua brought to us all. His presence was like being fed, deeply, down in the very depth of the soul; a food that made us doubly alive, even when we were hungry for more common things. He had the same kind of power that money has, to give substance and energy to things, to give consequence to souls who were thin and ragged and insignificant.

Being healed by him as I had been by then: it was a currency in its own right. He gave and he got. From the very beginning, he could attract money; get it behind him even without trying. He could reject it too. It was the devil he ran against, the devil he always had to outwit. Some called him a gambler. In the end he gambled his life; gambled it and won.

I have told no one of this. I have told no one of anything. If I were to speak, I would not talk like this. I would say instead he was a poet, a prophet, someone whose language was like the word of heaven[x]. His words made you forget common hunger. You forgot all that part of yourself, felt only the fullness of his presence.

Our secrets, he called them, the illusions and tricks and miracles, the way common reality bent itself time after time to create an effect that was hard, afterwards, to explain. He put his mind deep down into things; something in them we didn't know was there answered back. Things felt his power on them and became conscious, enlivened, the way the women at court, when his eye was upon them, used to act up and flirt with Herod. The eye of power: I had come across it once before, with Felix, but this was of a stranger type. Yeshua looked straight at and into things, and into people too as if their surface barriers and deceptions were hardly there at all.

Appearances are complex, more complex than we know. He saw the shallow glow in me, the difference between my inner self and how I appeared to others. "*You are an easy person to misunderstand*," he told me once. "*So many lights inside you, so many shadows too. You are like a watchtower, always on guard, always vulnerable; a lighthouse that cannot hold its own light. You cannot keep yourself inside. If I set you to guard the sheep, would you watch through the night or be the very thing that attracts the wolves?*"[xi]

Over those years, as our friendship developed, we had a lot of secrets, he and I. I even came to believe that I was in some way essential to his secret. Gradually, I learned that I was wrong about this. It was not he and I who had secrets. He had secrets with everyone. We were all part of one great secret so big that no one except himself could hope to grasp the whole: the secret of who he was, what his mission was and what, in three short years, he would bring into being. *The new kingdom*, he called it, the new age that was coming, an age in which that kingdom, inconspicuous at first, would grow so large it could house the whole world. He held every detail of it inside him, saw the whole field of his destiny in a single glance.

That destiny was inside us too, growing clearer every day that we spent with him. He was leading us to a new reality, he said, a sheepfold from one side but a gateway to heaven on the other. There was within us all a tiny space the size of a mustard seed. It was the seed of the kingdom we carried within us. His aim was to teach us how to nurture and cultivate this until we could exchange its flowers and fruits for the keys to his kingdom.

And the way he taught was part of this. He never explained things fully; just a touch of emotion here, a touch of sunlight there and a little scene to hold them together, but the ideas grew in our minds. You could see what he meant. The thoughts they planted in us; they grew like living things: we were their garden. A magical garden, one that knew no winter but had fresh fruit always growing: that was God's kingdom.[xii] Through his teaching, we would become this living, flowering truth. We were carrying a torch that would light us on the way to our true spiritual identities. We did not know these yet but they would be there waiting for us when we arrived in his kingdom.

Our place in that kingdom: it was what we lived for. Nobody doubted that. The difficulty was to find the right opening. So many doors inside us, that led to somewhere else.

"*I am the good Shepherd,*" he said to us once after a discussion that had set us arguing about the Way.

"*And we,*" I interrupted him, "*especially the stupid, confused ones among us, we are the sheep!*"

Sheep, we all knew, were not easy creatures to love or to lead. They are infinitely capable of going the wrong way, turning about in a blind direction, losing themselves somewhere between leading and following. They lack objectivity, find learning difficult. That is why they spend their lives crying out for their mothers: *Mère, mère, mère!*

Even so, it was an unfortunate comment. Peter took it the wrong way. He had no sense of humour at all.

He turned on me at once, brusque and hurtful: "Listen to mère…mère…mèrey Magdalene!" he said. "Mother of the sheep. Always bleating away."

They were not an easy group to live with, the favoured twelve. I travelled with them on and off for nearly two years but had places to stay when it became too much and I needed to escape. All of us had to break away like this at times; we had other things to attend to, or places we were sent when Yeshua needed something doing. We always came back to Galilee; always met up again at the agreed time.

Yeshua's secret, his great secret, was our guardian, a great white herding dog that held us all together and moved us forward, jostling blindly, one escaping here, another running off there, until we reached the place he wanted us to arrive at: a place of slaughter, sacrifice and betrayal. We should have known that earlier than we did, had not that conspiracy of secrets and all the miracles it was able to produce kept us from seeing clearly where we were headed.

I was his star pupil in those days. He was indulgent towards me. The thing between us, it was never entirely hidden. The men did not always like that. [xiii]Peter and I would spar often while Levi sighed and juggled the whites of his eyes between us: *"Give me the balance sheets any day!"*

Sometimes, we were sheep jostled up in a pen or fish twisting together in a net; sometimes, we were coin jingling in a purse, rubbing each other smooth, or up the wrong way. Children, he called us once, sitting in a market square and piping a tune we had barely learnt ourselves for others to dance to[xiv]. Caught up in our daily lives, just as children are who are still learning the ropes, we understood so little of what he was trying to teach us.

But he brought us into being like that, first through secrecy, then through fellowship and competition. *"Never tell anyone,"* he would say in the early days, whoever he was talking to. He spoke to us confidentially about secret things, but the secret was like a whisper around him, like a new-voiced wind to which everyone started to listen. *You hear that?* It was a wind that blew, and blew, and suddenly there were crowds around him, all listening intently, and he had become someone else, a public stranger.

Out there, in front of them, his feet lifting and sinking as he spoke as if to some kind of music, almost unrecognisable from his daily self. He even looked different, his own double in a disobedient mirror: a great flame whirling around itself, a vortex of energy that spun upwards until it dwarfed everything. It was as if his own body didn't contain him at all. [xv] No doubt he could slip free of it. He even did that sometimes, stamping his image on the mind of a crowd then vanishing suddenly as if he had just left himself behind. It could be frightening to see him do this, to catch a glimpse of what was hidden inside. Some called him a magician; others thought he was demon-possessed and shuddered at the wild license he seemed to allow himself.

He believed in it absolutely, the power of that secret. And the more of a secret it was, the bigger it grew. Nothing could dint his belief that he carried something of God's special love always inside him. It grew and grew like some rampant plant, the mustard seed he spoke of[xvi], bigger and bushier, full of amazing colour and life. He had only to look at you for you to be swept away. He could cast spells for empire. People watched and went under.

Then, just in an instant, the illusion vanished. He was himself again. An ordinary being, hungry, tired, inclined to be irritable, needing a piss. He rested in exhaustion sometimes but the energy, the drive was always there, it never left him for long. He made it seem so easy, being out there in front of the crowd as if he were entirely at home; as if he belonged to them and was theirs for the taking. But there was another side too: his need for solitude, silence, invisibility. Those times, he belonged to none of us.

It is hard to share someone you love with other people. Hard, because that special little bit of themselves they share with you is all you really want them to be. You don't want to recognise that it is only the small coin of their identity, a small coin in a larger treasure chest. He could make you feel special, his absolutely chosen one, with just a glance, a glance so warm and quick and full he seemed to be sharing his soul with you.

It was not the way ordinary men could make a woman feel special. His attention was like being looked at by God. He saw everything about you, but he saw it wonderfully, as it were, through his own eyes, as if you were a part of them, a part of who he was, endowed with his own spirit. The glance of most people is a weapon, bent on seeing you shrink. This was a different kind of seeing all together. He looked at you and you were no longer insignificant, a struggling, failing belittled thing but fully, impressively, lovably there. He could see you whole.[xvii] It was this most generous glance that made men love him. Made women love him too.

Jealousy, of course, was everywhere; it sprang at us from strange places. No one was free of it, I least of all. We were so bound to him; we were never free just to be ourselves. The aspiration was with us always to be his special one, to feel his love upon us. We all wanted it! How could he love each one of us so much and yet love all of us the same way? For years, I asked myself this question. And all the time he was drawing us more and more into himself. It started with us and then the world too started to bear his likeness.

This love was a radiant thing, something you never wanted to lose. The person I had thought myself to be was no longer who I was, but merely a diminishment, a distorted image, of my full being. He charged people with energy, just by looking at them. That's how he healed them too. He called them back from what diminished them, the sin or sickness that had straddled their psyche like succumbing to a demon. He pulled it off you, that parasitical demon. He pulled you free of it. Completely free, as if he knew it of old and could force it to obey him.

31

"You, devil of darkness, crippled imp of Satan! I command you to leave her! Leave her in the Holy name of God! You no longer have power here. She has taken back her own soul. It is in my keeping!"

When his breathing was like that, an inner snarl moving like a whip chord, they all had to obey him. The wolves, and jackals, and foxes, the warped and twisted spirits, the dark-limbed demons, the smug and smiling devils, they all fled when that great white secret obedience drew them into its order. He understood more about spiritual forces, spiritual beings, than anyone I had ever met. He recognised them for what they were, how we had allowed them in, the parasitic hold they had over us, how we fed them with our own fears. Fearless himself, he had absolute command over their world. He taught the brothers some of his secrets; with me he usually avoided that subject; he knew how frightened I was of it. We talked of other things, had our own secret world.

"Don't tell anyone, Magda," he would say after one of these sessions. *"Don't mention the vision-school. Don't even question it yourself. The time for understanding is not yet. Just fix your eyes on the stars. Remember that meeting point. All the wisdom you need is already there."*

He was talking about his kingdom again, but it was hard to hold onto what he said; it was hard at first to imagine going there. Later it became easier. I learned how to go deeper into myself; realised there was somewhere else inside me, a place inhabited by a person I did not know at all. She was calmer than I was, and much wiser. Her wisdom, on the rare occasions that I encountered her, disconcerted me. She was full of peace. It was as if she was living in the mind of God.

"Don't worry about yourself, Magda. Let the healing happen. Don't worry about the details. Don't take things too personally. Trust in the fullness of what is happening inside you, the fullness of the time to come."

Jealousy was one of those details, a demon not easy to be rid of.

Learning not to take things personally, that was a long, hard lesson. My life was a field that did not belong to me. I had to learn how to give it back, to the proper owner.[xviii]

*

Living '*personally*' for me meant listening to my dreams. Herod's court had been full of dreams and wise men were employed whose job it was to interpret them. Dreams were important to everyone. Sometimes our lives depended on them.

There was a time I used to ponder my dreams for hours, the big, wind-rushing washday dreams I used to peg out for myself so carefully. I used to lay them out like beautiful garments, smoothing out the ruck in their surface. I knew they were gifts from the spirit world: they came to me and wanted – oh, how they wanted me to speak their language, understand what they were saying. Some of them were so vivid, so full of colour! I called these my Sabbath dreams; they were pots of gold at the end of a rainbow. I would hover over them like an astrologer, or a physician.[xix] And then something bad would happen.

As I stared into their strange imagery, the outline of some disturbing thing would suddenly start to form, a crack of fear would open, a charge of anxiety running through it like a lit fuse. Then I would know, despite all its brilliance, that the dream was a missile bent on destruction, searching out the harm that hid inside me, filling me with dread about the future.

After a while, I ceased to care much for my dreams. They were no longer packed inside of me, a bright wardrobe of energy and emotion. They were outside me now, in the world I was starting to inhabit: Yeshua's world, one that had its own palate of colour. When I told him one of my Sabbath dreams, he would listen intently, inclining his head over mine to protect our privacy. He told me the dreams were prophecies starting to form, something I might have to say to the world. Then he would hold out his finger like someone trying to catch an escaped bird. He caught all of my dreams like that. *"Not ready to fly yet,"* he would say and handed them back to me.

But dreams won't do now. It won't be dreams that Marcus wants to hear. Not that I can remember many of them anyway. Some, a very few, of the details have stayed with me. They come flocking back through the sky like a herd of fleecy clouds, their bells jingling and tinkling across the valley. They are at my door, at every opening. Looking to me to shape them, to show them the right direction. He would know how to herd them, of course, how to lead them. He would surround them, race up and down until they formed a shape, became coherent, gathered, then he would drive them forward; pen them where they needed to be. Now it was my turn to gather what is left, to open that pinfold.

I fear him, this stranger called Mark. He has found me out. I fear that the secret I have kept so long is about to be let out, let loose in a land where it will no longer be mine. It will belong instead to the gallows tree of the world with all its craziness and cruelty. What I have kept in the depth of my heart all these years, kept in the darkness of my cave, it will all be changed, estranged from me, put to the test, judged. Found wanting, perhaps.

All these years of wool gathering, time spent alone, ruminating in the long solitudes, they must be called to account now, set up against opponents far more worldly and cunning than they are. The other ones: those hard-headed, nimble-footed goats who can scale impossible heights, use the magic in their heels to stand alone on rocks and promontories, free to make up their own minds, disbelieving the timid limitations of the sheep below!

People speak well of the dead; they fear their power. But if I am to be resurrected like this, called back into life, I must pass through the judgment gates that lead back into the world. Will I fail the test? Will the judgment go against me?

Unlike the sheep, the goats know how to take things personally. They have the knowledge already inside them. They ask a lot of themselves, know how to do it well. Sheep have a lower expectancy.

"Fix your eyes on the stars, Magda! All you need is already there. Don't worry about what the world will do or say to you. Just follow the path you have been chosen to take."

I think I understand now – at last – what he meant by that. But can I do it? Can I enter the world of the goats; join the fraternity, of which he was a part, the community of hard-headed, combative Capricorns? Out there, exposed, in a world that is every woman's enemy.

For me, this is Judgement Day. Of course, I fear it.

*

I knew it would come eventually, this day of choices. I have stood on the threshold for so long. Now I am being asked to step over.

Every solution creates a new dilemma. I see straight away the change I must make. Back then, in the land of time, I had to struggle to steady myself, to keep my balance, see beyond the pleasure of being alive and the measure of the women's dance in which I was a principal. He loved that. I was his dancer, he said, as Salome was John's. One of his cryptic sayings; it upset me at the time. Now I have learnt to steer by it.

Then, I lived in the moment, in the order of the dance. Now, I live up here, on the face of this eternal mountain where time is less troublesome, where I am beyond history and used to my own solitude. Now it is the world below, the world I have let go of, that troubles me, fills me with fear at the prospect of re-entering it. Then I was young, my feet had to be held back. Now they are where I drop things, drop things and want to let them lie. I must bend down to the world again; gather the strength to pick it up somewhere close to where it fell.

The reluctance of age! This is where I came in.

*

1.4   The Threshold

I stand on my doorstep, waiting in the warm summer dusk for Marcus to come back. But he is already there, standing with his back to the catalpa tree in the corner of the courtyard, looking out over the view that has been my world since I came here, tangled up in ends and beginnings, nearly forty years ago. A white owl calls once, then flies out into the darkness beyond the courtyard where the ground falls steeply away down the hillside.

Time has taught me one thing. I am not what other people would immediately call a 'reliable witness'. Women, in the culture I came from, are not expected to be. My enemies would say I had difficulty telling the truth, but they are quite wrong about this. The difficulty is that for me truth is such a vivid thing; always dressed in imagery and colour. Most of the time, I am entirely truthful. When I speak at all, I tell everything that is in my mind, and that is where the problem lies. I don't select, don't choose my words carefully, the way other people do. But the forum of the world requires choice, requires circumspection, for survival. Brightly dressed truths get mobbed and attacked just as brightly coloured birds do.

Still, even when I knew this, I dared to mix and make up the colour, dye the fabric and rejoice in its bright attractiveness. Rather than take refuge in the quiet camouflage of a common dress.

A coloured truth, then, for this is, after all, a day of celebration. It is the wedding day that Yeshua set us all to wait for.[xx] He has come at last, though not, it seems, as himself. Not as the bridegroom. He has sent Marcus as his proxy.

To have waited so long and still not be ready! Is this how he will find me? Undecided? Still trying to make up my mind? No, that cannot be. *"Watch and wait,"* he taught us. Be prepared for that moment! The bridegroom's sudden unpredictable arrival is a thought I have lived with for far too long.

Now I wonder if I am simply too old for marriage.

*

"Marcus!" I say, and hold out my hand. He takes it at once, raises it to his lips, then drops it suddenly and stands back as if hit by a small lightning bolt. He looks at me with alarm, no longer with compassion, and I can see the resemblance again. A strange phenomenon but one I can remember: the way a face would suddenly reflect a strong likeness of the teacher, like a blood relation. I wonder if the same is true of myself.

"I should have brought you a letter," he says again. "It's the way we communicate with each other now, between the churches I mean; our many different churches. You have heard of this? We are spreading our nets wider all the time and this is our Way, the way our members get to hear news of each other. We are a modern movement; we use the new technology of the empire. Letters travel further and faster than we do. The Romans have their uses and rapid road building is one of them. It has worked well for us. The Word can travel, it can get almost anywhere these days. Through our letters, we can share our gifts, our insights, our practices."

Marcus seems to have thrown what little caution he came with to the winds. No beating about the bush tonight. In his mind, a decision has been taken. He looks around, a slight expectancy of hand and eye, some characteristic expression. I recognise it as hunger, the sign of his excitement,[xxi] and quickly offer him a drink of the local wine, wondering what exactly it is he has come for.

"Peace be with you! You are welcome here," I say, having poured a little of the rich grape into both cups before filling each of them with water. The water instantly turns a soft blush pink.

35

"So, this is how we start our discussion, is it?" he says, with a swift smile of comprehension. "With a small miracle!"

I uncover a plateful of oatcake and honey.

"Sweet hostess of Christ," he says, as we raise our cups towards each other. I smile back cautiously, unsure of his meaning.[xxii]

Then something eases between us. We sit together at my evening table just as I sit every night in spring and summer, and for a moment we look out in silence across the valley whose every detail and every change I have contemplated for so many years. I came here in the reign of Tiberius. Many emperors have come and gone since then. Now even that madman Nero and his gang have followed them.

"How fitting," he says, "to find you in a place like this, so foreign, so far away, and yet despite everything, such a familiar beauty in the landscape. I can see why you have felt at home here."

"You must tell me," I reply evasively, "how you found your way here, how you knew where to come, but not tonight, I think. Tonight, we must both rest; you from your journey and I from the jolt, the shock, you have given to my peaceful life."

"And are you at peace?" he asks, as if genuinely curious. "Up here. So far away from everything, from all the life you knew before?"

No doubt I should reply that there is peace everywhere. Especially up here in the mountains. I have come to love this place. It has calmed me, taught me a kind of patience, a sunset kind of ease that comes every evening when the light starts to lose its intensity.

"You must have guessed already," he says, "that there are questions, many questions and one in particular, that I have come here to ask you."

"Tell me of your travels first," I say, as I try to guess which of the many possible questions he has in mind. I watch with pleasure as he reaches for another oatcake. For me too, remembering these things, being able to speak of them again, it is like unleashing a great hunger.

He talks of the places he has known, an active man, knowledgeable about the world. He has never been to this province before. His routes have always led him towards the great centres. We touch briefly – and without event – on the places we have in common, mapping each other's lives by the intersections that we share. He has a passing acquaintance with the towns I once knew well in Galilee: Tiberias, Capernaum, Cana, the Jordan valley villages, Jericho, Bethany, and of course, though we pause before speaking it, Jerusalem.

His world spreads further and more commandingly than mine. He speaks of Antioch, Alexandria, Rome itself. He is an educated man, a little unpredictable in his manner but a man of good family, wealthy, I guess, a merchant's family like my own, though he, no doubt, was a valued son, a privileged member as I never was in mine. He has worked, he tells me, both as a lawyer and as a scribe; the writing, it seems, interests him deeply, not just the copying of documents but the scope for alterations, additions. Something stirs in his eyes as he speaks of it.

We chat about different languages, both peppering the *koine* Greek we share with phrases from different tongues, getting a taste of each other's lives.

Soon he must tell me what he has come for and why.

These questions he wants to ask stir a trouble in me: old fears and insecurities never far away. Has he come here to find me? Is it as simple as that? Or has he another interest, something hidden below the surface, something I should be wary of? He treats me with respect, seems eager to win my trust, to gain my confidence. His voice is kind, cajoling even, but this is not a social call. Marcus is not a simple man. Behind that charm of manner, there is urgency, impatience, abruptness even, he knows what he wants, what he is here for. He is driven, ambitious for something. There is a hunger in him somewhere. Not a man who wants to waste his time.

"It would be easier for me," I muse, "if I knew who has sent you; what you have been told about me and why, so many years after the event, you have come here to find me."

"I come from John," he says abruptly, almost as if I had spoken aloud. "I work for John now, entirely for him. His older brother – James, you remember James? He was taken from us early.[xxiii] He died for our cause; a great death certainly, but tragic too, for John most of all. It affected him deeply."

But I can't take it in, what he is saying to me; just the one fact is enough to send shock waves through my heart. "John sent you?" I gasp. "John? You work for John?"

"Yes, John, Zebedee's son, you remember him, I'm sure? Not what you were expecting, perhaps, but what were you expecting? John remembers you well. At least, he mentions your name often, remembers you with particular…though he tends to ramble more as the years pass and he starts to reminisce."

John, so eager to hurry me to safety; John the promise-maker, the one who most of all persuaded me to leave.

Stunned, I make no reply.

Direct and plain spoken, Marcus reads my silence, the anxiety I cannot hide. "You want to know what he has told me about you? What version of …events? Believe me, there have been times when I have not always seen eye to eye with John, but where you are concerned, you should know he remembers you with particular…"

"Are there many versions of me then?" I am annoyed with myself for asking this. I should have let him finish.

"Yes, since you ask. There were many versions. There was no consensus. You were always controversial. People take different views, don't they?"

His bluntness is uncompromising, factual, but not, I feel, hostile.

I pass him more cake. *But surely there was some core of agreement? I had become important in Yeshua's movement by the end; along with John and Peter, I was a kind of leader. Surely someone spoke up for me?* I don't ask this. It lacks dignity, and besides I fear the answer. The long empty silence of the years has not been reassuring. It tells me over again that I was never really one of them.

They wanted me gone, even Philip, something of an outsider like myself, the one I cared for most. They preferred me elsewhere.

"You must tell me," he says kindly, "how it is you would like to be seen?"

It is an intimate question for a balmy evening, the night's quiet activities stirring around us. The white owl flies spectre-silent to inspect us, the insects chatter and confer, the mice and rats busy themselves in their runs and crevices.

I start to say: "I would like you to see me as he saw me—"

Then realise the impossibility of what I am saying, its hint of something a little too personal. Distance has never been my strong point. I answer as truthfully as I can, sorrows rising as my heart sinks.

"Most of all, I don't want you to think of me as a woman. Not any kind of woman. If you think of me as a widow, you will be wrong. Widows have a respectability I was never granted. If you think of me as a mother, or a sister, or a daughter, you will be wrong. I had no proper family. I was, for the most part, unwelcome in the one I had. If women are defined by their family roles, then I was a lost soul. I stepped away from those definitions and the wrong they brought me to. I won't say I stepped free, but I have become something else now, a part of this mountain if you like. Don't think of me as a woman."

"Not think of you as a woman?" he sounds incredulous.

"If you think of me as a woman—"

"But how else can I think of you? Surely—"

"Don't think of me as a woman. I'm not, I'm a—"

"What are you then? A priestess? A goddess of the mountains?"

The owl flies towards me. "Think of me as a ghost."

As I speak, a sudden wind stirs up towards us, come from nowhere as mountain winds often do. As if it has been listening, waiting to intervene. We listen back, conscious of a sudden chill, a slight catch in our breath.

"This reminds me," he says, looking round, then getting up and walking across the courtyard to the barrier that fences off the sheer drop beneath. For a minute, there is silence as he looks out through the darkness towards the dark edge of the land. Then he turns decisively. "There is something I must tell you. Something you must understand, if you don't know it already. It was the start of everything, the beginning of the way forward, the event that brought us all back to life. Something happened, something momentous: it must have been a few weeks after you left Judaea. We were certainly surprised not to see you there, in Jerusalem that extraordinary, unforgettable day.

"There was a meeting of those who had been closest to him, those who had been with him near the end and were witnesses to the last…events. We were all there: those who had suffered with him, those who had let him down, those who didn't know what to think.

"Everybody knew by them what had happened, how he had appeared to you…out of the tomb…how he had given you a message to take to the others, how John and Peter had found the tomb empty. How the teacher's sister had confirmed what you said.

"Other people in the group had had similar experiences; they weren't all the same, the meetings and sightings but they added up. Some said he just appeared to them; others that he spoke to them; ate with them even. He was quite alive, nothing spectral about him; you thought he was really there except that he…wasn't, at least not for very long. His body was different, as if he wasn't grounded in it any longer; as if it was a kind of memory of itself, not that important. There was a difference of definition. He never looked quite the way he used to, when he was with us. You know what I mean? Besides, he was always hooded now, his head covered as if he didn't entirely want to be seen. He had become, somebody said, like someone you know in a dream; though they look nothing like their real selves; you know exactly who they are. But these stories, reports, I should say, they weren't dreams. They were pieces of a pattern we couldn't entirely make out or fit together. Some said it wasn't him; some said he wasn't dead. No one could forget him for a moment."[xxiv]

"Yes," I find myself wanting to say something here but I'm not sure how to begin. Marcus continues:

"It was a month or so after the event, after his death, the Festival of Weeks[xxv]. We had met for a meal, quite an extraordinarily good lamb, with herbs and spiced dumplings; there were about a hundred of us all together, back in the same place, just as we had been told. We were expecting you to be there. There was a large group of women. Naturally, we thought you would be among them. Well, those of us, like myself, who were new to the movement, we definitely looked out for you. You were a kind of heroine to us then, a legend in your own lifetime, as they say."[xxvi]

Absence like a chill wind winds through my heart.

"I speak as a relative newcomer, of course, but I can vouch for the truth of this. Nobody knew what would happen. As we sat there, just after the meal, a great wind suddenly blew open the door and came rushing in through the openings. The drapes bellowed into the room like the sails of a great ship. I almost choked on a grape. I couldn't swallow it. The gust swirled around us where we sat, a strange wind, powerful, we all gasped, held our breath, gripped our neighbour. Then we just sat there and waited, shaken and fearful, it was so sudden, so strange."

"A desert wind, Marcus? In what way was that strange?"

"There were voices in it for a start, a huge congregation of the dead, sweeping through the room, the drapes suddenly billowing out and lifting like great sails. It was like being on a ship, the moment you cast sail. One of the women, it was the Lord's mother, I think, suddenly cried out. She began a sort of incantation, like a mourner in a foreign language. All the other women joined in – they are normally so silent – but now they began wailing like a group of mourners, or a chorus at a play, they were swaying, speaking with strange voices, prophesying, ululating, gesturing, a great volley of sound burst forth and then everyone was talking, as if they had all been given new voices. It was – unforgettable. As if the dead had suddenly found us out, found a way through which they themselves could make contact with us.

"We listened in astonishment trying to make out what was being said. Some of it was in Aramaic, some in Hebrew, some in Greek, of course, but there were other tongues too, some in Sumerian, or Persian, I certainly heard Latin, obviously in my profession I know it well; but different people heard different languages, whatever languages the dead speak. It was as if hell had suddenly opened and these voices came pouring out, souls released into life again as if they had something to tell us, some huge purpose to communicate.

"I can't tell you how strange it was; this sense of the dead filling the air. It was as if death itself was undergoing some change that none of us had ever contemplated before.

"People were standing, some even stood on the table as if they were orators giving an address. Others gabbled a soft, vowel-full chorus like children discovering the pleasures of sound. There could have been a rush for the door but Peter, I'm sure you remember all of these people, I don't need to tell you, Peter stood up with this new authority he had and shouted: *"God be praised! The Paraclete, the Spirit of Truth has come to us. The teacher has sent him just as he promised. This is the spirit who will comfort us, explain things to us, bring us the new wisdom; lead us where we have to go to spread his message. The kingdom is here. The spirit of our leader is with us!"*

"You have a good memory."

"I made some notes. It was one of the most extraordinary experiences of my life, and, as I said, it became our starting point. Afterwards, the appearances, the apparitions suddenly stopped; he had vanished from us, but that no longer mattered. We had our faith again.[xxvii] Peter had interpreted the event for us; it brought not just comfort but a kind of delirious joy. It was like nothing I had ever experienced. Our relationship with the dead was completely transformed. They were with us, but they were with us through Him, his energy pouring into us all. We had not been forgotten; our beliefs had not been destroyed. He was as he had always been, as good as His word. There was no room for doubt. It was the moment we all knew his resurrection was a reality in the world. He had risen from the dead and brought with him a great company. They were with us. They were with our movement. We had suddenly become strong again, full of certainty."

I sit transfixed with belief but asking the outsider's question: "And then?"

"People began pushing in from outside, crowds had gathered round the room. James, the teacher's brother, not John's, was at the head of them. He was not a friend to us, a critical man, sharp-tongued and sceptical, come to keep an eye on things, but the wind buffeted him, he lost his balance, fell heavily, caught the side of his head on the table edge. Someone pulled him out from under people's feet. I helped him outside. The crowd caught our enthusiasm. We all poured into the street together, talking at the tops of our voices. It was just as if we had fought some battle and won an enormous victory. That's the only way I can describe it. The sort of thing you get in the arena sometimes: when the right men have won, and everyone rejoices.

"The wind we heard just now, the one that came out of nowhere, it reminded me. It's one reason why I came, the fact that you weren't there. You had your own experience of course, you saw him *risen* before almost anyone, but you were alone. A solitary witness, almost. What we experienced then, we experienced together, as a group; it bound us together. You didn't share in that; you weren't one of us any longer. To us, to the new disciples, that seemed strange. You were his…we had all heard of you, seen you, met you and we wanted you to be there. I wanted you to be there."

"That touches me, Marcus. I live my absence all over again as you speak."

"So it was not of your choosing? There were different accounts. Some said, you had had enough; others that you were too frightened to stay."

But I am not ready to go there. Instead, I say: "Tell me about James. About Yeshua's brother."

"It's good you ask that. You must have known him well. He was sick and shaken, went home to have his wound dressed. The following morning, he came to us. He told us of a dream he had had, he was weeping as he spoke, not a man to do that often. He told us he saw the cross, the cross on which his brother had died, standing by his bed, growing taller and taller. Two men stood beside it. They took him from his bed and let him out of his house, but the shadow of the cross came after them, so tall now that it reached the sky.

The dream changed everything. James became a convert; he joined our movement.[xxviii] These dreams and visions and appearances, they had such power in them and such finality. James turned to the truth and never left it afterwards. He became one of our leaders, respected even in Jerusalem – at least until the final rift. The Sadducees turned against him in the end."

I listen to his words, but it is the dream[xxix] that speaks to me most, its images vivid in my mind.

To my surprise, Marcus reaches across the table and takes my hands in his own.

"And you, Magdalene?" he says. "May I at last call you that? Do you trust me enough now?"

I bow my head. Hearing that name again, like a stone thrown into a deep well, the ripples answer.

"This is strong stuff. I'm sorry. Have I said too much?"

"I am not going to prophesy, if that's what you mean," I say, carefully, releasing my hands, "Or speak with tongues for that matter."

"Too womanish for you, I suppose," he says mockingly. "But think about it: if you won't speak, if you can't find your own way of speaking, how will we ever know what it is that only you could have told us?"

He is circling round me with the hunting stealth of the owl. I sense just the touch of a talon. "After all," he says, "there are so few of us left now who can speak of what we saw, so few who can testify to who he was and what he taught them. Each year the number gets less of those who knew him in the flesh."

"What testimony does the rest of his family give? They were against him at first. He was not primarily interested in human families, and he let them know that. It was hurtful to them, I think. He taught a new kind of family, one that had his teachings at its centre."[xxx]

"Yes, that's true but they came round eventually. Once James came across to us, he helped them to understand, see things differently."

"And are they still…"

"Most of them are, yes, but James himself left us ten years ago. He too has gone to join the assembly of the blessed ones." [xxxi]

James is dead too? A leaf floats out of the darkness and falls on our table, making the small flame dance uneasily.

"It is getting late, Marcus. It has grown dark while we talked. You will have to find your way down these dark paths back to the village and that is not easy for a stranger. You must watch your step. The way is both steep and rough."

Silence folds over us. I offer him the last cake and an oil lamp that he accepts and promises to return.

"What shall I tell the people at the rest house?" he asks. "About why I'm here, what I've come for?"

I had already thought of that. "Tell them you have come about one of my garments, one of my *robes d'occasion*. They will understand. Nothing else is necessary."

He glances at me quickly but says nothing. After he has gone, I lie awake under my sheepskin, thinking back over what I have heard, my breath still tied up in knots around my heart. I don't know what Marcus has come for. Whatever else, it is not just to find me, to see if I am one of the few left alive. He has his own purpose; John's purpose too perhaps.

As my thoughts begin to drift in search of what that might be, I hear outside my cave the sound of a lamb, obviously lost and wandering along the ledges in the dark, looking for its flock. *Mère*, I hear it cry, over and over again. *Mère, mère*. I feel concerned, as if it has come to me for help. The mountains are dangerous at night. There are dogs and wolves that roam here. I get up and take my bed lamp out into the darkness. No sign of the lamb but I know it is myself and I cry until daybreak.

*

1.5   Magda Alone

In the morning, I reassemble myself again. I picture myself as I often do these days, having no brass mirror among my possessions. A woman in her sixty-seventh year, a woman for whom age and its problems are her main concern. Up here on the margins of history, she has not wasted what passes for time. She is resourceful, has turned her hand to many things. She is often solitary, often too tired to talk. Speech, like the act of dressing itself, wearies her now. Her passion for fine and subtle clothing has become a kind of penance, an act of contrition, ungainly and difficult to perform. Clothes no longer slide seductively over smooth, unresisting flesh. They ruck and twist and struggle, like being tied up by an enemy.

I picture myself: a spare old woman, her joints stiffening, her limbs no longer subtle, her skin weathered, her teeth not as bad as they might be, her hair still abundant, her hands no longer skilful with the combs, her arms too weak to lift for long without immediate exhaustion.

A woman who takes it day by day, craving the end of toil and effort, the comfort of sinking back into her own mind.

A woman for who silence has become her natural element.

*

I have told him to rest and to return in two days' time. He looked nonplussed, irritated at the delay. But, as if I have not had enough of it already, I need more of that time with which I am so familiar: the time of ghosts, time to weigh and ponder, to talk things over with myself.

You say you want to talk to me, Marcus, but I notice you do not tell me much of yourself. You do not tell me who you are.

Marcus: such a common name, Roman, but still a name that could be given to anyone. And you could be anyone too, except for that look in your eyes, a glint like something shiny and sharp; a hard, mineral shine. You have eyes that will cut things to shape. For all your charm and hunger, you have something hard and memorable inside you. And that is why I delay: memories can be a battleground. I do not want to be overwhelmed by them.

He will not understand this. It does not matter to him that there was once someone who was myself, someone with her own identity. Before everything, through everything, and now, changed though I am, even after everything, there is still someone that only I remember. Though she stands at a distance, the amber still in her eyes, she must be housed somewhere; I must make a lodging place for her here in these records I have started to keep. A place of safety, somewhere she can hide from the wolves that howl in the woods on the mountain when the moon is full.

*

How long has it been now, since I began to try and order my thoughts? Since I became ill, yes certainly since then, but that was so long ago and besides, the order of illness is a life apart, a life to one side. Illness encases you in solitude; it changes your way of remembering, makes you care only for yourself. A lesson I am grateful for.

Illness narrows your memory to its own thin channel. The time before is closed off, not entirely, but enough. Illness is the medium through which I mainly know myself now. It is neither accidental nor arbitrary. Though I cannot explain its origin or why it came, it fills my thoughts, has an interest-value all of its own. It is what I care about, this body of sickness I struggle always to cure. It is a companion of sorts. I would free myself from it if I could, but I do not possess the wisdom or the magic to reach deep into my own soul and set things to rights there.

Skilled in healing as I became, I cannot heal myself. Ointments have no power here. A sick mystery shares my life with me; a watery cross that holds me together. Sometimes, I think we – the illness and I – are working to achieve the same end, the same understanding. Sometimes I ask myself the ultimate question. If I could shed this cross inside me, would I be healed at last? If I let go of him, would the sickness let go of me also?

Time is fluid in my mind today. It moves in both directions. Just as I moved with it then, when it led me to this place, so I can follow it back in the opposite direction. I travelled in ignorance once, now I know the curves and the currents of the water. I can trace it to Massalia[xxxii], make sense of it from then, my new, thin, injured life.

But that is still not the beginning, not the origin of this strange trouble in my lung. The darkness owns it still; watery and unfixed; no memory can take root there.

Now Marcus brings another, more difficult hope. A hope that the illness itself might become closed off; brought to an end, become merely a passage in my life, a long fog of incomprehension, like one of the terrifying mountain mists that can suddenly envelop even the most familiar pathways. We wait, trapped in the moment, unable to move, until suddenly, if we can survive that lost time, the fog clears, and we have a landscape again.

Dying must be like that, I think. A place of darkness whose only light comes from the white snow that lies everywhere and goes nowhere, a ghost light into which we will quickly fade and become nothing. What is left of our intelligence struggles to find a way through; looks for a passage that might join life and death – and whatever lies beyond – in one continuity, a passage that will lead us to a place where the meaning of our lives is gathered up and restored to us. A hero might find his way through death like this, might stay alive through his own dying, but I cannot imagine doing it. Or what the meaning of my life would look like if I could.

I woke once in the night to a curious vision. I see them very rarely now but this one was clear in front of me. At the back of my cave, I woke to see a smooth-sided jar, pale as marble but solid, lidded, a container, hanging there in the darkness. Nothing illuminated it, nothing supported it, it hung above the ground shining by its own light as I stared and stared, trying to understand why it had appeared to me and what it meant.

I recognised the jar, of course.

In death, the soul, it seems, cannot survive that land of mist and snow where it arrives, naked, disorientated, without name or direction, unless there is something to hold in its perfume, a scent by which it can be recognised in the timeless realm ahead.

The scent of us, of our bodies and our breath; that is what tells us who we are!

If I could cure myself, if I could find that jar still intact, I might make the crossing, become whole again. But the jar was broken, forty years ago. All I can do is play with the metaphors, turning them this way and that in search of an answer.

Perhaps my illness is really a thread, something that still ties me to the life I had, the life I lost? Perhaps I should see it as a guiding thread like the one that Arachne spun when she challenged a goddess in the ancient world; the one that Ariadne used to unravel the labyrinth, a helpmate, and not a curse?

In the reaches of this cave, spiders have been my companions for many years. Of all the creatures that live here, they are the ones that speak to me most. Their intense and tiny lives have taught me how to survive, what to look for, what I need to complete my design, how to join my thin, frail life to that larger world in which I am not the only inhabitant.

As for Marcus, perhaps he really is an angel from the past come to help me find that thread again, the one whose meaning was lost long since and I have never been able to recapture.

"The cross," Yeshua told me once, *"can say two things. It can say: 'Enough! Stop here. You are pinned to an ending. You must stay and suffer!' Or it can say: 'Go on! I am the pledge of your continuance: I am the ladder you must learn to ascend. By the climb goes downwards first.'"*

*

It all began so piecemeal, this process of trying to order and understand. By the time I reached my refuge here, I had lost my certainty and I went on losing it. I had left my old life – my full life – behind so hurriedly that I took nothing with me and never lost the feeling that I was a scapegoat, cast out by those who no longer wanted me. When the months passed and then the years and I heard nothing, when no one contacted me and I had no idea what had happened after my leaving, that feeling of rejection deepened in me. It turned corrosive, ate away at my heart first, then it began on my soul.

I left Judea believing it all. I thought the world might end in sudden glorious fire; the kingdom he had spoken of might come and the figure I had so unforgettably seen in the garden of tombs would appear to me again. Instead, the mists came down, the kingdom did not come, and the world slowly emptied itself of everything, everything but that end. An inglorious continuation, the kind I frighten myself by contemplating: Darkness and its dumb comforts, anxiety, ignorance and wrath! [xxxiii]

Other experiences followed and began to affect and dissolve the ideas I had brought with me. It was not that I lost my belief, rather that I had lost myself and no longer had what it takes to sustain belief. That concentrated effort of the mind that first brought it all into being and then held it together in living harmony: it survived infrequently and only in patches.

My thin new life required nothing but survival, a shedding of every luxury, a thinning, a throwing away of everything superfluous, all the little pleasures and comforts, all that fed the soul with a sense of its own value, its own significance. On and on it went, that trail of losses. Colour bled away, feeling died, slowly, very slowly, with nothing to feed it, the energy drained away. What had once been myself became painless, hopeless, a bodiless vapour. [xxxiv]

There has to be some enduring foundation, some continuity. For me, there was only this sudden ripping away again of what I had become when he healed and remade me in his own image. That had been my salvation, my house above the river. Then the props were removed. I sank down. Discontinuities flooded in.

My year at the temple of the goddess in Massalia, for example: how do I understand that? Was it a betrayal of him, a betrayal that saved my life? The goddess rescued me from absolute shipwreck. Was that so wrong? She brought me nothing else. An arbitrary, piecemeal existence, a kind of freedom to be my old self again, to disown and betray the new image I had worn. It would confirm all Peter's reservations about me if he heard that. But I do not want him to hear it. This is why I must rehearse, must practice. Practice what it is like to seem alive again, not to be Miriam, not to be *Magda*, not to be the woman I once knew myself as, but the stranger inside her, the one who can rise free even of her own death.

For I had died; my life had become a ruined enterprise. I, who had died in so many small ways before, the fabric of my emotions torn first one way, then another, now found that fabric damaged beyond repair. This time, she, the one I had become, was dead, while I, the nothing that I was, lived on by force of habit, this ghost life across the water.

This is how I must speak then, not with tongues or as a prophetess, but as a soul learning how to lose the story it has spun for itself, learning how to let go of the outer garment, the thin clothing with which I covered myself when I came here forty years ago. These thin garments of recollected life, how will they withstand the touch of sunlight, the breath of living air?

*

As the memories and the faith began to grow brittle and break up inside me, as I began to break up, all that effort I had made, all the things I had done, all the people I had worked with, the ones I had helped and healed, everything I had learnt, everything I had given, it all began to disassemble, as if blown away from some cliff top in the winds of the ocean. I went through a period of complete inner blankness: the white shapeless void traced across the palm of my hand.

Nothing renewed. Nothing reaffirmed. An absence, aggressive, atrocious, reigned in its place. I was Queen of the Underworld, surrounded by shades moaning and bewailing their lost hopes, their fallacious happiness. These missing things, they took so long to disintegrate. The corpse held its beauty as long as it could, for twenty years perhaps; then it began its graceless decline into a stinking heap of rubbish on the surface of the earth. The dying took all of me.

Something, my spectre, that wretched, ragged ghost, dragged itself about from time to time; bit by bit it acquired a new language to speak with, a few crumbs of bread and comfort, a little knowledge of where I was and who my neighbours were, short excursions that showed me the lie of the land, the landmarks I could recognise. Every evening, I came up here and fed myself on the view. I drank the light in the morning when it was at its sweetest and somehow this was enough to keep me alive, to keep me altogether from the land of death.

I began to try piecing it together, putting it behind me like a track of footprints or placing it crumb by crumb in a line on my wooden food board. Each little bit, each piece, the crust, the crumbs, some bigger than others, I made pictures with them, little shapes and symbols before I ate. *Give us this day*, I would say to myself. *Dona-nos mei nostre pan de cada jorn.*[xxxv]

These were my crumbs of comfort, my daily bread, my memory of that great loaf, that God-loaf, vast and unbroken, still warm from the ovens with every intention of sustaining the world by its huge presence.

But it is an impossible task: to even dream of reassembling the whole shape of the bread, its crust and colour and texture, to reassemble its plenitude, from the crumbs into which it has fallen.

At the edge of the hill where my cave is, there is a small statue of a man, an *egregore,* they call it here, an effigy of power. A fine, sand-stone dust, the wind from the desert is always blowing it away, stroking its surface, changing its features, first this way, then that. As I knead the yeast, it watches me, curious but intent on its own task, of vanishing forever. Becoming unrecognisable.

For nearly a year, when the illness first took serious hold, I began to lose my voice. I could not, on the rare occasions when I tried to comfort myself, I could not raise a note of song at all. Half of the larynx, the vocal cords had become infected. A terrible cough rattled through me night after night. Eventually Pons banged on my door with his stick. He had lain awake listening to the sound. He heard it day and night. He could have left me to die but he was a lonely man and, since his wife died, he liked having a neighbour.

Pons was a good man, though melancholy, as the caves made all of us. He brought broth, and a medicine that soothed my throat a little. After a while it seemed easier not to speak at all. I listened. I learned what I could of this new strange language but for a year or so I gestured like a child my few communicable wants. Then the words started growing. I found a small dog injured in the mountains, it crawled out of a fox hole covered in dirt and yellow sand, its eyes huge and dark in the damp fur, whimpering with fear and exhaustion. I gave it water, a little dried bread, then I thought of a name for it: *Tobit.* It's a name from the Sacred Writings; I don't know why I chose it.

Tobit had already found his way out of the darkness. I decided to follow his lead.

One day, I told myself, speech will return. Not just these maundering thoughts but real speech in my own tongue, the true sounds of life, something that others could recognise.

Until then, well, I finger each piece of bread, rub it gently, knead it, shut my eyes, taking time back to what it was made from, in the beginning. The ingredients of life begin to reassemble. Bread is my miracle. It takes me straight back to that huge crowd with their insatiable hunger. This memory holds its place like a child's story; it never varies. Five loaves and two small fishes.

And before that, the uncooked bread, doughy and soft, waiting for the furnace.

I stand in my grandfather's bakery in Migdal Nunaya[xxxvi]. In the mornings, if I wake early enough, I am allowed to help. I touch the dough. I finger it. I start to stretch it, very gently, shaping a sparrow, a fish, a sun, no, it is a face, a body, firm and flexible, its arms stretched out, the eyes black as olives, the feet rising and lifting as if on tip-toe. A black shadow suddenly appears behind me. Another secret. Something else to be silent about.

The bakeries did well for us; we had the commission for the temple bread as well as the townsfolk. There were fluctuations in the market every year; sometimes there was so much left over you couldn't give it away. I used to take it to the shed behind the house then and feed it to the donkeys.

*

1.6   Young Magda's Story

Where it came from, that angry spirit, I can't recall. I must have been too young, but it was there, it was in me. It had a claw, sharp as a cockerel's spur. As the day wore on it would start to feel for me, it would touch my flesh, my arm, the outside of a thigh, and then suddenly it would go in. I would feel it start to tear at my skin, teasing out an edge, hungry for the blood beneath.

It loved the sight of blood. Blood was what mattered, what it needed to achieve. When the blood appeared, I could breathe again. The spirit had found me. Both of us knew that. Times were when it wouldn't stop. The blood ran, out of control, down my leg, onto my clothing. Trouble now. It was no longer secret. It would need a lie or a denial. But it gave me something in return, for the blood. Something like pride in myself: that I could manage the pain, that it really didn't hurt at all when I cut myself, or if it did, I liked the pain. It appeased that troubled spirit.

The hands of other people were to me a different matter. They were rough and clumsy. I was embarrassed beyond speech by the touch of others, their claim on my body made me vanish altogether. In the gap where I had been the anger came, subtle, black, comforting. Biding its time.

What was it in the blood we wanted so much, that angry spirit and I? The insects, the terrible bites, the scratches, the thick brown scabs lifting like tombstones! I loved that feeling when the first corner of the hard, brown scab suddenly gave up its grasp and started to lift, the little peep of bright red blood springing out from its hiding place. The queer sense of achievement it brought, of doing something secret, something wrong, of course and its own kind of punishment; that's where its power lays.

These dark things were one kind of secret, a secret I had to keep from other people, but I had another kind, a secret of happiness that was like my Sabbath dreams, something I wanted to share. It came rarely but it filled me with an enthusiasm my family had little time for.

There was the dark world under the bedclothes, at night where the blood was kept. And there was the world of bright magic with its beautiful brilliancy that would come occasionally and surround me with its sweetness; a world of tall flowers, intense scents, heart-stopping colour. In that lit silence I became someone else, the young bride of a bright magic that didn't seem to belong to the world at all. I sang all alone when it came to me.

These little powers, one that spoke of a sinful body, the other of a soul that shone its own paradise, they lived in me from my youngest years. I do not think they ever met, hardly knew of each other's existence.

But I knew of them. They framed my girlhood, made me intensely curious. About myself, mostly, as if that is what I was to myself: not a person in my own right, just an object of curiosity.

*

A drama was playing out in me from the beginning. I enjoyed being alone then and had little dependence on other people.

I was certainly not my mother's child. This was unfortunate for both of us. She wanted a nicer, better looking, less awkward version of herself, a good daughter; one whose beauty and domesticity would boost her social standing. It was hard to tell if she were a good or a bad woman; she kept so close to her role. Sometime though she too would describe a dream and her dreams were queer things, angular, eccentric, obliquely subversive. We might have found a meeting point there.

My best memory of childhood is of her cooking. She was not a good cook, far from it; she prepared food in anticipation of its end, sacrifice or excretion. *Burnt offerings*, the men of the family called them. She underestimated the power of flame; it was part of her unhappiness.

But this day, something altogether unexpected happened. I had been invited on an outing, a children's outing that required a journey and would last a whole day. Mother prepared a package of food for my breakfast. I remember that day as a day of special discovery. It must have been late Spring for the sun was everywhere but gentle, not oppressive. Samaria was beautiful at that time of year. We stopped at a place where there were trees, bushes, early flowers, a great deal of greenery. There was a network of small streams too, criss-crossing the tufted, tussocky grass in several directions.

I had never seen water like this before, little rivulets of sparkling clear water that we could jump across, the ground not boggy underfoot, leaving our feet dry and clean. There were so many other sides to the water and I at least jumped across them as if quite out of my ordinary senses. I'm not sure if the other girls jumped with me and shared my enjoyment or if I was entirely on my own but I seemed to be gathered together, entirely self-possessed.

After the streams, we walked along a path that had trees on either side and was dappled with sunlight. We came at last to an old temple, its hall half built into the local rock. A community had lived there once, and their roof-rafters were the highest I had ever seen, though the roof itself had gone in places letting in the air above our heads. As we sat on our benches at the long rough table, the room was full of sunlight. Though my strange self-possession still persisted, a giant smile seemed to pass through us all.

Instead of other children, I seemed to be sitting with the old eremites themselves, silent men entirely at ease with their surroundings but kind and unobtrusive. One of them sat opposite me and I, who normally never felt like this with other people, felt comfortable in his presence.

When I started eating my simple breakfast, the most delicious morsels anyone could ever have imagined seemed to have assembled on my plate. The bread was warm and mouth-watering, the cheese unlike any I had ever tasted. As for the pink jelly my mother had prepared for me in a little star-shaped mould, the taste almost sent me flying. This was angel food, nothing to do with human hunger.

I smiled at the man opposite and he looked back at me as if we shared for a moment some wonderful secret. For the first time in my life I knew the taste, the immense undeniable taste, of utter happiness. The high-roofed room with the sunlight in its rafters was full of this sensation. I was literally, word-savouringly, *over-joyed*, brimful of this new experience in which all the tensions of my young life, even the grim memories of war and brutality, suddenly vanished.

I carried the taste of that star-shaped jelly home with me and asked that I be given it again, but my mother laughed and said she had done nothing different; I must be imagining things. She often told me that, that I was imagining things. Her own preoccupations lay in a different direction, hard and material. She had no talent for happiness whatsoever.

Never again did any jelly she made taste of anything other than her usual lumpy confection. The incident had no fellow, but the memory of it remained.

I was still a young girl, several years before puberty, when she told me I was turning into a whore. It was her term, I suppose, for growing up, but she was an observant woman with curious hazel eyes that saw things about people they would rather have kept hidden. I knew at once she was on to something and I was quite defenceless against her.

Though I had no idea what the word meant, I was fairly sure she must be right. At the same time, the word she had used made me angry beyond saying. I was turning into something that attracted punishment and condemnation. If anything beyond myself was to be held responsible for this, I thought it must have been that pink star-shaped jelly, savoured once then vanishing forever, leaving only the lingering disappointment of its non-return.

None of this matters at all. Marcus won't want to hear a word of it.

But for me the questions remain: that young girl I was then, the old woman I am now, are our identities the same? Are either of them Miriam Magdalene?

Does that name unite us through all the attacks, all the vicissitudes, all the separations that invaded our lives, or does it belong rightly to only one time?

Is that pure happiness the core, the rest mere husk, mere accidental casing?

And our sexuality, that great serpent that appears on our path, is that part of the core too, or is it a wild card we are dealt, a name given us by others, a demon that we and they summon up, over and over again?

*

'It's all you'll ever be, my girl. A whore. If you keep on like that.'

I must have been about ten or eleven at the time, precocious, curious and clever in certain ways. I liked to be alone so that I could make up little stories and dramas in my mind and play them out to amuse myself. Mother didn't understand my love of clothes, a true love of mine after all! I liked clothes because they liked me. She didn't share my passion for dress, didn't recognise the discipline that clothes required, the courage they gave me. She saw only the money they cost, the quirk of independence in her daughter's identity.

The texture of cloth, the texture and the colour: it is a religious sensation they induce. Why else would the priests dress the way they do?

Yeshua understood this about me right from the start; it was something we shared. His words were like that too, visible, full of beauty and texture. As unlike John the Baptist as could be. When it came to clothes, John took more of my mother's view.

At some level, I think she might have understood me. She had married a cloth merchant after all. Perhaps that was the problem, for their marriage was not a good one and my father had always had what she used to call 'other interests'. When she called me a whore, I knew there was a twist of envy in her words. Like lighting a fuse, it ran directly to that other core, the hard core of anger and defiance that lived inside me as well.

Mother was a saleswoman, she wanted me to marry well, didn't want me becoming damaged goods. ^{xxxvii} When my father left on a journey from which he never returned, I became both her merchandise and her advertisement, a valuable commodity for exchange. The rich old man she and my brother-in-law betrothed me to when I was eleven years old, that was just what I needed, she said. He would spoil me; keep me in style. I could have all the dresses I wanted. My sister agreed. Perhaps they even believed what they said. But it wouldn't serve, whatever anyone said. I didn't like the man, couldn't bear the thought of marriage to him. To be his wife, that was not who I was at all!

I may not have known much about myself in those days. But I knew for certain what I was not!

*

1.7   Mèthamis

I try to be truthful, to keep my eyes fixed on a past of which I can only remember a little. The introspection is good for me. I try to remember myself with affection, but it is not always easy. I try to remember Mother with affection too. Harder still! She acted according to her lights; that is all that can be fairly said. It is more than I can say for myself.

Tonight, I grow weary of the task. Something about my conversation with Marcus, about the younger man still present in his voice and eyes, in the turn of his shoulders, makes me leave off my writing and come out into the warm evening air. I lean on my broom, sweep round the entrance to my home – not my cave this time but the little house I inherited ten years ago – at the top of the hill, where the path winds up to the village from the cave ledges down below.

The feral cats as always are everywhere. They watch me in lazy antipathy from their stations round the square, arching their backs on the steps to the little shrine house as I approach. There is nobody about. I look up as the stars begin to appear and, as always when this happens, I start to forget my cares and lose myself in the pleasure of forgetting, my best pleasure these days.

I contemplate my home from the outside, as a stranger might see it: a little house built into the rock with strange objects hanging from the roof that make everyone who comes here think I must be a witch. I want them to think that, of course, it gives me an identity, a disguise that keeps certain kinds of danger at bay.

Mèthamis. The moment I heard the word I knew it was the right place. Greek, to begin with; oddly, the Romans had left it alone, perhaps the sheer rock face on which it is perched reminded them of something they too wanted not to remember. In those days, you could still reach the village by boat; at least, you could reach the bottom of the hill by boat, travelling along the Nesque, that swift and surprising little river. From then on you walked, climbed, struggled upwards, as I struggled that night, nearly forty years ago. Now the village has become one of those places the river has abandoned. Depositing me here, it drew back, receded, bowed out along the valley where it came from, swollen by the rain of the pre-alps.

I was still a young woman then; twenty-seven when I left Judea, twenty-eight, it must have been, when I came here. I had known trauma, loss, degradation, extreme heartbreak but I had been given something too, though at that time it lay inside me like rock, a dead weight, heavy as a mill wheel. No one ever tells you about grief: how it feels so entirely physical, something now dead but still kept posthumously alive inside you, something you must wrestle to expel. I climbed the slow steep path up the side of the mountain, the grief of the world strapped across my heart, no one at hand to offer help or a word of comfort.

I came here that night, to Mèthamis, not knowing as I walked that it would be the end of my journey. First there had been the hurrying away, the sea bitter and heaving, two months it took us to reach land. And then, beyond my year at the temple in Massalia, a memory so shrunk in time now it seems almost nothing, a second journey, by river this time and up from the coast into this mountainous region, where the peaks are as jagged as the teeth used for carding lace: *Lou Dentelles* they call them, the foothills lying to the west of the great mountain itself.

I arrived in darkness; all I had was a name, *Joseph of Arimathea.* I knew him as a friend to our movement, but he was a wealthy man and, according to the Captain of the boat that had brought me to Marseilles, had holdings in this area. I pulled the shawl over my head and knocked against an open door. The man was a supervisor in the stone quarries; he arranged the local networks for supply and distribution. He looked at me incuriously and nodded, pointing to a curtain caught up at the back of the room. He left me alone. I went inside. *Just for one night*, he said. *Tomorrow you go. There are caves below for the likes of you.*

The next day, I woke up and looked out at my new world, the height of the village perched up on its hill, the extraordinary landscape and a sky full of golden light. There were tall, scented herbs growing in the cracks by the door; I had never smelt them before. I kept sniffing, wondering what message that scent would bring me. It was like a fortress here, lifted high above the world. Would anyone ever come to look for me in such a place? Here, I was lost to myself, as far as I ever could be, and immediately felt safe in that loss.

I had climbed out of the world, beyond time and space. Trans-historical, the Romans call it, for them a term of contempt, for me a respite. No one would ever look for me here. No one would ever find me. I did not come to this realisation at once. For years in truth, part of me waited. I did what he had taught me to do: I looked up, stared into the stars until I found the one I was looking for: the greenish tinged star, the one that came early every evening and hung on the horizon opposite my bench, as if it, in its turn, was watching me. We watched each other. The height made the pain in my eyes, the pain of the nails, less intense. Sometimes the view was so vast, so breathtakingly beautiful, I could hardly feel the pain at all.

There are many beginnings to this story. Coming here to Mèthamis, out of harm's way, out of the world's history, is one of them: an ending I thought might bring closure. The life of the woman I had been was over. I was a refugee like many another across the empire; a displaced person. The rest was meditation, meditation and the work of my hands; whatever I could turn them to. Though not entirely like the virtuous woman in the **Torah**, I had had a good education.[xxxviii]

Next day I went with my host to the largest of the quarries. After Golgotha, it seemed entirely appropriate; a mere step away. I had moved from a place of execution – tragic, extraordinary, too full of events ever to revisit – to this other quarry where death was entirely commonplace, where everyone was a criminal and all the stones had been rejected.[xxxix]

*

1.8 Magda and Marcus

I wake early. The sun dips into my shadowy home, a welcome intruder. Marcus is outside. I hear his footsteps approaching on the cobbles. He sits on the wall of the steps contemplating the view until I come out to meet him. We walk together round the ruined wall of the ramparts to get some water at the well then stroll out along the high path at the back of the village towards the long slope of the mountain. Here it is always quiet and private, and we can speak at ease.

He tells me a little more about himself, about the house churches he has belonged to, the meeting places where men and women whose names I still remember from that lost life began to form their fellowship.

He tells me there have been quarrels, disagreements; ruptures even. I nod sagely, taking in every word. "We know now who He really was," he tells me. "We are finally sure. We understand now what we only guessed at then, that he was God's Word, God's wisdom incarnate, *The Way, the Truth and the Life.*[xl]"

"And yet you say there are disagreements?" I lean back, brushing away one of the yellow butterflies that has lighted on my hair.

"There are," he repeats, "different personalities, different perspectives; aims that don't always coincide. I'm not sure how much I should say."

"Nothing you say will be repeated, Marcus. You speak of Simon Peter perhaps?"

He laughs. "Always obstinate. Always outspoken. He became the spokesman of the group, accepted almost at once as one of our leaders. The teacher appeared to him. Afterwards, he always spoke of him as 'our Lord'. It gave him renewed energy, brought back something he had lost. Though he could be hard on himself at times, harder still on others, he knew he had been forgiven for his night of betrayal. The Christ lived inside him again."

There is a pause. The butterfly is back. This time I let it stay.

"I see."

"Of course, a new movement needed a man like him at its helm, someone with honesty and conviction. He believed himself chosen. And he was strong; he knew what would work, the best way to protect our young church. He took over from Judas, handled the finances; to the surprise of some, he did it very well. Still, Peter undoubtedly had his blind spots; his mind had limitations; he acted quickly but he thought slowly. He was conservative, cautious in his decision-making; he didn't like offending authority, especially where the Temple was concerned. Some of us felt at times he was unreceptive to the subtleties, the nuances, the hidden profounder insights of the Lord's teaching."

Then Marcus tells me it was talking to Peter that finally convinced him that he should try and make contact with me: find out if I was still alive and could shed light on matters that were controversial, difficult for the new leaders to resolve. "John said you had a spiritual intelligence that others in the group often lacked. A *pharos*, he called you once, a light-tower.[xli] But the years went by, you didn't return, nobody knew where you were."

So my absence was my own responsibility then, something I had chosen for myself? I shake my head at this. I was a garment they cast off, one set aside and forgotten, too richly embroidered for their purposes. *"Make me a garment, Magda,"* he said to me once. *"One that is as easy as breathing to put on."* So I made it for him, just as he asked, its hem blue as the seashore on the lake. I wove it in my sister's house; made it of my own thoughts and feelings, put too much of myself into it, lost everything when I gave it him.

"At last, I heard a rumour," Marcus says, ignoring my look of protest. "All the other enquiries I had made, all the other places I had looked turned out to be dead ends. You had boarded a boat to nowhere. Peter said you had gone back to your distant family, the Greek settlement, somewhere near Narbo, he thought. Your sister contradicted this, said you were back in Samaria, near Caesarea, keeping a low profile, working for our cause; but there was no one who answered your description among our people there. And the description itself by this time was hopelessly out of date. People age, people change. No one knew what kind of woman you had become. What kind of life you might be leading. What reasons, after all that had happened, you might have for concealment and disguise."

What reasons indeed! I sense his innuendo and raise a sardonic eyebrow.

"I knew you must be somewhere. At last, because most of the evidence pointed to it, I came to the conclusion you must be somewhere in the Gallic provinces. But I thought you might have married, might not have been alone, might have…Anyway, I prayed for guidance, followed a few trails. And then came a series of strange coincidences, chance meetings, odd matches of fact and possibility."

I am thinking again: *he has reasons of his own for making this journey; some motive not yet declared.* I try to guess what question he will ask me first. I try to work out who he might have been, if I might have known him back then, however slightly, back in those days when there were so many young men fascinated by Yeshua's presence, the authority of his words, his inexplicable acts of kindness and power. They all wanted to be like him, to act the way he did, to have that kind of charisma, people hanging on their every word, fighting for a glimpse of him. But what is left of those young men after nearly forty years? We become strangers even to ourselves. Something boyish, a hard, greedy enthusiasm, lives on in Marcus's voice and expressions occasionally but the inner resemblance, the spiritual resemblance visible when he speaks of his faith: that is what I recognise most.

For one heart-stopping moment, I think: *Could it be Yeshua himself?*

Incorrigible, Magda! I laugh inwardly at this; he notices my smile.

Abandoning his search account, he says, abruptly:

"Well, shall we sit down somewhere and make a start? Where to begin, that's the question? There are obviously things I need to explain to you, but they must wait their turn."

His voice has changed. He sounds tense and determined.

"We will need wisdom with us," I suggest mildly, "for what lies ahead."

To my surprise, he seizes on this at once. "Yes, wisdom: that's it! That's how he described you once. Sophia herself, the fallen light of the divine feminine, her spirit weeping endlessly through the world and longing to return to her divine origins."[xlii]

I am swallowed by a great silence when I hear this: *Did he really say that?*

"Anyway, that was John's view, but let's begin, shall we?" He pulls out a piece of old sailcloth from his rucksack and spreads it out on the bench in the shade of the olive tree. "We should begin with you. Then, I'll explain more of what has happened since you left. What you said last night, it interested me, quite the opposite of what I was expecting. I want to know more about you…about who you were before you joined the Way, before you became his…"

Companion? Lover? Priestess? Accomplice? Who was I before I met God's son, his Anointed One, the madman or messiah they hung up and crucified with thieves and assassins? Just an ordinary girl, of course; as ordinary as he was himself!

"Relax," he says. "I'm not going to set any of this down. Not unless you tell me to. Not unless you agree. You can speak freely. I hope you will."

"Did you and I know each other?" I ask, determined to avert the impossible questions. "Did we know each other before, back in those days? There were so many people around him then, it's not possible to remember everyone. Did you recognise me when you got here?"

Am I still recognisable as the woman I was then?

"Recognise?" Marcus is uneasy with the word; he hedges at once. "Well, of course, I knew about you certainly. I knew who you were, by name that is. Everybody did! I knew something of your role in the group too, though only a little. After all, I was only there at the end, a neophyte; the merest beginner. Your age makes a difference, of course. But otherwise, well—" he looks at me closely, a slight smile twisting his lip. "Yes, and no. It is possible that we did meet once or twice, but they were such strange circumstances, weren't they, those last few weeks, so unforgettable in one way, and yet so difficult to recall in another! Emotion heightens some of the details. Then, the story changes every time someone tells it and I have talked it through a hundred times with Peter and the rest. You both are, and aren't, exactly as I'd…imagined you. A little smaller than the name you were given suggests and more centred in yourself than some reports had led me to expect. Luke's for instance."

"Who?"

He waves the name to one side. Then with one of his impulsive starts, he adds: "If I'm absolutely honest, Magdalene, I imagined you a lot."

It is an extraordinary comment, and we look at each other with a winning directness. The capacity to surprise and astonish can be very endearing. I sensed we both felt this about the other. He has a good face, kindness and warmth along with tougher qualities, someone not to be overlooked, a man who would have his say. His voice is difficult to read. He is educated, urbane but not easy to categorise, he does not come entirely from one place, many influences have shaped the man he is. There is something strange about the shape of his mouth, a slight hint of deformity. I am not sure of him. And yet, there is something likeable too, something masculine; he has an energy and an optimism that makes me want to trust him.[xliii]

"I see us both as people who have changed a lot since those early days. People whose lives have encompassed some quite fundamental changes. It's a thing we share. So tell me whatever you like, Magdalene. Put me in the picture."

He senses my hesitation, says, "I'm not here to judge you, you know?"

"Really?"

"Of course not. How could I? Besides, my mind is already made up!"

This makes me smile. He points to a red-tailed bird darting between the trees on the far side of the well. "I've not seen one of those before. Is it rare?"

"More common than you think!"

He nods. I take his point.

"I could tell you a little about who I was, in my youth, before…"

"If you like," he says. "Yes, alright, tell me something about yourself before you met him, something not too difficult to summarise. It's the meeting itself that matters most, of course; the change he made in us, in all of us, myself included. The past is important for some things but for others it's hardly worth trying to recall. We live in a new age."

I hear what he is saying: *Before* doesn't matter. At the same time, he is trying to protect me from embarrassment. He has heard things about my past and is trying to keep them small and marginal. Perversely, this only makes me want to speak of them more.

"Tell me about *before* then? We have all the time in the world to talk today. In fact, I'm thinking we should have brought something to eat. The air around here, it's so fresh. Like drinking on an empty stomach!" He eyes my basket and I set it down on the grass. Bread, cheeses, fruits, green olives. A pastry. "I'm sure there are things you won't want to tell me about, Magdalene. You may think I won't understand much but I do understand the difference, between then and now.

"Then we were young, of course, but it is not just a question of age. My own past, my behaviour, my attitudes, they have all changed; vestiges remain but that is all. I used to be obsessed with food, you know, always hungry. I've conquered that now; well, more or less! I don't crave luxury or miss my old life in the days before I met the teacher. I was a spoilt brat; that was the long and short of it! There are many things in my life I'm not proud of. But he understood, didn't he, that those who are searching are often those who have taken the most wrong turnings to begin with."

I turn out my hands like someone about to begin a prayer. "I've lived the life of a woman," I say instead, trying to mute a note of defiance that challenges his assurance that things are as simple as he suggests.

There is a pause; he looks away. I feel the contradiction start up in me. "Perhaps I should say I've lived the life of several women. But that life, it's not simply, not only, that of a woman."

"Ah, the mystery again," he says. "As you mentioned last night."

We are both mocking each other slightly, trying to find our positions. At the same time there is a truth about myself that he will not see, that I need to defend.

"Is it your age you are talking about, when you say you are no longer a woman?"

"No," I say, lowering my eyes to hide the annoyance this remark has caused me. "On the outside, I may look like a sick, old woman, but you do not see my thoughts, my inner life; there I am a spiritual being[xliv]. One you will not find easy to recognise."

He scrutinises me in silence, weighing my words. I meet his gaze.

As we face each other, it occurs to me that, though I am a sick, old woman, other people do not see me that way at all. And today, for some reason, I don't even feel like that myself.

*

1.9   The Life of a Woman

"The life of a woman is an inward-looking labyrinth; you meet yourself at every corner. It is hard to escape from that: the repetitions and reflections, the serpentine cycles by which we are bound."

"It all sounds very complicated, Magdalene! You guard your meaning like a minotaur. I haven't a clue what you are talking about."

"I'm talking about the sexual life of a woman."

He drops the cheese he was lifting onto his bread and busies himself looking for it in the grass.

The truth was, though I don't say this aloud, I had a liking for sex. Almost straight away, and despite the psychic damage it caused me, almost without exception. I think my childhood experiences came in useful there. I could never understand when I heard women complaining about 'that side of men', the drawbacks of married life, the difficult duties of a wife. Recalling with cold fury my mother's strictures, I became an adept in seduction. I liked the ritual clothing, the dimming of the lights, the sense of intimacy. More than anything, I liked what the Greeks liked: a goddess phrase, I heard once and always remembered: *Venus,* and her *eternal laughter.[xlv]*

As a girl, I found sex in a garden, the right place, after all, to discover the small taste of paradise it seemed to offer. This taste never left me; I had learnt, in the hidden places of my mother's garden, how to enjoy myself. Hot afternoons, the call, deep inside myself, the furtive preparations, the binding of the stems, the finding of the right tree, the hot hard pleasure of that orchard love! I accepted it as part of what I was, part of my curiosity about the world I was waiting to explore.

"Ah!" Marcus twists away as if he has spotted a serpent. "Mistress of surprises," he exclaims, then knocks over the water jug. "I had not expected such directness."

"I don't know what you've heard about me; I would be surprised if you had not heard something about this. And now you have come, I find myself wanting to talk about it. To make a full confession, even."

"Oh Lord!" he says.

"For a woman, it's not always easy to manage her own sexuality and combine it with self-knowledge; there are so many pitfalls, so much condemnation. It has its own voice, a will of its own. We are taught to deny it or become too bold for our own good. We have so little autonomy, so little choice. The labyrinth is full of choices that seem to offer us freedom, or variety but often lead us wrong. Our spiritual lives are disregarded, of no interest to anyone except ourselves. Our bodies pollute the domains of holiness. That is what we have been taught."

He sees that I have set him a test.

"But marriage, surely, is the answer to that? Didn't your parents set you a good example, try and find a suitable match for you?"

I sense the muscles round my eyes and mouth tugging my face in different directions, trying to settle on the right expression.

Marcus takes another pastry and pushes it into his mouth.

"My parents were married, yes. A mixed-race marriage, it is true, but a marriage, nonetheless. My father was Greek and clever, my mother from a wealthy Samaritan family. Neither was very religious. They met at Sebaste in one of my grandfather's bakeries, not that bread-making was his only occupation."

But the ground between us has suddenly shifted. Marcus moves out into the open, taking aim.

"You misunderstand me," he says. What I wanted to ask was whether you yourself had ever contemplated marriage? If a marriage…between the two of you, that is…was ever in question? As the rumours have suggested."

So we are here, straight to the point: the vanishing point, the question to which he wants an answer. He is not talking about my earlier past at all.

It is the test I have set him. Now I must set him another.

"Certainly, I contemplated marriage. Doesn't every girl? I contemplated it often. There were times I did more than contemplate it. Five times at least."

"Five years of contemplation, that suggests caution. At least you didn't rush into anything!"

"Not years. Times."

Marcus looks blank. "So, you thought it through…um…and then…you finally decided—?"

"I decided to marry my cousin."

"Your cousin, oh, I see! That's not what I'd…but it's a conventional enough choice, I suppose, to marry one's cousin. It's only one step out of the immediate family and the property is secure. So why did it take you so long?"

"The other four were still alive."

"You play a game with me, Magdalene."

"On the contrary, Marcus. I wonder, from the crumbs you pick up, how much of the loaf you really see. I have been judged falsely so many times I want to know what it is like – just for once – to be seen as I truly was."

"Of course. I understand that. Our pasts, as I said before, are not the issue here. So, this cousin you married before you…I mean, was he anyone in particular?"

"He was Nathan," I say, "Nathan from Cana."[xlvi]

A sudden hiss. The little serpent has reappeared. It is bigger than he thought. His eyes focus on me more carefully. I can see a shape start to appear in them, not one that I like.

"Nathan? You don't mean...Nathaniel, do you, the one who...His family owned a vineyard in Galilee, didn't they, wealthy folk, they had orchards too?"

"I was not just a small-town girl, Marcus."

"No, I see that. But Nathaniel, wasn't he..."

"A disciple? Yes, one of the earliest, though he wasn't around for very long. And he was Jewish too, though he never made much of it. He could have done, perhaps he should have done because I wasn't, you see, I was mixed race; we had different blood. And besides, Samaritans like my mother's family are from the old kingdom. They see themselves as the true guardians of our heritage even if the ancestral wells had all become defiled. Purity is a mixed blessing; it is never what it seems! The Jews damaged our inheritance, they destroyed our culture, but it cost them too! Our history is a bitter one. There was a deep-rooted division between the two sides of our family, animosity smouldering just below the surface. Nathan and I married across this divide; we were of an age, we thought we could overcome the past, heal its wounds. We were quite wrong. All we did was injure ourselves."

"The marriage must have been a very short one."

"Oh yes, they all were. About a month and a half. Divorce, you see, was so easy. At least, for men it was, and Nathan always took the line of least resistance. He liked the idea of having been married to me more than the thing itself."

"I heard he had settled in Lebanon."

"Yes, he went back there – to his first family – when things didn't work out in Galilee. He saw me as a wild girl, himself as my rescuer but that was only half of the story."

But I can't go on with my explanation, can't explain how wrong things were with Nathan. "He was an intelligent man, honest in his intentions but indolent in the extreme, entirely lacking in energy. We had been kissing cousins in our youth and I had mistaken him then. He used to gasp for breath when he kissed me as if the sweetness was overwhelming. I was only a young girl then and I thought him so passionate, so grown up!"

"And was he? A passionate man, I mean."

"Actually not. He just had asthma."

I hear myself sounding for a moment like the girl I used to be, flip and funny and perversely immoral. Marcus is studying me carefully, checking back with what he's heard: *This is what they warned me about. A difficult woman, careless and loose! Dangerous if crossed.*

"Poor Nat, he meant well. He had come back to Galilee after his father's death to claim his inheritance and that's how we met up again. It was a mistake for both of us. He wanted to sit complacently under his olive trees, looking down on the local folk and enjoying his patrimony. But vines have to be grappled with; they require hard graft and commitment. Wives too, no doubt."

Marcus is not enjoying this any more than I am. I can feel him trying to tack back to safer, shallower waters. But I am eager to get my confession over. If I am to be judged one last time, if I am to be seen truly, my faults were many and must not be hidden. All I can do is blur the boundaries a little, try to explain the woman I became.

He begins to feel his way forward again, in the direction he wants this conversation to take: "And so this wedding…to Nathan, it must have happened…sometime before you met the teacher. Am I right?"

"Yes, just before. And the wedding before that, if that's what you're asking, I married a gypsy."

His turn to gasp. "A gypsy?" He turns the word over carefully. *Anarchic*, he is thinking. *Unstable. A bit out of control.*

"An Egyptian, you mean? You had already married an Egyptian?" [xlvii]

I do not correct him. He is not inviting comment, but I have caught his interest. Then he surprises me. "Actually," he says, "I can understand that. They can be very attractive, the Egyptians, can't they? Very compelling! An old culture; we owe a lot to them, far more than we are willing to acknowledge. I told you I lived there, didn't I, in Alexandria? I studied there for a while. And what a city! Nowhere like it, in my view. And good for learning too! Did you know it at all?"

I notice the increase of respect, but I want it over, this interrogation I have chosen to undergo. I shake my head: "That marriage was quite short too. He was a damaged soul, poor Mussa, quite literally so. His father blinded him in one eye with a chisel when he was a child and the injury went deep. The hashish got him in the end, but I never regretted marrying him. He taught me a lot, helped me a lot too, helped me deal with bad things I'd experienced in my childhood. I learnt from him, he was kind and undemanding, very much his own man. He had good table manners too. I always remember that about him. He was a good cook; I liked sharing meals with him. It's important, isn't it, sharing a meal? If you don't…"

I hit a silence, noticing the empty platter of honey cakes.

"Where was I? Oh yes, would you like to try one of these? My neighbour, Pons, makes them, in memory of his wife. She left him the recipe."

"Very important," he agrees, stretching out a hand. "For us, it's the centre of our fellowship. My word, these are excellent! Give them the right ingredients and your Provençals certainly do know how to cook."

Something about the way he indulges himself frees me a little from the strict truth. Enough at least to miss out the next two men in my life, which weren't in any case proper marriages, though I used to think of Felix as the love of my life, disgraceful though that had been, and I knew it was wrong, though not as wrong as marrying Nathan was.

"And the time before that, Marcus, I married a zealot. A revolutionary. He was a violent man. I hated him."

A line suddenly appears between us. A crack. I draw back behind it. Some things require a certain light before they can be made visible. Perhaps he guessed, or got some inkling, for he drew back too.

"It wasn't little Simon, was it?"[xlviii]

"Of course, it wasn't little Simon. What do you take me for?"

The frown line deepens between his eyebrows. "All these marriages, Magdalene, I wouldn't have thought you were old enough...Are there any more?"

My days as a concubine I'm not going to concede. I've said enough and offer him a sweetmeat instead. "It sounds bad, doesn't it? But I loved none of them, I didn't know what love was. It was selfish, perhaps, but my life was always my own. I didn't want to be any man's property. I was sure of that but I knew nothing at all about my own heart. My first marriage was the worst; it went on longest and damaged me most."

He notes my emphasis. We stare at each other. There is a slight drop in one of his eyelids. He is looking at me with the kind of horror I normally reserve for myself. I hear the eerie, airy lightness in my own voice, meant to deflect, to keep it at bay, to keep it still and dead, the mammoth in my cave.

"I got away in the end," I say trying to strike a cheerful note.

"Well, that's a relief!" he says, clearly not wanting the details.

We both laugh. Something in this conversation is beginning to intrigue us. In the small world of that distant past, paths crossed repeatedly, family connections were widespread, almost unavoidable. People knew each other; we had all met before.

There is a long pause. I finger the strands of my hair, the way I did as a girl.

"I wonder how much you know," he says, "about what happened? Three years ago?"

So this is the way we will approach it next.

"You mean...Jerusalem?"

He nods, his mouth tightening, turning in on itself. "Simon was killed there. It is hard to think of it. The whole city destroyed. The temple itself; it was Passover, so many arrived there who never left it again. I tell myself: *In time a new city must be build, a new temple different to the old.* We must concentrate on that; never let ourselves forget what was done there, or the great sign he gave us before he went to his death.[xlix] The Romans will pay for it one day; they'll know what it means to have a proud city destroyed.

"But what I ask myself still, Magdalene, is: *How did he know it would happen? Where did he get his knowledge?* When it came to things like that, he was not just an old-style prophet. He had real information. He knew everything about people, knew every detail in advance."[l]

I nod. Marcus, too, has learnt something of that network of secrets, wider than we realised, that surrounded Yeshua's whole life: how he saw every detail, how he fitted it into his plan, how he missed nothing. He had that rare kind of intelligence. It set him apart from other men.

"Jerusalem, yes," I say cautiously. "I heard about it in Veisoun[li], some at least of what happened there. The Romans enjoy boasting of their Caesar's implacable wrath, the brutality he can always count on from his soldiers."

I do not tell him that the fate of Jerusalem as a city left me oddly cold, that I loathed the city, remembering first the legendary loss of our own holy mountain in Samaria, then that final reckoning of the cross. The rebels had provoked the Roman to the worst atrocities; the fall of the great temple was their final nemesis. But it was more complicated than that. I identified with the city too, the fallen ideals on which it lived; its failure to be what the psalms promised, that *crown of beauty in the hand of the Lord*.[lii]

Suddenly it occurs to me that, had things been different, I too could have been there, one of the countless thousands of women raped and butchered in its streets. For the first time in all these years, I thank my good star I was sent away before that happened.

Marcus, still gripped by the horror of his memories, returns to the subject as if he could never stop thinking about it; as if the answer to all his questions lay buried in the temple ruins.

"He knew what was going to happen there. I heard him prophesy. It was astonishing to hear him speak like that, his words like a great eye opened on our world. He prophesied, and they crucified him for it[liii] and then his prophecy came true. People remember that. And of course, the fulfilment of his prophecy has helped our movement; many people have turned to us since the war. The destruction of the temple…for those Jews who survived, it was like the defeat of everything they had ever believed in."

"He always knew what would happen next, Marcus. He always read it right, as if he himself came from beyond the end and had lived it all backwards."

"That's a shade deep for me, Magdalene. He always said I should eat less and think more! But I know what you mean. I've come to see he didn't just live day to day; he held time in his own hands; he shaped it with his mind. What impresses me is how everything, everything, even the most appalling events, always worked to his advantage, always benefitted the Way. He taught me part of his secret, you know, one night right at the end. He initiated me, showed me a glimpse of his kingdom. I understood it in part, never entirely. I still need help occasionally."

"You lost friends there, people you knew?"

"My wife," he says shortly. "Her whole family too." I wait in silence, but he does not want to say more. His thoughts veer back to my own opaque confession.

"Let's stay with your marriages for the moment, shall we? There's a connection somewhere. The past has its place in our lives but too much of it at one time, that's not good for anyone. We aren't travelling towards the past. We should shake it off, that's what he taught us! All that history, our families, childhoods, what does any of it matter to the way we see things now? Think of Levi. He used to be a tax inspector. Now he's a saint. The past does not define us, Magdalene. I am sure that is what he taught. We are made anew when He enters our lives, born again through his…his…"

63

Marcus shakes his head, as if trying again to make sense of something just beyond his comprehension. As if it all fitted together somehow, if only he could keep hold of the pieces.

"Look at it like this," he says. "In the past, we all made huge mistakes, fell into error, made our pact with the devil: that's why we needed him. Not to judge us but to suspend judgment, undo its binding force. To free us from our own shadows, save us from the devil's grip. Under the Law, we were all guilty…of something. But he, just for the moment he was with us, he overturned that Law, reprieved us from the punishment we deserved.[liv] On one condition, of course!

"I know there must have been difficulties, for you, Magdalene, in your life, in every woman's life, probably. He came to save us from all that; show us a new way. Let's talk about that, about the time itself."

Intelligent, I think, *a bit of a sensualist*, not worldly the way Felix was when he had the government of it in his hands, but there's a wealth in his voice. He has a handle on experience. That shaping he noticed in Yeshua, he has the knack of it himself.

"I need the past, Marcus; ashamed of it as I am at times, it is still my anchor. Yes, I was changed by him, given back to myself; forgiven. But I was not reborn. Or if I was, I became an orphan again almost immediately. There was no new life for me, no way forward that I could find."

And yet, even as I speak, I know this doesn't sound right, not even to myself who wants to believe what I am saying. He hears the puzzlement in my voice and tries to explain what he doesn't fully understand either.

"You didn't need to be reborn, Magdalene," he says. "That new time[lv], it was you who gave birth to it. Don't you see that? And the only thing that matters now is *his* time; the time we share with *him*. Without that, we are nothing. We have our life in his name. So tell me what happened *after* you had left all your husbands. Tell me about the very first time you …"

"Gave birth to the future, you mean? How on earth could I have done that? I don't understand you!"

"You brought him back to us. So tell me about that. The first time you saw him…what was it like? Surely you can remember?"

"I remember. I remember the very first time I saw him: I remember the very first time we met."

He sighs, a touch of impatience. "And?"

"It was as if I didn't exist before, as if the woman I thought myself to be had suddenly vanished, as if she had always been an illusion, just a mask I didn't even know I was wearing. I saw myself differently."

"Yes," he says. "That was the moment you became the Magdalene. Others have said something very similar…Sidonius, for example. Though for him, of course, getting his sight back, it really was like that[lvi]. So go on then, tell me what happened?"

Say it! Say it! I tell myself. *Let him know how it was.* But still I feel stubborn. My lips freeze. I am too vulnerable to tell that story. It will change me again if I do. It will undo me in some way. I will be judged unworthy.

64

I meet again, exactly as before, the same failure of confidence that brought me here in the first place. I stare down into my lap.

"I know you have come a long way since that time."

"We have all come a long way. And yet it seems to me I have come no distance at all." Tears fill my eyes.

"Do you think it would be easier if we went somewhere else? Somewhere away from the village? I don't want to pry or make you uncomfortable. But it would help me to understand you a little. Help you to release the pain still trapped inside."

"I don't often leave the village."

But we both know that if we stay here, I will tell him nothing. A great circle of blue sky protects me here. I feel instead as if a wind had just swept over the valley, a wind that has in it the rising swell of a terrible laughter. I remember as if from yesterday its daemonic force. The power it has over me, that demon of laughter. Anarchic wildness. Uncontrollable. I will be sporting ground for demons again. Wild Magda on her impossible journey walking the same way all over again!

"Be strong!" he says. "A word from you might unlock the world."

"There is one place we might go to. But we must start early. It is over an hour's walk!" I glance across the landscape, pointing out the place. "There's a spring. We will have water. And the remains of an old temple, the Romans built it, but hardly anyone goes there now. It's very shady, the grove, full of oaks and mistletoe. But it has a bad reputation, a bad story attached to it, people stopped going. They think it is haunted but for me it is a special place. I like the darkness there. I have it in myself."

"Wherever you want," he says, his eyes suddenly hooded again. He glances to one side, then adds, "I'm sorry it took me such a while to find you. I fear you may have been left here too long, on your own, if that's how it is. Other influences, other people with different beliefs; other…"

I think for a moment he is going to say 'other marriages', and I shake my head furiously.

"Absolutely not! That was the last."

Suddenly we find ourselves laughing together. Strange how we keep doing that!

*

1.10 The Wedding at Cana

Time to think. Time to put another of the beginnings in order. These long hot summers, my solitude, the distant memory of orchards in Samaria, these things always wake in me a strange longing to narrate, to pick over the details of my life, re-dressing them as I used to dress, over and over again, the blue-eyed doll I had in my childhood.

The only audience I needed then was myself, but that is not enough now. I am speaking to someone else, someone with a whole community behind him. I try to imagine them, the nameless others who surround Marcus, who make up the Way, the faceless ones who are carrying forward the movement we started all those years ago. Imperceptibly, they move a step closer. Will they freeze and vanish if I turn towards them?

*

"The first time I saw him, Marcus, he was by the river, that broad, shallow stretch of the Jordan so beautiful first thing in the morning. But this day it was full of people, a crowd had come there to see John who was splashing about on the edge of the water like a great bird trying to wash their sins away. I didn't know who he was at the time. He had his clothes off and was just stepping into the water behind John. I did notice him though, but only because of an odd incident, I'll tell you about that later.

"But the first time I met him, spoke to him, that was a year or so later. It was a strange, brief, almost incomprehensible meeting: accidental, you might think. I could hardly meet his glance. But the first time he looked full at me with those deep, hypnotic eyes of his, the first time I really knew him: that was at the wedding. I wish it had been otherwise and if you speak of this to anyone else you must not repeat what I tell you. Promise me that!"

"I can't say I'll lie but I can certainly arrange it differently, if that's what you want. *Scribal circumspection,* we call it." There is a sense of foreboding in his glance: "So whose wedding was it, this time?"

A pregnant pause; he shakes his head slightly.

"I see. I thought we had agreed no more marriages. I'm losing count, Magdalene! What was your family thinking of?"

"Nathan *was* my family. All that was left of it, anyway. He was my cousin, a couple of times removed, on my mother's side. I'd known him all my life, not closely but occasionally at family gatherings and the like. You know how it is. Both our fathers were dead, or gone off, in my case. Then Nat's mother died, which was a good thing for him because he couldn't stand her and he badly needed the money. He put the vineyard up for sale almost immediately, but planned to keep his father's orchards. Nat was indolent by nature and wanted a life of ease, enjoying the fruits of his father's labour. We were both orphans by then, you see. My own immediate family had rejected me by that point, and it made a kind of sense for us to marry each other. Our last anchor in the family; *a safe haven*, he called it.

"Nathan was not a narrow-minded man. He'd seen something of the world, studied in Tarsus and tended to look down on his homelands. He used to say Galilee was good for nothing but providing his patrimony.[lvii] Anyway, it was a bit of a coincidence, really, but it turned out that they all knew each other, Yeshua and Nat and Philip; an old boy's network, that sort of thing. Nat and Philip had known each other at school. Neither of them had liked sport much, both were clever-minded, better with books than people and so they became pals."

"So, the teacher was a guest at your wedding, was he?"

66

Perhaps the old temple really was haunted. Perhaps the goddess still stalked the overgrown triangle in the woods. We are standing at her crossroads. Her *discrimen.* [lviii] I decide to speak.

"It was the day before the wedding, actually. During those weeks before the ceremony, I'd come to realise that nothing I had done in my life before could possibly be as bad or as wrong, or make me feel more ashamed of myself, than what I was about to do now in marrying Nathan. It's not that he wasn't an eligible or a decent man; he was both, and relatively wealthy too. I persuaded myself at first it would be healing, after all the strangers in my life, to marry someone I knew, someone who had connections with my early life, someone who understood my past and what had happened to me, and could accept it because, after all, who else as interesting as me could he possibly get to marry him? There were benefits in it for him too; it spared him the effort of a formal courtship.

"But the problem went deeper than this.

"I was angry with my family, bitterly angry. The hurts, the divisions, the bad feeling, it was everywhere by this time; it was how the family had become. Mixed race, mixed blood, mixed feelings! The damage was done and no one except Nat would help me to repair it. Only we, it seemed, could salvage something from those ancient feuds, walk through that damage, Jews against Samaritans, and not be hurt by it. [lix] I thought I might bury it all in myself, deep down amongst all the other broken things that clamoured in my soul. It was stupid of me to think this, stupid and wrong.

"All I was doing, as far as my sister and her husband were concerned, was adding insult to injury. They took it as a personal affront, refused to attend the wedding. What I had chosen to do, it seemed at the time my only choice. I could see no other way forward. And there were personal factors too, that made the situation worse. I could not overcome my own antipathy to Nat; antipathies of every kind.

"However I rationalised it, I knew what I was doing was wrong. It was an act of total bad faith, probably the worst thing I had ever done in my life. I'm not just talking about disobliging my sister and her husband, both partisan Samaritans, he especially; it was not just the fact that I was in love with another man and he a Roman officer to boot! It was that the marriage, in and of itself, was a travesty, a desperate summoning of the forces of chaos. Despite all the sins of my past, I was a truthful girl. This was the biggest lie I had ever committed.

"Nathan had family from his previous marriage back in the Lebanon. He'd gone there as soon as his father died to avoid having to look after his mother. It seemed now he was marrying me to avoid having to care for his daughters. He found parenthood exhausting. None of that bothered me. It was all part of the end of something, the terminal kick of a dying family. I had wealth to bring to the marriage; we both had wealth. I thought there was a chance we could make something out of it. Sheer folly, on my part! I couldn't stop myself from seeing that."

"Sorry, did you just say…?"

"The truth was, Marcus, I was in a river of grief so deep, that I had to do this, or go under. I had to do something. My way of life, the losses, the unhealed wounds, had brought me to the brink of suicide. Black water filled my dreams. It was there at the end of every path, deep and threatening. There was no way back from it but this.

"We both knew what we were doing was wrong but perversely we persevered. Years ago, Nathan had told me he thought it was his mission to rescue me from the gutter; he liked that kind of thing. *The good boy with the future, the bad girl with the past!* The week before the marriage feast, I had gone back across the border to the mountains near Sebaste, a place of special associations for me: there was a tomb there, a bakery, a place where memory dropped anchors. I came there to think, to find some order in my memories, but there was nothing but chaos and loss.

"I set off for Sychar, staying in the house of a woman I knew from my court days. She had made a dress for me from a design I had given her. It was an ethereal blue with a gold trim and tangled green vines embroidered around the waist. She was to be my bridesmaid and Nathan came to her house to collect me.

"As soon as he arrived, we had a terrible argument. It was about bread of all things. Whether it was right that the wheat that grew here could be used to make shewbread for the temple in Jerusalem. As if either of us cared! But we were shouting at each other, or at least I was shouting at him, as if it was a matter of huge importance.[ix] It seemed impossible to go through with the ceremony. He went off in a sulk while I was sat out in the little courtyard garden, feeling dreadful and with no idea what to do. To call off the marriage at this late hour would be a disaster, a complete admission of failure. I couldn't go back to my family. My sister would shame and humiliate me. To go through with the marriage would undoubtedly be a catastrophe but of a different, slightly less predictable kind.

"Suddenly, a bird flew through straight across the courtyard and into the house. I'd cleaned everything the previous night and the interior was bright and shiny, light reflecting off the washed stone. The bird flew straight into the mirror brass on the far wall. There was a sharp knock. I went in and there it was at my feet, a small yellow bird, its eyes hooded over, its pretty feathered neck twisted sharply to one side. It lay there quite still, quite dead and looking down at it I started to cry. I don't want to sound sorry for myself, it wasn't that, but big tears started plashing down my cheeks as if the bird's death was entirely my fault and would be laid at my door.

"I built a little pyre for it at the garden's edge, topped it with moss and a circle of petals and lay the soft, tiny body down on my best handkerchief. My bridal handkerchief it was, the choicest I could find.

"'Forgive me,' I whispered to the little corpse. 'I will bury you properly when I come back.' Then, my eyes all red-raw and puffy from weeping, I grabbed a light shawl and ran up the long street to the prayer house at the top of the hill. I was so paralyzed with indecision, I could feel myself physically breaking up, splitting apart inside, something I had never experienced before.

"The day was brick-kiln hot and the hill a steep one. My mouth was dry with weeping and I thought of stopping at the well for some water but there were too many others waiting already and I hadn't any time to spare.

"As I came along the path to the shrine, there was a bench under the trees and I realised that that Nat was sitting there, his head bent down and looking really upset. A huge feeling of relief swept through me. Despite all our differences, we had come, as if with one accord, to the same place to find help for our distress. Even though I was an odd ball and belonged nowhere, I suddenly thought: *Everything will be all right; Nathan understands. We are united in spirit.*

This comforted me so much that I thought it must be possible for us to talk through our difficulties. With a new life ahead of us, the problems – in my heart, in my past, in our family cultures – would soon go away. Something had brought us together and we were going to make it work.

"I slid down onto the bench next to him, hiding my swollen eyes and face behind a veil of hair. We sat together in silence. I decided I must tell him the truth, the absolute truth, explain how I had been – how I still was – in love with someone else but, because the circumstances were so impossible, I had to break free from him. And I had to triumph over all the hatred and condemnation of my family too. Perhaps it was not true what they always said, that 'Jews have no dealings with Samaritans';[lxi] perhaps we could prove them wrong.

"That was the easy bit to say. The personal things were more difficult. I had to find a way of saying them, too, because I couldn't stop myself thinking them, no matter how hard I tried.. *"The thing is, Nat, it's not that I don't love you, it's just that…I don't like your smell, I don't like being close to you, your body, your skin, it's so milky! I liked it at first but after a fortnight I find I can't…And, to be perfectly honest, I can't stand the noise you make when you're eating either, that munching, snuffling sound, it's…I don't know why it bothers me so much, it just does."*

"I ran it through in my mind, but it didn't sound quite right. Perfectly true as it was, I doubted the wisdom of such a disclosure. Even someone as disinclined as Nat to take things seriously might jib at hearing that. At best, he would make one of his lazy jokes, not believing for a moment I actually meant what I said.

"Then I noticed his feet."

Marcus is torn between amusement and disapproval. "What was wrong with his feet?"

"Nothing. That was the problem. Nathan's feet were terrible, a real stumbling block. No, seriously! He was always falling over. He had a curvature in the spine, you see. It affected his balance, made it difficult for him to stay upright. Normally, I never let myself look at his feet; they were quite beyond redemption. Whereas these feet, the ones next to mine at the moment, they were beautiful. So few men had feet like that! I stared at them through my hair for a long time, feeling more and more uncomfortable. Then they uncrossed themselves.

"I looked up.

"The man sitting next to me hardly stirred. He had short hair, extraordinary grey-brown eyes and a severity around his mouth that was almost a smile because his lips were full and finely shaped and his expression curiously sweet.

"'Oh, God!' I stammered, jumping up. 'I'm so sorry, sir, I mistook you for someone else.'

"'Your bridegroom, was it?'

"'How did you know that?' His effrontery was remarkable. I was quite thrown off guard.

"'Aren't you always looking for him?'

"He moved his head to one side slightly, in the direction of the prayer house.

"'Oh, yes, of course! Is Nathan in there? Are you the Rabbi?'"

"He made no reply.

"I looked at him quickly, trying to guess who he was, my previous panic rushing back. 'You must be one of Nat's friends, then! Excuse me, I didn't recognise.... Are you Philip, perhaps?' The truth is, I don't know many of his friends. Apart from his mother's funeral, we've hardly seen each other for years.'

"He shook his head.

"'Well, do you at least know where he is? I need to speak to him. Quite urgently, in fact! I've made such a mistake. We had a quarrel. It was about the bread. And then a bird flew into the house and killed itself. And that's such a bad omen, isn't it? And that's why I've come here: to ask God for a sign…a different one, that is. A better one! We're supposed to be getting married tomorrow. And it's so hot. And I'm so thirsty.' I hang my head and weep into my lap for very shame."

"He doesn't move.

"'You know who I am.'

"'No, I don't! Who are you?'"

At this point I turn to Marcus and seize his forearm. "Don't ever repeat this, Marcus, will you?"

"Go on!"

"Then he said, 'I am Yeshua. If you knew who I was you would share a drink with me now. I have been waiting for you at this well for centuries. There is no need for distress. We can put a stop to this at once. You must bring Nathan to me, as soon as he arrives. He will become my follower. I will send him overseas again. Then you will be free.' [lxii]

"'Free? Free from what?'

"'I am your salvation,' he said, just like that! 'You will be free of everything. Free from your sins, your family, your past life. You can dry your tears now, drink the water of life instead.'

"'Jews and Samaritans don't drink from the same vessels? [lxiii] Surely you know that! And I'm a Samaritan, at least on my mother's side, though she and I aren't on the same side about anything, really. My sister says this marriage will be the death of her and I hope it is! At least it will have achieved something!'

"He contemplates my defiance, my sinfulness with a terrible, steady stare.

"'Nathan is not your husband.'

"'How would you know?'

"'You have had too many like him already. Five is it? If you will drink with me now, you won't thirst for any other.'

"'Look!' I say, then remember the awful state of my face and turn away.

"But he was looking. Looking past me out across the plain, the long sweeping view down from the hill where the temples stood.

"He said, 'A relative of mine is buried near here. I come to pray at his tomb sometimes. He suffered for me. I carry his death in my spirit.'[lxiv]

"'I'm sad for you then! Everybody I cared about in my family is dead too.'

"His words have such sincerity, I suddenly find myself wanting to confide in him. 'They all died, my little brother was the first. Then my father's mother, then my uncles, all three of them in the last war. The ones who are still alive, they all hate me. That's why I am marrying Nathan. He is my last hope of keeping the family together.

"'I know it's wrong, but if you are a woman what other choice is there? You don't know what it's like! How can you? Sometimes it takes a really big mistake to find your path again. You have to die in spirit: it's like killing yourself, committing suicide. You have to die; the person you were, it has to die and go under. Go right down into the underworld, into the darkness where the ghosts and the shadows are, the lost souls.'

"'And then what do you do?'

"'Then? Well, you either stay put and become one of them, become dead yourself or – how can I explain this? – you will have the feeling that something is holding you, despite everything. As if something loved you – it might be God even – and will not let go. You are still attached in some way: to the world of the living. There's no mistaking the feeling! You just have to let go of your old self and trust this strange attachment to bring you through.'

"'And where did you learn this?'

"'From bad experiences; terrible hurt. I've died more than once in my life. You just have to trust the thing that loves you, the thing that holds onto you and knows more than you do. You have to call on the very depth of your spirit to carry you through, and trust that it will lift you up again.' I look at him then, but what I see is not his face at all but the tunnel of darkness ahead of me, the course I am about to take, the icy shaft of a hopeless marriage. 'Of course, there's no guarantee.'

"Then I look into his eyes suddenly, and see his expression change. A shudder of fear passes through me, as if I had put my hand into living flame.

"'And if you don't do this?'

"'I will die; I will drown in a well of failure and self-loathing.'

"'I am there,' he said. 'Even in that depth,' he said. 'Drink with me now and you will not die. I will save you. I will show you a new kind of family. Chloë can vouch for me.'

"'Look, I'm sorry, I'm sure you mean well and it's kind of you to take the trouble but, as I've tried to explain, I've come here for a sign – a sign from God

– not to share drinks with a stranger. All I want is a sign! I've come here to pray for one. And I have to go to the shrine.'

"He smiles slightly, unoffended. 'What kind of sign would you recognise?'

"His persistence is exasperating. I haven't time for all these questions.

"'A proper sign, of course! A sign that will tell me what to do! I don't want dead birds; I don't want strange men. I don't want another distraction. What I want is for God to help me, just this once! I want him to show me what I should do!'

"I get up and walk off along the path into the shrine precincts.

"Then a terror shakes me. A fear of what I have just said. There has been a demon in my heart for so long and now I have just betrayed him. The demon will punish me for that. He will leave me. I will be left with nothing.

"'*Magdalene! Mary Magdalene.*' I hear someone in the distance behind me calling a name I half recognise. Like a voice from the seashore. Quite eerie.

"I turn and glance back over my shoulder, but the figure has gone. The bench is empty. [lxv] Not a soul in sight."

*

John Mark is looking at me, his mouth half open. "Tell me more," he says.

*

1.11   The Bridal Chamber

"Tearful, anxious and desperate to be alone, I hurried off into the shade of the prayer house and sat down by the west wall under a memorial for those killed in the last Syrian war. Even in here, it is stifling hot and I find myself wishing I had accepted the drink.

"The sunlight from the window slides along the whitewashed wall beside me until it finds the bronze memorial plaque, then blazes it into sudden fire. This is a land of wars. Sometimes it feels as if every conflict is still playing out inside me: my parents, their parents, the bitter history of Jews and Samaritans. The unforgivable wrongs, the destruction of temples, the endless retaliations! I return to my meditations, stilling myself, trying to find some lucidity within. I feel deathly, on the threshold of another huge, ugly mistake.

"Just as I am settling down into my prayer, the door of the meeting room is shunted open. A priest of some kind ushers in a party of visitors, a dozen or so men and women, most of who seemed to be suffering from terrible disorders. Their faces are distorted and foreshortened, they are war veterans perhaps with burns as disfiguring as leprosy or those plagued by demons, their limbs jerking spasmodically. I wonder for a moment if the man I saw outside was their exorcist, come here to perform a healing. It takes one to know one, they say.

"Two men at the rear of the party are carrying in a man with a crippled leg; a woman points to the bench beside me and, to my irritation, they set him down there. He smells awful and I can't prevent a sigh of exasperation. The priest glances at me briefly before launching into a history of the building, pointing out its features of interest. He mentions the memorial stone, and everybody turns to look at it, with me praying for a sign beneath it. Finally, he comes to the end of his talk and says something about a tour of the burial field. Some local benefactors and a famous general have their tombs there and the town is proud of its heroes.

"As signs go, I am finding this one hard to interpret. The priest has disappeared down the stairs, his party filtering after him. To my alarm, I notice the man beside me has been left behind. He shuffles along the bench, sliding up the leg of his tunic, then nudges me with his elbow. 'Had this thirty-eight years,' he whispers, pointing to his cankered thigh, the bone protruding and twisted. He nods to himself. "Incurable!" he says.

"I glance at the yellowed flesh, the desert landscape of hair and wound, and nod sympathetically.

"'Want to see more?' he asks.

"As signs go, this has gone far enough. I stand up, pressing my hand firmly down on his shoulder, put an offering in the treasury and slip out into the garden again, relieved the stranger has not reappeared.

"But the choice I must make is still there waiting for me. I have to decide either to cancel the wedding at this late hour at dreadful cost to my reputation, or to go ahead with it to the complete mortification of my heart. Neither option recommends itself: both seem equally impossible to survive! Then I think of the poor people at the shrine and the terrible afflictions from which they suffer. The burden I am asking myself to bear is surely light in comparison with those.

"Back at my lodging, I sit with my head in my hands, desperately wanting to speak to Felix. *I still love you; don't you see! The attachment hasn't gone; it's still there inside me.*

"I have never believed Felix to be a good man, but he knows the world, he is wise in its ways and has great power in Samaria.[lxvi] There is no one else I can turn to.

"In a moment of clarity, I ask myself: *Is it really Felix I am talking to, or is it perhaps, my mother in disguise, she who has turned her back on me, refused to attend the wedding, always sided with my sister against me?* The pain of her rejection eats at my heart, causes me an anguish that never seems to heal.

"Thinking of my mother brings to mind the little dead bird lying unburied on its funeral pyre. Mother had a phobia about birds, but I do not, and I have promised to complete its funeral rite. I go back into the shaded garden and only then do I notice that the pyre is empty. The bird has gone. It has either revived and flown away, or next-door's cat must have taken it.

"I look about for evidence of what has happened. There are no shed feathers, no sign of bird or cat anywhere.

"My heart lifts in relief. *This can only be good,* I think. *This temporary death is the sign I have been looking for. We can go ahead.*

"Suddenly I remember who Chloë is. Her red-cheeked, wind-swept smile.

"Nat arrives, shame-faced, apologetic, awaiting instructions.

"At first light, after only a couple of hours sleep, we set off for Cana, wretched little place though it is, and the marriage goes ahead. The service is mercifully short, and I don't catch a word of it. Cana is the home of Nat's ancestors. When we arrive at the wedding banquet where our guests are waiting for us, we find a motley crew of people I have never seen before. With few friends of his own, Nathan had invited more or less everyone he could remember from his past, friends of his parents for the most part.

"He is very nervous about his speech and, as one course follows another through the feast he has laid on, he keeps glancing surreptitiously at his notes. We drink our toasts. By the time the spiced wine arrives at the end of the meal, over-sweet and cloying, our artificial spirits are beginning to flag. The heat haze over the table is thick with dust and sweat and flies. A pall spreads over the occasion. It feels more like a wake than a wedding feast.

"I long to be on my own again, alone at home in my thoughts, free to bathe my face and body in pure, cold water.

"I think I will never smile at anyone again.

"Our host, Nathan's great-uncle, must have sensed this. A middle-aged woman with white bands in her hair who is sitting with the dance troupe suddenly stands up and beats her tambourine. She rattles it twice and there is a scraping of benches in the corner. As if on command, a steward appears carrying a large flagon of wine; a late wedding gift, I assume. He sets it down before us, a fine, blush rosé freshly drawn, and, as another steward follows him with a tray of clean cups, pours it out with extraordinary care.

"Something special then! Not just local wine, not even the well-matured wine from Nathan's father's old vineyard. We drink a toast. The wine is lighter, finer than anything we have had before, with a soft honey taste on the tongue, then something more complex and mineral, subtle and refreshing, underneath.

"'I say, Nat,' shouts the old school friend who gave the final toast, 'this is quality stuff! Can't remember last time I tasted better. Really pushing the boat out here!'

"Nathan accepts the complement with uncomprehending graciousness and gives his wheezy, asthmatic laugh.

"I look away politely and notice a man standing in the doorway. "Who's that?" I ask Nathan. "The one over there who has just come in, the man with the covered head and the silver and crimson sash?"

"But Nat's gaze is elsewhere.

"'Why, it's old Stag-face!' he says. 'Well, I'll be blowed; he made it after all! His mother told me he was setting up around here – he's a beggar, you know, sweetheart, a true professional, completely lame, used to sit by the bath-house steps at the entrance to the meeting house. I told her to bring him along if he wanted to come, but I never thought for a minute she'd take me at my word. No, I don't believe it! It's not possible! Just take a look at that, will you? He's not just here; he's actually standing up…on his own two feet! It must be the new wine! Next thing you know, he'll be walking across. No, no, don't stare, we don't want to encourage him!'

"But I am not staring, I am blushing crimson, a novel sensation, one I am not used to. The man in the sash is standing among a group of men at the door but he is looking in my direction. His glance is serious and direct, penetrating in its intensity. He raises a cup of wine towards me.

"In a moment of astonishment, I lift mine in reply and discover that I am not only blushing like a peony, I am smiling too, I, who have never be known to smile at weddings, and certainly haven't done at this one. It is as if someone has handed me a cup of pure amusement and I have swallowed it whole, in one clean gulp.

"A gulp of laughter as it turns out, for it is laughter that is welling up inside me! The wine I have just swallowed breaks back into my throat in a torrent of bubbles. I put my hand over my mouth to stop it blurting out, but it is too late! The wine cascades through my fingers, streams out of my nostrils and starts pouring down my chin. People scrape their chairs backwards to get out of my way and I hear Uncle Simon muttering to the man on his left: 'She's trouble, that one! I told Nathan nothing good would come of it.'

"Mortified, I try to suppress my weird hilarity by drinking a goblet of water, but the laughter gets hold of that too and jets it upwards. I am turning into a living fountain. People are turning away in embarrassment but still I cannot stop.

"Nathan thrusts a florid, red-spotted neckerchief into my hand, and I clamp it to my face, still sneezing and snorting until the spasm subsides a little and I can look about me again. The man's gaze is still fixed on me intently. For a moment the room empties, the sound dies into silence as if the whole scene were taking place under water. He is looking at me as if into a mirror, seeing his own reflection staring back at him, drawing it towards him.

"I breathe in, then hold my breath. My heart feels light as air, as if it were floating upwards like a feather on the breeze. I think to myself: *But it is only laughter, after all!? Nothing to be frightened of; you are supposed to feel happy on your wedding day.*

"Perhaps everything will turn out well. The mood of the party is certainly changing. One of the young men, cup in hand, comes into the centre of the room and, giving me a moment's reprieve, starts singing a well-known wedding song. He had a beautiful voice, deep and rich. It gives me courage to do what I have not done all day: to glance at that up-turned couch with its three empty seats at the end of the table where my bridal party, my close family, my mother, my sister and her husband, should have been sitting. I take in the pure space of their absence. An unsteady happiness, gaiety itself, sweeps tentatively through the room.

"'I feel so part of this!' cries Susannah, my bridesmaid, when I meet her in the latrines, 'I feel so emotional, so tuned in. And what a voice that young man had! As for your dress…it's such a beautiful blue! I'm sure it won't stain. And you've got your train tangled. Here, let me help! Anyway, you look transformed, beautiful. Perhaps this marriage will be better for you than you think!'

"Nat made an excellent speech. His groomsman, Philip, stood up and spoke, briefly, of Nat's sterling qualities. Some nice words were said of me too, not in truth that he knew me at all. But the words were so sweet and gave me so much pleasure that I repeated them over and over again like a mantra until they felt like truth and I felt almost happy to be where I was. The day wore on. Nat got more and more drunk. When we got to our suite upstairs, he sat down on the settle in the dressing room, wiped the sweat from his face with the damp handkerchief I had given back to him and promptly passed out.

"I picked up the cloth he had dropped and sat beside him for a while, quite still and silent. What was to be done? Then I noticed that the door to the bridal chamber had come unlatched. I stood up very quietly and, still wearing my wedding dress, I pushed it open.

"Half an hour later, I found myself married to a complete stranger."

*

1.12   Across the Threshold

Marcus raises both eyebrows and looks at me long and hard. An appraising glance.

"You mean…?"

"I mean…just what I say. And that may not be what you think. There's a meaning on one side of a door like that, quite another when you go inside. I'd begun a transition, you see, from where I had been in my life to this entirely new place. Something had changed deep inside me. The flim-flam person I used to be had vanished. I knew when I left that room she had gone forever."

Only the sound of her voice came back to me occasionally, when I was miserable or tired. She sounded like my mother.

*

Within weeks, Nat returned to his first wife in the Lebanon. He sold his lands, gave the money for his orchards to a new charity.

Mother's message had said only: *I will not be attending your wedding. We no longer consider you a part of our family.*

For the first time in my life, after five husbands and this last 'marriage', I found myself completely alone.

*

"And all of that is strictly true, is it, Magdalene?"

But it is too late now to ask me that. I brush off his question. I have started to speak! I have told him something I have never spoken about before. What surprises me is how much life there is in it still, like a lively little serpent twisting about, as I try to describe those extraordinary days.

Whether Marcus will come back to hear any more of my story, I have serious doubts, but it is too late to worry now.

The door has come unlatched. I have pushed it open. Time at last to step across the threshold.

*

Back in the coolness of my cave, I expected to feel sad. Reliving those old memories, recalling that desperate step, I thought it would kill me with grief. But instead, the opposite has happened. I feel revitalised, as if all the anguish of that time had simply risen up like the little golden bird and flown away.

If Marcus does come back – and I am not saying I want him to – I must ask him more about himself. Who sent him and why? I must ask him too about the people I can still remember. Did any of them ever think of me again?

It seems impossible that I have been here for nearly forty years. Impossible that my life since then has been altogether contained in this tiny village on the side of the great mountain where only the sun and the winds play out their drama.

I lean over the railing at the far side of the square and stare out at the view as I have done every day since I came here. *I am a prisoner*, I think tonight, *a prisoner of all this beauty; a prisoner who has lost all thought of escape!* Better, surely, a prisoner of beauty than a lost soul in a fly-blown world, worms and maggots burrowing into the flesh of everything that lives. I could go back to that world, but *cui bono*? What would I do there? What good would come of it now? Everyone thinks I am dead. If I leave my hiding place, I must face the memories of other people, those who did not love me then and will not want to see me now.

I went where they sent me: that terrible rite of passage, the black waves, the sickness. Instead of an end, instead of a beginning, this white void I carry in my palm.

Don't touch me, Magdalene![lxvii]

Better stay a dead woman in a world of beauty, a lost soul in the blessed light of heaven, than make that journey back to a place I would know now only as a revenant.

I must make him promise, this man who says he knows the John that I knew when I knew all of them, I must make him promise never to speak of my hiding place to anyone.

False precautions! I know already that his arrival here means it is time for me to leave.

*

Poor Nathan. I think it for the first time. I lost touch with him. He lost touch with all of us. He went back to Lebanon. I went forward on my black raft alone. In the eyes of the world, this was another failure, one that confirmed all over again the lost and mistaken being I had become.

All I could think of to do in those lunatic months after Nathan left was to contact Felix again, Felix who I knew for certain I needed to forget. The woman I had been might have vanished forever, but she does not know it yet: deaths

77

such as hers are not instantaneous. She tries to go forward, but she goes forward helplessly like a ghost. She does not realise yet that her will is powerless, her spirit asleep in a chamber of change from which it is not yet ready to emerge.

With Felix, nothing has changed. He sees my grief, tears so copious he is sure I am drowning. *"Someone who cries the way you do must be ill,"* he says conclusively; a sure signal it is time for him to leave. *"You must get some help,"* he adds, waving his plump hand vaguely as if to show how this might be achieved.

The black, poisonous waters surround me again. I determine I will survive. Then I hear that my mother is dying, two weeks later I learn she is dead. My family labels me a ruined woman; when I ask why I was not told of the funeral, my brother-in-law's voice is icy with contempt. *"I didn't tell you before. Why should I? You are no longer part of our family."*

Suddenly, I am in trouble again. Serious trouble. Someone makes an accusation against me, an accusation of immorality. At my weakest, the accusation falls. Someone has informed on me, Nat's great-uncle I am sure of it. I live contrary to their laws and customs. I am a corrupt and sinful woman[lxviii] and do not deserve to live. Black crows descend and surround me; I am helpless against them; helpless against their lies; helpless against their power.

I stand accused of being what I am.[lxix] My luck has left me. The Law has me in its grip at last.

*

He stands there ignoring me, ignoring everyone, a deep furrow of thought between his brows. He bends down concentrating intensely and draws a strange hieroglyph in the sand.

Then he stands up again, turns towards us, and points to what he has drawn. He throws down the rule he was carrying. It lands at my feet with a soft thud.

An interval. The soft thud is followed by a silence so unearthly it sounds like the notes of some incomprehensible music. I listen stupefied. The silence continues; we are all listening. It trails off into a series of soft thuds just like the first, gentle as a drum tap, repeated over and over again.

Eventually I open my eyes. He is still standing there.

"Go home," he says. "Go and recover now. Forget everything."

*

"So," says Marcus. "Rather a bad start then."

I nod slightly. He doesn't know, and never will, the full details of that story.[lxx]

"I'm not going to repeat what you've told me to anyone, except John, of course. You must have been at the end of your tether."

"My tether?"

"To the path of wrong. Even so, I'm surprised that first meeting had such little impact. His advice was surely excellent. He understood what you were saying. He knew you were in need of transformation, that it would take one further, final misadventure, to achieve the change. A woman of changes, dramatic changes, that is how I see you most. It must be hard sometimes to recognise yourself. To remember all those women you have been."

"The path of wrong: yes, I fell free of it. That is why I say you must not see me as a woman."

But I am surprised at how quickly he has put it all together. He has accepted what I say, made no apparent judgment of his own.

"That personal past, Magdalene, it's not our concern any more. All those unreal selves! They are what he saved us from."

*

Once that great bolt has slammed shut, nothing will ever open it again.

*

1.13   Marcus's Story

"How did you find me?"

Today, it is I who must ask the questions. Speaking of myself as I did yesterday, I have made myself doubly vulnerable. There will be talk in the village about our meetings. Word will get about; tongues will wag. '*Our mystery woman*,' the villagers used to call me. They have got used to me now, but I don't want to have my life shrunk and twisted into a shape of their making. Not now, not in these circumstances when my life story seems to have acquired some value again.

Marcus has already told me he is John's man. John has sent him to find me. Because others have already done this, John too is thinking of writing an account of what happened, before it is too late, before people's memories become unreliable and invented stories take their place.[lxxi] Marcus has been a member of the group for forty years and seems to have known Peter well. Now, much later in life, he has become attached to John; [lxxii] become his chief scribe.

John, miraculously, is still alive. I store this information in my mind. I will ponder it carefully in the time ahead. I remember John, the young man he was back then, his soft glance, his sinuous, almost girlish side, something fine about John, something competitive too. He was my rival sometimes for the teacher's special praise. John must be an old man now. A survivor like myself; one of the very last!

"So, how did you find me?"

"There was someone back then, wasn't there? Do you remember? Someone who advised you, helped with the arrangements. He was a man of some importance in Jerusalem, a counsellor; he was important to us too. You would have taken to him, I'm sure; you, with your liking for powerful men!"

I ignore his innuendo. "You are talking about Joseph, aren't you? Of course he was important. He was almost one of us. It was his tomb we used after the…for the burial. Joseph was a wealthy man; he had his own set of secrets. We all did." [lxxiii]

"You went there with them, I've heard. You went to the tomb. And then came back. It was first thing in the morning; there were special herbs you were supposed to bring, herbs, ointment, something about a garment? Joseph knew things the others did not. John said you came running back to them, that morning. You had seen Yeshua, he said. He had given you a message to deliver. The men were still hiding out in Bethany and Peter said once that no one believed what you told them. John disagreed with that; he did believe you apparently. By the time they had verified your account, it was obvious you needed to be got out of harm's way, to a place of safety.

"Joseph had already thought of that, he had discussed it with others and had somewhere in mind. You knew too much for your own good; it was dangerous knowledge. He was willing to use his contacts; he had quarries in Gaul,[lxxiv] knew the routes that crossed the empire. He thought it was his responsibility to protect you."

"Yes, that's right. Joseph was involved. He did give me some names, several of them all in different places, but…that was after the group had persuaded me to leave. It wasn't Joseph, surely, who…"

"We didn't know whose idea it was, at first. We all expected to see you again, naturally. We didn't think you would have gone so far. Joses, apparently, had misinformed the captain of the boat you were on. He got his instructions muddled. Some of us expected to see you in Galilee but you didn't show. Peter was gaining control by then; he had received his own commission from our risen Lord; he had had his own encounter. It made a difference to everyone, that! It silenced the doubters. Peter and John, they thought at first you were being taken back along the coast, up to Samaria. It seemed the obvious place for you to hide."

"Then whose idea was it, to send me so far away? And what happened to Peter?"

"Well, we'd had your message, about going to Galilee. The teacher had said the same thing himself at his farewell supper. A group of the early disciples went back there, to Capernaum, just as he had told them to. I'm a Jericho man myself so I wasn't with them; I wasn't important enough at the time, but I heard what happened. I heard it from Peter himself, though it was a good deal later. It took Peter a long time to…remember exactly what had happened there, a long time to reconstruct it all in his mind."

"Quick to act, slow to think! I'm glad he saw Yeshua, glad he believed me at last."

"They were out in the boat when they saw him, quite a distance away. Yeshua was standing on the shore cooking a fish that hadn't even been caught yet! There was a small fire made out of driftwood burning on the shingle. Those out in the boat saw the smoke first, it was like a signal, and then there was a figure standing beside it. His head was covered so they couldn't see who it was at first. It was Peter who recognised him[lxxv], Peter who jumped in fully clothed and disturbed the nets so that a shoal of fish swam straight into them. It was Peter who spoke to him. There was a fish perfectly cooked on the fire by the time the others got there."

I did have a message, yes, but there was nothing about fish in it, nothing much about Galilee either. Complex emotions stir inside me, deep and dark and full of injury.

"Because you weren't there at that time, we all assumed you must have seen him again, on your own somewhere. There were mutterings about that. Others guessed you might have gone away for your own safety. You were so close to him, after all. Peter, of course, didn't stir in the matter. Once he had seen the risen Lord for himself, he didn't consider your whereabouts important. Some said he found you difficult to deal with. Peter was a conventional man, especially so when it came to women. He and some of the others, they weren't quite sure how you fitted in to the group. You had your place in the inner circle, but you weren't really *one of them*, were you?[lxxvi]

"So, it was Peter who…"

"Peter didn't know where you were, Magdalene; it wasn't he who made the arrangements, though I don't think he was entirely sorry you had gone. We all assumed it was Joseph; he'd had some dream, I think, about your safety. Others, myself included, felt uneasy about your disappearance, not that I counted for much among them then. Your not being there: it raised questions, suspicion too. You know how it was among the doubters!

"When I talked to John about it, he said he was sure there had to be an explanation, he just didn't know what it was. He had the insight of his jealousy, John, he was wary of everyone, even a newcomer like myself. It must be hard to follow someone who loves everybody, someone who is always finding new people to love him. It was a long time before I won John's trust.

"John thought at first the two of you might have cooked something up together. He feared some secret arrangement; thought you and Yeshua might have met up in secret, leaving them to…take things forward on their own. Then, when you didn't come back, it was as if you were the one who had died. It began to seem almost natural, as if you were so much part of him you couldn't exist on your own without him."

Tears again. All those years of waiting, wondering what had happened, what misunderstanding might have occurred? All the excuses I made, for everyone.

"So there was no arrangement then, between the two of you? For afterwards?"

I shook my head. "Nothing."

"You never saw him again?"

"Never. Not once."

"Nathan had a different story. He came back south about that time; he was there in Galilee with Peter and the rest. No one had seen him for a couple of years but there was a bit of a stir about him back then. You mentioned a spinal injury; that checks with what I'd heard before. But when he turned up on the lake with the fishing gang, he was completely cured. Straight as a die, John said."

"You mean, it was Nathan who knew where I was? Nathan who sent me?" I am reeling with each new revelation. "He checked up on me? Had some secret information?"

"Nathan liked to feel he was a controlling force, apparently. He thought of himself as a kind of *unmoved mover,* a superior intelligence directing events from a distance. Philip described him as something of a voyeur; he liked to check up on people, felt that kind of knowledge gave him power. He had contacts through his family wine-trade but little instinct for danger – apart from marrying you, of course, and no one ever spoke of that.

"I must have heard you had family connections. He was in touch with your sister occasionally. Anyway, he was the one who told Peter you'd gone east, into Gaul, one of the harbour towns, Narbo, he thought. You'd been in touch with someone there, he wouldn't say who, just tapped the side of his nose. And he mentioned your fellow myrrh-bearer, that extraordinary, extravagant man who first told me about the teacher and made me so desperate to meet him. Nicodemus, you remember?"

Another secret then, one shared, it turns out, with unimagined others. But how had Nathan known about Nicodemus, my fellow myrrh bearer; my own special guide to the underworld?[lxxvii]

"Anyway, with Nathan's hint in mind, we worked out, John and I, who it had to be, your accomplice, and then one day, John met up with him at a house church near Ephesus. He was very old by this time, close to death in fact, but lucid and quite unafraid. All he told us were the directions you should have been given: the journey itself, and where to go when you got there.

"The journey hadn't been his idea, he said, but he had a contact in Southern Gaul who could help you when you arrived. Give you some shelter, that sort of thing. As it turned out, you never met up with him. There had been an arrangement, but something went wrong, the captain should have passed on information to you when you arrived, someone on the boat. But it didn't work out. The contact didn't find you. He vanished entirely. You vanished entirely. Those few who knew where you were going thought you must have died on the journey. Joseph was the one who mentioned Massalia.

"Eventually, and I'll tell you why later, I took a passage across the Upper Sea and traced your footsteps. You were there for a while but it's a busy place, Massalia, quite run down, difficult to keep track of people. I've been looking for you on and off for three years, Magdalene; I want you to remember that.

"Someone I spoke to there – we have a small group of our own people at the port side now – they mentioned a story about someone of your description, standing outside the temple and weeping like a wayside statue. People had noticed you, wondered who you were and where you came from. Quite a memorable image they had: sea birds flocking around your head, hair blowing like wild cords in the shore breeze, and your uncontrollable tears. You sat down on the marble steps as if in a trance, weeping so hard they thought you might be a visitation from the goddess. I even heard that someone took you in, that you joined the temple, went on its processions, practiced the cult of the great goddess Artemis, had care of her emblems even."

I look away.

"Is any of that true, Magdalene? To me, it seems frankly incredible that you should do such a thing, so soon after…Surely, you kept the faith that he had taught you?"

"It is all true." I say simply. "The goddess saved my life. Her cult, it taught me the mysteries. Through her, I understood something of what had taken place, understood more of what I had been through, the role I had played in his own sacred death-drama. There were similarities…"

He listens carefully. "So it was true then? You worked at the temple? Did the rites of the cult, performed the temple services? A powerful goddess, certainly! The great emperor Augustus promoted her cult, I know, and it has never altogether lost its status. We follow, as you say, a little in her footsteps."[lxxviii]

I listen in silence. He does not realise where we are standing; whose little temple this ruin used to house.

He waits for me to speak but still I say nothing. I am awed by his understanding, his openness towards mysteries that few had access to. *He has had*, I think, *some initiation of his own!*

"I was told, a man had turned up in Massalia looking for you. It made me think Nathan's story must have been true. The man was persistent, found your role there very…interesting, wanted you to perform temple services for him. At first, they said, you seemed pleased, excited even, to hear of him but then it turned out he wasn't the man you thought he was, he wasn't the man you wanted to see. All very confusing! All very mysterious! All very Magdalene!

"One of the temple-folk told me you became frightened, that you left the place suddenly and vanished again. You had talked occasionally of going to the mountains, wanting somewhere that reminded you of your home. You had been waiting for someone in Massalia, but it wasn't the one who came. After that, they said, you gave up waiting, went inland, they thought, or back over the sea.

"So, there you are, Magdalene. I've walked the mountain paths, on and off, for nearly three years. The tremendous alps, the heights above the Bay of Angels: I thought you might be there, I thought it sounded right but no one had ever heard of you or seen a stranger of your description.

"The mountains got steeper and stranger and further away, but I followed the trail, from Alpibus until I came here, to the last mountain in the range and the biggest of them all. There was a shepherd who knew all the paths, all the trails, all the springs, and I met him one morning at an inn; he'd been pastured in a place where there was a pack of wolves and he and his dog had had to drive them off. He had a wound in one leg where he'd been badly bitten and had come to the inn to get some bandaging. It was a bad wound, it had become infected, but his dog had licked it clean and kept him alive. He was lucky, he said, to still be here. I asked if he knew these hills well. He said, he had been born here and herded the sheep and the goats all his life. There was not a stone, not a path, not a stile he didn't know."[lxxix]

"And did he know me, this good shepherd?"

"He said there was a stranger woman in one of the cave-houses who knew about herbs and could cook up medicines useful for healing. Said she'd cured a boy of snakebite once. Said the rumour was, she'd been a temple whore at Massalia. Sorry Magdalene! I'm only repeating his words. There was something about a child, a princess on a journey down the coast who had nearly died giving birth. Or was it the child who nearly died? Apparently, the princess had called on the goddess for help, but it was this woman who came instead and used her skills and saved both of them.[lxxx] She didn't speak much in their dialect but had a way with her, and she had been well rewarded for her services. She was not a pauper woman; for all she was a stranger in these parts, and she once had a yappy yellow dog with her. He knew this because he had once helped her rescue it from a foxhole. And then he said, 'She did some death-work at the quarries. Plenty of call for that!'

"As he spoke, I thought the woman he was describing must be you. The same mix of…And so I came up here. And here you were. Does that satisfy you?"

He is remarkable, this man, the way he assembles information and holds it close. I wonder how he knows, or remembers, so much about our lives back then. He must have been close to Yeshua's movement, one of the new men who have come to prominence.

He holds some of my history in his hands, a history I thought I had lost and let go of. There was a break, a discontinuity, the thread of my life snapped entirely in two: it seemed impossible the broken ends could ever be joined again. But he has picked them up, bound them together; made a bridge between them.

Being found again, what does it feel like? I see a history of tears, a cascade of turbulent water, a river over jagged rocks in which I have been tossed and battered and torn. The story of a lost life. Now I am baptised in it all over again.

I weep while he speaks, but the anguish is less keen than I had expected. His account brings some kind of healing. The conspiracy to be rid of me seems less universal than I thought. Not everybody wanted me gone. My paranoia turns tail.

Did I, at some level, want that too? Was this separation really something I chose for myself?

"Everyone thinks it would be safer, better for us all, and for you too of course, if you went into hiding for a while, until the time is right. We aren't sure we can protect you; you might not be able to protect yourself."

Suddenly it occurs to me, John knew of our marriage. He might have thought I was carrying a child![lxxxi]

The kindness of this sweeps over me like a wave.
The irony of it leaves me speechless, all over again.

*

1.14   Magda Relives (And Stops Reliving)

And so, I climbed up here that night, after a long and painful journey: I was learning, so I told myself as I toiled upwards, how to ascend. I came to Mèthamis and from here, from its clear, unbroken heights, I could see in one wide glance, the whole catastrophe of my life: it was all there in front of me, the wrecked and wretched enterprise from which I was lucky to have stepped free.

But then, after the early period, after a few weeks and months, I really did begin to experience some sort of ascent, in parts of my mind, at least, some lifting out of that long dark view behind me. Perhaps it was just that I was recovering from the journey, but it felt as if I was shaking off some miasma, some mountain mist that clung to my clothing, as if I were climbing higher than the wreckage itself, seeing it at least from some vantage point that gave me, if not perspective, then clarity of vision. I wondered if dying itself, once one had shaken off all the old suffering, was like this too: not as bad as one had imagined it to be. I felt I had undergone a rite of passage through death itself, and the goddess who dealt in such things, had lent me her assistance. Dying has more than one face; women do it differently.

My ascension had relieved something. The higher I was, the safer I felt. Over the first two years, even my tears began to change. Until then, I had waited for him to come. I had believed in the plan. I thought I would meet with Yeshua again. I thought he would come to me. I hoped, even sinfully longed, for him to come to me, so we could be together, once more at least, so that the pain of this love, the always unfulfilled longing, might finally find some completion. Find at least something that would help me understand who he was, who I was for him, who we were for each other and who, since our last encounter, he had now become.

I was so sure this had to happen, that the meeting would come. And yet, it did not. I waited and waited. Mèthamis became the place in which I found myself lost, left behind, a figment of some all but forgotten dream. It was as if I had lost him all over again.

But this is how it is here: the land is kind to certain sorts of memory. It understands, accepts, and even cherishes, the better type of heartbreak. I think of Pons, the young woman who gave him her recipes. It is a land that heals too. It is the quality of the light that does it: not the light of the world but the light of some higher place; a light that has bathed itself in joy. *Jocunditas*, the Romans call it.

My tears, the ones I shed night and morning, didn't stop but they started to change as if the stones they flowed over were no longer so rough and piercing as they had been but softer, smoother, flattened by the water. The wound that affected all of us, the pain, the rejection, the incomprehension, the sheer atrocious loss, all of this, started slowly to change its complexion. The cold blank that had seeped like death through my memory began to lighten, the memories themselves began to revive, take on life again. Suddenly, out of nowhere and quite unbidden, as if I were still living them, they would come floating back to me, vivid and bright as soft-winged butterflies or those iridescent dragon flies that live along the river.

I'd be doing some mundane task and I would suddenly step out of my life now, my quiet, hidden life and I would find myself in one of my other lives, just for a moment I'd be there, exactly as I used to be, at Herod's court, in Tiberias, with Felix first, then with Joanna. On the road, the shape of the dust in the distance, the familiar shores around Galilee, the path across the wheat fields, the curious silence of the olive groves; the different listening of the crowds, the faces of those who were healed.

They didn't stay, these memories, I didn't reconstruct them or try to hold them to me. I watched them instead: little living inconsequential things, but colourful and unembittered, no longer attached to the suffering of the time, no longer in thrall to those who had turned against me but free to be nothing now except themselves.

At least in the daytime, my anger began to subside too. I could remember things in this new light without the pressure of any emotional distortion. I could remember how Yeshua had been pleased with me, how he saw me as a conquest worth making, his *first fruits*, he said; how he was proud when I heard his call. I was his well and his watchtower; a kind of measure he used to judge others. [lxxxii] I could even remember how he let loose a bird and then caught it again and held it out for me. It could have flown away but somehow, as if he had tamed its wild free life in a second, it didn't fly. It sat there on his finger. Magic, I thought. To be able to do things like that. Without thinking. I remember shaking my head and how he nodded lightly and tossed it upwards again.

In time, I could even bear to re-inhabit, like suddenly slipping into a piece of fine clothing, the good memories, those that carried a promise of happiness inside them. He taught me to cry. That, I have come to realise, was his great gift. Gradually over the years the tears still fell but painlessly, like soft rain, like clear water over stone; emerald, blue, brown; all the eyes in the world could be washed by those tears! Tears of love; tears of joy; tears at the core of who I was. Water. Sunlight on clean water! A source bursting from the rock: a spring, a fountain, transforming, and with the power to transform, everything it touched. I cannot sit in any temple for long now before I find myself weeping inexplicably. People used to come sometimes simply to watch me cry.

At night, it was a different story. I began to dream and to re-experience in a series of recurrent nightmares, how it had felt, every stage of that bitter, incomprehensible journey. In my dreams, I understood nothing: I felt, and I suffered. There was an argument I could never win, never bring to resolution; an argument with Peter. Why must he cast me out? Why must he turn me into some kind of demon? Why must he deny all I had done, all I had been, all my love for the teacher, my love for the group? I had given everything I had to belong with them. [lxxxiii] So many times I had interceded, tried to reconcile differences, to soothe bad feelings. I remember Judas saying to me once: '*Giving is a short-term solution.*'

In these dreams, I am always pleading, always arguing, always reliving that pain of rejection, the pain of a wrong that always triumphed over me. Struggle with it as I did, I could never master it, or free myself from its enmity.

The healing didn't work inside me. It was superficial, bright and hopeful but without power to bring cure. As I relaxed a little into the sunlight, an old illness started up in me again. My lungs filled with water, liquid froth rose up in my throat, my mouth oozed saliva, bubbles spilled out of it and in them sometimes pieces of coloured fibre, rose pink, and grey and blue, and then I coughed up blood followed by small patches of coal-black dirt.

Terror took possession of me: spirit terror, fear of the demons I had always been frightened of and lacked the power to exorcise.

Years came and went; I tried with all the skill I possessed to heal myself. The problem proved resistant to every medicine and every herb. I who had survived so many ruptures could not find a way through this, could not transmute the suffering it brought into new strength. When the little memories started to come back, it should have been healing. It seemed day by day, little by little, I was recovering, putting in place the measures of a new life, a new reality, however reduced. I learnt the pleasures of work, the channelling of myself into what my fingers could achieve. Hours could pass in silent occupation. Something inside me had become reliable at last. Something I might count on. But it was not enough: the demons of the past inhabited me still. I was their empty house and, as the illness deepened, they took possession.[lxxxiv]

The illness became my preoccupation, my constant companion. The initial loneliness of the sick, that self-isolation, soon passed. I worked as I could and in my leisure hours, I devoted myself to my illness, tried to learn its ways and requirements, tried to overcome my chronic fear of its origin and tend to it like a child.

The gossamer memories, bright as dragon flies, which had relaxed my mind and lessened the anxieties of my spirit, flew off again and left me prey to supernatural terrors for which I had no remedy.

There was one demon that dwelt inside me against whom I was entirely powerless. I could neither overcome it nor lay it to rest. We both knew it was stronger than I and though our warfare lasted for years it never relinquished its grip.

*

1.15   Peter, Paul and Marcus: The First Gospel

"Surely, you kept the faith, didn't you?"

To Marcus's question, there was no straightforward answer.

There were times when I used all the cynical resources of my mind to break down the belief I had in him, the belief that Yeshua was indeed inspired by God, a miracle-worker both in the big, showy ways he practised for the crowds and in the inner lives of those he healed so momentously. He could summon out impurities, entities, rooted habits; all the demons that prise apart the fault lines in our psyches and fill our souls with their destructive evil.[lxxxv]

Yeshua had shaken off all influences on himself except for that of God. His whole being was directed to that one end: to be a pure channel for his power. No one else I had ever known was remotely like that and though what he claimed seemed implausible, impossible even, as ridiculous as it was terrible, there was a force inside him that kept pace with his words. He would do whatever God wanted, be strong or vulnerable, heal or suffer, love or condemn.

I tried not to keep faith. In my thoughts and my feelings, I rebelled. He was not the Messiah, the Chosen One; he had conspiracy behind him, he had secrets, he knew what he was doing. He planned it all, used people to that end; he fascinated them like a charmer, bound them to him; made use of them. He made use of me too.

But the mind is not infinitely elastic; it cannot war against itself beyond a certain point. A truth, a core of truth, still stands in the way of all its errors. And that is what he was to me. That truth. A great storehouse of spiritual energy lived inside him; even when death came, it could not extinguish that.

After a time, I gave in. I reverted to belief. Even in absence, his influence over me continued to grow stronger.

*

Now that Marcus has come, how does it feel to be found? I ask myself this every morning. It feels like an underground stream bursting up out of the rock in a green valley, the pure water piercing its way into the daylight for the very first time, lifted upwards by the sheer force of its own escape.

It feels as if I have come alive again.

*

"What I want," I tell him at our next meeting, surprising myself with the discovery, "what I want, after our talks, is to see it all put together somehow, reassembled, fixed in some final form, so it can't pull anchor again and go on endlessly changing its shape with every one of the mind's retellings. I want to know the meaning of that past life. I want to know what it was I lived through.

"I want to see it written down! I can't understand it all on my own."

Marcus says carefully, "I understand that, exactly. You are right in what you say. Many of us feel much the same: that we must preserve it, offer it to others, give it presence in the world. Not just in letters but as evidence, as a new kind of story told by the witnesses themselves, those who were with him from the beginning. It will strengthen our movement. Everyone who hears of us will be able to read the good news, know what happened and believe, as we do, that he was God's Chosen One.

"In fact," he says incautiously, "the process has already started. Much has been done already."

"But I don't understand. Who has done what? Have they put it in writing already, without any…"

After my burst of certainty, I feel apprehensive at hearing this, as if I might just have fallen into a trap. I remember the wild deer, in the woods outside Massalia, when they were led in for the sacrifice. Their look of having outwitted themselves, aided their captors.[lxxxvi]

But Marcus is clear and direct. My words have pleased him, finally touched something of real importance to him. There are, he tells me, several accounts already in preparation.[lxxxvii] Peter had almost finished his before he went to Rome. He knew what risks lay ahead, what he would have to face there.

"Did you hear about that, Magdalene? Do you know what happened to him?"

I shake my head, remembering how the dreams stopped suddenly. As if there were no one to argue with any longer, but still the argument was lost.

Marcus looks at me intently; I notice my fists are clenched tight in my sleeves.

"At first," he says, "Peter worked with Philip; Philip and Thomas had kept a written note of some of our Lord's teachings, and of some of his private sayings in the group. Then, when Philip left on his mission to Samaria, Peter employed a new scribe. You might remember him, perhaps – the teacher's last initiate?"

I shake my head, dismissing this as irrelevant. I want him to continue. I am burning with impatience to hear of this.

"Peter was not always an easy man to work for. He was true to his lights, immensely loyal in fact, but there was an argumentative streak to him when people didn't see things his way. He found some of Philip's memories and interpretations too…*philosophical*, is the best word. Philip was by far the cleverest of the group; he was schooled, had the Greek understanding as well as the name; his vision of the Lord's teaching, it was sweeter, wider, than Peter's. And he was kinder too, more humane. He cared about others. He valued women, had daughters of his own, taught them the practice of the faith."

I nod my agreement at this. Philip was my favourite in the group, the one who had accepted me without question.

"Peter," he adds unnecessarily, "wasn't like that. He didn't always appreciate differences in understanding. He was unsparing. He thought slowly but once he understood something, he could drive things forward, give them momentum.

"Peter and James, the Lord's brother, they were our first leaders; James, once he came over to us, a good man, just as you described him, so measured, so calm, so level-headed; Peter, on the other hand, was a cauldron of impulses but he made things happen, he had the energy of his impulsiveness, he made an impact.

"Rock-like?" I offer blandly, remembering Yeshua's old nickname for him, the contradictions it bound together. Peter could vacillate with the best of them.

Marcus laughs. "Like a rock in the water, shells and stones and minerals of every kind attached themselves to it. His thinking grew, the way a rock grows, through accretion. Things adhered to it or they were cast off. With Peter, you brought your own glue. He was hard on himself, especially. He knew his own faults, never forgot his times of failure. But he didn't always—"

"Didn't always?"

"Appreciate others, give them their due. He was under a lot of pressure to find the right answers, the right interpretations. And he was not a great man for the details. He could discount things, discount people; be as hard on others as he was on himself. He had certain ideas, you see, about how the story of his Lord should be preserved. The word 'story' for example: he didn't want it. *Just the facts*, he would say, but it was not that simple.

"Peter was a practical man; he knew his trade; he knew his own limitations. He never moved far from his own astonishment at what he had been caught up in. A great earth-changing spiritual movement: an ordinary, down-to-earth sinner like him! The tension in this threw him off balance over and over again. Peter never really wanted to be chosen. He never thought himself worthy. Then he went through some unforgettable rite of passage. A baptism both of water and of fire, and fire was not his element. Love was not his element either. He died to himself eventually, the way all of us initiates did. But it was harder for him than most. He struggled in the net."

"And so...what you are saying is...Peter was not the right man, not the best man, to—"

Marcus interrupts me suddenly. "It was the ending," he says, "the account of how the teacher rose again like that. Out of the tomb. For Peter, that brought massive problems. He could never agree, not even with himself, as to how it should end. He didn't want a story: he didn't want different versions, he didn't want—"

"He didn't want me in it." I square my chin, the old argument still alive after all.

"I'm sorry, Magdalene. This is painful for you, but it doesn't take you by surprise, does it? Peter was a man's man. He thought women were in some way less...less suitable, not the best messengers for the kind of truth that...What I'm saying is he thought it would be wrong to end his account of the Lord's passion with...that kind of testimony, with what he called *a woman's words and a collection of ghost stories.* In Jewish law, he said, a woman's testimony would not be accepted as real evidence. The stories of women weren't often believed. They could even have the opposite effect."[lxxxviii]

Alarm bells in the heart. Something warns me not to pursue this. Instead, I ask:

"And the ghosts?"

"Unmanly, he thought. The sort of thing that women—"

"But there were some? Ghost stories, as you call them? Was it a ghost they thought I had seen?"

"Yes and no. Something of that sort. It wasn't altogether clear what to call them. The appearances, I mean. Ghosts, apparitions, wishful thinking."

"The man himself?"

"These are the questions, Magdalene, to which we need an answer."

"Who else has written his witness story?"

"Levi. Matthew; a sound head; he's bilingual of course and understands authoritative writing. He's a good thinker, structured, in a way Peter never was. Peter liked short pithy anecdotes, hard as stones. Things you could remember. *Jewels*, he said, *hid in a field.* Levi on the other hand had a clear view, analytic; he's written a lot of it himself, and all credit it to him: You want to believe everything he says. It all fits together in his version, how the Lord's life fulfilled at every point what had already been foretold.

"Levi did what Peter couldn't; he gathered together all the prophecies, all the anecdotes; he made it clear that the teacher knew at every step what he was doing, that he was always in control of the script. You don't get that in Peter. He was never in control himself. He saw the jagged edges. But Matthew had a grip on things. Then he started working on the back story too, aligning it with the prophetic texts, a mother chosen by God, predictions in the stars, kings and magicians at his birth, places the Lord came from and went to."

"Yes," I say, "I remember how it was with Levi. He was always citing his scriptures, always checking the framework. He saw things like that from the start. It was something he had in common with Yeshua; they both knew the traditions; to Levi they were sacred and unassailable. There were no breaks, no revolutions, only the unfolding of a divine plan. He sat in the background, listening, putting it all together for himself."

"A tax inspector, wasn't he?" he says with a short laugh. "They never miss a trick!"

We sit in companionable silence for a while, our minds in agreement – until I say:

"But what about Matthew's ending? Surely, both accounts had to agree. And if Peter…"

I sit stark still like a hooded hawk, a blank darkness suddenly come down over my mind.

Marcus says urbanely, "Yes, a problem certainly. The ending has proved difficult on any number of counts."

"Did Matthew see a ghost?"

"He's an accountant, Magdalene. Of course, he didn't! But he did mention you. The earth moved. You saw an angel at the tomb. Do you remember any of this?"

"Is that all he said?"

"He said you saw the Lord. Risen. That he greeted you. Told you he was going to Galilee."

He looks at me uncomfortably; uncertain of what I will do, which of the many things he's heard tell of me is likely to come true. I stay calm, my face a mask of composure.

"You mentioned several accounts. Is there a third?" I try – and fail – to keep the suspicion out of my voice.

"Obviously, there's a lot of material, a lot of oral traditions. People made jottings about incidents they could remember, sayings that particularly struck them and so on. For Peter, it was largely a matter of assembling the fragments, putting them together, then ordering them in certain ways; it wasn't just a compilation: there were numbered units, meaningful in their own right, that the other gospel writers wanted to follow.

"So yes, you are right, there was a third: someone who wanted to provide a new account, bring it to life more, include more details, more stories, more dialogue, more women, if truth be told!"

"And this was—?"

"Almost certainly someone you won't know; won't even have heard of. He certainly didn't know you. Except by reputation, of course. I've met him on a number of occasions. We travel, you see, we circulate the scripts, so that each of the church communities should have the same…information and guidance. He was a young man when I first met him, full of Greek charm, suave, a professional healer, knowledgeable and gifted. *Under the sign of Apollo*, as the Romans would say. He's persuasive. Has an artist's eye. Everybody liked him. He could even melt Peter, show him how things should be presented to serve the best interests – the needs, I mean – of the young churches. As you can imagine, we have quite a few leadership issues now; difficult decisions have to be made."

"You have reservations about him?"

"About Luke? Yes, I do. I'm not saying he isn't the very best kind of convert to our movement, because he is. He has everything we might want. But there are still considerations that matter, reservations about his…orientation. Luke has come in from the outside. He is not one of the original twelve. He didn't know the teacher at all and yet he acts as if he did, as if he had received a special commissioning.

"He certainly won Peter over, even before Peter went to Rome, and that was not an easy thing to do. Luke was clever in the way he went about it. He read my first account, the one I did for Peter, then he set out to smooth it over, made it more *readable*, he said. He added things, graphic encounters, he saw bodies the way a physician does, as if they were there in front of you, you could visualise the scene. But the real thing was, he always portrayed Peter in the best possible light, he supported his authority in every way. He even softened the turbulence in him, his outspokenness, his tendency to disagree, go against himself on occasions. Luke's Peter is a reformed character. He has a charmed life."

"But who is this man? You say he never knew Yeshua?"

"He knew someone who had been healed by him. She was a young girl at the time, quite an amazing story. We all knew it. Luke copied it from me almost word for word, but it caught his imagination. He looked her up later in life to hear her story at first hand."[lxxxix]

"Is Luke a scribe as well, Marcus? Does he work for someone?"

"Luke is more than a scribe; he's a penman. He can write as well as he can draw. Gifted, interested in people, he can put a touch on things that persuades you he was there, even though he wasn't. He's our best writer no doubt, he speaks to people, gets their interest. The manuscripts we work on, they get circulated, we all keep checking with each other, but Luke always adds something; there's more human interest, less divine direction than you get in Matthew."

"I like what I hear of him!" I say impulsively. "I like it that he includes more of women in his gospel. Especially after what you've said about Peter."

There is a sudden silence. Marcus looks away, pulls his hat down over his eyes against the glare of the sun.

"Marcus?"

"There's a trust issue here, Magdalene. There's more to Luke than I've told you. You're right! He doesn't operate on his own. None of us do that. He had a sponsor too, a man who joined the movement after I did. He wasn't there in the teacher's time, didn't know the beginning, but he's someone who became very important to our churches. Luke travelled with him, worked for him; they were inseparable for a while. Talked together, worked together."

"And this man is…"

"*Saul*, as he was known at first, or Paul, to use the Greek version of his name he came to prefer. This man, Paul, he believed…fervently believed…that he had been authorised to encourage the writing of a new account. He believed the teacher himself had instructed him in this. He believed…"

I look up at him suddenly. I search his eyes. "Who is he, this Paul? What does he believe? And why does he believe it, if he wasn't even there, if he never even saw Yeshua?"

"He – Paul – Paul believes that he did see him. He saw the teacher not in his lifetime but three years after his death. This was no ghost story like the others; it was an over-powering vision of Yeshua as the Christ, God's Anointed One. Paul hadn't been with us at first, quite the opposite, he did his best to destroy the new movement, he pursued and persecuted everyone he could find. He was there watching when our dear friend, Stephen, was stoned to death outside the city. He held their coats for them, the murderers, Stephen's coat too when they stripped him naked and pushed him down. The thing is, he was left holding it. The coat, I mean.

"At first, the stoning of Stephen seemed only to intensify Paul's hatred of us. But then, quite out of the blue, God moved in on him. He had a vision that stripped him of his senses, literally threw him down on the great black stones of the Damascus Road. His horse shied away in terror, kicked him in the head. Then Paul, so he claimed afterwards, he heard the teacher calling him by name: *Saul! Saul!*

"He could see nothing at first. When he asked who was speaking to him, the voice of Yeshua replied. He identified himself by name, asked Saul why he was persecuting him. *Why Saul? Why?*

"It was then Paul saw his vision; it came to him in such a blaze of light, he could not look at it for long, but he knew for certain it was the Christ. He lay there, so the story goes, helpless and bleeding. And the teacher, who had healed so many, blinded Paul in an instant. It took three days for him to recover his sight."

"Ah!"

"After that, instead of being our enemy, Paul became was a man entirely opened to the Way. His mind was emptied of everything; his former life was blank. No one would accept him at first, his reputation was so evil; he went away on his own, out into the desert. The more he thought over his experience, the more he came to realise that he had been chosen for a special task. Though he was not and never would be recognised as one of the original disciples, he became convinced that he had been especially chosen to witness the very last appearance of the risen Christ.[xc] This final sighting, it was perhaps the most powerful one of all. Paul's resurrected Christ was no longer just the Messiah, the holy king of Israel; he was not even Jewish anymore. He was a spirit free from all those old human categories.

"Afterwards, Paul travelled the empire; he took his vision with him and with it he bought us the world. He was the strangest choice of all those chosen but the teacher, I believe, always knew his people. He knew those he wanted, he chose them for a reason, knew always what he wanted them for. There was nothing random in his calling; Paul was living proof of that. The more wrong he had done, the more sin he had committed, the more passionately he came to champion the teacher's work."

These words, so easy to understand, were a revelation to me. No longer necessary to ask in all humility, *Why me, Lord?* The better question was, *What for?*

*

"What did Paul do?" I ask.

"He took our local movement out into the world. He was a Pharisee by background, like Nicodemus, only madly clever, a prize student of Jewish rhetoric, he even studied with Gamaliel; Jewish teachers didn't come any better than that! Paul was certain – and he quarrelled with Peter and with James about this, as you might imagine – he was entirely convinced that he had been chosen to take the teacher's message out across the empire to people of every race, and every nation. Paul was not just convinced, he was convincing. He did more than anyone else to establish what both Peter and he referred to as the Lord's church – *Christianity* as they called it in Antioch[xci] – not just as a fulfilment of the Jewish Law but as a new faith, a church with its own rules, its own observances. It was not all down to Paul, of course, but I doubt it would have happened without him."[xcii]

I listen to what Marcus is saying as if my life depended on it. I don't know what to make of it yet. What I do know is that my new understanding and my memories of long ago begin to tally in some way; I can see the same force working through both.

"And this man, Paul, he was Luke's sponsor, was he?"

"Paul had that gift too, of finding just what he needed, the right man for the job."

I sense that Marcus is wrestling with some kind of envy, of Paul perhaps, but also of this new writer who is more than a mere scribe, someone who has his own light to throw on events. I sense in him the unease that envy provokes; then realise that I too feel almost faint with it.

"This vision Paul had, this appearance: tell me again, what happened?"

"He heard and saw the teacher. Yeshua spoke with him on a journey; the voice and the vision were a revelation of God's new purpose. The power of it struck him to the ground. Later it raised him to heaven.[xciii] He was blinded. His whole mind turned inwards. They took him to Damascus. Levi was there with some followers and the city itself was alive with visions; someone was sent to meet with him. When Paul's eyesight returned, he was the Lord's man, body and soul; the convert who understood conversion better than anyone."

"There is a pattern at work here, Marcus. You help me see myself as part of it."

He ignores the interruption. "Paul," he continues, "was a strange fellow, an irresistible force, eloquent and intense; some said he was slightly mad; others that he was not to be trusted. For an overt enemy like him to obtain such forgiveness, it shook us all to the core; put us on our metal too!"

"Sin," I say with feeling, "sometimes comes from ignorance of our true self. From a blind spot in our understanding."

"Paul wrestled with these issues for his whole life. He suffered greatly, knew a bigger struggle even than Peter's had been and he thought big because of it. He dedicated his whole life to our cause. He brought us Herod's brother; you know? Brought us Manaen. Can you imagine someone doing that, actually winning him over! Manaen even became one of our prophets! [xciv]

But I am somewhere else. I repeat the name: "Manaen? Manaen! Are you sure?"

I am struck dumb again. Somewhere inside me the familiar pain is starting up, pushing for emotional shape. *Manaen: Herod's foster-brother and friend, his counsellor, the only one he trusted, the one who tried to rescind the order for the Baptist's death? He sent for me once when he was ill and needed to talk over the horror of what had happened.* [xcv]

"No word of a lie, Magdalene. That was Paul for you!"

"And you're coming here now, Marcus…to look for me? Is it because Peter has a rival in this new man, a challenge to his leadership?"

I hear a sudden sharpness in my voice. It is not that I care about the rivalries of these men. It is not that, at all. *Paul*, I know at once, *has stolen my story. He has made it his own, pushing me further and further into the darkness.*

"Yes, I won't pretend otherwise. It does have something to do with that."

"Was it because they, Peter and Levi, that is, wanted to know if I…"

"No, Magdalene, no, it wasn't anything like that. They all thought they knew enough of the truth as it was. You had delivered your message."

"My message? And they thought that was enough, did they? Just a few words? As if that was all I was, just the messenger?"

Something I haven't felt before. A spiral of anger, growing inside me, becoming, I could feel it, a towering rage. Only one man had ever known the full force of my anger, had ever been able to absorb it into himself, calm it and tame it. And he is not here.

Before I know it, I am standing up. I can hear a woman's voice completely to one side of me starting to shout. I hear her shouting curses, obscenities, profanations. I listen to the voice with interest, then realise it is my own.

Marcus jumps to his feet and takes me by the shoulders. He shakes me as he speaks. "Peter is dead, Magdalene! You need to understand this. Peter is dead. And so is James. He was the first. And so is Paul, too."

I drop back into my seat as if struck by an arrow. I hear the voice again, the mad woman's voice, it travels and echoes along the steep gorge where we are sitting, I hear it crying again and again, "No...no...no!"

"Stop it, Magdalene! Don't do this to yourself. I know it's all still alive inside you but stop, stop and listen!" Marcus seizes my hands, prevents me pulling furiously at my hair. "It's because it is still so alive in you that I've come here to find you."

Suddenly, I see that his eyes too are full of tears. "Peter," he says, blunt and direct, not bothering to hide his emotion. "He was taken prisoner in Rome. It wasn't the first time. He died there, put to death, publicly like a...it was a glorious death, not unlike the Lord's only...no, I'll spare you the details. He could have got away, could have left the city and the young church there to its fate. But this time, he couldn't do it. He stood his ground.

"Peter had escaped from prison before. Talk about angels! What a moment that was! Like a great door coming open. Time, Magdalene! Great shapeless, ungraspable time, there on the threshold again, suddenly on our side, holding out its miraculous hands. Luke made the most of it, of course."

"Tell me!"

"There was a knock on the door. We were all inside, praying as usual, trying to keep our courage up. We thought our leader was lost. Then the maid servant, Rhoda, I think it was, anyway she comes in and tells us Peter is there at the door, standing in the street outside; that he has escaped from prison. We all think she must be mad. Mother Mary began to moan, she'd not been well, and I think she had some kind of seizure. Then suddenly, Peter himself walked in. We all thought at first it must be his angel, his spirit, come to tell us he has been put to death but in fact, it was Peter himself, there in the flesh. [xcvi] Something inexplicable had occurred. The door came open. And it wasn't just prison that Peter was freed from; he was finally freed from himself. *Released from the law, bound to Christ,*[xcvii] as Paul used to say."

I start to look away, but Marcus continues. Peter, I suddenly realise, meant a great deal to him.

"It took a long while for me to like him, Magdalene, a long time for Peter to accept me too but he had this quality, it grew in him, though he had no oratory, people fell silent when he spoke. His was the voice people listened for, the one they wanted to hear. *What does Peter say? What does Peter think we should do?* In himself, he was never that special; others were just as important, but Luke, you see, he began to build Peter up as the leader, even though he himself was actually working with Paul.

"That's the way he got Peter to see Paul, not a challenge to himself, but an asset to the cause. Luke is suave, he's a Greek; he can argue things both ways. He had already written his gospel and people wanted to know more. He set himself to write a follow-up, to write our first history. Peter was to be shown as the first leader; then when his escape from prison forced him into hiding, Paul takes over the story, becomes his successor. That's how Luke has drafted it, a brilliant work of course though I'm not entirely impartial. He certainly doesn't always show me in a good light."

Marcus shades his brow with his hand and stares out into the distance. He stares straight into the sun. Then he turns over one of the stones dislodged from the ruined walls. There is a coin underneath it. He scrutinises the image for a moment before putting it in his scrip.

"What is this place?" he says.

*

1.16 The Gospel of John

His question hangs in the air; then floats away unanswered. I have listened to his anecdote about Peter's return from prison with a sense of déjà vu. That maidservant who answered the door: No one in this world knows better than I do what it is like to deliver a message like that. '*He is alive! He's here outside! He has returned to us!*' The blank incredulity, the dismissive contempt, nobody willing to believe what you are saying! *It is **my** story, **my** message that is being repeated here.* In the fabric of this truth, I have become a patch of scrap material to be stitched in as the pattern dictates.

Marcus, too, is deep in his own thoughts; he has his own fish to fry.[xcviii] "I admit," he says, at last, "to a certain envy. If only I had been free to write the way Luke did when he began his long history. I was just a scribe, you see; at the time, I didn't have that sort of authority. I was young and new in comparison with the others. I did whatever Peter wanted. I was his scribe; I told his story. But Luke, he can write what he likes now. Paul is dead; he is his own man and the group accepts him because his account supports Peter, softens his faults, omits the hard truths that Peter himself always insisted we should include: his cowardice, his lack of understanding.

"Luke portrays Peter as loyal, tactful, a hero-disciple in the making. Then in Luke's second part,[xcix] in his history of their deeds, Peter becomes the real thing, a true hero saint. I don't have an issue with this; Peter was a hero in his way. But in massaging the facts as he does, Luke alters other things too; he undermines the importance of those the teacher himself had already chosen, chosen as his own leaders, his own chief disciples."

"John, for example?"

He makes no reply. Carefully, very carefully, for a dread is working through my heart, I add: "Something extra troubles you, Marcus. Is there something else in Luke's account?"

"Wanting to write like Luke, I'm not ashamed to admit that! But I have something that he didn't. For some of the time – not much, I admit – I was there; I was part of it; part of the group, one of the inner circle. I knew the teacher; Luke did not. He didn't experience the miracles, didn't recognise them as the Signs they were, signs that he was God's son. Luke saw them as doctors do, as a power that springs from inner calm and superior knowledge.

"I knew Peter too of course, worked with him for years, helped him, became his preferred scribe; there were several other men to choose from, but he chose me, and I was flattered by this. I wanted his good opinion and I came to understand how Peter saw things; what he wanted told; how he wanted the words to sound. I loved him, Magdalene, faulty and wrong-headed though he sometimes was. He was what men are, good men, that is, men who can acknowledge their own faults, see the truth about themselves and others.

"We worked together for years. He became like a father to me, something I'd never really had. And the work we produced in that early account, it was good: not clever, not very literary, perhaps, but it tells the truth. You can trust what it says. I didn't have much input; Peter knew what he wanted most of the time, but it was partly my work all the same. He let me make suggestions. There was one episode – one that concerned me directly – which I thought should be included because it …opened up matters that could become a stumbling block if people didn't understand them properly. He let me include that, so I did make some contribution to that first gospel and I'm proud that I did.

"But the point is, Magdalene, things are changing in our movement. It spreads all the time, even apart from Paul, even though he is no longer with us in the flesh. Except for John, the men of that first generation are nearly all dead now. And it's essential for us that the right things get handed down through our communities. People need to know the truth. They have faith, of course, but they also have questions to ask. Those questions need answers."

"I wish you had told me from the start, that you and Peter…"

"No, I couldn't do that, don't you see? Everything has changed since then. And I've changed too. I'm not now how I used to be at the start, glad to be included, willing to do anything they wanted. I have my own views now, my own way of seeing things."

"And this contribution you made? In your first work, with Peter?"

"It was about…he had a group of children with him. I saw the way he was with them. He had one by the hand. I barely knew my own father; he was too busy making money to take notice of a child. I was his heir, the little rich boy set to take over his business, become his second self. But that was not what I wanted."

"And your mother?"

"Died shortly after I was born. I didn't really know her at all."

"So it was Peter who helped you to find your own identity?"

He nods. I try to read the lines of his allegiances. Where I come into this.

"It wasn't Peter at first, though. Not at all! It was…the teacher himself. In spite of everything, in spite of who and what I was, he took me as his own neophyte. No-one thought he would but he did. He baptised and initiated me."

"And Paul, the great Paul, you say he is dead too?"

"Paul chose his course. He always knew where he was headed. He was a prisoner several times over before they sent him to Rome. He wanted that, to be tried there. He even dreamed of converting the emperor. But Nero was beyond redemption; he was mad by then, crazed by his own evil. Like Jerusalem, he had already destroyed his own soul. Now Rome was set to follow."

I listen to what Marcus tells me and it is like a transfusion in my blood, something comes alive inside me. I could sit at his feet for hours hearing nothing but his voice, just as I used to do.

"So many gifted men, Marcus! Yeshua drew them all towards him. Was this Paul a writer, too?"

"Paul was a man inspired. He spoke well, preached better but his writing was inspirational. While he was in prison, he gave his time to it. He had two years, that's all. Luke was with him sometimes, right there at the horse's mouth. Much of what Paul wrote then is unforgettable. It shines in the dark like candle flame. In letter after letter to the churches, he poured out such astonishing things, practical advice mainly, but in each one there was a nugget of pure gold, a wisdom that came to him, he always said, direct from the Lord. *The words of eternal life!* [c] It's Peter's phrase: Read Paul and you'll know what it means."

"Impressive! Very! It sums everything up, though I don't remember Peter saying it."

"I may have tweaked it slightly, but it's a phrase that sticks: five words and such a wealth of meaning! Anyway, Magdalene, Paul travelled halfway across the empire, spreading the gospel, building the churches. I'm not saying Paul's preaching was wrong, but his emphasis was…different, not the way we would have put it. The Christ Paul spoke of is not like the one we knew when he was with us as a man."

"You mean, he has become a stranger?"

"He has become a spirit, Magdalene, *the* Spirit, if you like. Paul's rhetoric, his *theology*, I should say, isn't always easy to understand but his language is so powerful that at times it could almost raise the dead! And that is exactly what it wants to do! Paul claims not only that our Lord came back to life – we already know that – but that everyone who believes in Him will be brought back to life too. In the same way!"[ci]

"What, all of us?" This is news indeed. I search around for the right question. "And does Paul tell people how I saw Yeshua when he came from the tomb?"

"No. He tells how he did. And how all the male disciples did the same. After Peter, of course. According to Paul, Peter was the first. The first to see him alive again…in the…"

He trails off. The silence that follows from these words is one I will never forget. It was a silence in which my whole life had been concealed. I have come to terms with Peter's attitude, but with Paul I know at once that something different is at work. Not something personal this time, something institutional instead.

I stand up, the breath tight and fiery under my ribs. Instinctively, my middle fingers curl inwards to the palm in the sign of the goddess. "What kind of man is this, that he should dare to do such a thing? Does he hate women just as Peter did? Is there no end to their blind exclusion? And if Paul doesn't mention me, how on earth can this Luke tell the truth? I mean, in his own gospel…"

"To be absolutely honest, Magdalene, Luke isn't entirely clear on the matter."

"But…" I stammer, calling up my ghost's dignity again to deal with this new blow, "that is not just an insult to me. It is an insult to Yeshua, too. How can Luke pretend to tell the truth when he can't even get his facts right? He is not a historian; he is a liar!"

"You wouldn't use that term so easily, if you had read Luke's account or knew what it was like,[cii]hearing Paul talk, hearing the words of the teacher come back to life."

"What was it like?"

"It is just as it was. Paul draws the crowds just as the teacher did. People listen. Houses take him in. The word travels. The houses in particular, the womenfolk, the way women talk, their networks in the house and the market, they have all helped him spread his word. There was a woman in the textile trade, Lydia, she was called, one of many such who adored Paul, his ugly charm, the way he made people feel safe with him; the way his voice alone could create trust.

"She had an important business, this woman, she knew the dyers and the weavers and the tanners, had a whole network of trade contacts, particularly those who deal in expensive cloths and fabrics; Paul's message speaks to them with particular force. When they weave and spin and dye and make their garments, it's as if his words run along the thread, become part of the fabric. I thought that might interest you, Magdalene, given your own…although of course, Lydia deals mainly in purples; it's largely the wealthy, fashionable people who buy her goods."[ciii]

I know he is distracting me with this talk, but I can't help but listen. What he says of the cloth-makers speaks to me deeply, despite myself. Yeshua used to call it *the perfect analogy*. I have seen it in action, the way good cloth can lift and transform a body, be more potent than medicine at recovering life. I had a dress of my own like that once.

But I am standing naked now. *Mother Mary, Rhoda, Lydia*: It's not that all women have been excluded from the accounts. It's just that I have. An old patch in their new garment! Unwanted, potentially harmful. Damaging to the cause.

Cold as ice despite the sun, I start telling Marcus the saying that Philip wrote down for me once, a saying of Yeshua's I immediately learnt by heart:

"In this world those who wear a garment are more precious

than their garment;
In the Kingdom of Heaven, the garments
Are as precious as those who wear them,
For they have been immersed in a fire and a water that purifies all.

"And there is another saying too, that I used to like. It speaks of God as a cloth dyer whose best dyes *become one with the materials that they permeate.*[civ]

"And what's more..."

I am about to continue, to repeat all the poetry I can remember, words I have got by heart or created for myself; prayers that I used in healing; the *Merkavah* hymns [cv] I learned to recite in my girlhood; everything that might say I, too, had a voice in their movement; that I too have something to speak of. Those words of eternal life: I call them all up! I will not be their primal silence, not if I can help it. I begin to chant and immediately the anger settles inside me, the bitter taste subsides; some sweeter herb begins its healing work in my mind.

Marcus lies back on the grass and closes his eyes, listening to my song. I look down at him, his black lashes fine against his cheek, his body full of life and energy, and have a sudden, shocking desire to lean over him and kiss him full on the mouth. It hits me like a revelation, some secret I had entirely forgotten. He opens his eyes, narrow against the sun and looks directly into mine.

"Magdalene, I've heard tell the teacher used to take you in his arms and kiss you sometimes. If you carry on like this, I might find myself wanting to do the same."

"What else do you want?" I say, caught quite off guard, my breath sobbing against my heart now.

He sits up, surprised and susceptible, something like pain in his eyes.

"What else do you want from me?"

"I want to write your story. I don't mean your life or your intimate secrets. I mean the truth of what you heard and saw that morning. Only you can tell me that. Tell me what happened when you saw him alive again, when you saw him on the other side of the tomb."

My mind fills with sudden colour. Like the first flowers of spring: virginal white, sun yellow, unearthly blue on their high stalks. Then, a sudden spill of violets: the colour of secret words spoken for the very first time.

Marcus himself is suddenly alight with intensity.

"Whatever the others do or haven't done, I want to be the one who tells this truth to the world. I know the teacher chose you for that morning, chose you to be his messenger, to be his apostle. Everyone knows this but some don't want to acknowledge it. Neither Peter nor Levi could decide how their accounts should end. Luke, of course, has made Peter, his version of Peter, the hero of that resurrection hour."

"What exactly does Luke say?"

"He says you saw a man, a couple of men actually, in shiny robes, and they gave you a message. To take to the disciples."

"And the disciples—"

"Thought you were talking nonsense."

The silence again: it looks at me like some magical creature made of impossible combinations. A Chinese unicorn,[cvi]perhaps! The strangest thing ever heard of, perhaps, but, for all its strangeness, it carries some scent of possibilities, some truth still in the making.

Marcus says, "This is why I came here, Magdalene. To talk to you, to hear what you have to say, and then to tell it to the world. No matter what the others have done or haven't done; if you will help me, I can do this for you. I will do it for him too, for the teacher. And for John! I will do it for all of us. If you will help me."

I want to tell him I love him. Only the fear it may be true prevents me.

Suddenly, he too opens up, begins to speak of himself:

"Paul tells us how he was transformed by his encounter with the risen Lord. But he was not the only one. I was transformed too, and I was there, there in Gethsemane, the night they arrested him. I didn't speak, didn't know how, just sat there all night and watched him from under my initiate's cloak. The others had all gone to sleep but I was his witness, bound to wakefulness. He was alone in himself, unable to rest or settle. He tried to pray; to find courage through prayer but his dread was palpable. He knew what was going to happen. And then the guards came. Judas was with then. He saw me and that's when I slipped away. Yeshua had instructed me to do that: to leave as soon as they came for him. One of them grabbed me from behind, tore off my clothes. I only just made it."

I stop myself from imagining the scene; begin for the first time to realise something of this young man's role in Yeshua's ordeal. He tells me more, tells me what really matters to him most.

"These changes, Magdalene, the way he changed not just my life but the very person I was; I became someone else. I became *someone*. I had an identity. Believing in him, I could believe in myself. And these changes, they are part of what it means: part of this resurrection, as we call it now. I try to get a hold of the meaning of this, but it always moves just out of reach. I don't have enough…skill like Paul, or Luke's assurance but…it's what I want to do. I want to explain the mystery of the resurrection. So that people can see it, and understand it, like a star shedding light in every direction. If I could do that, I'd feel I'd fulfilled my task. Justified his faith in me."

"Ah, that mystery! The mystery of who he was and who we are because of it." I murmur these words almost to myself. "Perhaps we aren't meant to explain it."

"I don't believe that, Magdalene. I don't believe you do, either. For me, the changes he worked have gone on happening, astonishing, since I finished my work with Peter. That was over ten years ago. I finished his gospel. He was satisfied with what I'd done. I've added one or two things since then, made a few small alterations but mostly I've been concentrating on what has happened since. I've studied more, spent time with one of the Essenes, one of the very few who survived the disaster of Jerusalem; he opened my mind, told me more about John – the Baptist, I mean. I get a sense of his importance now, how he fits in.

"I've been back to Samaria. Seen it with new eyes. Luke is wrong. It isn't a normal narrative at all. You can't tell it like that. There's the time and the place, yes, but what holds it all together is something different. It's what came from the tomb, came so easily in the end, like…I don't know…a woman might say *like a birth without pain*."

"A birth without a body," I say, twisting a rope of loose hair back underneath my Provençal hat, as broad as a halo against the sun. Half of my face is in shadow now. I can watch him in safety from under it. "A conception, the birth of an idea?"

But Marcus is ahead of me on this: "More like the hatching of something fully fledged. That's why, to get this right, I have to know exactly what happened that first morning. I want people to see – those who have eyes for this kind of thing – to see what this resurrection of his really means. It's not just the denouement of a story: it's like stepping into an altogether different dimension, waking up to a new kind of mind."

"Yeshua spoke of his kingdom as a place beyond time by which the world itself could be kept spiritually alive. The Kingdom of Hope, he called it."

"The Kingdom of Hope, yes!" Marcus's face suddenly breaks into a broad smile. It makes him look younger, much younger.

And that is when I remember something I had entirely forgotten.

*

That evening, when we had finished our walk, Marcus came home with me, entered my cave house, the first fellowship I had known there since I came to Mèthamis. We talked all night. I made supper and he broke the bread, offered the cup, just as my sister told me that Yeshua did at his final supper. We talked of this; he knew details I had not heard before. We ate and drank in remembrance of Him and afterwards we talked on through the night.

Though the moment for kisses had passed, our speech had acquired an intimacy now, a closeness and a trust. He asked me not to call him *Marcus* any longer, but to use the name he was known by in the movement now, one that signalled the initiation he had undergone.

John Mark. I try it out, unsure if I could get used to it, another John, a writer this time, not a Baptist or a disciple.

Much of our talk that evening and in the days ahead was about this man, Paul, who had spread himself out across all the boundaries of our former world, blending Jew and Gentile, Hebrew and Greek, across the vast territories of Roman rule. He had taken with him the idea of a new kind of power, one utterly unlike the merciless brutality of the empire at its worst.

John Mark told me stories of what was happening in Rome and Jerusalem, atrocities in the arena, a gradual hardening against us in the synagogues, the new converts who came from all classes of people and proved at times so difficult to assimilate. We talked endlessly of our hatred of Rome; a hatred tinged for both of us with fascination at their customs. Rome for me was a book I had read at a distance, read as the blind read, as Felix had taught me to see it until I could trace out for myself its logic and its power. *"I will show you,"* he said to me once, *"how the world really works."* It was the only promise he ever kept!

John Mark, on the other hand, knows it from the inside; he can use its language just as Paul could, both for speaking and writing. Paul, he said, even had the rights of citizenship through his father's profession. It explained how he could step so easily out of one identity and into another. We both admired him for that.

But nonetheless, he keeps insisting, Paul's viewpoint is not our own. He might understand the teacher in ways none of his closest followers had ever been able to do but Paul had never heard Yeshua teach, never seen him address a crowd, perform one of his miracles, drive out a demon[cvii] or heal the desperately sick.

Paul was not primarily interested in the teachings, not interested in Yeshua's life either, or who he had been as a man. It was the spirit of the Christ who had spoken to him, the spirit who had risen from the tomb and called him by name that was the focus of his devotion: the Christ his own belief had created inside him.

"It's a difficult matter," John Mark explains, "these different versions that are beginning to appear. We all create our own Christ to some extent, the way Paul has done, but that's all the more reason why we should remember the one he really was. We mustn't lose sight of that. It was our starting point."

"What about John in his gospel?" I ask. "Does he have his own version too?" I know as soon as I say this that I have touched a chord.

"For Paul it was the significance of what happened after the Lord's Passion, as we call it now, that mattered most. It was the resurrected Christ who spoke to him, stopped him in his tracks. For John and me, this is only a part of the whole, a part of the harmony that wound itself through everything the teacher did. There are details missing, crucial events, incidents, truthful witnesses who saw what happened at the cross, all these details are vital parts of the mystery of his death, a mystery that Paul, for all his latter-day insights, doesn't comprehend. The richness of the imagery, the wounds, the nails, his thirst, the spear that confirmed his death, the blood and water that poured from his heart, all these have a meaning of their own. They speak to us. Each one is an opening."

I put my hands over my eyes when he says this, remembering that thirst, the sound of his ghostly voice asking for a drink so that he could speak the only words that were left to him. That was the end of who he had been, that parched whisper. It was his lowest moment, the moment of his need. The moment of his reminder to me, the terrible reciprocity it demanded.[cviii]

Marcus draws me back into a different scene:

"John says there was a light in his wounds. When he died, when he entered into death, the light simply flowed back into him, through his wounds, through

104

his feet and his hands, through his heart and his eyes, into the divine core of his being. Doesn't that prove what I'm saying?"

I draw a blank on this so give a cautious nod and say nothing. If there was light in his wounds, I wish I had seen it, but I can't say I did.

John Mark says with a trace of bitterness: "Paul writes about our martyrs, about those who have died for our cause during the persecutions. Well, Paul should know about that! He looked on at Stephen's death. In his writing, it's obvious he wanted to comfort and reassure people about such deaths, just as he needed some of that comfort himself. He writes that those who have been united with the Lord in a death like his[cix] will surely be reunited with him in his resurrection too. It's a good point. He makes it well. Every martyr dies the same kind of death as Christ. But he misses something too. What Paul forgets is that there was a real death, not a death *like his* but a death that was entirely unique. And Paul wasn't there when he was crucified; he wasn't united with the teacher in his suffering. *It was John who was!*"

"John, of course." I lower my eyes, realising once again how easily I can be made to vanish in the eyes of these men. How they have put themselves in all the places where I once stood.

"Don't get me wrong, Magdalene. Paul's faith was put to the test time and time again. He suffered worse than death on some occasions. He thought he could usher in his Lord's Second Coming, his return to us, by the sheer extremity of his own ordeals. He wanted to do that. He was so strong, so possessed by Yeshua's spirit; he was so sure it would happen. But it did not. It has not. Or at least not in a way ordinary people would understand it. Some people even say Paul himself *was* the second coming but that's not right. The teacher's spirit works in all of us like that; it's what keeps Him alive. But years have passed and still we wait for his return. In truth, once we had learned how to do it, we enjoyed the waiting. We no longer wanted this time to end. We just want the movement to go forward."

John Mark shifts restlessly in his place. He looks at me intently, hearing a deep agitation in my breath. "What is it, Magdalene?"

"A picture is forming in my mind," I say. "It happens sometimes, not very often; I set store by it, though. I know it is not a dream but a vision, a gift of the spirit."

I see a dying man; a white dove escaping upwards from his mouth. There is an eagle close by, perched on a stump.[cx] It is watching them. I want to cry out, but the dove has taken away my breath too.

But Marcus does not respond. Instead, he goes on as if the image had transferred itself straight from my mind and into his: "I don't have Luke's skill in picturing," he says, "but there are things I have learnt since I worked with Peter. I have practised what the Lord taught me, the exercises, the meditations; the prayers. I can use the symbols now. That for me has been a great discovery. It is through those that I began to see into the mind of God a little, to feel my own mind opening out into His. They came to me, the symbols – my own gift from the spirit – after Peter's escape from prison. The time I told you about, when he came to the house where we were praying. That was my moment, Magdalene; mine as well as Peter's. It was as if something the Lord had tried to teach me when he was alive suddenly became clear. The symbols gave me a breadth of vision, raised my mind, to a new level, a higher plane of thought altogether. I use them in my writing now."

"So your writing will be different from Paul's. Did you know the man well?"

"Paul knew about my work with Peter, on our first gospel. Sometime afterwards, he wrote saying he wanted me to work with him too, to go with him and Barnabas, he's a distant relative, to act as their scribe on a mission to Cyprus. I agreed to travel with them, but it was a mistake. Right from the start, there was a twist to our talks, an opposition in our thinking. I couldn't get used to not being with Peter; I didn't entirely want to.

"What matters to Paul is what happens through him. He had such a sense of his own power, but he was not the teacher; we had no binding memories in common. Paul wasn't there at the beginning. Peter was.

"When I worked with Peter, I helped him to remember. Our gospel is short, strange, lit with his own astonishment at what was happening. It doesn't tell everything but what it does tell is the unmediated truth and I am proud to have worked on it. Paul, though, had his own life story to deliver, one in which he himself becomes the unlikely hero. And what a model it was too: the teacher's deadly enemy becomes the apostle of his resurrection."

A sudden sadness makes me sigh and sigh again. There is no getting away from it, this tale of wrongdoing redeemed that he speaks of. Once again, I see the similarities, the match between Paul's story and my own. I shut my eyes; make a space for forgetting.

"So what exactly was it you quarrelled about with Paul? You disapproved of what he said of himself?" We are talking like old friends now, things we could share with no one else. His tears for Peter made me start crying too. For who is my enemy now?

"No and yes, I didn't disapprove but I was wary of him. When I travelled with him things went badly. There was a deal of mistrust. Barnabas is a man always happy to be in the background, but Paul and I, we both knew things the other did not, secrets if you like, things not lightly to be spoken of.

"The tensions grew. There were issues about belief, about miracles and magic. Questions too – inevitably, there always are – about the teacher's resurrection. What did it mean, that last and greatest of his miracles, the conclusive sign of his identity? Was it his resurrection alone, or our own as well that we were talking about? Or was it both of those and, if so, how would that happen? When would it happen? Was the Lord's resurrection essentially a spiritual change, as Paul suggested, a visionary experience, or did he return to life in his own body, a body mysteriously healed of its wounds?[cxi] A body that we knew and recognised!

"I'm sure I knew more than Paul did about this, but he understood other things better than me, ideas about death, and salvation; things you can't always hold onto without his words. For those of us who followed the teacher, those who believe in him, does something different really happen to us when we die? Is our death different to that of other people, the many ignorant ones, the unconverted masses, Romans and such like? This is the question I always ask myself, but I don't have Paul's answer."

"Was it Yeshua's death you quarrelled about?"

"We quarrelled about magic, Magdalene.[cxii] Paul argued that if we insisted on claiming that the Lord's body had been physically raised, resuscitated if you like, we exposed ourselves to the suggestion that it was all some kind of trick, a magician's sleight of hand. That he hadn't really been dead at all.

"It all came to a head over a Jewish magician we met on Paphos. It was weird; he even practiced under the same name as the teacher. We talked with him. He heard that I had some knowledge of the…esoteric rites, that I was one of the *gnostikoi* who knew the 'secret doctrine', as they called it.[cxiii] He and Paul went head to head in front of the proconsul there. Paul got the better of it. He blinded his opponent. He crushed him, gave him the injury he himself had suffered on the way to Damascus. Anyway, to cut a long story short, we quarrelled furiously on the boat out of Paphos and I left them to go back to Jerusalem as soon as we reached dry land."[cxiv]

"And Paphos itself?" The dim memory of a name.

"For the Greeks, Paphos was the birthplace of their love goddess, Aphrodite. She was powerful, more beautiful even than the Roman Venus. I sometimes think it might have been that which triggered our quarrel: love and all its differences. I went back to my studies. Barnabas tried to sort things out between us, but Paul was angry and never trusted me again. [cxv]He wanted his own man, after that, his own scribe to record his adventures. To show how, under his version of the resurrection, he himself had become the living spirit of the Lord.[cxvi] I admired Paul, but I was never going to be his disciple.

I struggle to process all this, the curious root of disquiet and excitement his words have stirred in me. It is leading somewhere, bending in my direction but I still can't make out how.

"What happened then?"

"Afterwards, Paul's fame grew. As did the rift between those who had known the Lord as a man and those like Paul who knew him only as a living spirit, as the Risen Christ he became. That's when we decided that a new gospel might be needed, another account by a different witness, someone who could explain the teacher in a different way, show how his life had always been a new revelation of God, a great allegory of divine love. That's how John sees it: not as a final revealing of the ancient prophecies, but as a gift of divine love, a new wisdom that has been implanted in our hearts by the Lord, a gift that can never be destroyed in us, no matter what the injury."

"A heart without guile?"[cxvii] The phrase comes to me from somewhere.

"Yes, exactly, a heart like John's. John is almost the only one still alive who has the authority to explain from his own first-hand knowledge the true meaning of our Lord's life, of who he was, both for us and for God. John always believed that the teacher had a special love for him. He was ambitious for that love and now he wants it placed at the centre of his gospel, especially now Peter is no longer here to…"

"So that is your work now? You are to be John's – not scribe exactly – but his…"

"His eyes, yes; his co-author, if you like – but this time it will be different. Not little vignettes, not a seamless prophecy, certainly not a charming story told through the eyes of a painter like Luke, but the way John sees it. As the great mystery of love."

It is as if an old, rusty cage had suddenly sprung open. Inside it I see a tiny, curled up ball of fluff: it is Benji, my little brother's Syrian hamster. We found it, half-starved and sick with neglect, after his funeral. We tried to revive it, my sister and I, then quarrelled over which was most important, grain or water. It died anyway.

I shake my head free of the memory. This is not a moment for sadness. John Mark's account of the new gospel sends a thrill of life through me. I think suddenly: this illness I have, it is a creative puzzle I must solve. Piece by piece, I must put it all together just like a mosaic until the picture at its centre is gradually made clear. And if I can do that, I will have my own power again, the power Yeshua developed in me, the power that helped me bring him back to life.

*

"So this new work of yours then, would it be – I'm guessing, of course – something like the gathering back into a beautiful jar of a sacred ointment, a rich perfume, which, when it is poured out again, will sanctify everything it touches?"

We look at each other helplessly, searching for an irony that is no longer there.

"A mystery of liquids," I say, "of oil and water, wine and blood?"

"A mystery of the Spirit, Magdalene, and of words too, words as powerful as any of Paul's, and with the same alchemy. I thought I'd start with the money changers, a story of shekels changing hands in the temple, courts full of traders,[cxviii] how he came there in such a determined fury, turned over their stalls, and shook all of the birds out of their cages. So yes, something released, that gives me an idea; something released and then re-gathered, broken and then restored. The story of the wine itself; the crushed grape torn from the vine and stamped underfoot, the terrible alchemy that transforms it, that transforms us too when we drink it. Nothing will be wasted, you see. It can all be gathered back. Our gospel will hold inside itself a perfume strong enough to remove for ever the terrible stench of death."

"And all this needs is…" I stare at John Mark the way I have seen Yeshua stare, with a concentrated intensity unnerving to encounter. I have to see what is inside him, what it is he is hiding from me.

He meets my gaze steadily. "It needs someone who can give a true account of the moment when…when Yeshua too was re-gathered, brought back to himself, when we, wretched as we had become, were suddenly restored to ourselves again, our belief, our trust in Him still safe, still living inside us. The truth you see, not just the politics of our leaders but the re-constitutive principle itself."

"The which principle?"

"That is what he was, Magdalene; call it what you will. Call it light, if you prefer; call it love or hope, but whatever you call it, that is what he was. That is what he gave us. The spirit through which we can rebuild all that is broken in ourselves."

"And John is to be the transmitter of this truth, is he?"

"John, yes, his name is to be inscribed in the work. He's become more visionary as his eyes have weakened. He's an old man now, of course, but hale, most of the time, though his bladder still gives him a lot of trouble. John is convinced his memories can capture, not just the day-by-day history of the teacher's life but the truth of what he was, a truth more beautiful, more integrated, than the other accounts have provided. John sees the Lord as a man whose life and death embodied the cosmic mysteries of *agape*,[cxix] someone who became saturated with that love the closer he came to the tragedy of his trial. Socrates showed the way of course but he was a method, not a man. He had little real care for others. Yeshua washed our feet as if his power were really ours and he its servant. John is convinced it was the special nature of the Lord's love for us, first his choosing of us then his final demonstration of that love, his exchange of himself with those who loved him, which brought him through his death on the mystic cross."

He gestures with his hand, an orator's gesture. And looks rather pleased with himself.

"I wouldn't have thought John had even heard of Socrates."

"You tease me again, Magdalene."

"You have an olive stain on your palm."

He laughs, licks it off with his tongue; resumes more humbly.

"Alright, it's true; John needs a little guidance sometimes, to express the sublimity…the elevation of his thoughts, but he believes, indeed I have encouraged him to believe, that he can reconcile Peter's view and that of Levi with what Paul is teaching, ignoring the life story, setting aside the details of the ministry, concentrating instead only on the Lord's death and his resurrection. Paul has made this great event the one thing needful, the skeleton of our faith; it is up to us to put the flesh back on the bones.[cxx] John was there at the trial; he was witness to the Lord's suffering and to his death; he was the first of the disciples to receive your message, the first to believe it, the first to reach the empty tomb. Paul had glimpses, insights, visions; he saw vividly, in part, but John saw it all."

I nod in acceptance of this, replenish his water cup. He sips it slowly as if unsure of what he should say next.

"Now the end is near, John too has reached a new level of understanding; become receptive to the symbolic vision. He sees that the human body is not in itself the only reality, it is a projection, always, of what lives inside us, our voice, our emotions, our energy, our spirit. This weakens as we grow older, falls apart when we die. If the spiritual connection between us is strong, projected bodies such as these can appear to us as if they were really there. We must listen to what they tell us.

"Great spirits have conquered the secret of making their identities available to us. Their strength is there for us when we do their work. But this is love, not conjuring: I learnt that on Paphos!

"John sees the true nature of the Christ, that he lives for ever at the point of the cross. It is the point of intersection between the mystery of love and the evil of the world. On the one hand, corruption and death; on the other, the living light of the risen life! And one thing we know for certain, Magdalene, after what we have witnessed: our world is stabilised by our Lord's presence. Take that away now and our history will reel back into chaos."

I clap my hands. I cannot stop myself. "John Mark," I say sincerely, "this is wonderful. It helps me to see…helps me to see what I believe."

"People ask John and me all the time: how could this happen, how could the Christ come back from the dead? It can't be true. It's against nature. I say to them, 'But that is just the point. Resurrection is not a commonplace event. It is sui generis, as the Romans say! Of its own kind! It is, by definition, a unique event.[cxxi] There is only one Christ, only one death like his. That is his difference from us all, the sign of his divinity.'"

"And does that convince them?"

"Not entirely."

"There is something missing?"

"You are missing, Magdalene."

John Mark frowns, deep lines furrowing his brow.

"You heard, didn't you, of what the Romans did in Jerusalem? It was a reprisal of course, the zealots fermenting rebellion again. They never learned! The Romans destroyed the temple; they massacred the people as only the Romans can. It was barbarous, pure unadulterated evil. Women and children butchered, blood everywhere, the streets thick with corpses. It was an act of revenge, they said. The destruction of the whole city and everything it stood for.

"The temple was their main target; the towers were taken, the walls shattered, everything sacred completely raised to the ground. We all remembered the teacher's prophecy. How he had cried over Jerusalem as if he had seen it all in advance. How he brought death on himself by shouting at the priests, *'Destroy this temple and in three days I will raise it again.'*[cxxii] It was as if he were prophesying Israel's doom, and claiming that he, and only he, could repair the damage. In just three days, he said. That's what they thought he meant, the temple authorities, they took him literally, but John kept shouting: *'No, you don't understand! He's talking about Himself. The temple is Himself!'* That only angered them more."

I don't want to hear about this again, about what happened to Jerusalem. John Mark returns to it with an obsessive persistence hard to listen to. I interrupt his tirade.

"But perhaps Jerusalem is not everything. Perhaps it is not the answer to everything either. It's just the unforgettable starting point; the place to which the folk who worshipped there always long to return. But it was never Yeshua's home; it was the death of him instead."

His turn to fall silent! Mine, to gasp as I see that hidden resemblance surface once again in his face.

"You are right," he says at last. "But for John, Magdalene, this is the cornerstone. He himself is to be the architect of that new temple, the temple of the risen Lord, the true Messiah who can only be understood from beyond that catastrophe. That is what his gospel will be! It is still so recent but the teacher stands apart from all that history now. He marks the place where the new way opens up. It goes beyond the Jewish Covenant. He has changed the face that God shows to his people for ever, and his people are everywhere now; Jews, Greeks, Samaritans, Gentiles from across the empire and beyond."

"Yes," I say again, though I cannot hear Johannan bar-Zebedee's voice in any of this. "And so, John has sent you to find me because I'm not one of them, because I belong with the Samaritans and Greeks?"

"We are sure you have something to tell us. The point is Jerusalem was destroyed but our Lord was not. He is more alive all the time: not just alive in the way that Paul has defined for those who follow his teaching. Paul's is the way of sin and repentance, of dying into a new life, being born again with a new identity through the power of the spirit."

"Yes, that's not wrong though, is it?"

"John has a different understanding; his is not the way of guilt and forgiveness. It is not the way of martyrdom either. For him the Way is one of love. This is not achieved by suffering and death but by faith and transcendence, a love that lifts us free of the world then sends us back into it to do his work."[cxxiii]

"And am I part of this?"

"You are its sign, Magdalene."

"Not for Luke, by all accounts."

"Not for Luke, no. For Luke's people, Mary Magdalene is a woman too far, a witness too unconventional, too fallen, to reflect well on the teacher. This woman has to be broken up, separated from her past, because to describe her in her entirety could create umm…an erotic zone, as the Greeks say. And this, it was felt, might lead to misunderstanding of the teacher's spiritual mission. If you could read what Luke has written of you, you would not be pleased. You might not even recognise yourself at all. John, though, has far more room for you."

I hear what he says with mixed feelings. Recognising myself is less appealing to me than he imagines. Though my heart sinks low with foreboding, I remind myself that I was there during Yeshua's lifetime; I was close to him; had a knowledge of him and a love that was entirely my own. Whose interest this might be made to serve is far from clear to me.

"Can you tell me what is at stake here, beneath the politics? There is a lot for me to take in. I begin to understand it but..."

John Mark puffs out his breath but does what I ask.

*

"When I worked for Peter, he had his own memories, his own guilt and misgivings; he wanted me to put together the story of the Lord's life and death with some of his teachings, particularly the ones he understood and could still remember. Peter wanted me to describe the moment when he found the Lord's tomb empty; no body on the slab. When I tried to include your presence there, he was unhappy with what I had written; said what you saw was just another one of your visions. You found the tomb empty and your imagination immediately filled the gap: A gleamingly beautiful young man telling you, as always, exactly what you wanted to hear. *A typical Magda-vision*, he said. He tore up the ending and threw away the rest of the scroll.[cxxiv]

It is like being physically hit in a place even more vulnerable than before. To my surprise, Marcus seems unaware of the anguish he has caused me, the acid parody his words deliver. He seems rather amused than otherwise.

"The thing is, Magdalene, Peter didn't know how to deal with the aftermath; his own denial of the Lord the night of the arrest was always with him and he didn't know how to interpret what had happened, the occurrence we now call 'the Resurrection'. You might have entered a visionary space[cxxv]. Hysteria might have seized the other women but, even if so, where was the body? Peter didn't know, he didn't want to know, what to make of your role, your prominence, your commissioning by the risen Christ. He couldn't accept you as the teacher's messenger. For him, it went against the grain. So we left it there. The ending was broken off; we left a gap instead. It was the truth, as Peter saw it.

"It was wrong but what could I do? You were not there, Magdalene, to argue with him and he didn't want me putting my oar in. Peter was the captain of the ship by this time; I was only his scribe."

"It is hard to imagine you being so modest, so submissive, John Mark."

"There was a lot of debate among the elders, as to how the ending of the gospels should be written. Your sister had cast doubt on your testimony. She said the message you gave the disciples was a mere repetition of what Yeshua had said to everyone at supper the night of the arrest. She was serving at table and told you about it afterwards. She said that was where you got it from."

"My sister said that! They listen to what my sister says!"

But Marcus shies away from the feline hiss in my voice. "Levi," he says, "he accepted that you had seen the Lord; that he had greeted you in some way, but he raised another problem while trying to quash the rumours."

"Rumours? Which rumours?"

"Rumours that the Sanhedrin had bribed the guards at the tomb to say the body had been stolen away in the night by Lord's disciples."

"But why would the disciples do that? Why would they want to steal it away?"

"The temple authorities put it about that the disciples had stolen away the Lord's body so they could make false claims that he had risen from the dead."

"And…would the disciples have believed their own lies?"

"It raised doubts, Magdalene, among the followers generally, even among the inner circle themselves. For some, the doubts refused to go away. Even when the teacher himself appeared to them in the mountains, some doubted that what they were seeing was really him.[cxxvi] There was some strangeness about the figure, a problem of recognition. Could it be someone else, someone impersonating him, one of his brothers for example?[cxxvii] There was even talk of a twin. The family were implicated in the movement by this time, at least the teacher's mother was. They had a motive for keeping reports of him alive. Those who felt betrayed, cheated, might have taken their anger out on them."

My mind spins as Marcus goes on unpacking his case of complexities, a Pandora's box of falsity and invention.

"As the reports of these sightings grew in number, there was more, rather than less, mystery about them. Peter was one of those who doubted most. He doubted that a woman's testimony could provide the right basis for our faith. In fairness, he had a point. Serious-minded people might dismiss it, whatever the ignorant and superstitious thought. Peter needed to make some affirmation of his own but still he refused to do so."

"It was into this void – of belief, of understanding – that Paul spoke his testimony. His mind has subtlety, his understanding of what had happened to himself was crystal clear. The Lord had appeared to him, spoken to him, forgiven him; shown him the cross he must carry. Paul was a living witness of the risen Christ; he had no reason to lie. He was the last person to do so; he had been Christ's enemy. Paul's conversion persuaded people. Luke wrote in the light of this understanding.

"Luke claims you brought a message from some men in the graveyard. Your story is dismissed as…nonsense. There is no glorious young man, no angel, no meeting with the Lord. It is Peter who steps into the breach, who goes to the empty tomb, takes on the task of deciphering what it all means."

John Mark glances at me, a glance both shrewd and nervous.

"What's more," he says, clearing his throat repeatedly, "and this is another difficulty. Instead of your testimony, Luke adds a different episode. Two men, two of the Lord's disciples are hurrying away from Jerusalem when they meet a stranger on the road. It's like Paul's experience on the way to Damascus but this time, instead of blindness, there is illumination instead. The stranger walks along with them as they go, and explains to them the full meaning of what has just happened in Jerusalem, the full meaning of the teacher's crucifixion. When they get to Emmaus, the men invite the stranger to have supper with them."

Marcus wipes his brow; he is sweating with discomfort though the cave itself gets colder by the hour and we need our sheepskins. I ask if he is feverish; he waves away my concern.

"I wake at night sometimes, trying to get this scene out of my mind. It haunts me; it haunts everybody. And yet there is nothing of the ghost story about it. It is so natural, so down to earth: men walking away from an event they cannot understand, a stranger who explains it to them, a meal they share together: what could be simpler than this? Everything is there.

"The stranger sits down and breaks the bread. As he hands it to them, they suddenly realise it is the Christ himself who is there with them. The moment they recognise him, the figure vanishes."

A shudder passes through me as he says this. Someone is walking on my grave.

John Mark's face looks like an effigy carved in stone. "The scene," he says, "is absolute genius; it cannot be bettered. It is the Last Word, the Word that says everything without even speaking at all?"

"And that is Luke's ending?"

"Just one more detail. Luke has his own agenda. Despite what Peter testified, there is no mention of any return to Galilee. That message is utterly discredited. Instead, the disciples in Luke are told to stay in Jerusalem and that is what they do. The Lord appears to them there for the very last time. He is in his own body, wounded, hungry and palpably himself. He tells them all that has happened and all that will happen in the future. He commissions them to spread his gospel. The only nod in your direction, and it is a very grudging one, is that the Lord takes them out towards Bethany and gives them his final blessing there.[cxxxviii] Then he vanishes into Heaven and Luke starts work on his sequel, his history of Peter and Paul and their great deeds in the new church."[cxxxix]

John Mark watches me cry. Solemnly then he takes my hands and holds them, kindly, in his own. He says quietly, "I hope that you will help me, Magdalene."

My hands immediately start to burn, live coals in the palm. I release them from his hold. "And John?" I ask.

"John, too. He's alive, yes, still in Ephesus, but fragile now. His eyes weaken; his thoughts get more and more muddled. I do most of the gospel work for him so he can concentrate on another piece he's writing now, a visionary one this time[cxxx]. It's taxing on his Greek and altogether different in approach to Luke's **Acts,** more like a prophecy full of mystical encodings extreme images, surreal creatures, that sort of thing. Still, it keeps his mind occupied, gives him pleasure.

"And the gospel you are writing—?"

"It will be as beautiful as the truth itself and more moving to read. Even Luke will have to acknowledge that."

"Will it convince the doubters?"

"I believe it will. It will show the teacher as John remembers him, and as I remember him too, more loving and more human than in Levi's version or in Luke's. There will be no vanishing tricks, no excision of the people who mattered to him most. There will no doubt be some editing of the details; there are always others who have to be consulted. There is always a margin of controversy. What I want above all is to clarify the essentials so that everyone can recognise him, know who He was – even the doubters, like Didymus; those *twins of the faithful,* as Levi calls them![cxxxi]

And to do that, I have to correct the emphasis that's been growing in the church since the first writings: Peter's emphasis, Paul's emphasis, Luke's emphasis. I want you there, Magdalene. I want you included. Our theme will be incomplete without that!"

To my chagrin, I am suddenly seized by a fit of yawning, something I've not known for years. It isn't boredom; nothing could interest me more, but my mind is full; I have heard enough. It is not used to this kind of comfort. I need to stand up, to go outside, bring some refreshments; a midnight feast for us both. It occurs to me I have swallowed Luke's anecdote whole; I need a supper at Emmaus of my own.

*

When I return, John Mark maps out his new gospel. He wants me to understand that the way of Peter and of Paul, the way of physical martyrdom, is not the necessary, not the only model for Christ's followers. Living the love of Christ, being his beloved, as John believed himself to be, that is enough in itself.

"Peter and Paul," he says, "were men who fought and struggled against the Lord. Guilt was in their souls; they denied and persecuted Him. Such guilt is unbearable, a tomb of death in the heart. Suddenly, when the teacher returned to them, that tomb of guilt stood open and empty at last. They were free from what had imprisoned them. Where the guilt had been, there stood a vision of the risen Christ. That was their resurrection, the Christ flowing back into their forgiven souls."

"So I am not the only visionary then?"

"On the contrary! Paul had many visions; and, what's more, he acted on them too. They became his guide to forgiveness. Sinners such as he needed forgiveness; but you, Magdalene, you are like John! You were forgiven when you obeyed Yeshua's call. Forgiven everything because of your love for him. You were purified within."

"Did John say that?'

"Not in so many words but I'm sure that's what he thought. John had the love of the Lord. It was, he said, always with him, unchanged and unchangeable; he didn't need his body and blood as well, not the way the others did.[cxxxii] John hopes his own death will be a peaceful one; he will wait, he says, in Ephesus until the Lord comes for him. There is a continuity in such a death, almost as powerful as martyrdom."

"So John is alive in…Ephesus, you say?" I am struck by the association. I have heard of Ephesus, of its great temple to that silver-shining goddess whose unlikely servant I had once become.

"John is old now, but he has no fear of what lies ahead. He feels the Lord's grace is still with him and always will be. Most of the others are dead, martyred many of them but going to their deaths with trust and courage. John always had a knack for keeping out of danger. On the surface, he is still as smooth as oil.[cxxxiii] He said the Lord told him he was too precious to lose early. He had something to accomplish, something he must stay alive to complete. That's another reason why we need every testimony we can find, yours specially. John's gospel will deal with the Lord's resurrection in a new way."

"New in what respect?"

"We are concentrating almost entirely on the three last things: his passion on the cross, his death and burial, and then his triumph over death, the glorious triumph of the cross that leads to his resurrection and return to God.

"John takes a little from Luke, but he understands it better. Christ, for him, was the bridegroom: that is how people should think of him, as the fulfilment of love. For John, marriage, true spiritual marriage, is greater than funeral and that is what his gospel will show: the true teaching of love. Even to men like Peter who found this a hard lesson to learn!

"In John's view, death is merely the spilling of the seed from which new life, if the seed is true, must always be born. He claims the cross was the Lord's lover, the place where he spent himself, after which he slept until he was woken again the morning when you went to the tomb."

My eyes round in astonishment as I listen to this. *But he abandoned me! Are you saying now he left me for the cross? It was bad enough thinking that about my own sister.*

I draw on my old court learning to meet this new challenge. "And so the Last Supper was his Symposium then? That's why you mentioned Socrates!"

"Quite so! John wants the emphasis to fall upon the love that existed in our fellowship; how our understanding of that love changed us into what we have become, as brothers of Christ![cxxxiv] What it was like to be there, in the last days and hours, to experience it in its most intense form: that was our initiation. He emptied himself out for us then, taught us a love that was not the love of a servant for his lord or a disciple for his teacher but the deep love of true communion, of a spiritual bond stronger than death. Some might say it was extravagant what he did for us; humbling himself like that; washing our feet the way a devoted wife might do.[cxxxv] But no words could match that gesture, Magdalene, could they? He opened himself out for us, showed us a spirit full of pure grace. John said, no one apart from himself and perhaps one other, knew more about that than you."

We look at each other again with that curious directness and lack of evasion that exists between us now. This is too important for pretence, for strategy. John Mark's words flow into my mind like a healing balm whose source I can't quite identify.

"I'm glad he said that."

"John insists those last days, just before and after his crucifixion, are the key to everything, the real sign of who the teacher was. Paul said something similar of course but, for Paul, the Lord's resurrection was a spiritual experience. It was his own visionary encounter, the death of his old self, then the raising of consciousness, as his mind's body was lifted up by a glimpse of the divine purpose."

"It's quite difficult to understand, that."

"Exactly, Magdalene, exactly! But for those of us who were there it was not difficult, it was a physical event, almost entirely a physical event; he was there not as a ghost, not as a vision, not even as a stranger but as himself. Paul, who never knew him, is unable to speak of this. Peter, who denied knowing him, cannot speak of it either; he can only speak of angels and messengers. But you, Magdalene, you can speak of it. You were there. You are the key that turned this way and that; the first witness to that open tomb.

"And what is more, Magdalene, you were faithful to the end. You are like John; you have nothing to reproach yourself for!"

His words chime soft as a bell in the grey light of the cave. I decide not to disabuse him.

*

1.17   A Meeting of Minds

Hours pass; I renew the lamp only when it gutters in the last drops of oil, our shadows, large as angels, bending towards each other under the cave's arch.

In the early hours, as the darkness thins, he tells me how it has all happened, how the leaders of the Way have created an order and an organisation, several organisations in fact, not all of them easy to harmonise. Men who were born in small villages have gone out across the empire, becoming leaders they would never have imagined themselves capable of becoming. He speaks of the new teachings, the letters that Paul started to write and how important they have become, how important it has been to gather these teaching together, scribes copying them so that each new church can hear the same words and believe the same gospel.

Now that there are so few who can remember the people and events at first hand, records have been made to preserve the true story of what happened in Galilee and Judaea.

It's not that I have stopped listening, more that I have recognised something in what he is saying.

"I know you, don't I, John Mark? We have met before."

*

He is brought up sharp by my words. His expression, so animated when speaking, suddenly falters. "That is possible, yes. We must have met, as you say, but briefly, fleetingly. I was not there at the beginning, remember. I was a latecomer. One of the very last."

Something hard to identify starts knocking gently at my memory. But this is not the time to invite it in. There is more I need to know. "You speak of the true story, John Mark, the whole story, but my question is, *Do any of us know that, or do we only have it piecemeal, so many of the pieces still missing?* With Yeshua, there were so many secrets. Things we were forbidden to reveal. Things he or we never shared with anyone else."

"John's intention is that the new gospel should hold it all together. Not the way the first one was written, with Peter, all anecdotes and astonishment; there won't be parables for the crowd that couldn't understand them or a life-story from birth to death with angels at either end! It won't be a story at all in that sense. Peter was right about that. Chronology doesn't matter.

"We deal only with those signs that point to the true identity of the Christ; the outward signs that everyone could witness and the inward symbols that only those who have been initiated can recognise and understand. Ours is not a gospel primarily for a Jewish audience as the others were, Magdalene. Ours is a Greek Gospel, a Samaritan gospel, a gospel that folds both inwards and outwards and speaks two languages at the same time."

I laugh suddenly. "Like that special undergarment he wore sometimes, hidden under his outer clothing?"

"The undergarment of the High Priest! Yes, our gospel is like that, both hidden and visible. Authoritative, for those at least who can see the inner meaning! It's all a matter of weaving it together in the right way: from the beginning, from the end, backwards and forwards like a loom or both ways from the middle where the pattern is concealed. That's the seamless truth, that's what John wants. And that's what I want to give him, with your help, if possible.

"But I—"

"We are none of us just ourselves any more, Magdalene. After meeting him, we never were. We became his people; our lives took their meaning almost entirely from him. What we have to tell of is our meeting with him, how we became part of this great cosmic story that makes even the vast epics of the past look small. We meet him in different ways, of course. Paul understood that when he told the tale of his own adventures, talked about himself, boasted his hardships and his sufferings.

"Paul's sufferings will affect everyone who reads of them: his experience will become the blueprint for countless lives: new identities will be formed from this[cxxxvi]. Quite ordinary people, people like you and I, will become transformed by what Paul and the teacher have set in motion. We too will become patterns, great identities; great saints through whom others will come to know themselves. Paul's copy has become so powerful, John is worried we might lose the original!

"Our personal stories, they are the matter of salvation; the churches would be nothing without them. But we must chart a careful course, you see, in how we tell them: there is the inner truth for those who recognise it, and then there is the story as we must tell it to the world. Between the two there must be some slight... concealment."

*

"John thinks Yeshua is still alive?" It is a wild guess, my own personal story leaping back to life as he speaks.

"To the eye of faith, undoubtedly!"[cxxxvii]

John Mark gets to his feet, offering me his arm to help me up. We have been sitting too long; there is stiffness in every joint.

"There are three questions I have to ask you, Magdalene, before I leave. Don't give me your answers now but think about them while I'm gone.

"The first is easy: When you first knew Yeshua, did you know who he was? Did you know he was the Son of God, the one the Jews called the Messiah? The one the Greeks call the Christ?

"Or did you think he was just a man?"

I nod my head, turning to fetch the last of the lamp oil, a jug of water also for our throats are dry. I guess what he will ask me next and how it follows from what he has just said.

"You want to know if we…"

John Mark sighs. "I have tried not to ask," he says, "tried not to think it important, but, the more we have talked, the more of a question it seems, especially now I've told you John's ideas for the new gospel, about Christ as the bridegroom. There's a lot in that to consider, I think. So forgive me if this question comes out wrong and upsets you, Magdalene, but I find I must ask it. Were you together…as a man and his wife? Were you lovers as the rumour-mill suggested you were? As you yourself hinted earlier. Was there a marriage between you?"

Immediately, the dumbness grips me again, the impossibility of speaking, a tight paralysis in my throat. If I start to talk, the thing I do not want to speak of will take shape inside me again, it will come back to life, the horror that the years have gradually muted. It will get loose in the world, a great black serpent heaping its coils around something so precious, so unique only we could fathom its depths. And I will become the world's creature. It will twist and turn and change me into a million shapes. I will lose completely the little of myself I still possess.

I shake my head. He can make of that what he wants. For now, he sees the fear in my face and turns instead to simpler questions about my life up here in the sun's own solitude. He asks about the people I have met, about Pons my neighbour, about the quarry overseer.

There are things in my life that are hard to think on, things about myself I wish not to see: the question of love is a mirror-brass I dread to look in, whether back there among the dark images of the past or out here in the sunshine where every flaw is exposed and magnified in a dazzle of light.

Secrets: things I once promised never to speak of. *Am I free to speak of them now?*

Am I free to tell John Mark something of what we shared, the slow, uncertain, hooded journey we took towards each other, Yeshua and I? The mysterious dance we taught each other to perform, backwards and forwards, a world of guesses and uncertainties in every step?

We talk until dawn, John Mark and I, a passionate, urgent discussion of everything that matters to us most, beside that second question. At sunrise, we shake off our stiffness and walk together to my vantage point at the top of the village to watch the daylight rise above the mountain. It spreads like wildfire along the highest slopes, the light an unearthly pink as it reflects from the cold white shale at its peak.

"And your third question?" I ask him just before we part. "You said there were three."

"The question of what happened that first morning. I thought that was obvious."

"Yes," I say.

"And there is another question I cannot ask," he says quickly, bending his head over my hand as he raises it to his lips, "until I see you again." His eyes are hidden from me as he says this, but I feel the kiss burning like a blue flame on the tips of my fingers.

*

There was only one event: only one resurrection. A visionary space: time and eternity reaching out to each other, sharing some fresh translation of each other's language.

It was a new birth, visionary, in the depth of the soul. From the vision came the power of the idea.

The idea germinates, the seed blossoms. Suddenly there are many kinds of resurrection.

The reawakening of love in a deadened soul is one of them.

*

Peter, as John Mark rightly said, found it difficult to understand at first Yeshua's radical idea of love, its equality and interchange of roles and identities. [cxxxviii] Peter liked hierarchy, hard-edged definition; the traditional deference to, and evasion of, a full meeting with the divine. He loved the teacher deeply, no doubt of that; it was those who the teacher loved that Peter found difficult. Some in particular: *The bleaters*, he called them; the lost sheep. He was a fisherman to the bone, was Peter. And you knew where you were with fish.

It was hard for him to accept that loving the one meant loving the others too.

In Galilee, so John told his favourite scribe, Yeshua had to take Peter to one side, cast his loving spell over him there, teach him a new craft, not the catching and killing he was used to but the patient caring of a shepherd for his sheep. [cxxxix]

*

After he has gone, I wrap my shawl around me and walk this way and that, restless and agitated, picking a small handful of the sweet yellow flowers that grow here low and early, like the first footprints of Spring.

*

120

All day, until the sun sets again, I feel both exhausted by the intensity of our talk and full of excited energy. So much has been said, so much light has been shed, I am glad we have a week to think things over, and to recover our composure. John Mark has gone to visit one of the new settlements that he knows of, further south from here, back towards the mouth of the great river.[cxl] He will bring me news of what is happening there, put me in touch with someone I can contact. He promises too that he will try to bring a copy of one of Paul's letters back with him for me to read.

I settle down to work on a basket, bending the rushes with swift, decisive fingers. I love my work, my occupations. I put all my passion into its weave, so many things to consider; vibrations of desire, suspense and uncertainty still pulsing across my heart.

John Mark knows I will help him; he knows I will answer his questions. He does not know, no more do I, the other outcome. The decision, to speak of love or not hangs over my meditations. *Your testimony is so important*, he insisted, and the words are healing to me. They tell me I am needed, even at this late stage: I am no longer a silent exile, no longer the rejected one.

In the watches of the night, he confided something the teacher had once told John: that I was a wildfire, a self-burner like the seraphim, needing no fuel.

The comment, almost a compliment, made me uneasy, rang bells of alarm. It brought Peter back to my mind. I remembered as if I had never forgotten it, the mistrust that grew in all of us as soon as we got to Jerusalem that final time. How it became impossible to know who could be trusted. A sudden fear of betrayal was everywhere.

Was it paranoia when even those I was closest to, Joanna, for example, suddenly seemed dangerous, no longer the friends we had thought them? How had I ever believed she was one of us, she who, it now seemed so obvious, was Herod's spy, set there to report on us and keep him informed?[cxli] Everyone was twisting in a new wind. No one was safe. Nobody knew any longer who anyone was. Even Peter. Peter most of all, Peter who believed most but was full of obstinate fear. In the danger ahead, which way would he turn?.

I trace again the contours of John Mark's remark: '*John thinks you may know more than anyone else about the event that concerns us most. He has almost a jealous fear that you do.*'

Suddenly, a touch of the old John, the one I can recognise!

*

Or was it a *wildflower* he called me? Not a *wildfire*. Just a natural outsider; a seed that survives best on its own: self-germinating, difficult to cultivate! Perhaps I misheard.

*

1.18　Cana Again

The door was open. I pushed it a little further. There were two lamps burning inside. I went in and stood there, the open door at my back.

Yeshua was reclining on the bed, half sitting, half lying; he was wearing a short loose linen robe that left his legs and feet uncovered; he looked quite at ease.

I gasped.

There were two glasses of the new wine by the bedside, one almost empty. I noticed the flagon behind it.

He gestured for me to close the door and I did.

We stared towards each other, perfect strangers meeting by surprise, breathless and astonished.

The flame in one of the lamps flared upwards suddenly with a tiny hiss.

"You!" I said, and took off my headdress. I shook my hair loose, the whole past day shaken away with it.

He watched me as if he had never seen such a thing before. Said: "Come closer to me. I want to see you."

I stepped forward. He swung his legs from the bed and stood up; taller than I had realised. He put his hand under my hair and felt for my neck, loosening the clasp on my gown.

And then the oddest sensation. I seemed to lose all solidity, as if some massive power had just passed through me and turned my body to atoms, insubstantial, without form. I didn't know how I was even standing up. I was a column of shaken water, hardly solid at all. The soft blue silken gown slipped down and spilled around us both like shallow water. "Tangled up in blue," he said as I stepped carefully out of it, wearing only my light golden shift beneath.

"Now give me your foot." He sat back down on the bed. I raised one foot to his hand, and he smoothed off the slipper.

Then he bent over and began stroking the ankle, the sole, the high dancer's arch which he kissed, and then the toes.

"I have a gift for you," he said, and slid a small jar of perfume oil across the table. He tipped some onto his finger and touched the arch with it. "See, I anoint you as my own!"

The scent was subtle and unfamiliar. I could not identify it, just a hint of myrrh mixed with something much sweeter.

"Am I your own?"

"You are my exception," he said. "The world I must enter. This is something I have never done before."

Had he not let go of my foot at that point, I would have lost my balance completely.

"Hold me," he said.

There are some occasions, not many in a life, when something so remarkable happens it is like being told the secret of the universe. A moment that seems to shout out loud through your whole being, to call for you to come to it from every disconnected memory of happiness you have ever known. You can remember yourself, vivid as a birthday gift in all its finery, all along that trail of joy you were suddenly born for. So rich and exquisite is it, that for months afterwards you want nothing else to happen to you at all; no dilution, no addition. Anything else would be too much; it would be almost unbearable.

And it was lucky that was the case. For when morning woke us early, he stroked my hair and face and said, "Now, Magda, you must forget it all. You must speak to nobody about this. From here we must make a new beginning."

"But how?"

"Meet me in Capernaum. Wait for me there. In a month's time! I will teach you everything you need to know. You learn very quickly."

"You too," I said, then found myself blushing furiously.

*

But I won't tell John Mark any of this. It is a secret, for the writing's eyes only!

*

Part 2

Resurrection

Jesus said to them, "Are you asking one another what I meant when I said, 'In a little while you will see me no more, and then after a little while you will see me?' Very truly I tell you, you will weep and mourn while the world rejoices. You will grieve, but your grief will turn to joy. A woman giving birth to a child has pain because her time has come; but when her baby is born, she forgets the anguish because of her joy that a child is born into the world. So with you: now is your time of grief, but I will see you again and you will rejoice, and no one will take away your joy."

—John 16: 18–22

"From now on, therefore, we regard no one from a human point of view; even though we once knew Christ from a human point of view, we know him no longer in that way. So if anyone is in Christ, there is a new creation; everything old has passed away."

—Paul's Second Letter to the Corinthians 5. 14-17

aletheia (Greek)   truth
dy-aletheia the duality of truth [cxlii]

*

2.1   Three Questions in Search of an Answer: Recalling Galilee, AD 35

At the start, in those early days, there was such hope, such lightness of heart. There was excitement in the very air we breathed, rarefied and heady, as if it had blown straight from the sacred mountain[cxliii] itself. It was as if a great mistake could suddenly be rectified, as if time itself could be reversed and lead us back to an earlier innocence.

We were no longer condemned to walk a path of error. Everything spoke of that. All the horrors of the past, our own individual memories of wrong and the wrongs that had shaped our land and cultures – the wars, the rebellions, the great Pomposity's occupation itself,[cxliv] the imposition on our lands of that Roman name, *Syria Palaestina*, had suddenly been drained away, so that the river of time flowed cleanly on, free of all the filth that had been dumped in it.

One thing especially we knew we were stepping free of – those Roman gods that leered at us from every street corner, a multitude of chaotic cults, over-colourful, superstitious, mildly terrifying! You had to hand it to the Jews, when it came to religion, they turned the full power of their intellect towards it, shaped their understanding of it in the very depth of their souls.

There was a path that began here and there was no doubt that Yeshua stood on it, stood there and danced in spirit, giving off an energy so radiant, so unusual, that even at the time it was dream-like. These strange tales John Mark tells me of apparitions that have appeared to people since his death, they do not surprise me at all. In some way, he was always like that; it was part of who he was.[cxlv]

He was not bound by his body the way most people are. His body was strong, surprisingly so, but it was never static or heavy. His presence was thrilling. There was a light inside him, a charge of energy. It went forward with a momentum all its own, breaking rule after rule, subverting every practice that blocked the pure channel of grace that was flowing through him. He spoke of me as fire, but it was far more true of himself. There was a swiftness, a speed, a lightness in him. He could vanish like smoke, appear and disappear, be there one minute and gone as suddenly the next. People were always asking: *Who is he? What is he? Where has he gone?*[cxlvi]

There were times when he was spectral, when you looked round to see what was behind him or where he had gone. For us, he was…usually…such a joy to be with, exhilarating, liberating, but subtly frightening too as if the spirit within him was always close, a little too close, to its own borders. No wonder the demons were always the first to recognise who he was,[cxlvii] to see at once how far out of the ordinary, how far out of himself he could go. Like a magician in his magic circle, he went in with such command, with such vulnerability too, it was thrilling to watch him at work. He was a showman, some said, but showmen do not take the risks that he did. He assaulted everyone's boundaries; left himself no retreat; he saw what was hidden in people, drew it forth to meet him.

As for the demons, he went closer to them than anyone else: he was absolute master of that space, that circle, with no fear at all of what might be waiting for him. [cxlviii]Whatever it was, he saw it at once, with those swift, dark, conjurer's eyes of his, hard and full at times as the eye of a serpent.

Every day we were with him, he let the spirit drive him forward; he held nothing back for himself, just let it take him where it wanted; even when he knew for certain the terrible ordeal it was driving him towards. He trusted it completely, gave himself to it, completely. Like riding a maverick wild horse of immense power, he stayed on its back by giving it its head, becoming one with it.

Visceral, the responses he evoked from people! How dare he do what he did? Why did no one else ever dare to do the same? Take the same chances, the same blood-curdling risks? Sometimes he failed: he could not catch that demon by the tail, it whisked away from him; he could not gather it to his purpose. He had to capture its attention from the start, hold it still with the power of his eyes.

Like a huntsman or a gladiator even, he turned everything round like that; seized hold of something inside it, compelled its obedience. Out in the desert, I saw a man confront a lion once, witnessed that curious interval when no one breathes, the heart itself goes silent as the spirit takes stock of its opponent, assessing the power it is willing to risk. He saw in a glance how much of the fear he lacked could be transferred to others; fear of harm, fear of confrontation; fear of our own selves. When we were with him, he could summon extraordinary courage.

The energy and the courage, they were his first gifts. Matching himself to them, holding on to his human self, his daily identity, that was the challenge that held him always. No one can make the claims that he made about himself, claims of an absolute authority, a power given to no one but himself, without walking the knife-edge of mania, the mouths of madness snapping at his heels.

He did not do this at first; he was cautious while the power began building in him. I did not understand this at the time but looking back I see how it grew and gathered itself to him, became harder and harder to manage. He was walking a tight rope to eternity.

For us, at first, it really was like that, like walking on air, a freedom in our steps and in our hearts. He gave us the courage to be what he wanted us to be. Normal judgments, the frowns, the disapproval, none of that held us back any longer. He had only to smile, to start speaking, to hold up his left hand, one finger raised in that curious listening gesture he had, and we were caught up in his voice, his vision, his kingdom. He made it all true, what he was saying to us. He had that authenticity that genius has: everyone who saw it wanted to find it in themselves too.

But it didn't stay that way. He didn't stay that way. The times were always changing. Instead of that sense of unlimited possibility, that joyful assurance of faith, there was danger and mistrust, tension and quarrel.

None of this goes near to answering John Mark's question: How did I see him? Did I know who he was right from the beginning?

They confront me, those questions to which he wants an answer; they stand in a circle looking steadily towards me, but I am wary and confused, hardly able to meet their gaze.

I am kept silent partly by the knowledge of how much I have changed since then, so that I can barely recognise in myself the manic, edgy young woman I was when I first met him. What I understood of things while I was living through them is hard to remember now. There must be some continuity in what we are, some core of qualities, but my life has been thrown off course so many times I have lost the connections that hold it together.

Having been given so much, loss is what I have always known most. I have lived on this mountainside for so long now there are blanks in my mind I shall never be able to fill, things I have utterly forgotten, places where no memory has formed at all. But Yeshua was always memorable, and more than that: he was like memory itself, a memory not whimsical and elusive but capable of total recall.

John Mark's questions must be answered. There are things he needs to know; but the answers are not simple, and I back away as if memory itself had now become my enemy. Shadows come in its train carrying weapons of fear and accusation I will never defeat, things done I will never live down. How can I stand strong and truthful amongst things such as these?

Put me in front of a king, an emperor even, any emperor, and I will speak out against tyranny and injustice just as I did that day, shouting out that Pilate, who could have stopped what was happening, would face a reckoning of his own before long.[cxlix] His cowardice in front of the crowd incensed me.

When the cause is not my own, I have no fear of crowds. Something magical protects me. But for myself, to insist on my own truth, in front of others, I do not have that confidence. A lifetime of disapproval has diminished me. I remember suddenly the withered fig outside my sister's house in Bethany, unable to withstand its own doom.

Two nights after John Mark left, I had a dream. I dreamed of him, of Yeshua, as if he were living and we were to meet, go on a journey together. I thought I was at home, in a familiar place. I went to the meeting but somehow the names were all wrong, everywhere looked different. I didn't even know which country I was in, let alone which province. Was it Massalia or Galilee, Samaria or Judea? The more I repeated them, the more the place names became confused with each other. He told me we must meet in Arausio, that golden town on the great river where Caesar built his victory monument, but then I thought, no, it must have been Avenia that he meant where the river is too broad to cross and the bridge ends in a gallows tree where corpses bob up and down in the water. I became more and more anxious that I would never find the right place, that he would be gone before I reached him. There were signs everywhere but the directions on each side of the street were different. One side said *Aquae Sextiae* but the other *Vieux Sextiae*. Everything had two meaning, two sides that did not match.

The roads themselves kept melting into each other yet there were crowds all pushing in the opposite direction. I had only my baskets to protect myself from the soldiers. I tried to put the place together in my mind but the more I tried the more it seemed that I didn't know it at all, only some vague verisimilitude that was not reality. The impressions in my mind were not sharp and accurate but filmy and insubstantial. It was then I realised I was not at home at all but a stranger in my own dreams. I wished I had not even started on this reunion. *What does he want of me?* I kept asking myself. *How can I ever hope to find him like this?*

And then I saw a torn piece of scroll at the bottom of my basket. There was writing on it, but I could only make out a few words: '…*me tangere Magdalene.*' That is all I can remember.

There was a voice speaking to me, but I do not think it was Yeshua. It was more like the voice of John Mark, due to return here in a few weeks' time.

*

I think over what John Mark has told me, of all that has happened, all the extraordinary things, how the movement has gone forward, just as Yeshua said it would; how belief in him hasn't faltered at all but has been growing all the time. Each new believer, it seems, brings him back to life more powerfully than before. He always had that particular trick of making it seem that it was not he who was bending reality but we who had misjudged its strange materiality, its willingness to shape itself to our needs.

What seemed miraculous then is now becoming a certainty: something proved, no longer needing to be tested. Deaths that should have halted the movement have had the opposite effect, as if, with each death, some vital energy source were pouring back into the veins and convictions of those who followed after. As if his promise had been a true one, that whoever lost their life for his sake would become a living part of his glory.

Only I, it seems, have crept away to hide in a cave. What possible use could there be in that? What was it I thought I was protecting?

There was no child, no reunion, nothing I did that could help to further his cause or spread his teachings. Was my disappearance the best I could offer him? Had it been helpful to them in some way?

The very idea still twists my soul in anguish. *They wanted me gone!*

It is a strange bridge you are asking me to build, John Mark. A bridge of footprints that have left no trace! A ghost-crossing where all the ways back home have vanished in the snow.

*

2.2   Magda Begins Her Confession.

My story then: a living hinge in that cross-beamed doorway which opens two ways, into different places and planes of meanings that I struggle to reconcile. There was a man who thought he was God, a God who wanted to feel himself man. It was a point of intersection then, knowing both of them. He was a man always special in life, who was transformed by his death journey into something that gave to others a deeper and better humanity, something that crowned them, not with luxury but with grace.

I stand at the highest point in the village and look out across the steep ravine of the valley where the Nesque still flows rapid and turbulent in wintertime. Beyond the far bank of the river rises the long slope of the great mountain. This has become my sacred mountain, my ancestral home. It is my faith and my security. Today it is as if I am looking at it for the last time.

A vast landscape of green surrounds me in every direction as far as the eye can see. From here, so high is the place where I stand, the mountain itself seems almost small in the distance, its peak alone visible, a white triangle supported by two foothills, one on either side. This view never wearies me: it is as far as I am ever able to look. I stand in a small crowd, at a distance, watching that scene, the white mountain hung between two smaller peaks on either side of it. The view is exact, a finality, the true place of the cross.

Each day, I come here, to this precise spot, and look towards that distant place where the three mountain peaks anchor my memories. The mountain has become my God. It has become the place of God, like that holy one in Samaria, after the Judeans destroyed our temple.[cl] Sometimes it is my Mount Ebal where Joshua built his altar of unhewn stones. Such traces of our history we carry inside us, shaping our hearts and their search for consolation.

All I want to know of God is located here. The windy mountain[cli] they call it locally. The mistral hits heavy at times: a wind that haunts its slopes and has no other home.

Today, I turn my eyes away from its great green slopes and look across the steep ravine where the river circles one side of the village. Beyond that, in the lower, rocky reaches of the mountain, there are the *baume*, a row of caves that have been there since time began. I still go to them, they were my home when I first came here and I go back most days, sometimes at night, to pray and lose myself in their silence. At other times, I re-enter the village, inhabit my little house in the rock-face next to the temple.

We are so far away from any authority here that they have even given me its huge, iron key. I have become a kind of custodian. I look after the place, clean it and open it when there are rituals to be performed. Five gods have their shrines here, not that they receive much cult from the villagers who know their Roman overlords mostly from the quarries nearby, and they do not inspire much devotion.

The villagers sometimes gather outside of an evening; they talk and barter their goods and strike their bargains at the shrines. Sometimes I am a custodian of this place, someone who knows the ways of the temples and what needs to be done to keep the gods peaceful. Sometimes, I am a wise woman down there in my cave. I teach nothing but I listen, offer counsel and help and heal where I can. People bring me food and little gifts, to thank or to propitiate. I am a woman of two worlds now, and can move easily between them.

But beyond this, far beyond this protective circle of hills, there is another world, one with a beauty that is harsher, harder, and more argumentative than this. It is a land that lacks altogether the soft sweet vowels of those whose first taste of language came from Provence.

How can I summon back all that happened on the far side of that vast blue ocean where the world shows a sharper, more complex character? The land I fled from has become so displaced in my mind that I would not recognise it if I saw it again. There were no farewells: a great line was drawn between then and now, so quickly I stepped across it.

I am not trained in ordered thinking. I cannot set it all to rights as John Mark and the others are now doing. I cannot speak publicly of myself. It is not the custom for a woman, even a non-woman like myself who has no family, no father, no husband, not even my own child. Whatever my gifts as a girl, I have become a woman of few words.

The musing of my own thoughts, the memories I can summon, they swim in me like fish in familiar water. Now I must catch them, net them to the surface, set them out to dry and cure on a bank of hot stones as I used to watch them do when I stayed in Magdala as a girl. Lifted outside of myself like this, will they still hold their shape and colour? Will my memories still hold life inside the words chosen to display and preserve them, like the eyes of the dead fish that stared at me as a child?

When the sun goes down here, the light flushes like kindness, like the gentlest sort of love. It is no longer demanding but giving. It is the light that reminds me most of who he was. He had a humble and a gentle heart; I can remember him saying that.[clii] And what he said was true at times, those times when he was not called upon to act out his great identity. When he was not in front of other people, the crowds that flocked round him, he was oddly simple. Humble and gentle. Not assertive, not a firebrand. He could close up, like a plant, fold up his wings in a ball of feather, suddenly becoming peaceful and gentle and still. A resting shepherd, playing a few notes on his reed pipe while the herd gathered together and slept.

For a moment, not that there was anyone remotely like him, he could be – he could seem at least – ordinary, slightly vulnerable perhaps, his power taken off like a cloak and set to one side. He would listen, if you wanted to tell him something. Such attentive listening! His mind was always present, always awake to what you were saying.

What John Mark is telling me is this: Yeshua's life, his story – that is the great centre of us all! The only necessary thing is himself. We are the bearers of that story, carriers of the myrrh in which it is preserved. We only matter as far as we can remember him. As for our own stories, our own selves, they are of little importance: it is Yeshua, the Christ he has become, who gives them their meaning. That is what Levi would say, and Peter too. For them a great movement had gathered up their lives and taken them forward, inexorably, as the tide shapes the water.

But I have not been part of that. I have been here, alone, quite apart from the stir and excitement of those growing communities. The people that John Mark speaks of, those who came back to life again in the power of their faith and their new movement, they do not include me. I have not even gone out and preached the Way as they have done, as they were sent out to do. My voice has been silent; my only story has been myself. That is how little I count, how little of value I find in myself.

Is there anything I have to tell that I haven't spoken already? Anything important enough to break this silence so deeply embedded inside me that I can barely tolerate for long now the pressures of human speech? What was between us, Yeshua and I, was often unspoken. It was not a straightforward love affair. It was not a love affair at all perhaps, except for the love between us. There were gaps and absences and other things that preoccupied us and demanded our time, his especially. We were moving forward towards something and it was there, at that point, we would find each other. It was that which would define us most: the end of the affair. The closer we came to it, the closer we came to each other. The

130

end of our love: that was the true beginning of its story. All the details fell away from there.

For these others, for Paul's followers, it must be different. Paul, it seems, spoke of Yeshua, not of the man that John and Peter and I knew but as someone else, something else, something he has become by dying so wretchedly and yet being so untouched by this. It was as if death had clarified not cancelled his being. It was merely a rite of passage that he went through, transformed, as he was, into a self infinitely strange now, strange and yet still intimately familiar.

It was not as a ghost that he came back to us; he left almost nothing – nothing except myself, perhaps – behind in this world. Ghosts need peace in the grave, they draw us backwards to what they lack, for their repose. His return was the opposite of this: he wanted to draw us forward, to take us over that threshold into a new age. By dying, he has become for us the Christ, the Anointed One, the Chosen One, just as he always said he was, and I believed him to be. For me, whatever happened, he would always be that Chosen one. There were many other men who wanted to be what he was; but none who came even close to holding the secret of his power.

According to John Mark, this new man, Paul had a great understanding of the mysteries that moved through and around him wherever he went. Paul's writing tells us how his own life was completely changed, not by the man we knew, but by this other Being, this Christ who Paul had never known as a man at all. Here is the step I must take, between the one we knew and this other he has become now: this is the bridge that John Mark wants me to cross, a great seismic shift like a movement of the earth between one plane of understanding and another.

Somewhere far in the distance, in the scriptures, there was the Messiah, the priest king who would justify all the ways of the Jewish world to us and become its great leader. And then, somewhere in the future, there was the Greek Christ, a different figure from a different culture, a new hero from a culture that had given birth to so many already. And, in between these two, the Roman Empire and the man who healed me of my broken life. I thank my lucky stars for this mountain vision I have acquired; the long vistas of time and space that have become my familiar landscape.

How much did I know, then, of this otherworldly one, the one whose heart was neither gentle nor humble but bound to proclaim for himself the greatest of all identities? Whatever I say about those quiet moments, those gentle and humble times when we all rested, talked, ate, sang together, it was not possible to know the man at all without knowing that this great Other existed as a fundamental part of him. It set him on a course far removed from ordinary human destinies and desires.

He was, in any case, never turned entirely towards the world. He carried his own atmosphere along with him. He certainly never craved for himself the fame and celebrity his deeds inevitably attracted: the crowds; his reputation as a miracle-worker; the sensation he so quickly became! His family did not understand this about him: they did not understand how he had to keep growing to keep pace with himself, the massive energies that were rising all the time inside him, but we who were closest to him, we saw it, watched it sweep away his caution, his love of invisibility. Watched it claim him entirely for itself.

He understood the attraction of earthly power; he could have led a movement as many of them did: that Egyptian, for example, the one I heard of [cliii] who gathered a small army of thousands of ragged, disaffected folks and marched on the nearest city to raise an insurrection. Politics interested Yeshua a great deal but not as it interested others. It was something he had to know about but he saw through its mechanisms, its repetitions and predictabilities; the way it cankered and warped the soul. Leadership for him was a pure ideal, an idea brought down from heaven and still in direct contact with its own origins. Leadership was the sum of its vast parts, every detail contributing, falling as if by divine compulsion into its own place. Keeping earthly power at bay while never losing the force of its attraction, that was one of his daily tasks, the food he forbade himself.

He reached as far as he could away from all that, into an emptiness where only the heart could be heard singing. He could go there, into that emptiness, almost at will. It was the lesson of the desert, unforgettable. The power he cared about was concentrated inside himself; an opening like a wound that was always with him, a vulnerability that attracted envy, uncertainty, hatred. This openness, this purity of spirit made visible to the outside, it was in him like a glow, palpable, obvious, an affront to the world because it dared to show itself, did not feel the need to hide, and so challenged the powers of the world to injure or destroy it.

It was not like the slick sheen of evil that carries the opposite message, a warning like the orange diamond in a viper's eye. It was softer, subtler than that; it was grace itself, a kind of presence that surrounded him with its glow. Everywhere he went people tried to touch him, to touch some part of the light in which he stood. Even the clothes he wore were charged with it at times, an intense concentrated energy! He had destiny like an angel at his side; it was always there, he never forgot it for a moment.

People took their sick and injured into the market place and he went among the stalls like a spirit oblivious to barter while those in pain cried out to him, begging for the mere touch of his cloak so they could be healed. [cliv] It was counter to everything, a market where only the soul could be exchanged.

Above all, he was the one who could forgive us the wrong we all carried inside ourselves, some more than others; he could wipe it away, that imperfection, that twist of wrong inside us; it was astonishing to witness but we all saw it happen. We all experienced it in ourselves. He could open that other kingdom he spoke of, God's kingdom, the kingdom that was always there beyond the horror and atrocity of earthly power. There was something else that mattered more, something as small as a word and yet so supercharged with wisdom, compassion and love it could always speak to us. Something *Christ-like* Paul would say, at the core of everything.

Through his teaching, Yeshua could roll us back, like a polluted river, to some origin that was not the passion of our parents; that was not human lust and sexual begetting. It was there before everything. He set us on the threshold of that otherness. We lost ourselves at such moments, became offspring not of this ordinary, earthly life, but children of God. As if we came straight from him as Yeshua had come, bright in spirit, a new creation! We believed in this as we believed in him and it was not a delusion.

Whatever we had been in our lives before we knew him, however far we had strayed from the best in ourselves, he brought us back and there we were, standing on the threshold of a different world, a world inhabited by angels and full of happiness. I understood quite early on that his power to do this came from the death he had chosen for himself, from that opening into his spirit, that willing wound unlike ordinary circumcision. The two were held together in a constant tension, the grace and the danger, like a great equation, a balance that swung backwards and forwards between them like some strange fluid, wild mercury perhaps, or blood.

There was this point between the two, an aperture closed to everyone but himself, a wound that only he could open; words full of light, poetry as close to truth as anyone could get, poured through him when it did. He could make himself disappear, like a conjurer, disappear and become invisible. He did this in so many of his healing miracles, gave something then entirely vanished. All his healings brought a kind of death with them. They emptied him out, channelled all his energy; sometimes afterwards he had to struggle to get his breath. He made it look so easy; but it was not. It was not easy at all.

Of course, he knew the tricks of the magicians, knew their formulas and deceptions, these things were common knowledge; you could buy them in the market place. Yeshua did not work with them, except on certain occasions; he was always there at the line, the trick itself, not the magician. The magicians borrowed from him, tried to copy what he did. [clv]

I saw a man once – he cropped up in my life at odd moments like a kind of jinx – he had been ill from birth, his legs crippled from a twist in the spine. He shuffled about trying to get close to people, poor soul, begging for kindness, complaining that no one would help him.

One of the men who was there watching at the time told me what happened. Yeshua turned to the poor cripple in that curious fury that took hold of him occasionally. He ordered him to stand up, to help himself, to straighten out his spirit and pick up his begging mat. The moment the man stood; his healer was gone. So few understood what it was that had healed them; so few showed any gratitude. It was easier to heal their bodies than to teach them love. "Who did that for you?" an on-looker asked, suspicious with astonishment. The man looked about, he lifted each leg carefully and shook his feet. "I've absolutely no idea," he said. "There was this man…"[clvi]

Once, he was translucent and alive and the light shone through him so that we knew who he was. All of us close to him knew. We knew what he was in part but not the limits to which he could go. We understood him in time, in the power of each moment. What he might become confused us; we didn't know how to imagine that. Everything alive has the potential for growth and a species mould that sets limits to that potential. A sheep cannot become a horse. With Yeshua, it was different. He appeared to us both man and angel; the bound of his spirit was something for which we had no measure. He was heir to himself alone, an inheritance he shared with no one. We came in time to understand the prophecies; we understood the feasts and processions that proclaimed him our leader. But beyond that – there was a wall. Sheer incomprehension. Nobody understood what was beyond it.

Then came the time when he entered the darkness; we had seen it coming towards him like a dark storm approaching, but he passed through that also, and, with the darkness of death behind him, he could be seen against it, not as a lamp lights up the walls of a cave but as a new dimension, a great projection forward. Suddenly there was more to life, more to him than we had seen, and with this a new sense of possibilities. He had pulled it off, won some enormous gamble that cost him the world, such a small stake as he made that seem! It was unexpected; we didn't see it coming, I sometimes wonder if we saw him at all.

But that is what he told us, what it seems now they are all saying, that he had won for himself something he would keep forever. He had won a people who had been born of God as he was and would follow him back to his home in paradise. He had become that part of God we could encounter for ourselves; a God we could see at work in our own lives; a God we belonged to. Belonging to ourselves we were nothing; belonging to him, we had a destiny, an identity too for he became the guarantor of what we were. And the story of that belonging is the story I too am now being asked to tell.

It is a strange thing that, by killing him, by nailing him to that cross, his enemies only made him more himself, made him the very one they condemned him for claiming to be! The sacrificial lamb: he was given to us and for us; he bought us with his life. That was the cost. He brought something of us to God as well and in this new likeness, God came closer to us, with a face in which we can recognise something of ourselves. Yeshua had become our way of understanding God. We can speak with him in prayer. We no longer hear his voice in wrath and terror as the old prophets used to do, shaking with dread when they felt his power upon them.

God gave him to us, and we made him bear our sin because he alone was strong enough and pure enough to carry it without injury to his own spirit; he took it all; left it behind in hell and then rose free of it. His death cleansed us, I think; changed what we are, changed what we can become if we keep the memory of his love alive inside us. He lifts his cup in our direction. It is the wine of God's vineyard. Every time we drink with him, we renew the energy of his spirit inside us.

I think this is right, though it hasn't always worked that way with me.

This is my answer to your first question, John Mark. I have struggled to set my understanding straight from what I knew and what you have told me. Perhaps I have got it wrong in parts; perhaps it is not quite what you were expecting! But this is how it was for me when I carried heaven in my soul.

Though you must have guessed by this time, it was the man himself I loved.

The man that I am being asked to give up now, to let go of, no longer cling to in my heart.

Perhaps if I do this, the God inside him will become clearer, the God that now carries the imprint of his own, beautiful, human image.

*

Quite the theologian, Magdalene!

I can hear John Mark's voice saying that, the irony in his tone. See Peter's bushy brows lifting in heaven!

I decide to continue anyway.

*

I must think over what I have heard of Paul. It was easier for him than it is for me. He only ever knew the resurrected Christ, not the man Yeshua. He saw the Christ in a blazing vision and was blinded by it, but though the voice he heard may have been the voice of Yeshua, and the face and body may have been his too, Paul could not recognise him as we would have done. Paul saw him only in spirit; did not know him when he was alive in the flesh.

For those of us who were closest to him, those who knew Yeshua in his earthly life, for myself at least, this will be much harder. To understand the Christ he has become, we have to let go of the human person. We have to learn to let him rise, to let go of what we once held so dear, then see how we have grown more like him by doing this.

I watched a small child in the square yesterday morning. She was sitting, playing with a toy; she dropped it, then threw it away from her. She started pulling herself up, holding on to the wooden bench where her mother was sitting. The mother was not even watching; she was talking with a friend. Suddenly, the little girl takes a step forward, then she takes another. She lets go of the bench. Suddenly, the mother notices what she has done; her face fills with pride. She smiles as she sees me watching, then lifts up her daughter, and sits her on her lap.

I see the change that has taken place. Think how I must be changed too, no longer *Magda* as he used to call me then, but *Magdalene*, the name John Mark knows me by. I was changed when the first hint of his great identity was whispered between us; our secret at first; I carried it with me to Cana. And if I speak now of what I know and remember, I will be changed again, changed into whatever John Mark, in this new gospel of his, wants to make of me. I will become his *Magdalene*, the unknown woman who knew Christ from the inside.

James and John, Simon Peter and Andrew, Matthew and Philip we were, first and foremost, his followers. We existed in relation to him as he was then, and he belonged to us and with us. We had left everything, just as he wanted us to do, simply to follow him. He loved that: that we would walk away from all that defined us, our homes, our families, our work, our friends, simply to be with him, simply to be part of what he was doing. I remember Peter suddenly speaking up for us one day, reminding Yeshua of how much we had given up simply to obey his call. [clvii]

Now he is no longer ours. After the crucifixion he no longer belonged to us; death changed him, made him harder to recognise.[clviii] Death does change people like that; severe illness or ordeal can do the same. Is this what John Mark is saying? That people who saw him afterwards often saw a stranger? It wasn't just that his head was covered making him hard to recognise; it was that he was different. He was the same person, perhaps, but the life he was living was no longer the same as ours. He had stepped free of all that; stepped free of himself at the same time. Isn't that what death is? We don't know what death did to him, what the change was. And yet something must be written to explain this transformation. John's gospel will try to do that.

I think of it like that and I ask myself: *Was it the risen Christ we found hard to recognise, or was it the man himself who fooled us into thinking we knew him?* There is a stranger hidden away in all of us; someone who can suddenly appear and walk free of the self that other people thought that we were.

I have lived here so long, a lonely old woman brooding over her own thoughts, thoughts that have become, if they had not always been, her main consolation. Self-absorbed, introverted, frightened of everything beyond this cave, this tiny rock of selfhood, that has held me high above the treacherous waters of the past. John Mark can shake me loose from this. He can make me re-enter a history I still dread to remember, a past whose very passing calls up the stuff of nightmares.

I stand and muse, until the sky is quite dark and the stars are thick all around, as if I lived not in this distant place where no-one comes and nothing happens but as if it were a city of stars, full of light and action, everything going on there but incomprehensible, to me watching, with my disordered thoughts, impossible to interpret or make sense of. Like a foreign language you have no idea how to read. Writing a history, finding a way across that field of tiny lights, looking up but understanding myself, as it were, upside down.

*

"Oh yes," he told me, during that long night of confidences, "yours is a story that must be told; it is the essential threshold. No doubt of that. Think of it, Magdalene! He chose his witnesses just as he chose his scribes, and you were the one who saw and spoke of him first.

"No matter how unlikely a choice we might seem to ourselves or to other people, we were chosen precisely because of that, precisely because we were unlikely. We were part of his power to astonish, to create an endless astonishment, like the making of new worlds, one from another. In his world, it was not the obvious ones, the righteous, the elite, the best educated, who turned out to be the best qualified for the task he had to achieve. He himself was not the obvious one, not a prince, or a mighty warrior but an insignificant man from Nazareth. Nazareth – of all places! Many might seem more suitable than he. But the more suitable one seemed, the less…"

He stops there, suddenly hesitant, and changes tack.

"I have heard," he says as day breaks at the entrance of the cave, "of your work in the quarries."

*

My work in the quarries then: should that have got a mention? Not the brooms and brushes and crude sandals I sold there, just the work of dying in which I became involved. I told John Mark a little of it, before we parted that last morning.

A small group of men: slaves yes: but that is not their only category. Among the slaves were people of strength, intelligence and other kinds of distinction. Some of the prisoners were wellborn, educated, skilful. Despite the hell they worked in, they did not lose themselves entirely; they organised a group around them, became the ones the overseers spoke with. They knew how to bargain, how to sway the outcome of things. Even the quarry had its limits. Inhumanities beyond those limits could rebound in unpredictable ways.

One of the overseers became sick; he believed himself the victim of a curse. Not just one of the hundred curses he heard each day but a curse that filled him with terror. He had blinded a child, deliberately gouged out his eyes, then cut off both hands and fed his dogs with them. The little feet he hacked at with a cleaver. But the filthy, soot-blacked child still lived. It is amazing how much pain it can take to kill a human being. Finally, he seized the child by the hair and hung it from a pole over one of the drops. His own eight-year old son was watching the atrocity. As the scalp tore and the child's body began to fall, someone, no one knew who, pushed the son over the same ledge. The two children flew down to their deaths like ravens. Everyone agreed they looked like ravens.

The following morning, when the overseer came out to his work, there was a group of those birds, the ravens who pecked out the eyes of the corpses, perched on the dusty tree that marked his territory. They were waiting for him; they spoke to him in curses. When he screamed at them, threw stones at them, they cursed him more.

After that, the men said, they needed someone to help with the dying, especially with the children. 'That might lift the curse,' they said, but no one believed it. The madness had him. He was too far gone. The madness took many of them like that.

There was very little that I could do. I gave them, perhaps, a sip of sweet wine, a little clean water, mostly they were too sick for food, a few crumbs to choke over. I said almost nothing to them. Certainly, I did not preach. There were very few words of comfort, though I spoke sometimes of a father who waited to receive them in the place to which they were going. Sometimes I sat beside them, gently massaging their feet and hands and heads. But mostly what I did was cry, sit beside them with their hand in mine and cry.

What they liked best, those who watched at least, were the tears. I had so many of them. They watched if they were still able to take notice of what was happening and it seemed to ease them in some way, the feeling that they were not abandoned, not alone; that whatever they were suffering, someone was sharing it with them.

Eventually, there was an incident. Someone attacked me, attacked me verbally and then physically, as I was coming home. I had thought I was recovering, my lungs clearing out whatever substance had damaged them at first. Afterwards I became ill again, I became, though slowly at first, very sick. My lungs choked up with the dust. I started to cough, uncontrollably. Pons, my neighbour, thought I was dying. The blood I kept coughing made it impossible to continue. I did very little for them really.

I helped the women give birth, slaves twice over many of them, to a life that few would consider worth having.[clix] My time at the temple gave me the necessary knowledge.

*

That is all I had to say of the quarry. The sickness of a hell I had no power at all to transform.

But I see that it fits in somehow; that it is not, as I had thought it, the opposite of my life *before:* there is a thread connecting them, a queer kind of continuity. It is part of the same fabric after all. I put away my half-finished basket and think about my writing instead.

*

Good news! The order of what I have to say has come to me in the nights, sleepless or sleeping, since I saw Marcus last. It came of its own accord, this ordering of my life – my life as it became, my life *afterwards*. After I came to Provence, *unrisen*, as Paul might say.

I shall tell it to myself; I shall rehearse it, write it down perhaps! It will be, after all this time, a valediction, my way of saying what I couldn't say then, a farewell to those, myself included, who I never saw again!

I wish it were true that I had no self, for it is the self in me that sickens. Perhaps when I have finished telling its story, imposing an order, that self will disappear with the sickness and I will become laundered, washed clean of the rags that have choked my inner life since I left Judea. It will start in Massalia, after I had crossed that endless water, stepped out of the boat and onto a new shore.

Hard to recognise, perhaps, but a continuity nonetheless!

138

2.3   AD 36, Massalia: The Temple of the Goddess

I left Jerusalem; I left Judea, hurried away by what others had chosen for me. I let myself be led as they directed and then could not forgive myself for my loss of confidence. Nearly every action of my life has affected me like this: no sooner performed than it seemed either sinful or silly or both.

If anything was going to happen there in the afterlife of our movement, that happening had no need of me; I was no longer a part of the action. I was alone now.

No, repeat it as I might, that is not how it was. That is not the truth. I left Judea believing we would meet again. All of us.

I saw nothing clearly, just a long, dark journey by water ahead. Nicodemus, was he involved in the arrangements? If so, he told me it was not his idea that I should leave; it was not Joseph's either, someone else had thought of that. I am spirited off, quite literally taken as a corpse so nobody should try to stop us, back on that long night journey to Samaria and on to Caesarea. Beyond that the sea, my dark companion.

Months it took, that journey, but I have almost no memory of it. Just the islands we sailed past before I gave up hoping for land. Paphos, the white temple rising beyond the foam of Venus: I sat staring across the water, wondering if I was travelling forward in time or being drawn back into some remote past, in some previous life, some earlier culture.

Then Crete, home they told me of some bull-headed monster that haunted my dreams just as it destroyed young men and women turned loose in a labyrinth longer and darker than the catacombs of Rome. Malta was where I saw a green parrot in a cage that cried: *Repent! Repent!* at the top of its voice and made me laugh in spite of everything.

After a while someone put a cloth over the wires to shut it up, but it pulled the cloth off and began tearing at it with its beak and claw. A man, one of the sailors, brought a small monkey on board too but it died before we saw land again. I watched its small body, its frightened little face, sinking slowly beneath the waves.

I decided then I wanted no more memories. I was a soul in the charge of that grim ferryman that Nathan had once told me of, crossing the waters of forgetfulness.

Afterwards, at sunrise, Massalia:[clx] city of wrong choices, some called it, for it had chosen the wrong side in the Roman war and been slighted by their Caesar ever afterwards. Provence, *the Province*, as the Romans called it, was a land even more beautiful than their own. It had become the land of Artemis, Diana, the family goddess of their greatest Emperor, Augustus, that young hero whose statue is everywhere. The goddess herself, I was told, had been given a miraculous temple at Nemausus,[clxi] where she and her nymph Egeria[clxii] presided over waters not wild like the sea but sweet and ceremonial, its streams flowing through the city in finely crafted channels. I never saw this miracle though I imagined it often. I saw only the sea beyond the temple steps in Massalia and once also the great river that took me north from Arelate.[clxiii]

When I first arrived in Massalia, Artemis was everywhere, her shrines still under the protection of the former emperor's mother. Do not think it strange that I became her servant. It was not so. I spoke the language of her cult. She had temples in many places that we knew of. I went once, with Felix, to her great temple at Jerasa. Her shrines were everywhere and as a woman I was familiar with her cult.[clxiv]

The goddess was important to our times, even in Judea she was part of our culture, though the men mostly disregarded her. She helped me understand myself, helped me understand the turning wheel of female experience, the dark places that women have always inhabited. The emperor Augustus made her part of the order of his empire, more restrained and complex than many of the more popular Roman goddesses. [clxv] Artemis had a Greek restraint and chastity, but she was also fertile, a virgin mother who presided over the mysteries – the pains and dangers – of childbirth; she could heal, she could resolve disputes, she was the goddess of moonlight and of caves, of lakes and rivers and water, she was the goddess of wild creatures and those who hunt them too. Her cult had its share of savage aspects, especially in the great centres: Aricia in Italy or Jerasa across the Jordan. It had a wildness that appealed to those who had little to lose; those on the far side of the law, homeless men, criminals and foreigners.

Something fascinated me about her priest, the white-faced phantom who held his power on such precarious terms and knew more than most about that terrible threshold which the dead cross once and from which they long ever afterwards to escape.[clxvi]

Like the great moon that was her emblem, the goddess had a dialogue with human time; they spoke to each other in cycles; if only we understood how, it would all come round again.

The goddess had a care for strangers just as she had for me when I came to Massalia, a stranger myself, uprooted from everything I knew; she had a care for that too, for women who were estranged from themselves, enduring the ordeals of childbirth, and the wild febrile emotions of our monthly contamination. She understood death, and all its rites: the killing, falling; encrypting, perfuming, washing, re-clothing. She knew about grave clothes, both what one must wear and what one must shed on that journey. I remember learning about that, how I paid it special attention. "I served you as your robe, but you didn't know me."[clxvii] There were seven garments in all that had to be shed. And with the seventh garment, the goddess vanished, and the winds blew fierce and the storms came, and the sea heaved up like a woman in labour.

And then, three days afterwards in the rite, there was the stepping up from the water, one step, and then the second, before the greeting of the children. These were the children of Egeria, the lovely water nymph whose appearances were always heralded by a golden light. This light was her presence, a gold light cast over silver, her face dimmed in it. Then too there were the mistletoe groves at the back of the goddess's shrine where the oak trees grew so thick it was hard to find her pathways. Somewhere in that grove there was a crossroad: those with difficult decisions to make always searched for that spot, the *discrimen*, it was called, where futures were decided, paths chosen. The white-faced priest was there too. I saw him often when I tried to explore that crossroad for myself; it was the place I came to where I made no decision at all.

Massalia then: it happened more or less as Marcus described it to me, when he tried to follow that thirty-year-old trail. Unless I had honoured the goddess and given her my service, I cannot believe any trace of me would have been left at all. What could anyone remember, except that I had been her priestess for a time? After that terrible sea journey, months of dread and separation and sickness, I gathered up my few surviving possessions and came to the temple steps where I could still see out across the water. For a while, I simply stood there and looked back across the strange blue waters. Concentrating hard, I could see far, but not far enough. I had crossed over: gone from myself, gone from the life I knew, gone from the one I loved and the many who had not wanted me to remain.

I sat down on the steps crying, I sat there past caring, the hungry gulls circling overhead, crying too in a tongue that had nothing to tell of kindness, only of harsh, raucous survival. I cried until sunset. Then the great goddess took me in.

I found her healing at first. Like coming home, not that I ever knew this feeling, coming home to a loving mother. I shared her feast day,[clxviii] understood her cult; performed her ceremonies with the other women; the teachings I had received from Yeshua helped me make sense of everything. I knew the order of the ceremonies and the observances, as if they were my own.

I had learned the laws of the temple, listening to all the talk that had surrounded us when I was the companion of one who knew those laws from beginning to end. I knew the language of the temple too, easier to read than our own. I thought I would be able to speak it, until the day I tried to do so, the day I tried to stand on the temple steps and speak of Him, tell of a greater one than their goddess; to share his message with sea-folk for whom the anchor was their only home.

It wasn't that I couldn't do this: on the contrary, in those days I found it a natural thing to do. I could both teach and make myself heard. I could remember by heart so many of his sayings; I could tell of his healing powers and I could practice them too. I had the touch: a concentrated heat and energy in my hands. I could even touch at a distance if the vibrations were right. Exorcisms I could not perform. I tried once or twice but with no success at all. The demons would not listen.[clxix]

These activities did more harm than good. Passers-by began to see me, not as a priestess but as a woman of the temple courts, a courtesan who talked there to attract men. Anyone who understood my words recognised the anomaly; here was a servant of the goddess who preached the power of her 'brother', Christ Apollo, *Sol Invictus*.[clxx] Sometimes people claimed to know me, to have met me in another life, another place. Sometimes this was even true. Occasionally, I saw the new followers of the Way, the Christ's Way, gathered in small, impoverished groups. There was secrecy, secret codes and symbols; secret places of meeting and stories of persecution; they saw enemies in wait everywhere. I debated with myself whether I should join them, approach and tell them of myself. I hesitated, uncertain.

And then I saw him again, the one I least wanted to see, the one I wanted never to see again, and, what is worse, he saw me. That was the moment that made my decision for me and brought me here, to my hideaway in the mountains.

Perhaps the goddess was angry. Perhaps she had her own kind of wisdom. Perhaps she did what I tried never to do and recalled my past life; the terrible choice I had made which seemed so real and exciting at the time. I was not the first well-born, well-brought up young woman to find she had thrown in her lot with the revolutionaries, the avowed enemies of Rome.

The fact that I did not chose this – any more than I chose to come to Massalia – made no difference at all. It had happened anyway.

But there it was. I saw him again, the mad zealot I had once married. Something about his righteousness, his conviction, his anger, his daring, something too about that dangerous, dare-devil gift he had, his mad beating of the drums when night fell and he summoned up the great demon who was his own, calling his name in every language that he knew. *Diablo! Diablo*! I was fascinated too by his reckless disobedience where authority was concerned. Devils need you to make that trespass, to overstep the line, to defy and keep on defying. That, and only that, is what keeps them on your side. You have to hide your fear, go further every time. He was like that; he kept going.

It wasn't that I loved him. Not ever. Truer to say, I hated him but what I hated about him most was his confidence, his determination to charm me like a snake, to bind me to him, to capture and to dominate. I knew how much that meant to him, the chase, the hunt, the killing conquest. He was like the fearful priest of Diana, master of the golden bough, determined to conquer.

Determined to domesticate too; he wanted me as his slave, bound to his fortunes. Eventually I turned on him like a wild animal, hunted beyond endurance, pain and fear made me desperate to escape, whatever I had to suffer to get free. I got away from him. It cost me my family. No one ever really cared for me again: I had besmirched myself in being with him, marrying him and they never forgot it; they let me know they never would forget it. I was damaged goods; the only way back was to come as a servant, the lowest of the low, little better than the slave they, like him, now wished to see me as. What I did was a wrong, to myself no doubt but also to them, to the honour of the family. My death would have been far more acceptable, far more respectable. Why had I denied them that satisfaction?

And so, in Massalia, in the temple precinct, it was seeing him again, the shock, the completely unexpected encounter, that was the final straw. That was when I started to break. I had held up through it all until then, through the agony and death of the one I loved and followed and believed in. It was the coming back to life of the one I hated most, the one who was his substitute; the one I could not endure. Even now, I cannot say his names for fear the snake will get my tongue; a fear that if I do name him, it will summon him again, summon too the demons that surrounded him, that surrounded both of us when I broke with him. Some people fear to use the name of God; for me it is the name of the devil that must never be spoken, never, for fear of summoning it up, giving it that power of being which exorcism seeks to remove.

How could I speak of that to anyone? I could hardly live with the horror, for years a nightly visitant, a staring demon whose evil eye was fixed on me again in the dark cave of my own conscience. What right had I to try and preach of salvation to anyone? It's not just what we do, it's not our actions, bad though they may be, that draw those demons to us; it's the trap in our own story, some fault-line of our own, that springs us through into a hell we must then try to make habitable. Myself alone, I was a miserable sinner no doubt, but I never *was* alone. The world was always with me. I was not strong enough to stand against it, not strong enough to turn my back on it and walk away. I was always half its creature.

This sin would be laid at my door for all eternity, the sin that, once written down, would define me forever. It wasn't Judas who was to blame. And anyway, Judas was dead, that I did know. Judas knew that for him there would be no forgiveness, no chance of redemption or resurrection. I saw his body swing on the tree, heard the creaking in the wood where the anguish in his soul was imprisoned. It was almost the last thing I did see before I was hurried away. I understood Judas, his motives, his irritation, his huge sense of inferiority, the way he tried to compensate for his fate, to be the one who knew everything, who saw further than the rest.[clxxi] They had that in common, after all! Judas, I thought, was easy to explain. For him I was one of the levers that had turned him away from salvation. Now he was turning me.

My guilt was a subtle, serpentine thing. It had been with me since the beginning of time. And he who had the authority to forgive the sin was no longer here to do so. After that short encounter in Massalia, I knew I would never feel safe again. The man I hated would hound me, hunt me, haunt me in my dreams. And so, the goddess was angry and I, who could preach with a voice that drew people and made them listen, really listen, suddenly found myself growing sick, my throat drying, then turning into a culvert of slime and saliva. I was like a pythoness in her cage, foaming at the mouth as she tossed out the cryptic riddles of the future.

The sickness got worse. I did the only thing I could, I turned away, found a path to escape by, a boat that would take me up river, beyond the water into this wild, mountainous quarry where the slaves were sent when they reach port, a place barren as a desert, steep as an amphitheatre, inescapable as the pit itself. I travelled with a convoy of them, half of a mind to go with them to their prison hell, hewing the limey white stones that were the basic building blocks of the region. The bowels of the earth, white dust over everything. I thought of Lot's wife in her casing of salt.. I wished that I could turn back too.

In the end, I did not stay there. I was not Judas: I remembered his words: 'A town built on a hill could not be hidden.'[clxxii] I found this place instead, this cave where I, sick sinner that I was, could hide from the light that Yeshua had given me, the light that no longer illuminated anything.

I found Mèthamis, an old Greek settlement where they made cheap pots and jars and vases from the white clay that was quarried here. *Mèthamis*. I liked the name, its Greek sound reminded me of the goddess. And beyond the name, there was the view I discovered on my very first day in the village, a view of the mountain, one particular view, visible from only one place, a place not easy or obvious to find. I looked across the deep ravine of the river from there and saw the mountain's great shining peak and one smaller hill on either side of it. This was my station of the cross; if he ever wanted to find me again, he would know where to look. But the years passed, and he never did. The man I hated was still alive; the man I loved no longer existed. Only this view, this freedom of the eye that was given me in his place!

I waited: I learned how to live with absence, profound absence. But the absence also took away my fear: I began to feel safe, hidden from my terror.

What was I waiting for? Was I waiting for him to come and find me? Was I waiting for the world to end, or was I already in the kingdom? This queer, empty beginning where I was nothing and he was gone, and I knew we no longer belonged to each other. Instead of him, this absence that was always with me, vast as the blue heavens in a lonely landscape of one.

Very slowly, very gradually, the illness that had brought me here began to abate. I thought it might have gone forever. As long as my life remained empty, the sickness could be kept at bay.

*

2.4 A Reed Shaken by the Wind[clxxiii]: John the Baptist and the Court of Herod Antipas

The sickness that has become my daily companion had its origin much earlier in my history, long before I came to Provence. I must go back there.

Becoming ill again, set apart for more than five years in the sorrow and isolation that sickness brings, meant living a life so meagre, no memory formed, and I can hardly remember that I lived it at all. But consciousness is never wasted: it is always a privilege. That was what I told myself and the telling kept me alive.

What surprised me was how little I could recollect of my earlier illness. That time back at Herod's court in Tiberias: such memories as I had seemed to belong to someone else. Then, I shared the sickness of the world. Now I was set apart in a world I shared with no one. Illness isolates, it locks you up in yourself in a constant self-preoccupation. I searched and searched to find its origin, some cause for which I was perhaps responsible.

My illness was strange and shaming and unsightly; no one could explain it, least of all myself. I relived each scene until there was nothing left to look for and I still could find no explanation. "Quarry dust," they said, when I tried to find help. "Have you seen anything like this before?" I would ask, but the answer was always, "No. Never."

144

This second illness, the one that came from the quarries, was like the first only worse, the symptoms more severe, and nothing seemed to cure them. My lungs filled up again and again with strange frothy liquids, and the froth and phlegm and hair and dirt ran out of my mouth uncontrollably. Twice a day with intervals, then it would start up all over again. I became a total recluse, convinced that sin itself had made me incurable. There was something evil inside me not even Yeshua had been able to cast out.

There were people I knew, both men and women, whose souls were beautiful: you could see that, in their every gesture, the way they spoke, the goodness within. Gentle and humble. I was not like that. I was full of faults, things I could neither change nor accept about myself. I was impatient often, full of queer angers, and worst of all inclined to harsh judgments, to thinking ill of people. My tongue spoke amusing, uncharitable things about them more often than not. There were so many people I could never look at through the eyes of love. Peter and I, we had the same difficulty. It was more visible in him though!

These things about myself, they told me something: not just that I was sinful but that I was ordinary. Something ordinary was wrong inside me; you know when that is the case and how worthless it makes you. My sister was my worst judge; she and her husband had been set against me and I took their condemnation into myself. The fact that they disliked me no matter how hard I tried to please them made me dislike myself too; it made me especially vulnerable to their hostility. I wanted to change myself. I wanted to be different. I injured myself, operated on myself like a physician, crammed myself with food; then vomited out my self-loathing in secret. I turned more and more inward and made my outer self, my other self, a mask and a stranger; she acted badly but she did it rather well.

I was subtly off the rails: noticeable but not likable, desirable but not lovable: a damaged mind unable to connect well with the world of other people. If not an entirely bad woman, then certainly not a good one! I was wrong in my spirit.

I think of that sick and sinful self, clever, in control, unlovable; carrying inside itself a place where demons dwelt, one especially. It had a strange power, a strange kind of luck. I could do all kinds of things that would bring disaster down on other people, but I could get away with them. I could get away with murder, rebellion, damaging liaisons.

The demon protected me: I could take risks, risks that would appal the well-thinking but which, by a kind of devil's luck, always paid off for me. I could expose myself to dangers that made normal people shudder and I could get away with that too. "The devil," they say, "takes care of his own!" You have to respect him for that. Like Tobit my little dog, the devil was my familiar.

It taught me how to suffer, how to endure biting physical and mental pain without a murmur. I could make myself do all kinds of things that ran against my instincts. As a result, I could frighten people. They didn't see my own fear: they only saw how I didn't respond the way they expected me too. They could make me suffer but I could ignore the pain, treat them – I speak of course of my family – as if I loved them still. The more I did this, of course, the more I ignored my suffering, the more I attracted what I wanted to avoid.

There was a man – after my years with the zealot gang, after the gentle gypsy who helped me escape from their leader, 'my Egyptian' as Marcus calls him, after these, and after John the Baptist, – before and after John if I am truthful, – there was a man who I loved. He was a Roman; a high-placed official, Felix, a man used to command. I met him at Herod's court where I had come as a dancer, all legs and lips and eyes, to teach the local dances I had learnt for visiting dignitaries to gawp at.

He was a Roman, that says it all perhaps, but he knew the world;[clxxiv] he had hazel-green eyes that were full of this knowledge.

"It belittles you in some way, being here," Felix said, almost as soon as we met. "You don't belong here."

Partly he wanted to help me escape; partly he wanted to keep me in thrall to himself. The stories of my life, the wild, colourful escapades, the dangerous people I had known, fascinated him. He thought me beautiful, saint-like, evil: a serpent in a carnival mask; a fairy from some non-human sphere. He couldn't quite pin me down but the pain of that pricking, probing search was a torment to the nerves. The entanglement had me in a hopeless bind. I had no power against him, not even the power of saying 'no'. I became his concubine.

I loved this man because for a while, unlikely though it seemed, he loved me. To start with, it was a good kind of love, one that raised my standards. He cared for me in some way, experimented with me, toyed with me, put me through all kinds of trials: I came to believe, so much of a liar was he, that he was the devil incarnate – and perhaps he was. Certainly, he taught me a great deal and used me both very well and very ill. I couldn't go abroad as Nathan and John Mark had done to study the art of rhetoric. I leant from Felix instead, the way of the world.

A sea of pain started rising inside me at this time but whenever Felix hurt or humiliated me, I found some clever, amusing way of retaliation. I could outwit him, out-dare him, refuse to be victimised, confront him with himself. Resilience like that can be very seductive. His anger drew him back to me: I stood up for myself when I should long since have broken down and begged for mercy. He began to encourage me in a kind of devil-may-care wickedness; fed me something to live on through those desert years at Herod's miserable provincial court in Tiberias. But it was bad food, poisoned sweetmeat; I always knew that.

Later I leaned the reason why. In that great show city[clxxv] Herod had built to honour yet another new emperor, he had ordered his own palace to be constructed over an ancient Jewish burial ground. Graves and corpses had been dug up en masse and unceremoniously re-buried in a builder's pit. Herod's contempt for his own people, his toadying obsequiousness to their Roman oppressors, it was written in that palace for all to see.

Disturbing the dead like this, in a place where they have already been enshrined, it activates some strange force in them, brings their angry spirits back to life, both envious and vengeful. Once disturbed, they can be very troublesome, very injurious to the living, difficult to lay to rest, resistant to exorcism. Herod's court was a sporting ground for such things, strange occurrences which increased if you acknowledged them, unaccountable signs and disturbances, sudden chills and repulsive odours, footsteps and whispering, the malevolence of guilt and revenge.

There was a fear about the palace like a miasma, a fever swamp whose vapours penetrated people's minds. Herod himself was the prime example. He was terrified of the ghosts he had conjured back to life by his own evil and duplicity. Being around him, we all became infected. The air, the water, the food, it was all contaminated. Uncontrollable angers and perversities would suddenly appear in people for no reason. It was difficult to appease them without bloodshed.

Then the sickness broke out; a slow poison infected the atmosphere. Manaen, Herod's friend and foster-brother, the only adviser he actually trusted, fell sick one day and seemed likely to die. He asked for me, to perform a ritual healing dance he had once seen. I tried to help him battle the demons that had seized upon his soul; he had developed a loathing he dared not express for Herod's rages, his pointless cruelties. I did what I could to heal him. I even tried the spells and potions I had learnt from my gypsy husband who peddled cures for the sick as part of his road show. I knew a few of them. All my education came to me through the men I had tried to love; perhaps that way I learnt what most women aren't often exposed to.

But I was not strong enough to drive away those evils. I never have been, not entirely. I have a vulnerability that makes me fear those demons and fear is what they live on. I lacked the right defences and could not exorcise the spirits that plagued him. Though Manaen recovered, the spirits took possession of me instead, like an empty house with no true owner.[clxxvi] I caught his sickness, became more and more disturbed in my soul. I knew there was evil in me and that I could not release myself from it. It set me further and further on a path of wrong and I could not stop walking. Felix was both my torment and my rescuer: I was with him at the beginning, later I went back to him again, deeper and more desperately entangled in his coils.

When we first heard of the Baptist, he was out in the wilderness, a wild man but a true prophet, his voice unforgettable as he denounced the evils of our time. Israel had lost touch with its prophets; few had the spiritual strength any longer, so John was a novelty, rare and remarkable. He lived on nothing, took no heed for himself; cared only for the voice inside him and the gospel of repentance that he preached so ceaselessly. He called the local people to come to him for baptism, to be washed clean of their sins in the River Jordan, to make a fresh start. The whole court went out to him, curious but desperate too to experience his sincerity and conviction, his steely purity of soul. It was so long since we had had anything to believe in.

John Baptist: *Johanan*. I still cannot think of him without anxiety, cannot even speak of him easily to myself. I hurry past his memory like someone running past a haunted house. He exists in my heart like a piece of broken glass, jagged and painful, never to be removed. His death, a bitter milestone in the lives of all of us! You cannot kill a man like that without consequence.

Marcus will ask me about John. He will want to know what I knew of him. He will want to know if I was there at the beginning, if I saw the first great sign of what was to come. I must think carefully what I must say.

John made a great difference to us at first. We thought he was the one we had been waiting for: the one to save us both from ourselves and from our oppressors. We were wrong about that. John was a prophet who shook with God's own fury when he spoke; he was a burning brand, fiercely critical, both of people in power and of the evil done in their name. His truthfulness was breath-taking. To hear him speak out so boldly, so openly and with such fierce oratory, it was as if one of the ancient prophets had come back to life, Elijah himself, they said: the great teacher who could part the waters and drive the *Merkavah,* the fiery chariot of God.[clxxvii] John, so the legend went, was a storm-child to the core, son of a priest and a hag, a woman who believed herself too old to conceive a child.

But the Baptist was not quite what he seemed. He had his own part to play in what was to follow: he was Elijah come back to life on one of the goddess's great circles. That is what had been agreed for him; that is what he had been bred for. John himself was so remarkable, everyone overlooked what lay behind his birth, his priestly father sworn to silence about it, his mother too compromised to tell the tale. [clxxviii]

That John was a prophet, we all knew. That he was Elijah himself, come back to prepare the way for one greater than himself, that we understood only gradually and in part. John spoke of a great change, a new future that was about to burst upon our world and destroy our certainties. Prophets don't mince their words. People loved to hear him speak; they listened horror-struck with interest and excitement. He had set himself to purify the present, to transform the court, to strike a road through the desert along which a new future, a new deliverance, a new king could be rolled out. The King's Highway[clxxix] would bring us a leader unlike any we had known before, a spiritual man who would in time defeat all our enemies.

Listening to John talk of this new leader, we became mad with excitement. A Great Something was about to happen; we had to prepare, transform our lives, wait in readiness for someone who would be far more important than John himself; a prophet chosen by God to surpass his master, just as Elisha, in ancient times, had surpassed the great prophet from whom he had learnt.[clxxx]

He knew exactly what, and who, he was talking about. Though we did not know it at the time, he was describing his own cousin. It was all to happen just as they had planned it. And they had planned it just as it had been written. Written in the Holy Scriptures, proclaimed by the prophets, it had to happen! John and he were actors in a drama that had already been scripted, young men dedicated to the roles they had been taught since childhood how to play. This was the biggest secret of them all.

148

Herod was completely fascinated by John at first, his Hebrew intensity; his ferocious moral vision that defined, beyond the rite of circumcision, what being a Jew was really all about. And what that was, in John's view, did not include divorce and certainly not a divorce that broke faith with another Jewish king, a king more devout than Greek-speaking, Roman-obeying Antipas would ever be. John favoured this man, King Aretas, Herod's father-in-law, the father of his first wife. The Baptist's fierce criticisms of Herod's behaviour were dangerous in themselves; then he denounced his new marriage too. It was, he proclaimed to everyone who could hear him, un-Jewish, contrary to law, because Herodias, his new queen, had been the wife of Herod's own brother.[clxxxi] Herodias was too insecure and too ambitious to tolerate that. When she saw her chance, she had John arrested. That was when the turn came. Something unpredictable had intervened. We lost all hope of salvation.

After John's murder, Herod's court became for me a dance of death. It was as if I had become her pupil instead of she mine, Herodias's doe-eyed daughter. I got sicker in my soul, not physically ill but morally sicker: I waded back into a river of wrongdoing the very opposite of the Jordan's cleansing waters. The spell of John's baptism was broken. It seemed I had no good choices left. Caught in a weird coil of self-destruction, I became obsessed by the thought of suicide. Planning my death, practicing it, this became my entertainment, an arrogant denial of my own sufferings, a determination not to be broken by them.

The power of refusal never presented itself to me. I lived, as it were, off my own blood. I was possessed by an active evil; layer after layer, flowing all the time through my dreams and my veins and my actions. A toxic anger had me in its grip, left me without any boundaries of my own. It is not just prophets and mad people who cry in the wilderness. People began to sense there was something inhuman inside me; that I was being controlled by a dangerous force. Still I did not break down. In my saner moments, if I can call them that, I saw only one means of escape, only one way of freeing myself, from a sinful entanglement that was eating me alive, like a great black lion in the arena. I'm describing Felix of course, my Roman lover and tormenter. Death was one option but – just as before – it was not one I was ready to take.

I chose instead to marry Nathaniel, my clever, lazy, guileless Jewish cousin.

They had a saying at court: *Women never turn to God until the devil has finished with them.*

*

And that was when I got to know him first.

*

2.5   Bad Timing: The Lesson of the Fig Tree

A complete stranger: someone nonetheless who knew all about me, must have heard of me from somewhere. He knew at once where the fault lay. Spoke straight to my condition. Said only: *I will be with you – in that still small voice of calm.*[clxxxii] A different kind of prophet: quieter, a teacher who watched me with interest when I was doing wrong.

There must be some explanation for why Yeshua cared for me, why he gave me his time and his attention, but I never could quite understand what it was. He came, they said, to save sinners and I certainly fitted that description. There were stories about me, a kind of half admiring notoriety. Not good for a woman to be known that way. But the stories were drawn to me, nonetheless. Perhaps the Baptist, John of the wilderness, had told him my history: a woman from a wealthy family but one who had so much of the wilderness, so much of desperate poverty, within.

This is more difficult to speak of than I thought. I will not tell John Mark of this; I will write it instead, in my secret book.

"You have a good spirit in you, Magda!" Yeshua said to me once. *"But you have hidden it! Where could that be? Ah yes, over there! Look at that field you knew in your childhood. Do you see that golden light where the moon daisies grow? If that's where you lost it, that's where you must find it again: in that little wedge-shaped field with a well in the corner."*

How did he know these things? How did he know about the moon daisies? Does everybody have them, these same incidents; these same special places of memory? Or was it always he himself who was really hidden there?

Yeshua knew that I had a voice, knew that I could speak out; that some kind of truth was in me. He said once I was a prophetess, a prophetess of God's hidden treasure, though he never would tell me what that was! He told the others I was worth listening to. He listened. Sometimes, quite often in truth, I amused him, a man not easily amused. It was as if he was learning something, as if the path of my wild escapes was a way he had never thought of before but could somehow understand. And so, he never judged me; was never angry when I spoke out. Or said a wrong thing.

I wonder if he heard me that last day screaming below Pilate's balcony: *"If you do this, if you don't stop it happening, I will go to Rome and tell them the evil that stands to your account. I will go at once; I will tell the emperor in person."* There was a stir in the crowd. Everyone around me heard. People turned and stared. I am sure he heard too. But all that day, the day I was most there, he never even looked at me. Not once. So I stood back. I kept my distance. But my throat went bone dry. I felt some of his pain in my hands. I watched his feet, he had beautiful feet, unlike most men's, the bones so strong and sure and fine, like a fine Arab horse, dancingly alive. Now I saw them bound together, tightly roped like an animal slung on a pole, one heel pierced by a nail and running with blood and dirt.

I do not want to do justice to this scene.

I stood next to his mother, that cool, strong-willed woman watching the fulfilment of what she had agreed to thirty years before, watching her part of the

150

bargain brought to fruition. She had agreed to this – she had chosen it for him – and he knew that was the case. She had given birth to a child whose death and destiny were known from the beginning. However special it made him, he always, in some part of his being, resented her for that.

Everyone grew uneasy as we watched his suffering; even the two wretches who shared it with him. Time itself seemed to hang from the cross, every minute excruciating and slow. The crowd that had at first bayed for his blood, angry, and disappointed that their Messiah had failed them, began to shift and suffer. After the first hour, the power drained away from them. They had made their call, their frenzied insane condemnation. Suddenly, they went quiet. There was no longer strength in numbers; there was ebb, exhaustion, fear. I am quite sure of that, of the animal terror. Even the soldiers were uneasy, the dogs slunk back; there was a strange concentrated silence. Even now I can re-inhabit that experience. I can re-enter it, the fierce burning pain in my foot, that queer, suspenseful silence; everything that hung there. It has never left me.

If I concentrate on that, if I focus on the sensation, on that pain, sometimes it will open for me; it will take me back to the day itself. The place I need to go.

I only ever saw him stumble once: a stone gone awry beneath his foot. My heart pulled down with him. Some terrible mistake; a force stronger than he had anticipated! Something had gone wrong; some vulnerability after all. Someone bent down to pick up the stone, one of the black-hooded women, wanting a souvenir!

While I was literally beside myself, he was withdrawn, his body almost devoid of presence, his spirit concentrated on the small cross where spine, neck and shoulder blades hold together.

But why am I describing this? I am supposed to be telling it from the beginning; from the time we were first together. Why then have I gone instead straight to the end time, as if that was the only important thing? I will never get on like this; make a story that others can understand, if I lose the order again. And yet, the lines of this loom are strangely set. You cannot understand the beginning unless you see the end as well! I am like John Mark when he starts speaking of Jerusalem. The weft comes apart there, the pattern gets lost. The reed cannot hold them together.

I can never untangle the threads of my life from his; they are fixed on the same heddle. I must return to that first question, the one from which all the threads started. The single eye of God in a diamond triangle: what did it look like from there, our human attempt at interpreting his purpose?

I thought I had answered the first question, but I see now I was wrong. That question of Yeshua's identity, it is the thread along which the whole history of my life was strung. Beginning to end. End to beginning. The loom goes backwards and forwards; in and out, the shuttle is thrown between taut wires. I must go forward in time before I can find the design, the threads I must separate out, before I can make sense of the past.

Who was Yeshua? John Mark's first question is the easiest one to answer. Most of us know only in part what we are; our identity is a riddle that throughout our lives we try to solve. But it was not that way with him. Even in the early days when he was filled with the joy of his own teaching, his own healing, his astonishingly easy performance of power, his identity was an open secret. A rabbi, a teacher, a spiritual master of astonishing gifts and extraordinary audacity! Yes, *astonishing,* that is the word for him: Marcus was right about that.

By the time I met him, he knew exactly who he was and who he had to become. He amazed us all, took our breath away. There had been many others who believed themselves to be the One that Israel was waiting for, but he was in a class apart. He belonged with the *aristoi*, the best, those who excel, those with the deepest power, the stamina, self-belief, the unstoppable God-given capacity that sets them apart from the others. They go way beyond the norm. You know when you have met such a one. You know when you have met the One. Nearly everyone who met him knew. But there was something hidden so deeply inside him that even he himself did not know, something he learnt only gradually.

The shocking secret hidden even from himself was that he was not that One; he was not the One that Israel thought it was waiting for: it was only at the end when the Greeks came calling for Philip and wanting to be introduced to him that his identity finally became visible. [clxxxiii] He was no longer the Jewish Messiah. He had stepped across that line, become the Christ instead, just as earlier he had stepped across the borders into Samaria, back to the beginning, the true origin of the race, and beyond that too into Canaan itself, the land before the beginning, the land that God's people had been promised, the land they took from others for themselves.

He grew with the gaining of this knowledge, that his boundaries were not those his mother had taught him but were incomparably greater. He was not circumscribed by her vision of his future.

Something of this must always have been with him, but opaque, without definition. I knew from his mother that even as a child he had known who and what he was. She knew how unique he was but there was something in this difference, the way he acted it out, which jarred with her. He had a certainty all of his own, a lack of obedience to what she had imagined was to happen. There was a curious friction between them, actors in some drama of their own, some knowledge they tugged at between them, some disagreement, quite fundamental, about the way things should be done and when it should happen.

About the timing of things they were often not in agreement. It was as if she were hurrying him, wanting to make sure he did not get too attached to the wrong things or take his own path. At times she clearly thought he was mad; at times I thought what he felt for her was a kind of hatred. His anger towards her was a disquieting part of his magic. [clxxxiv] She tolerated me as if, after the error at the wedding, she held herself partly responsible for how things had turned out and accepted I had become a fixture.

The tension between them really went back to John, his cousin on his mother's side. After John's death it became for a while a war of nerves between them, a battle for control. She had the power to begin with but after John it was different. The Bapist, living or dying, made a difference to everyone. Once she came, twice in fact I remember, when he was teaching and he denied her access, insisted that she no longer owned him; that he had chosen his own family;[clxxxv] that hers no longer contained or defined him. He had escaped her grip and she knew it.

I aided that shift of power between them that came when he worked with John and increased after John's death. Yeshua could not escape the blueprint of his own identity, but he was determined to live it out in his own way. He chose me perhaps to tell her this, a woman so far her opposite she could not help but recognise in me some shadow of herself that she did not want to see.

So it was that once our companionship became established, I who had freed him from one set of circumstances brought him difficulties of another kind. There were times when the temple lawyers and the Pharisees who had their own agenda, goaded him about me, trying to catch him out on some moral trip wire. I made him vulnerable to this kind of provocation and there were times when he raged against it.

One morning, very early – it was the second morning of that last week in Bethany – he left the house in a blind fury because of me. I had overstepped the boundaries that defined our relationship; I had challenged him about Martha, told him she wanted to have his child; that she was scheming to become his wife. I knew it was wrong to say that, even though it was true. I did not dare say it of myself, I who was his soul mate, the one who lived on the inside of his mind, part of his spirit, he once said. They were so strict, the Naassenes; nothing must get in the way of their dedication. But women threw themselves at him all the time. "Don't touch me!" he used to whisper, feeling weakened when they did.

The tension in him had been growing throughout the previous weeks, in that period of restless travelling before he returned to Jerusalem. This week when he got to Bethany, it was palpable, acute, impossible to diffuse or alleviate. I could not always find the right way. This particular day, after I had angered him, he went out early without eating or speaking, went out and turned his anger on a tree by the roadside, an innocent fig that had just come into leaf but not yet produced any fruit. It was not the season for figs; none of them were ripe.[clxxxvi]

It was not the tree's fault, but, according to Peter afterwards, he blazed into a rage and cursed it for its barrenness. *Barrenness*, was that the real issue? By the end of that day the tree was withered and dead. The force of his anger was terrifying, demonic almost. The incident brought back again that sense that the timing was wrong; that something – in him perhaps, or in the world – was not ready. It was not the fig's fault: it was he who was not ready. But he always harvested his anger, drew something from it, turned it back to its source.

His fury remained with him all day. He went into the city, making sure everyone knew he was there. Then he turned on the stallholders in the temple courts where foreign currencies were exchanged for temple shekels, where taxes were collected, and birds and animals sold for the sacrifices. Doves were special to him because of John. Down by the river the birds had congregated around him like seagulls, waiting to be fed by the people who had nothing else but a few corn seeds to give in exchange for their baptism.

Thinking back on it now, it was as if John himself had come back to life again, as if Yeshua, normally such a different character, had summoned up his spirit and taken it into himself.[clxxxvii]

John's spirit was with him all that day. There had been an incident on the way down from Jericho, something to do with money, a new initiate with wealth to offer who had created fear and jealousy among the brethren. They lived in constant dread of losing their leader to some new disciple wealthier and more sophisticated than they were themselves. As ever, the stories of what had happened, of Yeshua's deeds, had gone ahead of us and set people talking.

John's death was part of this. Before returning to Jerusalem this last time, Yeshua had gone back across the Jordan to the place where he had been baptised.[clxxxviii] Questions continued to circulate there. If the Baptist had been so important to him, if John had indeed been such a great prophet, why had he, Yeshua, who could perform such miracles, done so little to save him from the ignominious death that ended his career? Why had he left him there in prison? Why had he left him for dead?

Why indeed! I knew of these questions: some of them had been my own. After his execution, many of the Baptist's followers had joined our movement but others had remained, divided and leaderless, uncertain whom to trust. They thought Yeshua had failed him, not spoken of him with enough respect; downplayed his importance and done nothing to save him. There had been sharp words, a falling out amongst us as to what should be done. Yeshua knew how he had benefitted from John's life; even more perhaps from his death.[clxxxix] He had taken but not given, not given John his due, not defended him from his enemies.

Some unease remained about this. We had gone back across the Jordan to settle the disputes, reinstating John's pre-eminence among those who were counted as Yeshua's disciples. In winning John's people over, he also made more enemies for himself. The temple hierarchy was alarmed. The stakes got higher; the Way more dangerous.

It was all waiting for him when he got to Jerusalem, all the issues that were rapidly coming to a head: arguments about money and pre-eminence, about John's ministry, about human marriage, the true purpose of the kingdom of God. As John's death had made clear, prophets like kings needed heirs, someone to follow them, to inherit their power, to take forward their work. The fig tree raised the spectre of the future: its sexuality a temptation, its barrenness a curse.

I couldn't help but identify with it.

Later that day, he recanted and preached about our need to overcome anger, how prayer could help us to do that, prayer that must always include forgiveness.

But it didn't end there; his enemies wouldn't let it. There were so many of them now and they could sense his tension. They tried to draw him further into their trap. The Pharisees sought out his weaknesses, that threshold where wealth and spirituality confronted each other like non-identical twins; they goaded him with questions that touched his fear of the unknown time ahead, the end time, that vague and unspecific future in which Jerusalem would suffer calamity and he would lose what he always had: that extraordinary and carefully orchestrated control of his own life.

Outside the temple courts, the Sadducees were talking about death, and against that afterlife in which they, so wealthy and well placed in this life, had little real interest.[cxc] Some of the scribes and lawyers who felt less certain, baited him with case law while the crowd gathered for another of those public contests it was their delight to witness.

After the resurrection, one of the lawyers wanted to know, whose wife would she be then, that woman, the serial monogamist, the one who had married and buried seven brothers, one after another? After the resurrection, in the afterlife, which one of the men would she belong to, given that she had had them all? Judas was scowling and glancing backwards to where the women were standing, listening. I guessed he thought they were talking about me. Perhaps others thought the same.

No one would be married in the afterlife, he told them. *The souls of the chosen lived free as angels from the constraints of their earthly bodies. God's kingdom had its own lines of succession: its heirs were the living who had faith in his teaching.*[cxci]

It was a theme he often spoke on and he was sure of his ground. He dealt with their questions easily and silenced his interrogators, but the anger was still twisting inside him. He raged again, first a rant about the downfall of the Holy City itself, then a dark prophecy on the way back to Bethany that evening, a prophecy directed at pregnant women and nursing mothers who thought there was a future ahead of them for their children, instead of the apocalypse that was coming.

Nobody understood him or what was driving him so relentlessly towards that unborn future. Suddenly, there was the fig tree again; Nathan's fig-tree,[cxcii] I suddenly thought, glimpsing a man who looked like him half hidden in the throng. Yeshua held up his hand, as if he were signalling a greeting to someone at the edge of the crowd. But it was the tree he was pointing at. "*The lesson of the fig tree,*" he said calmly as if the colossal energy of his mind and the perturbation in his spirit were once again back under his own control; "*it had something to teach us*"! The fig tree itself was a sign, he said; its fresh green leaves a reminder that summer was on its way; it offered us a lesson in certainties, an illustration of how we would know his *parousia, his* Second Coming as *Israel's judge*, was imminent. The tree was his prophet, his words the eternal ripening of its fruit.

I knew I had something to do with his rage that day but in truth it was not possible to understand him or explain him simply through his dealings with other people, people like his mother or Peter or myself; situations, the Sadducee priests, his debates with the Pharisees, the misuse of the temple, the way he understood himself, the strands always drove together. No one person or group of people determined his course. He wanted to hold it all together, to be the lynchpin, the corner stone. Every secret had him as its moment of disclosure.

*

2.6   The Anointing in Bethany

I must tell the end first then. It was that which defined us most. The beginning can only be understood from there.

*

It was impossible for me to forget the week he came to Jerusalem for the last time. He was to stay six days with us in Bethany and for me these days were full of trial. In my sister's house, though he had brought about reconciliation between us the previous year, I was never at ease. I felt as if I were a kind of servant there, allowed only on sufferance.

My old self, largely quiescent when I was with the disciples, reasserted itself when Martha was around. Partly because I saw the way she looked at Yeshua, the way they spoke to each other, I felt the need to claim him as my own, to want him as my lover, not just my teacher. There was jealousy between us; suspicion too. She disapproved of the life I led and saw my return as an attempt to regain status after years of disreputable living.

She was a widow now; a woman of considerable property and she despised my lack of material wellbeing. I was her ne'er do well sister come back to the roost. He had talked to her, charmed her immediately and brought about a reconciliation between us, easier because both our parents were now dead, and she no longer had a husband. He stayed with her whenever he came back to Jerusalem; it suited him, and she made his followers welcome too.

The house was large with lots of outbuildings and it was useful to him to have a safe place close to Jerusalem where he could come and go, dealing with the temple by day, dealing with his destiny until prayers were over and then at night folding up into himself again, and folding into the dreams of those who slept around him. It wasn't that he asked us to arrange things for him exactly. He was as secretive about his movements as ever, but we all knew that the following day was to be momentous, the day of his proclamation, the day everyone in the city would know at last who he was. The white colt would be waiting for him, just as the prophecy demanded.

I had been sent on ahead with Thomas and Bartholomew and my share of secret tasks. I had arranged for Uncle Zeb's white donkey, Cherub, to be there at the gate with her foal when he arrived with his retinue on the first day. He greeted us and we thrilled with pride as he rode off on her, followed by the sort of crowd that always assembled in Bethany before each of the three main temple festivals.[cxciii] We walked along with them watching as the people of the town, who had heard the whisper of his coming, began lining the road with their palm branches ready to greet him.

Everyone knew. Everyone recognised what had been building up around him for so long. It was the great moment: the moment of clarification for everyone, the moment everyone had been waiting for. He was coming in the name of the Lord. He was the Lord; he was God's chosen one. He took in the crowd, who was there, exactly where they stood, every detail as he always did, his eyes, Levi said, sharper than a tax inspector's when it came to detail.

At one point, he turned and saw me following, dancing behind him, like Miriam.[cxciv] Perhaps I did something to amuse him. He smiled. Suddenly, the colt took fright, tripped on a stone, for a moment there was silence, a gasp from the crowd, then suddenly it was righted again. The procession headed into town and all day he was there, noting everything, the stallholders setting up round the temple, the women who worked there, the bird sellers, the herdsmen in the open courts and merchants and money changers of every kind.[cxcv]

When he got back to Bethany that evening, he was high on human energy, filled with the joyful reception he had received. It was his supreme achievement. He had become a king at last, fulfilled the prophecy and been greeted as the Messiah.[cxcvi] I understood that; we all did. It was his night of temptation too, ours as well. He had drunk a little more wine than usual; he had eaten one of our best suppers, Martha had excelled herself in the preparations. Then he asked us to give him time alone, to pray for what was to come.

"Not you, Magda," he said. *"I want you to pray with me. We will walk outside together first, before it gets too dark. There is something we must speak of. Then we will pray together."*

I don't know what happened. I don't know what possessed me. I was wearing a new blouse, a cheerful, velvety black and I don't know why but, as if it had some magic in it, real magic, the moment I put it on, I knew I had been transformed. I had stared at my reflection in the brass and seen myself as if I were a different woman, startlingly beautiful. I had never seen myself like that before, so I knew that something had happened; I had become the kind of woman every woman dreams of being. A legendary queen, perhaps, or the high priestess of some mystical cult!

"Yes, rabboni."

I sat down on my stool close to his knee; it seemed lower than it should have been. Two lights flickered by the door. He came back from seeing his followers disperse and stood over me, his shadow bending towards me on the wall. Then he leant forward and gently removed the comb from my hair. It tumbled down like a waterfall. I knew a feeling of happiness like no other in my life; except perhaps for that happiness I knew as a child, eating my star-shaped jelly at the inn of the ancient temple.

I knew with absolute certainty that if I looked up now God himself would not be able to resist me.

"Magda..."

I looked up. And as I did so, I found myself rising to my feet, standing so tall that instead of me looking up into his face as usual, he could look straight into mine.

Will I have to tell Marcus what happened then? Will it be an important part of the story? The profound intoxication of that kiss? Not a public kiss, not the kiss of the initiate or the clever student, not a reward for insight or the right answer. A private kiss, intimate! The feeling of being taken in his arms, such strong arms as they were, carpenter's arms, a man used to working with tough, intractable wood. It had been so long!

And then across the threshold my sister appeared, her shadow preceding her.

"Oh, so you're here, are you? Both of you, it seems!"

"We were just going outside to—"

"Look at the stars, I suppose?" She spoke sharply, her voice full of exasperation. "Or were you going to take a walk to the tower, again. The way you did with Salome that night?"[cxcvii]

My sister had an unshakeable conviction that knowing me was bad for Yeshua; that I would hurt or harm him in some way. She thought I had already done this with John through my brief spell at Herod's court. But if I was the dancing mistress then, this time I was mistress of the dance. I would not be intimidated again, not endlessly have guilt heaped upon me by association, for things that other people had done.

I stood looking back at her, unabashed, my eyes huge and glowing. Tonight I would dare demons for what I wanted. She glared back in return, then started to bluster and busy around, asking if Yeshua had everything that he needed for the morning. She began to rearrange the couches, collecting cups left on the table.

"Time you were in bed, miss," she said, as if speaking to a child or a maid-servant. "I won't be needing any help from you tonight. And the teacher must get his rest too. You shouldn't be keeping him up any longer."

I heard Yeshua sigh impatiently. "She listens to my words, Martha. You are wrong to scold her. Magda seeks wisdom as you seek mastery in your house. You have each your own spheres but now there is something that especially concerns her. Listen to your own counsel, Martha; listen carefully; the hour is indeed late. Your work is over for the day."

He said goodnight to her, then turned back into the shadows momentarily.

He bent down and whispered through my hair, *"Come to my room, a few minutes before midnight."*

And then, as if in a vision, I suddenly remembered: moon daisies in a meadow full of tall grass, grasses almost as tall as I was; a willow tree, oddly shaped, bending its green-lit branches over a small well in the corner of the field.

I was there with my dead brother and my sister, the youngest and smallest of the three. It was my first glimpse of heaven!

An hour later, I sat waiting in the dark well of the stairs, with my grey shawl over my head. I watched as Martha came round the stair post, quietly lifted the latch and went on up into his room.[cxcviii]

*

There was never only one truth with him, John Mark. I learnt that a long time ago.

*

The following morning early, he found me sitting in the garden under the jacaranda tree.

"She wants your child," I said. "She wants to be your wife. I saw her!"

Wrong of me, I know. He saw the truth of my jealousy and his brow darkened. He left the house without a word. I stood up and followed, my shawl tight as a winding sheet around my arms.

He waited out in the road until Peter and the others came out to join him. They were going up to the temple where he would be preaching all day. It was the second morning; all the exhilaration of the day before had vanished as if it had been an illusion, an unhealthy dream. I watched in horror as he cursed the fig tree. I felt it was myself he wanted to strike down.[cxcix]

*

It was the third day. We all knew something of what lay ahead. If we didn't understand what was going to happen, it wasn't for lack of telling. We knew that the end was getting near. The suspense affected all of us, made us behave strangely to each other. He had told us all that he would be taken prisoner in Jerusalem and handed over to his enemies. He had told those of us who were closest to him that these enemies would put him to death and that he must endure this at their hands.

The men were not willing to believe this, especially not after his triumphal entry into the city. They had seen him proclaimed by the crowds and greeted as their long-awaited king. But I believed it. I knew he was going to die. This was why I behaved as I did that last week in Bethany, that final week in the city he had wept over with such passion.

I stayed at home that day. Martha and I prepared the evening meal, a simple one tonight as we expected guests again the following day. We said nothing to each other about the matter closest to our hearts and our hearts themselves were far apart. We waited for the menfolk to return, listened avidly when they did to their accounts of what had happened that day, what he had said and done.

There had been a blistering attack on his tormentors of the day before; there had been parable after parable that Levi was keen to note down and store in his memory. He was strangely jubilant. The tax collectors had been praised above the temple hierarchy: "He called them *vipers*!" he told me gleefully.[cc] "Imagine that, Magda! He called them vipers while we…"

"Such fury!" Andrew interrupted, mopping his brow as he spoke. "It was just like hearing John again out there in the wilderness, so righteous, so angry, so full of God's own fury. He was not himself; it was not his usual style at all."

Everyone brought away with them strange, unforgettable vignettes of those days in which money, death and the great black hole in time ahead of us shifted around him in a macabre dance of anticipation. The smell of blood that perversely marked the feast of Passover was already in the drains; the streets were crowded with animals as before, but the stallholders had moved their wares into the outer courts of the temple.

John was white faced, obsessively twisting his hands like thick strands of straining rope. "I saw him sitting by the offerings box," he said, ignoring the wine cup I held out to him. "He was sitting absolutely still, his face stiff as an icon. Instead of the moneychangers, he sat there alone as people looked away from him and dropped in their coin.[cci] I can't get rid of the image: him sitting there in the treasury, still as a stone and listening to the sounds as if intent on counting some incalculable cost. An old woman came up and put in a couple of small coins embarrassed by the amount. *"It's all I've got, Sir,"* she said.

"We are the same, you and I," he said to her. *"We have given everything."*
She gave him a toothless smile. *"We still have the hope of salvation, Sir. Don't you forget that!"*

*

That night our supper ended early. Everyone was tired and went their own way afterwards. Very little wine had been drunk with the meal. Yeshua had asked for water and the rest did the same.

"Don't forget, Magda," he said quietly into his shoulder as he stepped past me. *"Come to my room tonight, a little before midnight."*

*

I should stop there. Go to sleep now. Forget myself again for a while. But first there is something I want to explain. I want to explain it to myself, one last time before I decide what exactly it is I should tell John Mark.

*

It is the following evening. He had been teaching in the temple courts again, but in his own voice this time. I went with them to listen. All trace of the Baptist had vanished.[ccii] Many had tears in their eyes as they listened. He spoke quietly, like a compassionate judge, of the stark choices in our lives, what we make of what we have been given and what it is that we must give to others. We had to get it right on both counts but the balance between them kept shifting so that we were always in uncertainty. There was nothing lax about his compassion.

That evening he was peaceful, poised, immensely centred.

We sat at supper with our guests, just as we had rehearsed it. The table was full for Yeshua loved to share a meal in company, loved food, loved talk, loved wine, just as he loved solitude too, his mind feasting alone with God. Tonight, despite what lay ahead, he seemed full of happiness, a happiness that overflowed into the *agape*, the love feast of those around him. He praised the food. It was Martha's particular hold on him; she loved to cook, loved to preside over and serve at one of her generous banquets. Simon, who had once been in the Leper House, was there too as another guest of honour, his skin healed almost beyond recognition. Since his recovery, he had developed a strong attachment to Martha and a dislike for me in consequence.

I was not in my element in my sister's house and always aware that this might bring me trouble. I couldn't help noticing that there was something unusual about our guests this evening, some were complete strangers to me or people Yeshua had cured during his travels: another former leper who had actually come back to thank him, one of the blind men whose sight he had restored, a couple of former cripples, some neophytes I didn't recognise and, now perfectly himself again though inclined to silence, one of the demoniacs he had exorcised in the tombs. What were they all doing here? I began to wonder if my wine had been drugged, as if I were hallucinating some sinister festival of healing. Judas, for instance, was wearing a new cloak, not his usual threadbare moss green; it was red, I remember, strong-coloured and expensive. It didn't look right on him somehow, and he was drinking more than usual.

My task this night was not to sit and listen as I loved to do, but to help my sister prepare and serve the meal. I carried out my tasks just as she ordered me to. I waited until the food had begun to relax people, until the sound of their talk became settled and even in tone. Then I slipped out, fetched my jar from its hiding place, and came back into the room, pausing a moment on the threshold. Then I walked towards him, steady and deliberate, set my jar on the table and knelt down in front of him, just as we had agreed I should.

I waited there until the guests had fallen silent, then I rose again and, while everyone sat looking at me, cupped my left hand and poured some of the nard into the palm. The perfume was dizzying. I touched his forehead with my finger, then placed my hands together in a steeple on his crown and gently rubbed the ointment into his hair and scalp. Finally, I raised my right hand in the sign of a blessing and spoke the Greek words he had taught me straight into his eyes: *"Behold the anointed Christ!"[cciii]*

The scent of the perfume was intense, almost overpowering, and, stepping back, I knocked the jar off the edge of the table where I had left it. It hit the floor with a crack. A gasp, mine perhaps; then a shocked hush, benches pushed unceremoniously backwards. As the jar rolled loose under the table, the perfume started seeping out. This was not supposed to happen. This was not what we had agreed. I was to keep half of it for later. Sudden tears sprang to my eyes. Martha's fury was like a torch beam thrown across the room.

In that moment only one thing mattered to me; the perfume was for now and none of it should be lost. I went down on my knees and wiped up the ointment from the floor with my loosened hair. Tears were coursing down my cheeks and spilling onto his feet and sandals. I began unlacing one of them, washing his bare feet with the tears and perfume and wiping them with my hair like a slave. Once I had begun, I was in no hurry to finish my task. The perfume was too precious to be lost and I dreaded standing up again.

Was it an accident, a sudden clumsy gesture, or did I do it on purpose? So many times I have asked myself this question, as if something hung on it, something I still need to understand.

At the time, I felt I had made some terrible blunder, destroyed a ceremonial rite. I had named him; I had anointed him as the Christ. It was my job to do so. Then, as if some devil had pushed my hand, I had knocked over the flask. The perfume spilt out; the scent filled the room.

I can still relive that moment, but I no longer castigate myself. However clumsy I have become I was not so then. It seems to me now there was some kind of protest in what I did, a protest I made in spite of myself. That there was extravagance in the gesture, I recognised at once. It was an extravagance I would pay for, an extravagance for which I would be condemned. But there were too many emotions in my heart that night and defiance – my old defiance – was there among them, as if, despite everything, I had done it on purpose.

But defiance of whom? And why?

I need to understand this. I knew what I had done would be used against me, used to explain the betrayals that followed.

It was a moment of clairvoyant certainty. I seemed to see and acquiesce in a train of consequences that all collapsed unstoppably into each other, like cards in a pack.

Yeshua lifted me gently to my feet, raised me up, held my elbow lightly; then let me go. I pushed back my hair, wiped my face, blotting up the tears as best I could.

I knew in the instant I had brought trouble on us by what I had done. Once again, I had placed myself in a circle of controversies. I had been over-dramatic; I had not been discreet or sensible; I had drawn attention to myself. I had brought hurt upon myself; the old demons had never entirely gone away and my sister's example always seemed to summon them back. She would think I had up-staged her. Deliberately made myself the centre of attention. She would be angry. And rightly so. But I could not stop my tears: any more than as a child I could stop myself cutting the flesh on my thighs.

But it was Judas who shouted out that my actions were a disgrace, and it wasn't the first time! He banged his fist on the table and pushed it forward as he stood. Extravagance, showy extravagance, a woman who couldn't stop pushing herself forward, parading her sinful past, her ill-gotten wealth, her disdain for all they worked for, their care for the poor, their disregard for the things of this world. His exasperated tirade continued: I felt like a child who had broken some rule of the table, rebelled against the tyranny of family custom. Clearly, I had done it on purpose. And what he said about me, it was not untrue.

I wanted to defend myself but as so often, the motivation for what I had done was obscure to me at the time; it would remain an embarrassing blank until the terror of the action was over. I did not mean to make a display of myself or annoy anyone; I did not mean to be extravagant either, at least not in the way that Judas claimed.

But something in me protested the role I was being made to play, the drama I had to act in, the interpretation of my part by others more ignorant than myself. Yes, there was defiance, but only a streak, a small wire to cut with. What Yeshua asked me to do had separated me from the rest. And there was something I wanted to say.

Yeshua's love, that was the real extravagance. So much had been poured out over so many of us who did not deserve it and that extravagance, that generosity, had been the healing of many broken lives. Some never even thanked him for it, never acknowledged what he had done. I wanted to show that in some way I understood the strange economy of his being, that I could match the love he showed us. I could even symbolise its return.

There had been so little gratitude. So many people whose lives and bodies had been completely transformed had gone away, rejoicing in their recovery but as if it was something they had accomplished for themselves. And that was just what he had taught them to think, that it was their own faith that had healed them. As if they were the ones who had given something to him. I saw for the first time that this was, in that strange economy of his love, exactly the case.

Many took from him; took wisdom, healing, salvation itself. It seemed inexhaustible, that giving grace of his, but still the exhaustion was there. The splendour of those lilies he had spoken of, there was only so much beauty one could admire; only so much grace the world could assimilate. There was impermanence too, a limit on the splendour, it was not meant to last.

There was a moment when it changed, reached its capacity, spilled over. It came that night, the night of the perfume oil. He understood that of course, even though we had not rehearsed it. And it helps me too, to make sense of myself at last.

All those people who flocked round him, wanting this, wanting that, impossible things and yet the work of a moment, for him who was giving out of the depth of his own spirit! I pondered over this endless love he so often preached, the love of God – for people who were not worth what he gave them, who were not made better by what he did for them or by the example he showed them. And then, how they all and always wanted the same thing, over and over again: a sign, another sign, a sign they could really believe this time, more signs to convince them, to keep the excitement levels high.

I wanted to show him he was not alone.

We had prepared for this moment, of course. He had made me his priestess, the one who had momentarily taken on some of his own power, his own authority. Just as, at the beginning, John had been the one chosen to baptise him, so now in John's place I was the one to anoint him, to unlace his sandals, to wash his feet. The roles had been reversed; the debt to John had been paid. He who needed forgiveness had been forgiven for everything, for all that had been done, for all that he had asked of us and for all the suffering, great as it would be, that lay ahead.

The love he had shown us, it was not, after all, a hierarchy of power: that of a master for his servants, of a husband for his wife; it was this capacity for reversals, for a change of places that seemed so risky but could still hold the bond steady.

I would always be the one he had rescued and redeemed: my thanks and my gratitude for that would never come to an end. But I had something to give in return and he had accepted that gift. In the days to come, he was to give himself as a sacrifice for others, for many; but I had something as precious as he, I had a wife's love, I had the man himself; that was my sacrifice. Not even Mary his mother could do more, or say fairer, than that.

I poured the perfume into my hands and anointed his head, my fingers working swiftly through his hair and into his scalp. It was a technique I had learnt, one intended to close the anxious eye of the future and it brought instant sweetness through his taut body.

Washing his feet, weeping over them, it was simple really.

It was my way of saying goodbye.

*

Judas banged his fist on a plate and pushed himself free of the table, pointing at me as he left. He had had enough; enough of enough, enough of too much already! Enough of signs and symbols, of posturing and preening, of jostling for our places in heaven! And enough too of women like her who don't understand the importance of money![cciv]

Yeshua stood up and blocked his passage. "Sit down," he said, so sternly that everyone including Judas did so at once. "I tell you the truth: what Magdalene has done here, it is a beautiful thing! She has given the world a sign that will always be remembered of her, shown a love that you do not understand or begin to recognise. She has lifted the cup of heaven for you to drink. What she has – no, Judas, listen! – what she has done will never be forgotten."

"Too right, it won't," he spat back. "The perfume, the ointment…don't you realise, it cost at least 300 denarii. Money that could have been given to the poor. Isn't that what you taught us?" There is contempt in his voice, a sneer no one has heard before.

There is a whisper among the disciples. Yeshua silences them.

"The poor will always be with you, Judas, but I will not. Magdalene bought that perfume with the money she was saving for my burial, to say goodbye now the time has come for me to be taken from you. Her perfume will sweeten my death; it will be there on the threshold of my kingdom. And where that is, she will be also. What she has done will always be told of her.[ccv] What will be told of you, I wonder, Judas? How will you say goodbye?"

"You kiss her, Lord. We think you love her more than you do us."[ccvi] Peter intervenes, trying to strike a balance.

"Judas must choose his own sign!"

Judas left without another word. He chose the fig tree, the tree whose blossoms have no scent.

Suddenly the spillage was everywhere.

*

I think I might leave some of that out, Magdalene, if you don't mind. Beautiful as it is, it's quite complicated. Not everyone would understand.

Marcus is back in my cave tonight; he is standing over me, listening to my thoughts. *Too much detail*, I hear him whispering in my ear, *at least for our purposes.*

*

I have a shorter version.

*

I accepted the role Yeshua had given me; I understood what was about to happen: I knew he was going to die; I knew he had chosen that, chosen not to open the door of human love to me for long, chosen his own farewell.

Human love, earthly love, a love that was personal, yes, he could do those things, he even wanted, when the stars were bright and the radiance was on him, to do them but now he needed all his strength, all his passion to face what lay ahead. I wanted him to see that I understood and accepted that. I would be his priestess not his wife; I would act the part he had chosen for me in the terrible drama that lay ahead.

But another thing was true too, my own story, my truth to myself. The spillage was the story of that, and the something he did not know.

The perfume jar has cracked across the neck of its opening. I pick up the broken body that still has some ointment left inside it, and hand it to Martha.

*

He dips his head over a smile as I leave the room.
He had that kind of love that can explain you to yourself.
He could bring out the goodness hidden away in our faults.

165

That spillage, it is what I am recording here. These words, warm and profuse and scented with something of that extraordinary time, they symbolise my imperfections, partial actions, things not fully understood at the time and still striving for that perfect explanation, that completion which only the deep silence brings.

It was just before midnight. I climbed the stair quickly and knocked twice as he had told me to do. He stepped back from the threshold to let me in; then closed the door. He held my arm; I wondered whether I should lower my eyes but decided I did not want to. Instead I looked at him with the same direct gaze, a more complicated adoration, than he had received from me before. His rested his hand gently on the back of my head for a moment. I could feel the hair slip loose under his touch again. He sighed then, suddenly weary.

"You understand, Magda, don't you, what has to be done? You understand what is to happen."

It is not a question

So I nod, dumbly. But actually, I didn't know, not really. I didn't even want to imagine. I knew only what he had told us all, told us repeatedly, about what was going to happen. There were as always, a few secret details he had not told everyone, so no one was entirely sure of what lay ahead. We all had our allotted tasks. The herbs I must gather. The ointment I must prepare. "I understand what you have told us, yes." I understand, that is, in theory. But I can see a huge incomprehension coming towards me, like a runaway horse. He is asking me to stand in its path.

"Are you able to do this for me? Are you strong enough? It is very important, Magda. There must be no mistakes. Can you remember what I have told you?"

I begin my recitation: "I will do what you want me to do. I will stand in the crowd when…I will walk to the hill where…I will stay close to your mother. I will stand there and watch…the…I will remember everything we have talked about. And then. When…" My eyes suddenly swell and blur with tears. "And then, when she goes home with John…."

"Then, when it is over, whatever that is, you understand, Magda, you will go with Joseph and with Nicodemus. You know the man; you can trust him completely. You will follow them and take note of the exact place they go to. No tears, Magda. We are past that now. You will go and you will stand there as long as it takes, and you will listen to what they tell you. They will tell you something important. And you must do whatever they say.

"Afterwards, you will return home, rest as much as you can and pray just as I've taught you, the exact words and they will keep your mind clear. Clear of everything except that green star, you remember – that strange star low in the sky that is yours to follow. The following day you will remember my instructions. You will collect the herbs, just as I've told you, including the rue, and arrange them together. And you must bring the ointment too, what little is left of it, and the myrrh for help with the healing. You will have time before the Sabbath ends, to do all this. And as soon as the Sabbath is over you will come back to the place that Joseph has shown you. It is the tomb where I will be laid, where you will leave what you have brought. You will come at first light, just before sunrise. Is all that clear?"

"And when I do this…"

"And when you do this, Magda, you will become my beloved companion again. You will become one with me, one with my spirit, you will join with me in God; we have seen other priestesses who claim to do the same but yours will be a harder task than theirs. And you must tell nobody. Nobody. After tonight, it is our secret."

"And then? Will I see you again? Will I ever see you?"

"You will see me again. I promise you that. But first, you must do what I say. Everything may depend on it. Repeat the words to yourself every time you feel frightened. Stay composed, as I have taught you. Find that place in your mind, your vision space, just as we have discussed. Watch, pray, remember. Then go back; prepare yourself, prepare the herbs. Bring your jar of myrrh; it is a signal. And bring a companion. Someone reliable, someone you can…trust." He smiles for a moment. "Not your sister, perhaps. She will be needed here. When the others return."

"Are you as frightened as I am?"

"I was born for this, Magda. And you have been chosen for it too; always remember that. The pain I can bear. It is voluntary suffering. It is what I have agreed to. And you will bear it too. You will bear it with me. It is the time I fear most, the sufferance of it, time's final hold on me. Then it must let me go. No more talking now! No more words. We must be ready."

He draws me towards him, leans forward and presses his mouth to my forehead. There is a tap on the door. John comes in, looking uneasy and self-important. He has with him a man I do not know, though I recognise him as a priest by his robe. His head is covered, and he looks down, he does not look at us at all. Another stranger stands by his side, whose face I cannot see.

"Yes, we are ready," Yeshua tells them. He too draws his cloak around him. He is hooded, unrecognisable. "We will proceed as agreed. The service must be brief, as brief as possible. And you, John, you are our witness for this night and for this night only. Afterwards, you are to tell no one. It is our secret alone."

John casts a glance at me, a sideways glance: I cannot read his expression. He knows something I do not. He nods, accepts the terms. Whatever they are.

The man beside him adjusts his headdress. We stand in front of him; he joins ours hands together, places a cloth of woven material across both wrists then lays his hand on top of the cloth. He touches our foreheads with oil. The words, a shortened version, follow. When it is over, I stare into Yeshua's eyes for a moment, their mesmerising brown depth, looking for my future. Our future.

But I see nothing.

He kisses me, takes the palm of each hand and kisses them, kisses the place between my eyes, the top of my head, and then finally my mouth.

The moment of the kiss. Yeshua's moment.

Afterwards, I return to my room and stand stock-still by the window looking out towards the olive groves on the mountain. Something has happened to my breathing, but I don't know what. My breath comes deep and slow, as if from outside of me, as if I were listening to a silence flowing in from a source that is extraordinarily still and quite empty of time. There were no angels anywhere in sight. Someone is here but it is not myself. This breath that flows into me, it is not my own. It is not my own at all.

Of all my wedding nights, this was by far the most extraordinary.

*

"Magda," he said to me, during one of those last sittings, when he tried to help each of us find our special gifts, the strengths we would need, our own special resources, "Magda, yours is a different way. It has always been with you, a rough and stony path, a thankless way, no flowers offered you as a lasting tribute. It will be yours again, you have taken pain and stored it inside of yourself, learnt its secret, transformed it into strength. It is a spiritual strength you can always rely on and I can rely on it too. You know the secrets. You must become the grieving mother who suffers my death in order to give birth to what is to come, my future life, my new family, my spiritual children." [ccvii]

This was not the first time he had spoken of this new family; how we were all being remade to belong to it. His seed was the word: it grew inside us, it kept on growing; it grew in our minds and hearts; it would grow in the world too, he promised us that. It seems his promise has come true.

I understood some of what he meant. Later, with the goddess – she whose priest was a terrible being, a convict, a rebel, a murderer even, his face moon-white, covered with a sacred cloth as he fought off the perils of the night – I understood a little more.

*

There was something else I learnt too. I learnt it from John Mark just before he left. He told me Judas, before he came to us, had wanted to join the Essenes. He admired their teaching, their purity and abstemiousness; he aspired to live like them but was rejected by them. The Essenes were holy men, strict in their observances. They rejected many of the pleasures of this life, one of them was marriage; another was perfumed oil, the touch of which they regarded as a desecration, polluting to the spirit. [ccviii]

And that Judas himself secretly yearned to be the Messiah.

It helps to know certain things. It was only when John Mark told me about this that a memory of my own came back to me. When the jar of nard fell with a crack on the marble floor, all I could think of was another sound, one I had heard many times as we went from village to village, the sound of sharp stones landing against each other.

It was after we had met again in Capernaum, just a few days after. Someone made the accusation. Nathan's uncle.

I lay at his feet that day, blood in my mouth, dust in my eyes and hair. He raised me up then. Though I was not injured, I could not stand on my own; his spirit did this for me.[ccix]

Eight is my number. I had forgotten that moment; it has been buried inside me. The shock was so great I neither slept nor spoke for days. I gave him my life then; never until now realised how few men would have done what he did. Not just saved my life but stood beside me, turning the law that condemned me back against my accusers.

It was like living in a far-off century, a different millennium far ahead in the future, when laws were more generous and a woman's place not always in the wrong.

*

2.7   A Short Digression on Angels

Bad dreams. Dreams that make me anxious; make me cry out in my sleep! I don't know whether my fear is of the past, of its coming back to life again; or of the future, of John's man, Marcus, and what he has come here for. What will happen if I do what he asks? Will past and future coalesce around some new event, some other victim? Will something be brought back to life only to undergo another burial, the darkness lifting in one place to fall in another?

Today, I remember John. After all these years, I call his image to mind: not John the wild man of the dessert but John the disciple, John the favoured one, with his subtle self-importance, his sweetness of mind and swiftness of body, his smooth tongue and his talent for survival. John was lovable; it's a quality some people have, like a well-shaped head. He was fine-limbed and good-looking, his mouth beautiful, his eyes warm and full of charm. He and I were never opponents; I used to think there was some special understanding between us. Both favourites in our own way, we made a show of friendship. Now I am not so sure. Now, I think I was wrong. I was a rival. He never tried to intervene as Peter did or prevent what was happening, but he made sure than when it did, he was always in the best place afterwards. Things always worked out well for John, despite his faults.

It was he who persuaded me to leave. He was our wedding witness. He knew far more about us than the others did. He had been trusted with our secret, but he had contacts and connections of his own that I knew nothing of. What is John's plan in all this? Does he simply want to hear my story again, straight from the horse's mouth, or use it to set some record straight, settle some score within the group? Somehow, this is not how I remember him, but I cannot help but ask myself: *What will John make of what I tell him? What will John Mark tell him of what I said?* These two men have become so close that they even share his name, a sign that hints at something I cannot decipher.

Must I tell him one story and keep another for myself? Should I keep a proper record of my own – just in case these two men who work as one cannot be trusted? Mistrust shivers inside me: objects around me take on a peculiar life of their own, they move in the night, fall unexpectedly; hide themselves in inexplicable places.

*

After the dreams, I could not go back to sleep. I lay awake until daybreak; know from this that the cause of the anxiety is not just in my mind.

John Mark returns here today. I have missed him greatly but still I do not welcome his return. He knows what he wants from me. I do not have that certainty.

I sit with my back to the sun, waiting for him to arrive. I don't anticipate today the questions he might ask me. I can't concentrate on that. I let my memory idle instead, give it freedom to choose its own past.

Massalia then. I will go backwards from there, my landing point; back along the sea lanes to Judea, to Galilee, back to his time, Yeshua's time, the time before anyone knew where all of this was leading. I recall without pain now the day I stepped ashore in a foreign country, finding my way to the temple for shelter, torn and distraught, an exile from another world.

They speak of the scapegoat but that was never Yeshua's role. Though there was a mystery about his birth, something foreign in his appearance, he stayed where he came from, in life and death anchored deep into the dry soil of the land. It was I who left; left but then, strangely, in this bewildering foreign port, found acceptance again. Though the language was new I acquired it easily, almost as if it was something I had known before and simply forgotten. It was a language that welcomed me: the soft vowels, the sweet lift of the voices, a hint of caress in each of them. I sat down on the temple steps, faint and fearful, looking back across the water. When some kind soul offered me a drink, I wept uncontrollably. Someone laid a hand on my shoulder. Asked why I was crying. Took me to the shelter of the goddess.

*

He comes carrying flowers. "I picked them," he says cheerfully, "early this morning. They are to tell you my thoughts, in case they don't get spoken. In case we don't have enough time."

We greet each other with a warmth I take to be genuine, wary though I am of the frisson of excitement that exists between us now.

"Shall we talk about miracles first?" he says bluntly, kissing both of my cheek in the manner of the people here.

"Miracles, yes, plain, honest to God miracles, so much less complicated than people!"

He laughs. "They happen sometimes, Magda. Ordinary life is never as secure as it seems; it can always be taken by surprise, ambushed by something it never dreamt was there. There are ways of unsettling it and the teacher could always find that way. John says he could bend the laws of our understanding as easily as the weather changes on the lake."

"Sometimes a miracle *is* necessary," I say cautiously, "to attract attention, to set us free from our previous habits and assumptions. Miracles stay in our memory. They speak to something very deep in us; we never forget them. They are a sign, a communication; the most powerful one we know! Miracles speak of a spiritual path inside us, one we are perhaps in danger of forgetting."

He hands me the flowers, misty blue and white, two flame coloured roses in the centre. He has been to Veisoun then, where they sell such things! He is cheerful, caressing, persuasive. "Did you forget me, my sweet mistress of *Perhaps*?"

"Neither you nor John."

I parry his directness; it makes me nervous, as if he were certain of his success. "Yeshua was a thing of miracles," I say. "All the angels loved him." [ccx]

Though, of course, my own mind whispers, *it all depends what you mean by 'angels'*.

"I understand," he says, looking at me intently. "The question is, Magdalene: Do we begin with miracles, John and I? Do we start with his acts of power?[ccxi] According to Levi, miracles are a necessary way of beginning, the great door we must leave and enter by. Luke agrees, he starts his account with miracles too, Mother Mary and the miraculous birth etc. Of course, he didn't know Mother Mary as well as I did. For Luke, miracles are a kind of cosmic charm. 'They happen,' he said to me once, 'because some charm is upon them; they can make us do whatever they want.' Then smiled his untranslatable smile!"

"So that's Luke. What about Peter, when you were working for him?"

"Peter thought differently. 'We must start,' he told me, 'with the first great sign of who Yeshua really was. This is what we need to steer by, the star of his divinity. That will be enough to keep the wonder levels high.'"

Nail your eyes to the stars, Magda! I remember Yeshua saying this and fall silent again, wondering as ever what he meant.

*

Miracles and signs, they have two faces, one opens into heavenly joy; the other swings down into the darkness where the lost souls stand. Two doors with no fastening. They swing open when they like. We enter by one but leave by the other. Miracles are the stars that light our way. False stars, some of them.

If I were writing a gospel, I would choose a different beginning, a beginning from this side of time, a beginning from history, from what John Mark calls the ordinary. I would open a different door. I would start with a father, a man who knew how to work the wood from which doors are made. This will not be John's choice. He will have his own beginning; God will tell him what that should be.

"So why not start with Joseph?" I say anyway. He was there, after all; the very first convert."

But on the subject of converts, it seems, John Mark himself has much to tell and he is eager to do so. A new community has started; they have found a place of safety, a place, he says, so high and hidden, it is almost out of this world. He has brought me more than flowers; he has brought me good news too, the copy of a letter from Paul. We are to read it together. The excitement ties us in knots; we are in such a hurry to begin, just a little reluctant, given the novelty of seeing each other, to make a start.

There is something I want to show him: a place I have found, half an hour's walk into the foothills, on a stony track that takes you down to a spot we both recognise as numinous, close to the kingdom. When you stand there and look back at the mountain, with the little villages sheltering in its vast wing, you understand what it means to have faith: you see the immensity to which faith is attached.

Though nothing has been built here, it is a natural shrine. Perhaps one day I will help to set up a little chapel here, a chapel to our new faith. Instead of our former rendezvous at the abandoned temple with its Roman ghosts, this will be our Meeting House now, for as long as John Mark remains.

When I tell him this, he encourages me: perhaps I have misjudged him. Perhaps he wishes only to please or distract me – from the vexed question of beginnings and the great ambiguity of ends. We both know that Yeshua's beginning did not conform to the usual Jewish conventions, that patriarchal lineage that has held their long and troubled history in its grasp. Yeshua's beginning was Greek in its fluidity, its openness to the divine.[ccxii]

"Actually, John and I think that the beginning is not the most important thing. What matters more is the meaning, the end to which it was all heading. We can leave the rest to the story tellers: to people like Luke."

"It was certainly the end-time that worried Yeshua most too," I say, chiming in with his mood. "He knew he would return but, apart from the Judgment Day which all Jews fear, he lacked a model for what was to come. That was God's secret; he had no access to it. In some ways, he was against finality. He wore its sternness like a cloak sometimes but his thinking was never end-stopped. His God was not a tyrannical Lord or ruler, threatening vengeance on his enemies. Sometimes he called himself 'the Son of Man', as if he were the pattern and prototype of all humanity.[ccxiii] And it was that pattern which would judge us in the end. Our handling of the power we had, the way we used and shaped it: the way the Romans had done with theirs. God would judge it and he, Yeshua, would be the measure of that judgment. Rome would fall in the end. When he looked into the future like that, you couldn't be entirely sure he wasn't..."

John Mark cuts me off, my doubts unspoken.

"He thought on the grandest scale, that was only to be expected. But are we in any case looking, already, for such an ending? It was Paul's view that we were; that the End-time was imminent, the final judgment about to happen. But we, surely, we, Magdalene, understand it differently! For us, he has already returned! Not as a priest-king or a warrior-judge; not even as a saviour-hero, but in a more familiar form. For John he will always be the bridegroom, the one whose love knows no ending."

I tremble when he says that, tremble and remember.

"You saw him, didn't you, Magdalene? Everybody—except Luke of course, who speaks for Peter on this—agrees that you did. You saw him. You saw his resurrected self. The one event, remember! But the point is, this one event: it keeps happening. It will always happen. He will be drawn back to us again and again by the angels of the presence until his kingdom really has come."

"Do you mean—"

Distress is taking hold of me again; I can feel my troubled lung filling with froth. I need to be alone to cope with this before it starts spilling from my mouth. I struggle to suppress it, say as calmly as I can:

"The truth is, John Mark, he was not sure of how the future would unfold. He knew he would return to us, he said that he would, and he kept his promise. But that return was just after his death. As for any other return...any final ending whether happy or terrible, that was still to be written in the stars.[ccxiv]

"Any mention of his Second Coming and Yeshua would stare into the distance, his eyes searching for something he could neither see, nor recognise. It was the only time I heard him admit to a doubt: the only time I heard him say 'I don't know'. His doubt tended to make us doubtful too. There was a void we all stared into."

"John calls it *the sublime gap.* He takes a long view of things, as you do too, Magdalene. For John, the cross itself is our bridge. The immensity of its reach, across the nations of the world; across time itself! But for now, that's enough! We have gone in too deep too soon. Let's begin instead by celebrating my return, in the here and now, just as we are. I have the cup with me. Shall we begin as He told us too, by remembering him?"

The frothing inside me abates as we share our simple, ceremonial meal. I give him bread; he gives me wine. We remember Yeshua as the Christ; we name ourselves his followers. We ask that he should be with us. Today, especially!

Here at this unsanctified altar where nothing is killed, I taste for once a peace I have seldom experienced; new things are gathering in my heart. While John Mark prays, I let my eyes travel with the spring breeze across the scrub oaks, the brown slopes, towards the white-headed mountain majestic as always in its circle of clouds. I see it today as a tomb, spacious and white inside and resplendent with lamps, the tomb of a king whose body is lying there, embalmed on a marble slab, as white and still as the stone itself. Someone sits beside it, waiting for something to happen. But the body does not move.

*

My lung grows quiet; the trouble temporarily subsided. I come to myself again. John Mark is speaking to me, kneeling towards me, offering reassurance.

"It's all right, Magdalene. We are all right. Our understanding is good and true. I have a few more questions to ask you in the light of what you've said. You spoke of a father you dreamt up together. Do you know whose son he really was?"

I stare back at him in surprise. He is changing his tone again, asking me for the gossip. We are back in the human world and I am glad of it.

"Didn't Mother Mary tell you about that? About what happened to her? With the angel?"

He looks serious suddenly, speaks formally again: "There have been differing accounts about this...this...what shall we call it...this break with tradition. Matthew has been factual but subtle; he doesn't draw attention to the break in the patriarchal line. You could miss it altogether if you weren't looking. Luke does draw attention to it; it's the painter in him, I suppose. His version will include this angel you mentioned, Mother Mary's angel. He knows people like that sort of thing. An angel coming down to her in the night: you can feel the hush, almost imagine it happening,...though, of course, it's not the sort of thing we want people to start imagining. On the contrary!"

I can't resist. "Women everywhere would be imagining it," I say, trying to keep the laughter from my eyes.

He shrugs expressively.

"John's view exactly! We don't want that kind of thing! We're at a point, you see, where the oral tradition – the memories of men and women and what they have said and done or wish they had said and done – that's no longer enough. We have to move beyond that, have to frame it all with something more permanent, something that shows knowledge of God's purposes, one that is *theological* in the Greeks' sense. We want 'God's word alive in the text, not just a people story.' John's been devising a new cosmology, a philosophical scheme that..."

"Yeshua's father was an angel."

John Mark looks at me dubiously. "I'm not sure you understand me, Magdalene. This idea of a beginning, it's not just the birth of a human being, not just a break in the Jewish tradition. This beginning, John's beginning, it was there always, from the start. God always intended it."

"John the Baptist's real father – he was an angel too!"

"I see. And you know that for certain, do you, Magdalene?"

"It's John you should talk about, you know. John the Baptist. His angel started it all. John's birth was the true beginning! His parents were temple people;

174

you must have heard. His father was a priest, an old man, no longer able to give his wife a child. He was appointed by Herod Antipas himself, chosen to leave Galilee and move south, to become a priest in the great temple at Jerusalem. And this promotion, it created opportunities…"

"I don't understand your insinuation. I heard it was the Baptist's mother who was infertile."

"Men always say that, don't they! That it was the woman's fault. Herod's spies probably made that up or Zachariah blamed her for his own infertility. But Elizabeth, John's mother, was still young enough to attract an angel, an angel that came down from the old Northern kingdom, the one that was torn apart and destroyed. It was an angel from the ancient tribe of Naphtali perhaps, one that wanted to re-establish a connection with the great Southern temple in Jerusalem. Angels are not without ambition, you know. It probably dreamed of unifying the old kingdom of Israel again, making a kingdom strong enough to drive out all its conquerors. It would have taken a miracle to do this, of course, but angels can fly against the grain of history. Or so I've heard.[ccxv]

"Naphtali?" he says. "I wouldn't have thought…"

"The Galilee region," I tell him, gleeful for knowing, just this once, a little more geography than he.

"Interesting!" he says, sucking meditatively on a stem of grass. "Are you suggesting a conspiracy of some sort, Magdalene?"

"Do angels conspire?"

"A plot then? Is that what you're going to say?"

"I'm going to say that Elizabeth found herself pregnant and that's when the real break with tradition occurred. Instead of naming her son after his husband, Zachariah, as she should have done, she called the baby 'John'. Perhaps she found it easier to spell; perhaps the angel chose it for her. Disrespectful though it was, Zechariah, poor man, was unable to say a word against it. The angel struck him dumb. His voice was taken away from him. He only got it back on condition he agreed to her strange choice. When they asked him in the temple what his son was to be called, he wrote down: 'His name is John.'" [ccxvi]

"You make it sound like a plot and a conspiracy."

"Well, it certainly was a coincidence. John and Yeshua: their mothers turning out to be cousins, like that! And both knowing angels too! Both of them getting pregnant at the same time! I'm sure they must have noticed the coincidence. They certainly met up to discuss it and what it might mean for the future.[ccxvii] It turned out to be a real family affair! Perhaps the angels knew each other too, came from the same…background. Perhaps someone from the great temple had summoned them both."

"Go on, Magdalene. This is most entertaining! So our Lord was the son of an angel too, in your opinion? I think 'plan' be a better word for what you are suggesting, a divine plan, obviously. the sort of plan John has in mind for his starting point; a plan God had in place from the beginning."

"The thing is, John Mark, plans—human plans that is, the sort of plans the women might have been party to—they sometimes go amiss. People can intend one thing while angels have quite a different idea. The Baptist's angel was conformist; it did what it was told to do. Yeshua's angel, on the other hand, was more independent, it had a will of its own."

"Free will, huh?" John Mark makes a note of this. He looks up. "Tell me about Mother Mary then. You should know that John isn't interested in her; he's gone his own way on this one. Mary is too human for John, altogether the wrong sort of mother. In the bridal chamber of heaven, divine wisdom is the lover. According to John, God's plan is what really matters."

"Don't underestimate Mary. She was a force to be reckoned with. She did what she was told to do; she waited in the darkness of her room until she heard the door open, felt the breeze entering her chamber. When it blew upon her, she lay down on her pallet, lowered her eyes, felt a feather-soft touch on her thigh. Then she closed her eyes tighter, kept them closed for as long as it took. "[ccxviii]

"I have to say again, Magdalene, John won't want people reading that sort of thing. It's far too…Besides, it's the theological truth that he's after, not the biological. It's interesting, what you are saying but…there's something distracting, something misleading, about it."

"Shall I stop?"

"Certainly not. Go on…about the angel."

"Let's just say Yeshua's father was a messenger from God, an angel who, just for a few minutes, could take human form. It must have done that, mustn't it, because, as Yeshua himself said, angels in their own bodies don't do that sort of thing.[ccxix]"

"By *angel*, you mean an impulse from the Divine Plan?"

"I'm suggesting there was a human plan too. And that they didn't always coincide."

"Enough, Magdalene!" he says, mock stern. "Stop there. You let your imagination run away with you. You have told this story before."

"I've told it just as I heard it from Mary herself. She did tell me things like that occasionally, especially when there were speculations and rumours afoot. And yes, as it happens, I think I did mention it to Philip. I used to talk to him when we were travelling together. There was a lot of talk between us on the road, or in the evenings when Yeshua was praying by himself. Obviously, there was talk.[ccxx]

"But the point is, John Mark, when Yeshua first learned the truth from his mother, he came to terms with it in his own way. He took what some might see as a social stigma, his being a *mamzer* without a proper father, and he turned it to his own good. He turned what was missing in his life into a heavenly power that was larger and more powerful than any real father could ever have been. He took what was missing and turned it into something that everyone in the world wanted to: a father more loving, more perfect than any the world could offer; a father whose greatest purpose in life was his only child.

"There was no limit to it, you see, the affirmation of that distant father's love. Yeshua had no boundary to himself, no limit of the kind human fathers impose on their sons. No wonder some of his ideas grew larger than life! I sometimes

176

wonder if that is why the end-time troubled him so much. The idea of finality threatened everything he was."

Marcus looks at me stupefied, as if he might suddenly have had an inkling of why Yeshua chose me as his companion. Something I have said has touched a chord in him.

"How do you know all this – about the angels, the temple conspiracy?" he asks. "Where does your information come from?"

"I know because John told me. John the Baptist, I mean."

The angel concerns me too, but I do not tell Marcus this. For my father was no angel either and my mother's father even less. I too closed my eyes and thought of angels, learned an anger that was almost like love, just as Yeshua learnt a love that could blaze out like anger. We were all children of a secret, John and Yeshua and I. The laws of family life were strict with us. For very good reason.

*

"Yeshua had been told of his birth when he was quite young, not everything about it but enough. His mother had told him quite early on, perhaps a little too early, that he had been chosen – as she too had been chosen – for a great destiny."

"Being chosen? What did she mean by that?"

"She meant she had been chosen to give birth to a son unlike any other, a son whose destiny it was to be the salvation of his own people. They all knew about it, that little clique at the temple[ccxxi]; they knew of Zachariah's experience, they knew about the angels; in fact, I think they might have known the angels quite well. They knew Yeshua was the child spoken of by the prophets, the one for whom the whole nation was waiting. He was marked out from the beginning. Most mothers seem to feel this about their firstborn sons but in Yeshua's case there was supporting evidence. Even Mary felt uneasy about it sometimes."

"You say he had a spiritual presence for his father? An angel, is that right? Not just a human absence? I can see how John might find a value in this."

"You can?" I sense he is deliberately missing my point.

"Yes, it matches John's idea about the family, that spiritual family that has been gathered in God from the beginning. Yeshua's true family."

"Is that a Jewish family, you mean, or are Greeks and Samaritans included?"

"John sees beyond those kind of divisions. Just as the teacher himself did. That's why his natural parents, his birth parents, don't matter to us. When it comes to birth, John and I aren't interested in the people-story. That's Luke's domain. But just as a matter of interest, what else do you know?"

"Yeshua was not the son of Joseph, I know that. Joseph was the wood in the story, there to give it backbone and credibility. He was there to silence the gossip, to give things an air of respectability. He was a master craftsman. He built houses in the new towns around Galilee and Samaria that had sprung up in honour of the latest emperor. Sometimes he was asked to provide poles and crossbeams for

177

the Roman army, asked to provide the very instrument that would be used to humiliate and subdue his own people. He was a good man, a true believer in his religion, prone to visions and dreams that he took very seriously. That was why he was chosen; he was a true servant of God; he did what was asked of him.

"Mary found his work a touch distasteful; she was of a higher family, temple-class, aware of her status. She spoke with a clear-cut superiority that people always took notice of. There was an aura about her; she was self-composed, spoke little but always to the point.

"She told me once of a time when they had been to visit Joseph's father, Eli, in Jerusalem. The boy, now twelve, had always been very fond of him, adored him the way small children do with their favourite grandparents. Just before they set off on their return journey, Mary decided that Yeshua should be reminded once again that Joseph was not his real father, that he was not to get too attached to that side of the family. She thought he might have forgotten what she had told him before; that he might have put it out of his mind, as something he was not ready to think about yet. She was wrong about that; her reminder only served to anger him, and irritate his soul.

"When it was time to travel back to Galilee, he hid himself away.^{ccxxii} They thought he had gone on ahead with his mother's sister and her family. After a day's travel, busy looking after the younger children, they suddenly realised the boy was not with them and had to go back to look for him. Eli told them the boy had seemed upset when he saw him last; believed he had been forbidden to come and see him again. He had let the boy stay an extra night, certain that Joseph would soon return to find him. Instead of this, Yeshua had taken himself off to the temple. They eventually found him, sitting listening to the teachers in the inner courtyard. He greeted them coldly; made it clear to both that things had changed between them. He no longer regarded them as his parents. Instead, he had decided to forge a new relationship with the God who was his real father.^{ccxxiii}

"He could be, at times, surprisingly literal like that. He always had his own way of understanding what was said. That's why things didn't always go smoothly in the family. His mother confided this to me one day, half proud, half wistful; it was a tale that rebounded on her in a way she could never quite justify. Had she done wrong in giving him that warning? Had she done wrong in telling him at all?

"I learned later this had been a turning point for Joseph too. The whole family were shaken by it. Joseph turned more to James, his second son, his real son and James became his favourite, the one he loved most. James went into the business with him, became his partner and took over from him eventually.

"James was his father's heir in religious matters too. Inevitably perhaps, he developed a curious, difficult relationship with his older 'brother'; he used to goad him sometimes, test him; turn the other children against him. They both saw themselves as leaders and James had an uncompromising rightness and sense of duty about him that you could only trust and admire. Many fathers might have thought him the better son."

John Mark marks his tablet again. "Do you happen to know," he says, "what became of Joseph? It's not relevant to John, of course; he's above that kind of gossip but still you can't help wondering." [ccxxiv]

"I know some of it."

"How do you know, exactly?"

I note again that current of mistrust that springs up between us, like the surreptitious tightening of a noose. He is wary; thinks I am inventing a story, making things up. And I am wary too because he does not trust me.

"I knew Yeshua's sisters slightly. Especially Chloe, the eldest girl, she died quite young, but we were friends for a while. She used to tell me things, about the family. Women talk, you know, they share things, about themselves, about the people they know. And Yeshua talked to me occasionally too, when we were alone together; mostly about his mother."

"Was there a breach in the family, an open quarrel?"

"Not exactly a quarrel; more a small tragedy, something that was never properly explained. It was the time of the Baptist's ministry, when he was across the Jordan and at the height of his fame. John was a sensitive subject for Joseph. Mention John and it stirred old troubles into life again. Joseph was a straightforward man, essentially truthful, and he always felt, I think, a little used, never quite allowed into the secret.

"They all knew – John's parents, John himself – but Joseph did not know the full story of what lay behind Yeshua's birth. The story of the angel, I mean, so don't look at me like that, John Mark. It was a secret story, obviously. Joseph only knew that there had been a cover-up; that he was a substitute, someone put in place of the truth. He had been chosen by *them* – whoever *they* were – to be the man who wasn't the real father of his eldest son."

John Mark tells me suddenly of the old Greek practice where eldest sons were always dedicated to a God, even sacrificed sometimes, because with the first child the father could never be entirely sure that it was his. There had been a time before the new wife became his property. A man never quite knew for sure what had gone on before then. .

A sudden glimpse into the male psyche! I'd never heard of this before. It gave me confidence to go on with my story: "When the Baptist got his calling and went out into the wilderness, when he started getting a name for himself, the first real prophet we'd had for so long, Joseph's position became more exposed. There were questions asked, about the family, about the circumstances surrounding John's birth and the name he had been given. Joseph felt the questions getting closer to himself. He and Mary had come to some sort of arrangement. They'd half-forgotten the circumstances at the start of their marriage. Daily life takes over! They ignored the obvious fact: you could see at a glance, hear it the moment he started speaking, that Yeshua was not Joseph's son. There was a refinement in his bones, an authority in his stance, a subtle tone in his voice.

"What troubled Joseph most was what the old temple people had said of Yeshua when they had taken him to Jerusalem to be presented. [ccxxv]There was an old prophetess there, Anna: she made a big impression on Joseph. She and an old man prophesied that trouble would follow this child, that he would inflict pain on the people who knew him, and bring suffering to the world. It was more like a curse than a prophecy and their words haunted his dreams.

"Joseph didn't know what to do for the best, so he did nothing, just let things take their course. Yeshua didn't show much interest in the family business. He was not by nature a craftsman. Though his hands were good, he preferred to work with his mind. He loved the scriptures, wanted to teach, to become a rabbi.

"Mary didn't interfere; she watched from a distance. They were both pleased when Yeshua went away for a while to find teachers, attracted, just like his cousin John, to the Essenes and, even more so, to the Naassenes[ccxxvi]. He absorbed their teachings; always keeping pace with John but determined to go beyond him.

"He was not concerned with worldly success; he did some work at the prison, found he had some healing skills, then moved to the lazar house[ccxxvii], getting to know the people in Bethany who ran the place, including, of all people, my sister's husband who ran it as a tax break. It was this experience that changed him most: the lepers, people imprisoned in their own skin, a horror to look at, anathema to touch and yet, despite the chronic nature of their condition, occasionally subject to inexplicable cures. Illnesses at the interface between the inner soul and the outer body had a special fascination for him: the blind, the paralyzed; the shrieking, self-harming demoniacs; those with women's troubles.

"He had an Arab instinct for the treatment of injuries too, knew some of their wisdom, picked it up quickly just as he'd picked up much both of the Hebrew and Egyptian prayer magic. He knew how to use the formulae; he practiced them until they were second nature. Most of all he knew the magic of touch. He could place his hands on someone's body and listen to the trouble inside. His hands used to whisper back some healing command the body chose to obey. Yeshua knew exactly who he was by this time, but he was still working out how to direct his mission. How to take over from John too, in that brief period when the Baptist became his rabbi."

*

2.8   Baptism

"I saw him for the first time, out there in the desert around the Jordan. He had just started working with John."

"I thought you told me you met him at your wedding. The one in Cana, remember?"

"It was at the Jordan that I saw him for the first time., He was there with John. I didn't know who he was then and I only saw him from a distance. It was later – almost a year later – when we met again. That was when he spoke to me, knew my history, seemed to know everything about me."

John Mark nods, corrected. I like this about him. He does not over-rule me without listening closely to what I have said.

But then comes the difficulty. Not the angels this time, but the demons, harder to speak of them, they are so…under the skin; so dark and shapeless. Angels always have a purpose; you can tell what they want of you. Demons are not like that.

To tell or not to tell? It is one of those accounts that have to be introduced right from the start as *a long story*, one that carries its own inbuilt weariness. There is a twist in the tale, exhausted energy flags at the thought of it. It took so much longer than it should.

I decide to keep it short.

*

"I survived the ambush, I even made my way back to civilisation eventually, but that is where it started, the moment our caravan was suddenly stopped and surrounded by a gang of lawless men, robbers, rapists and killers the lot of them. And how grateful to them I was! Three of my guards were killed in front of me; then the camel driver who I had known since childhood. I watched as they stole everything they could lay their hands on, including the beautiful silks for my wedding dress. Including me.

"I was twelve years old.[ccxxviii] They had, quite inadvertently, saved me from a fate I dreaded, marriage to a man my brother-in-law had chosen for me, a merchant richer and older than he was himself. [ccxxix] I had met him at our betrothal two years earlier, and spat at him like a cat the first time he laid a hand on me. To my amazement, I quite enjoyed doing that; it was a discovery that I had my own boundaries and wanted to keep it that way.

"What I experienced after the ambush should be called rape, I suppose. Rape is certainly what it set out to be. But I had this twist to my fortune. Dangerous things loved me best. I could always find my way with them. My sexual initiation was not the ordeal it might have been. I thanked him, child that I was, weeping on my knees and offered him one of my best wedding gifts, the blue-stoned ring I kept hidden on my person, as a present for rescuing me. He was so surprised he held back, stopped the others with a curse; said he wanted me for himself. They were a political group, bandits or zealots as they came to be known, who robbed to fund their work, hating those who prospered under Roman rule. I was travelling with part of my dowry. They kept us both."

I fold my arms and meet his gaze without any appeal in my own. He must form his own judgment, little as men know of a woman's life!

"It took me a long time," I say, "to get away."

The truth was I lived with their leader for nearly five years, until I was seventeen. Eventually I became his wife; he had developed a kind of obsession about me, grew extremely jealous; practiced on me a kind of sexual mysticism in which I was his killer and our roles had been reversed. I made him cry out with erotic pain, but still I hated his body, I hated his feelings, I hated the touch of his skin, dry and flaky: worst of all, I hated the pleasure that hating him could give me. As a man, he was quick and capable and passionate for change. He set his own rules and was committed utterly to the revolution that would overthrow his enemies, those he hated with such unremitting intensity. Ours was a bond of hatreds; that was how it hung together.

I tell John Mark some of this, explain how this new captor saw me as his talisman, how holding on to me meant his revolt, especially against the Romans, would be successful. He played it all out on me in his fantasies. I was the order he would over-throw, the system he must smash. I must be beaten by him in spirit, subdued, conquered and yet it was not as simple as that. He admired and lusted after the very things he hated. He made me hate myself too. He took to beating and violating me, convinced I was unfaithful to him. And in this he was right. He may have rescued me from my family, but I would never belong to him either.

Damaged goods? Yes, for sure, and the damage went deep. "Eventually, I escaped. It was a desperate time and I suffered for all I had done and all that had been done to me. I wanted to get home because I could not think where else I might go but I knew they would never want me back there. I met Masud, *Mussa* as we called him, on the road one day; he was a *qibt*, an Aigypton, a gypsy who had a travelling magic show and people stopped to watch him because his acts were different, sexual of course and more than a touch frightening. [ccxxx]

"He wanted a volunteer from the crowd, someone to take part in a strange comical dance which told people when they were going to die and what they might do to save themselves. I had to lead them, make movements that the crowd who followed had to copy and then suddenly when the music stopped others ran among them dressed as devils and tried to capture as many as they could. So it went on.

"The man I was married to had heard the drums and was watching from the roadside when suddenly one of the devils took hold of him and wrestled him to the ground. It turned out they had been robbed by him earlier and saw their chance for revenge. They beat him badly; one of his gang was killed. Mussa threw a devil's coat over me and took me with him. "Quick," he said, "he is bad man. It is right you leave him."

"I left with nothing that time, but I got away.

"'We need a good dancer,' the Egyptian said. 'Free meals, I cook, you do the costumes when they need repair.'

"I learned a lot with Mussa, skills I could use, things I could do and make that gave me a kind of independence. He was poor and on the road but he had a brain and a poor man's passion for knowledge. The hashish got him in the end. And so it happened. That is how, two years later, I came to Herod's court and met Felix and my life changed again completely. I became one of the women of the court; thanks to Felix I even regained some of my inheritance. I wasn't popular exactly but there was always a demand for what I could do.

"From knowing some of the outlaws of our world, I now began to mix with those at the other end of the scale, the wealthy and powerful. They called me Mariamme after the old Queen. I recovered some of my former self, but only a little. Felix controlled most of it and I saw him so rarely. Mostly I was left to my own devices.

"I loved fabrics and could work with them; I knew the sort of things that women wanted. I knew oils and perfumes too. I could read and write better than most. I had my father to thank for that. I could dance as well, the ritual dances for which there was always a demand. I had few friends but those I made were women who knew the court and were high enough placed to keep out of Herod's way.

"It was then that I joined a group of people who were headed for the river; they were looking for the prophet, John, a river god some said, who could bring people back to life, wash away their sins and make them whole again. Most of all he could bring them back to God.

"John was a craze back then, and we all caught it. Though my spirit was damaged, though there was evil in that damage, evil that I held in check, I longed to be free of it, wanted to shed the filthy coats of experience I trailed behind me. I didn't know it of myself then for court life was textured with deceptions and self-denials but there was a sense of loss inside me; I knew there was a better way of life. Being with someone I cared about, knowing someone I trusted, I found such things impossible to imagine. Until I met John, that is! John the Immerser, as he was called!

"Most of the year, the waters of the Jordan were easy to pass through; at other times the flood became deep and rapid. My heart was in my mouth, just as if I'd swallowed a frog, the first time I tried to get across. I had to go back to the bank twice before I found the courage to wade through that deep swathe of current in the middle of the river. Baptism was not a simple ritual; it had its dangers and it required preparation, though John knew at a glance when you were ready. His eyes were famine sharp.

"As for the man himself, wild man though he was always portrayed as being, I found something in him I had not encountered before: a strong, inner light, a pronounced spiritual being. I could be with him entirely without my habitual fear of men. Though I cultivated a hard, ironic exterior in those days, I had little need for it when I was with him. I could be, not the self I had to perform at court, but someone simpler, quieter, able to listen. John spoke to me as he spoke to many of the women who had what he called *an edge* to them. He wasn't frightened of me either as many people were. Instead, he found, he said, a sweetness stored in the corners of my eyes. It was like wild honey; he always had a taste for that. John saw the vulnerability in me too, knew I didn't belong with the others from the court. His way of seeing things, his way of speaking touched me; it made pretence impossible.

I had a dream about him once; I never forgot it. I dreamt my little brother Eleazar was still alive; he had been lost for years but suddenly I found him again. He was going ahead of me into the water of the Jordon and encouraging me to follow. He looked so unhappy, so disappointed when I held back. He made a strange mouth at me, then suddenly it filled with water and a wave took him; next moment he was gone. I rushed forward into the water, but John was there instead. He stopped me from going deeper. 'You can't go there yet', he said, then pointed to the opposite bank. Eleazar was standing there, waving at me. He had his red spinning top in his hand.

"After a few day's preparation, John baptised me himself along with a group of other women from the court. I used to come and see him sometimes, to watch him at work. He liked that, even talked to me alone occasionally. He was so far outside the usual reach of Jewish politics that many Samaritans were drawn to him; he had a clear affinity with their lost ideals.

"Some drew back subsequently. The movement that had looked to him as their leader lost him soon enough and there was bitterness on this score. I never drew back. I watched and learnt instead, even did some ritual anointing for him once or twice, with women about to discard their clothes before entering the water.[ccxxxi] John had the rarest of gifts: he could simplify people, strip away all the rubbish from their minds; create instead a hunger for purity: a passionate hunger for having less.

"Better the little that the righteous have," he used to quote at us, "than the wealth of many wicked."[ccxxxii]

"We had something in common, John and I: we called it *the wilderness factor.* "Your soul is among lions," he told me once. "But for you, unlike the psalmist, it is a blessing!"

"The terrible scale of my past, my sins, my suffering, diminished when I told him about them. And I did tell him about them. You could not talk to John and lie. You could not hide who you were, you could not pretend or conceal. I told him things I had never told anyone. He took note of me, kept me by him when he wanted company occasionally. The truth was we liked each other, a pair of odd balls together. I used to bring him things, little gifts for variety's sake. But John did not want variety. Every day he chose sameness, the same basic food, the same hour, the same place. He was a creature of disciplined habit, John. He wanted nothing for himself and there was no changing that.

"'Sit with me, Mariamme,' he said to me once when he had finished his work. 'I will instruct you and teach you in the way you should go; I will counsel you with my loving eye.'[ccxxxiii] Then he would bark out his strange desert laugh. 'There is nothing to fear with me; nothing to hope for either. I am no one's bridegroom.'

"'You are my brother,' I said in reply. 'He would have been like you. He would have been a great prophet, just as you are.'"

I felt safe with John, entirely free of that struggle and self-assertion that other men induced in me. Finding John, finding someone I could trust, it healed something in me. Though the change wasn't permanent, he changed what I had become. His baptism had power over all of us; many named themselves his followers. Through him I came to know people who became important to me later: Joanna especially became my friend and took me under her wing when we returned to Antipas's court. I was so impressed by her sophistication, her knowledge of the world. I had already met Felix by that time, but he was there

184

so seldom I had need of a friend who knew that world better than I did. She knew Felix a little too, the worst and best of all my bad lovers.

That was a curious time, but I have noticed how new things always burst in upon us, they come and claim our attention and what had once seemed new and important drifts slowly away. Our daily life, the sphere in which we have our being, moves and alters like the pattern of birds in flight. I never grew tired of John, never did other than admire his strict and narrow routine. I loved him without intensity, watched him at his work for hours on end, became thoughtful when I was with him. Then life began to make claims on me again, to draw me away from his austere simplicity of outlook; we heard of his arrest, his death in some distant tower, the location kept secret, the horror spreading everywhere.

I tell John Mark some of this. About the river mostly.

"And you say you saw Him there? Our teacher? At the Jordan?" John Mark's eyes are keen and piercing. I fear I shall disappoint him.

"I saw him once; the cousin John spoke of with such reverence. I had come with Joanna, there were crowds of us that day, Yeshua was just beginning his mission but had not yet made a name for himself; he was simply John's disciple. His sister was there with him and we found ourselves jostled together in the crowd. She was a bright, merry girl with red apple cheeks and a wind-swept smile. *Lovely*! I thought, a touch envious. Later, we met up again and established a kind of friendship. There was a fascination between us, instantaneous; we looked at each other almost like lovers. It was meeting Chloë that impressed me most that day.

"I remember standing beside her, excited at the meeting, feeling she had taken a liking to me too. She had seen me before with John and noted our friendship. "Listen!" she said, seizing my arm suddenly. "It's about to start."

"A young man, not handsome especially, but with that weird, indefinable kind of Jewish beauty that eons of spirituality have bred, stood surrounded by a small crowd. He was standing in for John this day, preaching to the crowd and holding them almost as if he were singing to them. It was his voice that held me too, that and the flow of eloquence that poured from him. His voice was remarkable, an instrument in itself, intimate and soft to begin with but full of modulations, where love and anger, compassion and contempt, even at times a snarling condemnation enmeshed themselves in a kind of yearning vulnerability, so that he was master and victim almost in the same breath, a man whose suffering mixed with an authority that not even John could muster.

"I had never heard anything like it and neither had the crowd. The performance silenced everyone as if his voice had conjured up a dimension of reality we had never even imagined before. His version of things mattered immediately; our own no longer did. He laid it aside for you the moment you started listening. That is how he fascinated people; he disconnected them from themselves with a couple of astonishing phrases. His voice, his slightness, even the way he moved, full of restless energy one moment, the next self-contained, poised and inscrutable. This was the real thing. Everyone else was commonplace.

Within seconds of hearing him speak, you felt as if scales had fallen from your eyes."

"'Who is he?' I asked. 'Where's he from?'

"Chloë gasped and clutched my hand tighter.

"We noticed John gesticulating in our direction. Not that anyone needed to gesture. We couldn't take our eyes off him. People in the crowd were sobbing, some even down on their knees. John himself had started baptising again. A naked man clearly anxious to avoid the gaze of the crowd was stepping gingerly into the water.

"I strained forward to get a better look at him but at that point the young Rabbi said something that made the crowd murmur and grow angry. The snarl reappeared in his voice and the waves of anger seemed to gather round him like the spin of a great top. He stood in a vortex of energy, as if a great flame was rising above him.

"'It's my brother,' said Chloë. 'Free as a bird, isn't he?'

"Her face was bright, two crimson patches on her cheekbones; but as she said this, her expression changed. There was a sudden look of fear in her eyes; her mouth turned down at the corners, she looked momentarily woebegone. I wanted to hug her, protect her from her own thoughts whatever they were.

"Instead, I took her arm and we pushed forward through the crowd, to get a better view of what was happening at the centre. A boy with a broken shoulder, his arm hanging limp, was standing in front of him, his parents on the other side. There were people all around and though Chloë called out, we did not have the confidence to approach closer. He was standing with his back to us when one of John's pigeons, disturbed by the baptism, came flapping noisily across from the river and crapped on his shoulder as it flew past. Everybody froze. But the anger had vanished; he grinned and grimaced. 'It's good luck!' someone shouted, and the crowd hooted with relieved laughter. Even Chloë caught the mood. 'That was really funny,' she said, her cheeks redder than ever, tears of laughter in her wide, grey eyes.

"It was as if the universe had suddenly broken free of its chains and done something infinitely amusing, setting off a ripple of laughter that would go on multiplying through time. The change of mood was extraordinary. The great world tree had suddenly been shaken to the roots and its strange, brilliant fruit came tumbling down on us. [ccxxxiv] Perhaps it did even start to rain then, a suddenly heavy shower. I can't actually remember."

John Mark shifts uncomfortably. "That's an arresting description, Magdalene. A first impression, obviously. I've heard a slightly different version."

"Yes, I'm sure there must have been more than one. People see so differently. No one understood it then, the strange dislocation of that event. They were both him, weren't they? The great public performer on one side; the silent, invisible spirit in the water with John on the other! He was both of them. I think Chloe realised that; it's what frightened her. The different fates that lay ahead of him;

all the adulation, suffering and ridicule the public performer would have to endure! We laughed then but we were blind to what was really happening."

John Mark touches my hand. A kind of apology, I think.

"Anyway," I continue, "the thing is, we all trudged back to court afterwards, high and happy as if it were the very best of times and we were lucky to have been born into it. Joanna had bright red goose bumps down her arm. She kept pulling back her sleeve and showing us. 'This rash,' she said, 'on my arm, it's like a burning brand. Do you think I've caught something?'

"Then, shortly afterwards, John was arrested. The news spread through the court like wildfire. He had been locked up in a remote tower somewhere to the east, across in Samaria.[ccxxxv] Herod wasn't taking any chances. He had mixed feelings about John, knew he was a prophet, certainly didn't want to offend or upset him, despite his wild outspokenness about political matters. Herod liked listening to him at first. He wanted to discuss the things that John said. Could it be true, though, that a new Jewish kingdom would come and sweep away all the dead wood of the past, all those who had collaborated with the Romans? The idea made him nervous; his spies became more vigilant.

"We heard John had been thrown into prison for speaking out against Herod's divorce from Phasaelis. She was a Nabatean, the daughter of a Jewish king who John approved of and Herod had thrown her over to marry the unscrupulous, seductive wife of his own brother. John didn't countenance divorce. Though the Greeks and the Romans thought nothing of it, he considered it un-Jewish, an impurity. Celibate though he was, marriage had a huge symbolic importance for him; it was the linchpin of the law."

"Marriage, yes," says John Mark, "the Baptist was right as usual. John the apostle, he sees it as central too: the starting point. He believes in the bridegroom, in the sacred marriage, the miraculous transformation."

"Does he?"

There is an awkward pause, for both of us. "All men," he says quietly, "can identify with that. The bridegroom is there in all of us who follow the teacher."

It makes my head spin to hear this. Something I had never realised before.

We change the topic. John Marks says, "So how did all this affect Joseph?"

*

"Joseph knew, of course, that Yeshua had gone out across the Jordan to be with his cousin. The alliance troubled him. He remembered the words of the old man in the temple; saw destructive forces about to be unleashed, on his land, his faith and his customs. The secrecy that had bound the Baptist's parents – that had bound Mary too – had trapped him also. Something terrible would come of this, he was sure it must be so.

"He heard that John was turning away anyone who lied to him, anyone who hid the truth, refusing them baptism unless they made a clean breast of their sins. Joseph had the old anxiety on him again, not knowing what he should do. John disturbed him as he disturbed everybody. He shook men's complacency, shook it to the roots; opened people to themselves. He himself stood naked under the heavens, thundering away like a force of nature. Sin had given him a wide birth.

"Suddenly, Herod moved on him, threw him into prison. And then it began: the rumour that John had been murdered, a hideous ritual murder at the whim of a daughter who was not even Herod's child. Another of these troublesome stepchildren! I knew her slightly and had taught her once; Joanna knew her very well. She made a strange *moue* with her mouth when her name was mentioned.

"News of John's murder was one of those moments, those unique incidents: everybody can remember exactly what they were doing when they heard the news. It tied us all together. Chloë came to court asking questions about her father. I remember her rushing in, her colour heightened as usual, a white and purple shawl over her head. She had heard of John's death; now Joseph was unaccountably absent too.

"He had been working on a new construction project on the outskirts of Tiberias,^{ccxxxvi} it was Herod's show piece, his signature town. There was lucrative business there for builders like Joseph and both James and Jacob were with him. Jude, of course, was off with his older brother. When Chloë went to tell them the news of John's murder, Joseph inadvertently sliced off the side of his finger, frowning at her words. As the day wore on his temper got worse. Suddenly he flung down his chisel and went outside. Evening came, the boys arrived home for their supper, but he did not return. The following week, one of Herod's men rode up asking for Mary. She was pregnant with her seventh child, and frightened for her children.

"'You have found him then?' It was not only her husband's welfare Mary was concerned about; she feared some discovery. John's murder had sent terror through the family.

"'We found him in the river, lady. Drowned and swollen and floating like a log. That's what happens when people don't stick to what they know. Meddling with our affairs, it never comes to good. We found him caught up in the branches of a dead tree; thought it was a log at first, one of those birds, long-necked things – what do you call them? – was perched on the corpse. Bad omen, I'd say. Didn't sit there for long.'

"James stepped forward in the workshop. He was obeying his own instructions.

"'And what about his work for Herod,' the man said, 'that's what I want to know? He was under contract; who's going to deliver on it now?'

"'I will.'

Herod's man slapped the scowling young man on the shoulder.

"'Better get started then, hadn't we? Or we'll take our business elsewhere.'

"Mary had her sons to comfort her; her daughters though turned more to Yeshua and became his followers. When Chloë died of consumption a year later, Mary S and I became friends instead. She was a nice girl, not prone to jealousy and totally devoted to Yeshua. She liked what he liked, accepted everything at face value.

"That's when it really started for him. Down by the river. That's when word got around. Suddenly they were both gone: his cousin, John, and the father whose son he was not. His favourite sister had gone too. He became himself then, stepped forward, took John's place just as John had always told us he would, not that I really understood what that meant then. He was to carry on John's work, just as James took over from his father.

"I lost track of the family before that. After John's death and against my own better judgment, I left court and went to join Felix at his new posting. He invited me and I needed somewhere to go, to get away from Herod and his new wife. I grieved for John; his death unsettled my whole world. He had been the one we believed in; we had taken on his strictures, tried to be as he wanted us. Then it was all over, brutally, violently over, as if no good could ever triumph again. All we could do was to make the best accommodation we could with the evil that surrounded us. I can't recall much about the months that followed, my shameful back-sliding, my…"

"We don't need to talk about this." Marcus wears his startled look again; I have put myself beyond the protective circle; first one side, then another. "What about Yeshua's mother?" he asks, changing tack quickly. "Did you have much to do with her?"

"Mary talked to me once about his childhood, how he'd responded when she told him that Joseph was not his real father. After he had gone missing in Jerusalem as a young boy, she tried to repair the damage she had done by telling him a story, to make both of them feel better. She told him of a father who could not be named but who cared for him beyond all other children and had chosen him as his only son and heir. Mother and son, they both came to understand it that way.

"Many children fantasise about such a thing, don't they, about parents they might have had, parents who were an improvement on their real ones? Mary told him again about God's messenger, the one she liked to describe as an angel who had come to her in the night, just like the angel who had helped her cousin Elizabeth to conceive John. They were doing it, all of them, for the good of Israel. Once Joseph was dead, the story took on a life of its own. Then it became more dangerous. She was in a difficult position, had her family to think of.

"It's possible," Mary said to me, "I didn't explain it to him as clearly as I might."

"Anyway, Yeshua grew up with this image of an ideal father who loved him so abundantly that all he had to do was to share that love with others, with all those who needed the same kind of love. It turned out there were so many of us who did!

"As time went by, Mary forgot exactly what it was she had told him. As he grew older and stranger, she began to distance herself from his preoccupations, seeds she herself had sown in him. The Baptist's death finally caused her to turn her back on the past, to draw a line through its expectations, its obvious dangers. She wanted above all to be respectable, to be respected. With Joseph gone, the burden on her was greater: not just coping with the family but having to cope with the whispers, the sneers, the humiliating stories that she was not as holy as she liked to pretend, that her past was a little suspect, not all it might have been.

"Yeshua was no one's son except his mother's and he found his own way of reminding her of that. He was always at home with women; he liked them, got on with them easily. Because of his mother, he made a special point of getting to know women with a bad reputation, sinful women, good time girls, the wild ones, those whose lives were lived outside the law, outside the family. It was a cruel caricature of herself."

There, I am in the circle again. Now he will ask me what he wants to know.

"You have a gift for story-telling, Magda." John Mark speaks a touch sardonically. "It is all very interesting, very...moving. And this was your first encounter, was it, out there by the Jordan? And you didn't recognise him when you met again?"

"A lot can happen in a year like that. I had seen him only once and then from a distance; my thoughts were elsewhere. By then I had become absorbed into a different world, Felix's world in Syria. It was not easy for me there. He wanted company and entertainment. So many adjustments, and most of them I failed to make. I had exchanged one bad situation for another, but I hadn't forgotten John or the difference his baptism had make in me. When I met Yeshua again, I knew him as one of Nathan's friends. The contexts were so different, I had my own problems to deal with."

John Mark listens without comment, without reproof.

I say, suddenly, "He lived with impossibilities all his life. The stories his mother told him of his birth, the expectations that were laid upon him, the way he accepted it all; demanded it of himself."

"Don't you believe those stories?"

"Yes, I know for a fact that some of them were true. He was born with a strange inheritance: I saw the gifts given him as a baby. Gold, you would never have expected from a family line such as Joseph's. It did not come from Eli either; it was temple gold; and the incense too. A gift from 'the angels', from the sponsors who stood behind them, far out of sight. It all told him who he was, how his life must be spent. There was myrrh besides, a strange gift to give a small child, yes? He gave some of it to me, the rest to Nicodemus, to take care of until it was needed."

*

"When you write, John Mark, when you talk to John about this, you have to make it clear what it was like for Yeshua to grow up with this all-giving, all-demanding father on the one side and death always so close on the other. It made him feel like Moses, a target for attack every time Herod had a panic about his astrologers' predictions, and sent his men out to fix it. To know that you are the survivor when others are killed in your place: that is not easy for anyone. He bent all his thoughts towards that perfect father, the one he believed in absolutely. There was hardly anyone else he could really trust. It helped him face the death that dogged him from so many directions. Throughout his mission, he shared Herod's fear of conspiracies, of people plotting to kill him. It was there in the background right from the beginning. When John was murdered, he could have stayed away but he went back, and it worked for him. John's people were leaderless and what's more they knew that John had named him as his heir, as the longed-for Messiah. People thought John might be rescued or reprieved. Nobody thought he would be killed. But Yeshua, yes!

"There were attempts on his life, by men from his own village who were so incensed by him they tried to drive him out down the rock face. And then the physical attacks, the volley of stones he often had to dodge. After that, the plots and entrapments with which they pursued him, important people, dangerous people: all this trained him in a way, made his mind move faster than ever, made him see his own death as an integral part of who he was. He learned how to tame his fear of it, to see it as a kind of twin. Just as God was his father, so death was his dark cloak: personalised, an accessory, not a terrifying maniacal stranger.

"I heard Peter once tell of how even the worst of sea storms failed to frighten him, how he could swim through the highest waves, ride their crests almost standing on the surf, but of course it was the wood, the wood was always there beneath; he knew from Joseph everything that could be done with it. Like the gods of ancient time, trees were part of his magic, a language he could speak.

"He tried to be cautious, to be true to the time. He found ways to avoid his enemies, ways to outwit them; he had to be there and not there at the same time. He could slip away into a crowd as if he had vanished, his movements as swift and sinuous as a serpent's; he could disguise himself, make himself invisible, appear and disappear in an instant. He knew his own death; went towards it at last like a …like a bridegroom.

"And there it is again: our first meeting. A nightmare wedding, Nathan and I, nothing holy about this: the bride and groom walking towards each other as if towards some inescapable disaster, some grim destiny we had both chosen.

"It doesn't matter, you know," Felix told me. "It doesn't matter at all. If it doesn't work out, I'll write from Syria. Let you know my next posting."

"How many times must a girl look down? How many times? I can feel the curious twisting in my arm as I try to wrestle with it; I can feel the cells of my brain start to fly apart, like a peaceful aviary when a sparrow hawk flies past. It is unmanageable: I can't face seeing who I was. Making myself do those things: the injuries I inflicted on myself as if I lacked part of my own face, part of my own brain. Other people wore faces that were their own. They made choices, lived lives, had a story that fitted them. But my story was inhabited by demons. As a child I knew them; as I child I lived with them, tried to avoid them; just as I tried to hide from the great serpent that pursued me in my dreams. I could never summon the power to speak to them direct, call out, 'Leave me alone! Get out of me. Be gone!'

Because I could never summon that voice, I could never stop them from hurting me. And so I married them, over and over again. I found people who resembled them. Perhaps I was trying to learn some control. But every time, articulate though I was, muteness would descend like a fog: I became invisible to myself, of no account. Everything I have done, all the places and all the people I have known, they are just veils of experience, trailing behind me like sullied finery. Unlike Salome, I never learned how to dance through them, how to cast them off. From error to error, I went. Lady Folly incarnate.[ccxxxvii]

Demons I do know about, and about spirits too. I know how difficult it is to master them; how rare it is to find someone who can.

There is an encounter of this kind ahead of me. Someone I must see again. Someone I tried to leave behind. My time with demons: it is here with me still. Waiting to put me to the test.

*

"So this wedding then," says Marcus, "the wedding at Cana, it was pure folly, was it?"

"Folly, pure and unadulterated! And yet, call it that if you like but it was a strange kind of folly, one that has wisdom at its back, wisdom was waiting for it at the end of its fall. Some follies have an element of the miraculous and that is how this turned out for me. It brought me back, back towards something I had glimpsed before but failed to realise properly; it brought me back towards something that was good in myself. It was folly, yes, but there was a kind of miracle in it too.

"Just before I went into the feast house with Nat, while I was standing at the top of the steps and taking my last look behind me, I noticed there a green enclosure, a small field I had not seen before. It struck me like a vision and might even have been one, for what I saw was a small, wedge-shaped field full of moon daisies, almost invisible from the path. Walking into the wedding feast on Nathan's arm, the sight stilled my heart, took away its misery and panic. Heaven was at my side; there was something to have faith in after all."

*

"And then, you see, it was astonishing too! How, after everything, after every bad experience, every bad choice, after I had drained my cup of sin and sorrow right down to the very dregs, not that Nathan was the dregs exactly, it was astonishing to find that then, of all times, a cup of such great goodness had been set before me. A young bride might have found this at the beginning of her life but for me that pattern was reversed. All I had to do was reach out and touch it."

"And did you do that? Just reach out and touch it!"

"Not that simple. There was a long period of solitude. After the wedding at Cana, I was strangely alone. I didn't even know how to think about what had happened. It wasn't another impulsive love affair. It came to me more slowly, the realisation that the cup was there, and that it was mine to drink from."

John Mark draws himself up slowly and magisterially.

"I heard someone mention, someone in Alexandra it was, they spoke of a dramatic ritual he performed for you, an extreme form of…exorcism?"

He sees the blankness in my eyes.

"Seven devils," he prompts hopefully. "Cast out? Was it when you…"

But I am shaking my head slowly. He has not understood what I have told him at all.

"Don't get me wrong," he says urgently. "It is Luke who thought this was important [ccxxxviii]; he thought the episode should be emphasised. 'It set you apart,' he said, 'gave you definition.'"

I fold my arms conclusively.

"Or demons, perhaps? Seven demons?"

"That was Salome," I say. "And by then I had already left court."

*

2.9   Apostles of the Resurrection

Today, for a change, John Mark is doing the talking. He tells me first about his work with Peter, then with Paul, the outsider who had been given access to the secrets of the kingdom. Twice they had tried to work together. Twice they were unsuccessful. He shakes his head.

"For Paul, the thing that mattered most was the great mystery: the Resurrection mystery, how the Lord had triumphed over death. He called this the central doctrine of the new faith, and he believed it was. Paul's Christ was not the popular messiah, not the saviour king that Israel had hoped for. The Christ for Paul was entirely spiritual; his death had freed us from sin, led us into the grace of the one true God. A God who was everywhere and in everything!

"Paul was convinced he had met this Christ, three years after the crucifixion. It was a visionary moment, one of utmost clarity. There was no mistaking the presence. "I am Jesus," he said to Paul, the one you are persecuting."[ccxxxix] That moment of recognition was for Paul the moment of the resurrection, the moment he stepped free of his old, sin-laden, death-ridden self and into a higher consciousness, born again into a body that was dead to all his previous errors, alive now only to God.[ccxl]

"I don't deny that Paul was chosen by the Lord: his faith moved mountains. It was superhuman. He might have been hearing those words said aloud, wherever he was, whatever he was doing. Some power not his own drove him forward. Even now, I can't really think of him as dead. Paul, that is. His words and deeds bear eternal witness to his faith.

"A writer prays for moments like that, for a revelation, that lights up the whole mind with the speed and power of some new truth and then, through the grace of God, finds the right words to express it. Yet some people have doubted Paul. They say what happened to him was his own guilt burning out his former sin through some massive inner conflagration; that his own mind produced the vision; a vision that announced what something deep inside him had known all along: that the love of Christ was already inside him. "

193

"But surely," I say, "explanations like that don't really change anything. Beneath the vision lies the hard fact. That moment was Paul's *resurrection*, if you like; it lifted him out of his old life. He never looked back, did he? It's not what he saw but the power it charged him with that makes the difference. Paul's vision brought him a lifetime's strength. That's how we know that it was the truth."

"Yes, but it is not as straightforward as that. Visions are inward things; they lack…materiality." Marcus looks at me with those shrewd, deciphering eyes of his. He is thinking, weighing up my words. "It's significant that you call Paul's experience a *vision* then, not a real physical encounter."[ccxli]

I sense an issue here; a fine line being drawn; sides to be taken. Paul's dramatic encounter remains dangerous ground.

"I thought you said he had a vision. Is there a problem in that?"

John Mark picks up a stone and skims it far into the distance. "First and foremost, Magdalene, it's the problem of trying to match Paul's oratory and the great authority it has given him. Vision or not, Paul makes everyone else's testimony seem infantile. Look at Peter. I was trained in one of the best Schools of Rhetoric, that was to have been my profession, and working with Peter we found a way of telling things. It was crude but it's convincing. It even sounds like Peter.

"With Paul, it's different. You have to aim higher, reach up beyond that common level of understanding. I studied with Philo for a time in Alexandria[ccxlii]; you probably haven't even heard of him and I didn't always get what he was saying. It didn't make much sense to me then, but the more I've thought about it, the more I see a new way of understanding, a new way of explaining. I couldn't have done it without my work with Peter but that first gospel of ours was like a first draft. It was rough and literal. Paul has lifted our minds beyond that.

"John wants his gospel to reflect this development. He wants it to excel, to go beyond; to rise to the highest level of the Lord's resurrection. To go with him into heaven! That higher, wider view, it's like looking out from this mountain, time seems to matter less when you view it from here. As for Luke, he has great qualities, qualities that carry conviction. He knows how to shape people's testimonies, especially women. He got to know Mother Mary too. We had a house church in Rome; she was important to him; she influenced his view of things."

I look up quickly, alert to something in his tone. He notices my glance but doesn't hold it.

"So John wants you to better Luke at this, just as he wants you to rival Paul's dazzling abstractions?"

"Ah, Magdalene!" he says. "And you wonder why I have come to find you? I am here like Prometheus, to steal everything you have."

"Fire?"

"Inspiration."

And so, we come back to the central issue: Yeshua's death and what Paul and Luke have made of it; what, most of all, they have made of his *resurrection.*

"John and I," he continues, "and you too we hope, we have to redraft that ending. What we need now is a fresh pair of eyes, authenticity; a genuine illumination."[ccxliii]

"And for this *illumination* you have come to me? I'm not quite sure why. You want me to outsmart Paul, correct Luke's bias; the bias of Mother Mary too, from what you are suggesting? Is that it? Or is there something more?"

"Yes, Magdalene, that's it; the matter in a nutshell! You don't always know, in this world, who your enemies are or see what is at work against you. But John and I do know. We see how…certain facts have been shaped to…favour others, how some details have been omitted to give a particular impression. I have come to correct this bias, to supply what is missing.

"But there is something more to it than that. A new level of understanding, a greater freedom from the confusion of the past. We're not interested, you see, in the details of our Lord's birth, his human birth, that is. What John and I care about is the second birth, the one the teacher spoke of to Nicodemus. That's where we are; that's our starting point: the need to be born again, a birth not of the flesh, not of a husband's lust but of water and the spirit."

"I'm not sure I understand. quite…Where do I come in here?"

[ccxliv] You are the birth giver, Magdalene. The woman pregnant with his spirit! That's why your meeting with the Lord after his crucifixion is the key to everything. Luke has suppressed it entirely."

"Suppressed it? My meeting with…?"

"Yes, entirely left it out. That's why I've come here. I've come so you can put it all into words for us, your own words if you like. You are the one who saw Him first outside of the tomb. You are the one He chose to be there. Everyone knows that to be true, however much they wanted something different."

"Tell me again what Luke said? About my meeting with the teacher?"

He takes me by the arm, as if to ward off evil.

"He said there was no meeting. Just a message you were given by some men at the tomb, a message not one of the disciples was prepared to believe. Until Peter confirmed that the tomb was empty, they assumed you'd simply lost your way, gone to the wrong tomb."

"He said there was no meeting…that I had mistaken the tomb? You mean…"

"Correct. As Luke tells it, the Lord only appeared later in the day; to two men, on the road out of Jerusalem."

"Two men?"

"Two witnesses, yes."

Like Paul, I am struck down; struck by a bolt of that lightning so strong it brings no illumination at all.

"Don't take it to heart. John knows it's not right. We know it's not what happened. Trust yourself here! Trust us too. So what if the others didn't believe you at first! They were wrong. Paul's writing has made it clear that the early accounts were inadequate and misleading. John's gospel will give true witness, help our people to understand what really happened, so there can be no doubt at all that our Lord and leader really was the Risen Christ.

"You do believe that, don't you Magdalene, that what you saw was the truth, the absolute truth. Not just some subjective vision of your own, a sort of dream that anyone could have had?"

*

John Mark sees the shock in my eyes and reaches for my hand. He folds the fingers in his own, stroking my wrists reassuringly. Then he tries again.

"Could you try and describe it to me, Magdalene, from what you can remember? Was it obviously a physical resurrection? Was he there for you in the flesh, there as a man in his own body?"

A body you knew better than anyone!

"It was forty years ago, Mark. I can't…"

"Or might it have been a vision you saw, something like Paul's only more…detailed? More accurate! Not just a voice, or a blinding light. You do have that faculty, don't you?"

"What does John think?"

"John thinks that what you saw was…a something in between, liminal; a something still on the threshold, no longer entirely a man but…not yet, not altogether become a spirit."

He pauses; I breathe deeply, let myself remember that strangest of all nights, the curious wedding guests, the midnight ceremony. I see something I had not seen before. I see how it all fits in. The ointment I spilt like the sudden opening of the birth waters. That hadn't occurred to me before and it didn't make much sense to me now, but it made some. It explained the overpowering impulse that had come over me, even though I knew I was doing something in public that was shameful, uncontrollable, distinctly feminine. It had had the imperative of birth.

Afterwards, Yeshua copied me. He performed the same act with his disciples. He went down on his knees, Martha told me, and washed their feet, just as I had done for him. "Only with him," she said, "it was done in a controlled and orderly fashion." No one was embarrassed. Except Peter of course. Anything remotely womanish always got on his nerves.

But John Mark has more to say, "You know of course that others saw him too; in fact they went on seeing him: on the road to Emmaus; through the walls of a locked room; on a mountain-side near Bethany; even at the end on the banks of Lake Galilee where it had all started. They went on for forty days, these sightings, these appearances, and then, after the incident I told you about, when the Paraclete[ccxlv] came to us, they stopped suddenly. It was as if he had finally gone. Gone out of our world, because by that time we had something in his place, the Spirit of Truth he promised us, the great Comforter. And that was all we needed. Until Paul, that is! Until Paul came along and reopened the matter, confused us all, confounded our understanding. These resurrection appearances have been controversial to say the least. Some people refused to accept the evidence of their own eyes. Others insist that what the disciples saw or thought they saw was some kind of ghost; a grief-induced phantasm.[ccxlvi]

"When it comes to the resurrection, people don't know what to believe, or even whether to believe at all. Some doubted even as they saw.[ccxlvii] And yet, this uncertainty, it's the centre of our faith, the central mystery, as Paul called it. It must be made clear, Magdalene, that to those he wished to be seen by, to those who loved and followed him, he was really there. In the body he had as a man. Not just a vision."

But it is no good. My illness comes over me. I feel the frothy liquid rise in my lung and my throat. If I try to speak, I will froth at the mouth like some sick old python and the white bubbles will spill down over my chin. And he will see, with disgust, the illness I try to keep hidden.

John Mark presses on. There is something about his interrogation that makes me shrink inside. The pressure on me grows unbearably. Is it on my word that the truth of this new faith is to hang? Am I to be the only one who can answer these questions? And still they come, insistent, obsessive, altogether unanswerable.

"In what sense did he survive death, Magdalene? Was it 'survival'? Is that the right word? Did he survive death in the sense that he was *resuscitated*, brought back to life the way he brought others back on a few occasions? Is death an illness that can be recovered from? Did you, or Joseph perhaps, do something, did give him something to help bring him round? Was it arranged between you? Did you know what was going to happen?"

I put my hand over my mouth and try to contain what is happening there. It is as if my mouth itself were the tomb and the body, decomposed beyond all recognition, was still inside it, still trying to escape.

"Put it another way. What you saw, outside the tomb, was it him, Magdalene, just as you knew him? Or had he changed in some way? Those who saw him have said they didn't recognise him at once. There was something queer about the way he looked; he was both familiar and, at the same time, unrecognisable. The way it happens in a dream: you know who someone is even though they look completely different. And for you, who had been through such a lot: well, it wouldn't have been surprising if…the mind can play strange tricks, can't it, when you lose someone you love?

"Just tell me what you saw all those years ago? Who did you see? Was it the man you had known, in his own body? And if so, was his body…injured, crucified, naked and broken? Or was it whole and healed, glorified in some way?"[ccxlviii]

There is such anguish in his voice as the questions pour out there is no doubting the sincerity with which he asks them. And yet-and yet-he seems suddenly to have become a madman, one of those demon-possessed men who haunt round tombs crying out for someone to release them from their torment.

*

2.10 The Touch of the Magdalene

I hold up my hand to stop him. "He was clothed," I say. "His body had clothes on. The robe had a blue hem."

"Clothed?" John Mark starts and looks round suspiciously. "Why do you mention that?"

"Because I made it for him."

"Still, I don't see—"

"When I saw him, he was fully dressed. He wasn't how he looked when they…took him down, all naked and bloody; he wasn't how he looked when they put him in the tomb."

"What are you implying?" Again, that sharpness of tone: something has touched a raw edge.

"A man's naked body might come back from the dead. But his clothes don't, do they. He was dressed when he came out of the tomb. The robe was new."

*

I need to be alone. I ask if we might meet again later when I have had a short rest. But still the questions continue.

"Did you touch him, Magdalene?"

John Mark's face, for a moment, looks oddly young as he asks this, but his tone is no longer conciliatory. He is tense, almost threatening. The warmth I thought at first he felt towards me seems to have vanished. Something else is there instead.

I turn away from him, indicating I need time to think of my answer, to empty my mouth of the froth that is building up inside me. I gesture along the path; I start to walk away.

He sighs but takes possession of himself again. "Take your time," he says. "Forgive my impatience." He leans back against a mound of turf and stretches out his legs. The sun is high now and the air full of bright May sunshine. He shuts his eyes against it, suddenly calm again. "I'll be here when you get back. Whenever you are ready?"

I struggle with my doubts. What, after all, do I know of this man, even though he has come to seem so familiar? The familiarity could be an illusion. I don't know how far I can trust him or his sudden championship of what I have to say. First, I was the problem, the one nobody would believe; now I have become the solution, if only I knew, after so many years of silence, how to tell what I know.

Paul, it seems, had certainty. He knew what happened when he was struck down; knew who it was when the vision spoke to him. All you can do is believe his testimony. It was not like that for me. I was still in the middle of things. And yet I know I must be clear in what I tell John Mark. Once it is written down, the writing will fix it forever; it will become unchangeable. There will be no second draft.

I deal with my lung, spitting and retching behind a tree as if the filth of the world were trapped inside me; gradually I close it off, gain control of myself again. I drink some water, wash out my mouth over and over again, then walk back slowly, considering my words. But I can think of nothing, rehearse nothing. I am being torn open inside.

"John Mark?"

He makes no answer. Just lies there with his eyes closed. My chance to study his face, then! I sense a great stillness in him; think: *Perhaps I am not such an unlikely witness after all!*

And then the stillness starts to move. It starts to spin round me too like a great whirlwind descending from above. I know this feeling. It came to me once before. Some presence is with me. Is it the golden serpent again,[ccxlix]the one that surrounded Eve as she reached for that forbidden apple? Or is it a higher power? Is it the *Merkavah* again, the Chariot of God himself?

Though it seems a mania, a madness, I feel quite calm, unusually self-possessed. I know at once that my identity is here. The one I have always had inside me, even when I didn't know it; the one that was shaping me, slowly transforming me into itself. Yeshua always knew who he was; knew also who it was he must become. But I am a piecemeal thing, bits of a pattern broken off, a pattern-less kind of pattern and I have gone on like this, sensing something, knowing a well of power was in me but hesitant, unsure of what it was.

I think suddenly: *This is the star that he has nailed me to!*

I am here in this moment, all my wandering thoughts, all my abstractions and imaginings, suddenly concentrated, sharp and focused in this vortex of energy.

As soon as I start to speak, as soon as I tell my story, something will be let loose on the world, and what it is will have a life of its own. I will not be able to stop or control it, this identity that is fixed on me. It will take a shape I may not even recognise as myself; and once that form has come into existence, hundreds of women in the future, thousands, perhaps will be shaped in its image. Knowing Yeshua as I did, it has given me this other identity, this shape that is gathering round me, like it or not!

I let the swirling energy spin and settle: I make myself at home in it. Even though I do not know what John will say of me in his gospel, I know who I am. Every glance, every word, every kiss, every reprimand told me the same: I am the woman Yeshua loved and trusted, the woman Yeshua chose and defended. I loved and trusted him in return. What that love was, and what it meant, the world must be my judge.

Mary Magdalene: patron saint of lovers and sinners! Emblem of all who loved him!

I, who promised not to speak of this to anyone. Ever!

*

"Are you asleep?" Still John Mark does not answer.

For the first time in years, my throat has become bone dry. I clear it as best I can. I start to speak:

"'Mary,' he said."

"The tomb was empty. I saw the great stone pushed to one side. Nothing. Just silence all around. Not even the birds were stirring.

"Then, in that chilly lightless dawn, the sun not yet risen, I noticed a figure standing among the shadow of the trees, the outline of a man leaning on a rake or a long-handled scythe. I turned to him, desperate for information. 'Where is he?' I cried. "What have you done with him?'"

John Mark's eyes are open now. He is sitting up, his eyes intent on me, long and narrow as a huntsman.

"That was not the first thing, Magdalene, was it?"

"No, it was not the first thing. I thought you were asleep. I was testing you."

But if no one else was there, how does he know it was not the first?

"Let's go back a bit further, back to his death and what you remember of it. Tell me everything from the beginning." John Mark seems composed again, pats the ground beside him, inviting me to sit close, to whisper my story.

"What happened then? Tell it in your own words."

"He said he was thirsty."

"Yes."

"He wanted some water." I stare back through a crowded horizon of tears. Those were his words, I am quite sure of that. They were his signal to me: the living water he promised at our first meeting. It had run out now. It was my turn to supply it. "Yes, he wanted water but it was not what they gave him. He drank it anyway; he sucked at the sponge. He wanted to say something, but I don't remember…it was hard to hear; his voice was so faint. Some words about…"

But my memory holds nothing. I held up my jar, just as he had told me to, the lid wide open.

"That was when he died, wasn't it? Do you remember, Magdalene? John says there was a centurion's spear thrust in his left side. Blood and water spurted out everywhere, it flowed down his leg, onto the ground."

"Yes, yes," I say obligingly, though in truth I do not remember the spear at all, only the blood running from his wounds. I caught some of it. "He cried out, like someone in his sleep. And then there was a kind of sigh, only sharper, rasping, the sound of someone struggling for a last breath. And then a shudder. Blood gushed from his mouth."

John Mark is insistent: "But it was the spear that killed him, wasn't it.[ccl] John says there was no doubt of that, no doubt at all that he was dead. The centurion checked it himself, to make absolutely certain." I make no reply.

He prompts again, "What did he say, that centurion? Can you remember?"

"He said, no, something else. That last breath, it drew away the heat, there was a sensation of great cold. We all felt it. Because we had been suffering with him. His suffering spread through the crowd, as if the pain were being drawn from him, as if we were all suffering together. Then, we saw him writhe and try to raise himself and then sink down as if his spirit were finally broken. In that great shudder, we felt the life going, as if the sun itself had suddenly gone out. The way it feels just before sunset. That sudden chill that comes out of nowhere.

"The centurion had his hand over his forehead. He turned to me and said: 'God was with this man, wasn't he? He was truly a son of God." Then his face twisted up. He said: "What have we done this day? What have they made us do?"

"For a while nothing happened. Nobody can remember that time and if they say they can they are lying. There was a blank.

"Then eventually the other Joseph came up, the one who was not his father or perhaps, as I thought then, that's who he really was, the other Joseph: his real father. Anyway, he came. He helped lift down the body when the guards pincered out the nails and the cross fell backwards. It hit the ground with a thump. The head swung loose. One eye seemed to be still open, the other, the right one had shrunk up into his head. There was blood and water and excrement everywhere.

"He no longer looked like himself. He looked terrible: I stared at him, now that I was at last allowed to do this, to look at him freely and openly, not as my teacher, not as my lover but as an object entirely naked to the eye. I could look at him just as he was, without any life of his own to come between us. His neck hung to one side as if broken; he looked utterly defeated."

"Did you help in any way? Were you close enough to see the details?"

But I can't answer. A sudden intense nausea twists my stomach, so I don't know if what I am saying is true. I hardly even remember myself as being there. Then Joseph, the other Joseph, the Joseph who might have been his real father, pulled me up, helped me, I must have been on the ground somehow and he told me to follow him, and take notice. He had a brown donkey; there was a litter for the body and I walked beside it while he and Joanna, Mary Salome, was it? Or was it the other Mary...I can't swear which one it was...there was a whole gang of them, weeping and moaning. Joseph sent most of them away. [ccli]

"So you walked to the tomb? What happened then?"

"Let me think. You are not giving me time, John Mark. It was so long ago, not like yesterday. It's more like trying to remember tomorrow."

"Tomorrow, then, yes! We are both exhausted. Shall we take the last question then?"

We start walking back together. I am mute. I wonder if I will ever speak again.

"Thank you," he says. "I know how difficult this is."

"Do you?"

Something touches me. A small prod. I stop walking, turn towards him.

"Funny about the clothing, though! Wasn't it?"

*

How do you describe the final twists of evil? They too are serpentine, they slide past so swiftly, one after another, all of a heap, knotted together. Every word of betrayal, every event suddenly jumping out of its hiding place; every blindness suddenly staring you in the face. Things you hadn't seen before.

I kept looking at the body laid across the litter, a bundle of old rags pillowing the poor injured head, the hair matted with dark reddish-brown blood, a rich gold and purple cloth laid over the body. A covering for a king, Joseph's, I guessed, noting the brilliant colouring, incongruous after the darkness of that day. One eye was still fixed open as if he had suddenly thought of something he wanted to say and now there was no time left to tell us what it was.

Joseph, who was holding the donkey's head, bent towards me and whispered: "Don't bring Joanna when you come back," he said: "Just Mary." He didn't say which one. It didn't seem to matter.

He put his hand on my shoulder: "You don't look strong enough. Do you want to ride?"

I shook my head, sick and giddy at the thought.

He passed me a small vial of liquid and I hid it in my sleeve.

Our little procession made its way to the burial garden where this other Joseph had a tomb, a new one as it happened, one never used before. There were trees to one side of it but the tomb itself had been cut out of rocky ground and the entrance hadn't been smoothed over properly. We were joined by a handful of temple guards and a couple of Joseph's friends who were waiting near the tomb. Joseph told the guards to stand further off while they carried the body in; we woman were told to sit around the entrance while they disappeared inside and started preparing it for burial. They worked fast and we were not allowed to watch them. It was all done so quickly, so efficiently. The Sabbath was beginning. There was no time to linger or say any words of goodbye. They were still in my throat, those words, when I woke after half an hour's sleep, the following morning.

Two of the guards were inspecting the entrance stone; it was rough and heavy, not rolled smooth like some of them. Mary and I looked at it too, making mental notes of everything we saw. Both of us were numb with grief and shock and tiredness; barely recognisable to ourselves in this new situation. Joanna[cclii] walked across to the guards and spoke to them briefly.

"They want to seal it," she said to us, shaking her head. "Orders!" they claim."

"Don't make any fuss," Mary S said quickly, putting her hand out to draw Joanna back into our group. "Don't say anything at all. We'll worry about that later."

Strange how the event itself, the necessary actions, carried us through for a while! Joseph came back out of the tomb. His friend, Nicodemus, a man I liked and always felt a particular affinity with[ccliii], watched from the entrance as he told us to leave now, to go back and prepare for the full ceremonial burial due as always on the third day when the death had finally been confirmed.

*

We walked back in silence, weeping as we went.

"What's going to happen?" said Joanna as we crossed the death field, darkness already beginning to fall.

That was the question we would all ask ourselves repeatedly through that weird week's end. No one answered. The silence hung round us like a dust cloud on the road.

Judas was waiting for us on the way to Jerusalem, a dark presence barely visible among the olive trees. He was in a state of high excitement, the right side of his face twitching, his right arm jerking up and down as if it had been cut off at the elbow.

He stepped in front of us and I thought for a moment he was going to hit me:

"I blame you for this," he said, his eyes a glaring red, "you and your damned…stink oils! If it hadn't been for you…" He was too angry to say more and spat the last words at me as if they were poison. "We were alright …until you came."

I turned round, went towards him and to my own horror, spat back at him like a serpent, full in the face.

It always seemed to me that that was when it started, the illness that developed slowly in the time ahead, the illness that gradually took over my life.

*

I didn't go home that first night. I stayed with Mary S and Cleopas and we spoke little. My own sister, I knew, would be waiting for me like another coiled serpent, the house full of followers, all grieving and angry. Just before dawn, I fell into a short deep sleep, then woke up to find myself crying out aloud. But the words made no sense to me. Next morning, I waited until the men left for the synagogue or went into hiding outside the city.[ccliv] Then I wrapped my cloak round my head and made myself invisible.

Whatever else I have forgotten; I remember that walk. Time hanging there, like dust in the road, no one to walk with or towards. I walked like a ghost barely touching the ground. The solitude that engulfed me, I felt I could live in it forever; time was so thick with meaning, I would need nothing else.

I slipped into my sister's house and went straight to my loft; my special possessions were there, the things I would need for the following day. For a while, I sat in a trance among the herbs, the fresh linen strips and the ointments, trying to remember who I was. Martha looked in once and set some bread and olives and goat's milk on my table. Neither of us spoke. She was kinder than I expected. I noticed she had mended the broken alabaster jar and set it beside my bed. Eventually I bathed, my face, my hair, my entire body. Then I sat alone, knees drawn up, trying to find him, somewhere in my mind.

I knew I could do this. I had done it many times before when he was somewhere on the road and I needed to find him. Concentrating, breathing as he had taught me, I could enter a state where everything was bodiless; there, if I listened acutely enough, I could sometimes find a line of his energy, the pulse of his heart. As if he were, because he was, my own soul, I could feel the contact.

For a while there would be nothing, an inert kind of silence, one that voiced my own need. Then like a fish in the great deep I would sense a disturbance, a sudden fine tug on the line. When he was on his way back to me after a period of separation it was as if the sun itself was rushing full tilt on its chariot towards me and I would no longer be hooked thin, stretching across a vast absence, looking for him, but back in my body once again, full of life and joy.

He hadn't told me to do this; he didn't need to; he knew I would. I needed to know what had happened to him. Whether he was still somewhere, a living soul in the silence. Or gone completely. Out of reach.

At last, just as I was about to give up and let the depression engulf me again, a light appeared in my mind, a small intense rose-glow of light. It seemed hesitant, wary.

"I don't care what you look like," I said. "Or how you appear. Just tell me you're there. I won't be frightened of you."

I think this might have been a lie for the light blinked and faded as if I had shocked it somehow, not said the right thing.

Then, twelve hours after his burial, I performed my rite. I filled my jar with water and the liquid from Joseph's phial and watched it turn red. Then I started to drink. Every hour of the next twelve, I drank from it again. By midnight, there was none left.

It did me good, knowing I had done that, knowing also that my other preparations were complete. I began brushing my hair, over and over again, touching light oil on the curls. Then I noticed the cloth package leaning against the foot of my bed. I plucked it open nervously. The fabric was costly, green-coloured, but I could not bring myself to unwrap it for more than a glance. What was it? Some present from my sister, a belated wedding gift perhaps? Something I should wear when I entered my husband's chamber for the first time? A resurrection dress perfumed with myrrh and bitter to the touch.

Or something she knew about that I didn't?

*

The talk was stirring like a dust storm. People were whispering everywhere.

"Six hours," Pilate had said on the morning of the event. "That'll be enough. They've flogged him half to death already."

He had glanced down at a message from Herod. Herod and he were, it was rumoured, in agreement about this. Complete agreement. Herod had enough on his conscience with the death of the Baptist. And as for Pilate, his wife had had a vivid dream the night before, a dream that warned him not to get involved with this man they called the messiah. She was a descendant of the old Caesar's family, one of the Julii women; they were women who had learnt the hard way to take their dreams seriously.[cclv]

Pilate had been shaken by what she said. He looked about him, so the whisper went, and gave a few last-minute orders.

"And give him a drink, if he asks for one. The soured wine vinegar. Take a flask along. Just in case."

The centurion on duty that day was already uneasy. Obeying orders was never as straightforward as it seemed. There were nuances, inflections, asides. Everyone had mixed feelings about this rabbi fellow. He already had doubts about what he was being told to do. The honeymoon period between the Roman command and the Jewish authorities was already turning sour. There was hidden play afoot. You never knew which side was trying to undermine the other.

*

"Mary," he said.

When I heard that name my blood ran cold.

Putting that to one side.

Let me try once more to reconstruct it. Piece by piece. The five ghosts.

Then suddenly there is one more.

*

"So, that's who you are!"

John Mark's turn to look sheepish, extremely uncomfortable. He nods his head. Looks tired suddenly. "I wondered if you would recognise me at all. I've changed quite a bit since then."

Momentous. A great peak of excitement rising inside me.

"It was you, wasn't it? You were there in the tomb. We spoke to each other. You were dressed entirely in white; clean, white linen. I didn't recognise you then. I thought you were an angel."

"I know you did and so I was, in a sense. I was the messenger."

"Of course. Of course! You were there all the time. You went in with Joseph. You were hidden away like a *deus ex machina*, on the inside. I never thought..."

"I was his tomb servant, Magdalene, yes. His *shabtis*, the Egyptians call them. In Egypt, it is the custom at a king's burial. A king always takes his servants with him to the tomb. Even the Romans recognised his status. They crowned him King of the Jews, didn't they, in three different languages. Why should you, why should anyone be surprised? Such things are entirely customary."

So obvious, I had never even thought of it. *Did the disciples know?* Something told me they did not. "Surely, you were..." I was going to say *a strange choice,* but he corrected me before the words were even formed.

"I was chosen, yes. He thought I was the right person; relevant experience and so on. He had prepared me for it, of course. Tested my credentials. The night before the supper, the final one, I spent it with him. We were alone together; I was his last initiate. He taught me the secrets of his Kingdom."

205

"The night before the supper? You mean, the night when…" But I cannot go there. I cannot revisit it, this additional twist of complexity; this unlooked-for secret. [cclvi]

All I can think is how little we saw! We understood nothing because we looked only at our own little piece of the puzzle. We were his details, details in a living picture bent on shaping itself around him. Just as he intended it should!

I say instead: "What you mean is: you were there the night of the arrest! You were there in the garden, at Gethsemane? With the others?"

"Yes, I was with him all week. I stayed as close as I could to him for six days, listening, learning, hiding. That night, the night of the arrest, I didn't speak to him once, but I stayed awake, I watched and listened while the others fell asleep. That's how I know what happened. I stayed at a distance, didn't dare to comfort him. It was terrible to watch, his anguish was…Anyway, I told Peter about that. It's all in the first gospel. At dawn they came with the temple guards to arrest him. The scene turned ugly at once; I only just managed to get away. Someone grabbed hold of me, tore off my clothes!"[cclvii]

"You still have a look of youth about you," I say, eerily polite, hiding the shock his revelation has caused me.

He nods, acknowledging the complement. "You too," he says.

*

What he has told me changes things in ways I can't begin to unravel.

"What about Peter? And Judas? Did they know you were there? In the tomb with him?"

"No. Neither of them knew; only Joseph, and his friend, Nicodemus, who guarded the door. Except for Peter – and John of course – I have never told anyone. It was my initiation secret. I had to keep it for ten years."

I can't contain my dread any longer: "Judas said it was all my fault, that I was the one to blame. Do you and John think that too? Is it what you will say of me?"

"Mother Eve again! That's madness, Magdalene, and you know it. I've thought of you so often, you have no idea. Even when I was a student in Alexandria, I'd heard of you, imagined you. And no, not as my long lost little sister; not like that at all! Now that I have come to know you a little, I understand so much more. If it hadn't been for you, the teacher would never have taken me. He would have sent me away, ashamed and humiliated."

"What do you mean, if it hadn't been for me?"

"Don't you remember, that last long journey down from Jericho? When he crossed the Jordan that final time.[cclviii] He'd been baptised there and went to meet some of the Baptist's old followers. There had been trouble between them, and he went to sort things out, to effect a reconciliation. He came into the city afterwards and it was there in Jericho that I met him for the first time. I had heard of him, of course—who hadn't by that time?—but I'd been away in Alexandria for much of his ministry, finishing my studies.

"When he came into the market square, I was determined to seize my opportunity. I went up and spoke to him, asked if I could become one of his followers. He was both kind and very impatient with me, as if he had already gone too far ahead and there was no time left, no time for compromises, only absolute choices to be made. I was simply too late to be teachable.

"It was you who intervened for me, Magdalene. I can't believe you've forgotten it! You didn't know me at all, just that I was a rich kid, terribly spoiled by his sister and so badly hurt when he rejected me, made a show of me in front of everyone, as if wealth were some kind of unforgivable sin I couldn't help committing.[cclix] As if money corrupted everyone, everyone except himself, that is.

"I could tell he liked me, it was obvious from what he said, but still he refused me, said no, I couldn't come with him, I couldn't enter his kingdom. Not unless I gave up all my possessions, everything I had. He sent me away with the whole crowd watching, astonished at his teaching. James and John, they were there too; pleased no doubt to see the rich boy humiliated in front of everyone."

"His closest disciples," I tell him truthfully, "it was their biggest fear: fear that they would be supplanted by other, richer, more intelligent men. This fear grew worse towards the end, when Yeshua was at the height of his fame."

"I couldn't believe what he'd done to me. How cruel his dismissal had been! I went off in a deep sulk and shut myself in our family tomb. I wouldn't come out. I thought, *I'll show you all!*

I stayed there three nights in that dark hole before my nerve broke. Then I found I couldn't get out of it. The damn stone had got stuck in its groove. In the end, my sister sent a message to him, asking for help. And it was you, Magdalene, who brought him to our house. Surely you remember? It was you who persuaded him to come, persuaded him I was worth helping."

"What did I say?"

"You spoke up for me, told him I was genuine. You said, 'If you help him, he will repay you double for what he has received.' The teacher shook his head but still you insisted, you shouted at him, said, 'Not all our debts have to be cancelled. There are some who will repay.'

"Still he deliberated. According to my sister, everyone was watching to see what he would do, whether he would sell out as the men seemed to fear. Then you hit the nail hard on the head. You said, 'And how will your teaching go forward, Rabbi? When you have left us, and we can't count on your miracles any longer? Surely then we will need the help of men like him?'

"I had a point!"

I don't suggest there might have been an element of drama in all of this, a kind of playing to the crowd. It happened occasionally. I say instead: "He knew that if he accepted you as a follower, John Mark, your journey with him would be very short. He knew he was going to die."

The incident he speaks of stirs some kind of memory, but it is the meeting with the Baptist's followers that I remember most. Yeshua and I had our only serious quarrel there. I would not take his side because I too felt that John had been dishonoured in his death. The debt I was speaking about was the one we owed to him.

John Mark suddenly jolts me with an extra detail:

"We sent you some money afterwards, my sister and I; a messenger brought it secretly, just for you, not to be shared with the others. You may say this was wrong of us, but I wanted to thank you. That week I spent with him it, it transformed me, turned me into the man I wanted to be. He taught me secret things: showed me the powers hidden in myself, hidden in other people too.[cclx]

"I went out and bought a chalice for him, silver-gilt, the most expensive one I could find. I don't suppose you know what happened to it, do you? The money would be useful to us now; we have so many mouths to feed. At the last, he taught me the secrets of his kingdom. And I belonged to him. You and I, Magdalene, he was different with us. We were his cross at the end; his human support. We saw him through."

I cry again at this, strange, human tears. My thoughts turn back to our meeting at the tomb.

"I want to ask you," I say between a sob and a smile, "the same question that you asked me. What did you do to help him? What part did you play? You owe me the truth now, John Mark. I think you should have told me all this earlier. There have been so many mysteries, so many secrets."

"I had to find the right time, the right…"

"It is now!"

He looks at me with a smile, sudden amusement in his eyes. "*Mea culpa*, Magdalene! I did the costumes, brought fresh clothes to the tomb. I certainly needed some! You were quick to sense that. Resurrection has a dress code all its own."

Suddenly, a wild spirit of hilarity seizes us both. It is as if, after years of incomprehension, we have finally seen the joke!

"After all," he says, "it's clothes that bring us back to life every day. We sleep like the dead but then we wake, we dress. Suddenly we are ourselves again."

We both laugh. I hear myself laughing. Laughing. It is unbelievable. Exhausting. Yet both of us laugh, without restraint, like children at a party.

"They took the robe we wove for him; you know: his high priest's under-garment. They played dice for it, one of the soldiers won."

Even this shocking detail has a lining of hilarity.

"And that's why he needed new clothes. We both did."

A moment's thought and we are quickly sober again.

"So, you brought fresh clothes for him…to put on if…when…he…came back to us? You spent the night in there with him: two nights in fact. You sat with him all the time?"

"Yes, I sat with him. I sat with his body, just as he had told me to. I sat with him and prayed for two nights and one very long day. He taught me the right words. But that was all, Magdalene. I knew a fraction of his secret but that's all. Until…"

"And the stone…when I arrived, the tomb was already open. You must have rolled it away from the other side? From the inside?"

"Yes. It was not difficult. Tombs like that are meant to be opened. At different times, whole families get buried in there."

"Who else…knew of this?"

"One other. Joseph. It was his tomb."

"But Peter? And John?"

"They didn't see me. Had no idea I was there. I was not to speak to him, or to them or to anyone else except you."

"Can you speak of it now, tell me the whole inside story?"

"I don't know. You came and glanced in, to me the first ray of sunlight across a dark threshold. You gave a cry when you saw the stone rolled back. Then you turned away, went back into the garden again. I waited in the tomb for a while, tidied up the grave clothes, then crept out and hid round the back until I saw Peter and John arrive and find the tomb empty. [cclxi]They looked about briefly; then left in a hurry, both shouting at each other. Obscenities actually, a volley of them."

"But that can't be right! Peter and John weren't there when I was. They came afterwards."

"Ah, yes, indeed. Good point! Possibly I've got some of the sequence wrong. I've talked it over with them all so often, you see, I might have got a few details mixed up. Luke's fault, of course! He wanted Peter to be first and he could be very touchy over nuance. To give you an example: he insisted there had to be two of us inside the tomb. Two messengers of the resurrection! As he saw it, he and I were both evangelists so we both had to get a mention. And then of course the different accounts had to be harmonised. What I wrote with Peter, that was closer to the…but as I've said before, that text was incomplete.

"Anyway, shortly after you turned up the first time, you came back again. You looked inside properly then and saw me sitting there. I gave you the message. Told you he was not here, that he was back among the living! I shone the light on the stone to show you he was gone. And that's it, that's all I have to tell. You turned away, wandered off into the garden, completely dazed. I waited until you had gone, made sure everything was as it should be, then slipped away as quickly as I could. I had played my part. I was not to wait. For me it was over."

"And now you want…"

"I want what you want. I want the truth to be told, from both sides, if we can trust each other. I've explained already. John has been preparing his account. He needs help at times, especially with the language. His grasp of written Greek isn't …Anyway, I encourage him to concentrate on his visionary piece[cclxii], his *Revelation*; it's an *epistolarium* to the churches, a bit like Paul only less concerned with practical advice, more with…Let's just say it's a mystical text, all about his dreams and so on, but sound on his main idea: a celestial marriage, the New Jerusalem, a new Holy city to become the Lord's heavenly bride. *A new heaven*, as John puts it, *for a new earth!*[cclxiii] It will end almost where our gospel begins; on a different plane of course but it all fits together. Just like Luke, with his *Acts,* only the other way around."

As if some heavy stone had rolled away in my heart too, I hear at last what he is saying. I see it in my mind, the work they are doing together, until I realise there is something I don't see, something secret still hidden in the tomb.

"Yes," I say, "I understand what you are saying but…what about you? Did you do something to revive him? Did you give him something, to bring him round?"

I thought again of my herbs, their individual properties; the warm, healing ointments, the spices. I call to mind the moment I got close enough to see that the stone had been rolled back, the guards had gone, and the tomb was open. The stab at my heart I try not to recall. This was not in the plan.

I knew at once that something had gone wrong. I had imagined quite a different scene; thought I would be alone with him in the tomb, Mary S standing guard outside while I…assisted…in some way, performed my part as his grieving wife, his mystical priestess. He had prepared me for that. Not for this though, this emptiness as if everything had already happened, without me. As if I had no necessary part.

I understood at once John's jealousy, his fear of being supplanted.

"Did he teach you some secret? Was it you who brought him back to life?"

"Would that it were, Magdalene, but I did nothing. Don't you see? We were just his back up, you and I, in case he needed help. There was no secret between us of the sort you are suggesting; only the esoteric secrets, the *deep mystery* that John hopes to…encode in his gospel. We haven't quite worked that out yet, but, given your help, I'm sure we will.

"My task was to bring clean clothes for us. I had some oil for the lamp, a flint, some bread, a little water, no wine in case it me sleepy. All I did was to sit in the dark beside Him, waiting and praying. He had taught me one of his secret prayers, more a chant than words. It calmed my mind when the nervousness took hold. It can do strange things to you, sitting in the dark like that, watching beside a corpse. Your sense of time, for example. I started to think that I might be dying too.

"Towards the end of the second night, I lit the lamp. I shone it on his face for a moment, then dropped it again, hot oil spilling all over my hand. The cloth that covered his head had been lifted slightly. His eyes were open, both of them, and he was looking at me. I saw Him raise one arm and pull the cloth away from his face. He handed it to me; I folded it in half, neither of us spoke. I wonder sometimes, I even wondered at the time: was this a dream? The darkness, you know, the cave, the mix of terror and excitement; the heightened threshold of anticipation. Had I simply fallen asleep? Was I imagining things?

"Neither of us spoke. I handed him the clean garment, helped him to dress, though I was shaking so badly I nearly put it on inside out, then I opened the tomb for him and watched him go out. It was still very early; there was hardly any light. I heard the guards startle up and shout, one dropped his sword, there was a clatter on the stones; then they ran away. That was shortly before you turned up.

"You were singing to yourself, very softly. Or praying. Then you went quiet. You saw the open tomb and cried out. I think at first you were too frightened to look inside. You went away and I heard you shouting in the garden. I renewed the light and shortly afterwards you came back and looked through the opening. I asked why you were crying. I gave you his message. Said he had risen from the dead. And that was it. You turned back to the garden. My first account ends there: just the tomb, empty; the body gone. No conclusion.

"Peter, you see, didn't like my original ending. I had to scrap it. He tore it across, mid-sentence. He wanted his gospel to finish with the message the Lord had already given his followers at the supper, that He was going back to Galilee and that He would meet them there. But you didn't pass the message on. You were too frightened to speak of what you'd seen."[cclxiv]

I try to grasp the implications of this; "Peter wanted his gospel to end with that? With my silence, my failure to deliver Yeshua's message?"

"I know; I know; it wasn't right at all! It wasn't a very good ending either. But you see, we hadn't decided amongst ourselves what kind of ending would be best. How do you tell something like that, describe something so…miraculous, so story-like, and yet make it believable, so that people believe what you are saying is true? There were objections, insinuations. We had to help them understand the mystery that Paul was already teaching them. People were curious about it. They wanted to know what really happened."

Anger: its finger on my pulse; my blood racing. *I will not be silenced like this!*

The anger sets me free at last. Free to speak of what I can remember, even though I must struggle with the shame of what I have to tell.

I confront him angrily; I confront all my enemies. "I was there!" I say. "I know what happened. I turned away from the tomb. I turned back into the garden."

"Yes, that's right. You were twisting backward and forward, like someone caught in pain or indecision, looking inwards, then looking out again. But what happened then, Magda? What did you see? And if you saw Him, really saw him, what did He say to you? What were his very first words?"

"But you were there, John Mark! Why do you keep questioning me?"

He puts his hand over his eyes, his face drawn and ghastly. "I saw him dead, Magdalene. I sat with him. But then, then there comes a doubt. A terrible thought. I haven't told anyone, and it doesn't go away. I was still so new to everything, so new to him as well, don't you see. After the ordeal, watching by his side all that time in the dark, I sometimes wonder if, if it wasn't…me, who got up, who put on the cloak, went outside…"

"You?"

"That's why I question you. That's why I have to know what happened. Your meeting that morning: are you sure it was Him? That there wasn't some…terrible confusion?"

My knees buckle. I fall forward heavily, as if I had been pushed from behind. Pain jolts through me. At last, I know what to do.

I opt for speech, years of silence vanishing like smoke. It was as if everything was happening for the very first time.

*

At first, nothing! It was still dark. There was a dawn wind in the trees. The leaves rustled. At first nothing, then a whisper. I had seen that the tomb was open, I'd heard your message but I'd turned away. I thought I could make out a figure, in the shadows. Watching me. It was a man, an old man, I thought, hooded and slightly bent. He was leaning on something. He spoke to me, mumbled something. I couldn't hear what he said. I thought he might be a guard or a caretaker or something."

"What about a gardener?"

"Alright, yes, a gardener. I ought to have been frightened, but somehow I wasn't; it didn't matter anymore. The tomb was open; I knew it was empty. I shouted at him: "Where is he? Where have you put him?"

"When he didn't answer, I went up to him. I pulled his sleeve, said again: "Where is he? Where have you taken him?"

But still he said nothing.

"Alright, don't tell me then," I said and in my anger, I gave him a sharp push. The figure crumpled up immediately and the hooded robe slid to the ground. It was empty. There was no one inside it, just a stick with a cross bar for arms. I jumped back, my heart beating madly. I turned back to the tomb…"

"And then?"

"And then, I heard someone say, '*Mary.*'

I mean, almost nobody calls me that!"

*

A bird suddenly startled up, loud and piercing as if night were an argument it was just about to win.

For a moment I thought there must have been a mistake, some kind of mix up and the name was meant for someone else. For Mary S, perhaps. Then my blood ran cold. I knew that voice. Turning again, I saw a figure, a real figure this time, move out of the darkness, stepping out of the shadows towards me. He was standing up straight now with a hood over his head and I was suddenly filled with terror.

I knew at once I had walked straight into his trap without even thinking. "*Mary M, marry him!*" It was the old joke: Barabbas's joke, something they used to chant round the fire in the evening. Barabbas in person, not even, as in the past, one of his gang hissing out a message. Barabbas. Hiding, lying in wait, knowing I would come here. The past rolled across my path like a stone, I would never be free of it. I went rigid with cold, intense cold, my very blood seemed to freeze in my veins. Judas had been right about me. I was the cause.

212

As if it read my thoughts, a snake suddenly slithered across the stones in front of me, inches from where I stood. Evil to evil. I was born its creature. Otherwise I must have screamed.

"Mary M! Miriam! I need your help. Take a message for me, will you! To Simon! Tell him to meet me in Galilee. Two weeks from now. Tell him: same place, it's all arranged. Don't let me down."

I had heard that kind of message before; Galilee was their headquarters. The Zealots often hid out there. I must have lost my grip on reality for a moment; my whole being was flooded with some wild emotion I couldn't even recognise. I knew Yeshua had said something to the men about going to Galilee. Martha had told me about it after the supper, though it seemed a lifetime ago now.

I lost my balance; half fell where I stood. Then I looked up at him, just growing visible now as the grey light thinned away.

He stepped closer. I saw his feet. I stared at his feet. He wore no sandals and it was easy to see why. The arch of his foot was smashed in; the toes drawn up like the claw of a dead bird. I saw the hem of his robe, the one I had woven for him, its blue hem visibly embroidered with blood, beneath a long grey cloak. I looked up and saw a hand held out as if to lift me up. He drew it back quickly but not before I had seen the shattered palm, the finger bones bunched and twisted like that of a cripple, a picker up of rubbish in the street.

A sinister black wound like a slave's brand had been burnt into his flesh. Compassion flew out of my breast. I could see his face now, hurt and bruised, almost unrecognisable, one eye grotesquely swollen, the other shiny with liquid though his voice was hard. I reached out towards him.

"Don't! he said quickly, pulling away. Don't touch me. I'm not ready yet.[cclxv] I'm still too weak. Neither of us is ready."

It came as a command, yet he looked so vulnerable. I put my basket with the herbs and ointments down on the ground beside him and bowed my head, ashamed of myself, of my old demon of anger.

I wanted to ask: "Are you in great pain?" but I knew what he would answer.

I'm not here to recover.

I could see this was true, that he would never recover but there was something else too: he was changing as I looked at him, literally changing in front of my eyes. It was not recovery, it was rather as if, in the grey light of dawn, he were sloughing off the skin of his ordeal, peeling it away as we stood there, like an unwanted mask. It was Yeshua himself; I knew he was alive; I was certain of that. But the life he was living, it was…no longer the same as before. It's hard to explain. We weren't as we had been; we were more like a memory of that. It would never be the same again. We were separated, and yet…there was a new kind of invitation. I couldn't grasp it.

He feels no anger! I thought. Nothing has touched him. In his spirit, his emotions, he was quite detached, quite uninjured. He was un-injuring himself even as we spoke, stepping free of his human life. What he seemed was…not peaceful exactly, but composed, *majestic* even. I recognised that in him immediately, that he had acquired a different …status, if that is the word. Like someone from a different realm. A king after all! I could not reach across.

"Where will you go?" I asked.

"I am going home, Mary," he said simply. "To my Father's house. I am going to make it ready for you and all my brothers. Take this message to them. Tell them I am alive, that you have seen me. Tell them all: *I have done it! I have come back, I have kept my promise.*"[cclxvi]

I nodded dumbly, too shaken to admit I wasn't entirely sure about the first part of the message. Did he really say 'Galilee'? Or was it, 'alibi' I heard? My old dread of Barabbas had confused me, conjuring him up as if he were there in person.

I could hear movements. The sound of voices; someone panting as if they had been running hard. I turned and ran too, my heart finally flooding with relief happiness. The suspense was over. *He had done it after all!* When I stopped to look back, both he and the herb basket had gone.

*

Hard to remember the sequence. The time it took. Was it me who ran back then? Or was it the other Mary? Or did we both go? I remember I stood in the doorway and gasped out my message. They looked at me queerly, as if I was holding out to them some magical apple of temptation that they did not want to bite. Then Peter came in, sour and angry, to hear the news. Good though it was, it was clear he did not want to hear it from me. I was hurt by his brusqueness, his tone of contempt but I held my ground. I had spoken the truth. They all stared at each other, trying to decide what should be done, what should be thought.

Soon Peter and John were racing down the road together like a pair of Greek athletes. I went after them to the tomb in the garden, trembling as if a lightning strike had passed right through me. By the time I caught up with them they had been inside, discovered for themselves that it was empty. I repeated his words. Peter kept peering at me, pushing me, trying to make sense of my message, and whether or not I should be believed. "He called you his brothers, Peter!" I said. It was that which persuaded him.

*

"I saw him as well," said Mary S when we got back. "I saw you talking to him. He raised his hand to me. He greeted me. I'll back up what you say."

She looked pained. I put both my arms round her, and we hugged in a little dance together.

"Yes, he did, didn't he! Of course he did. He greeted both of us. Almost as if he couldn't tell us apart."

The other Mary. His sister, this one! A listener, not a talker. Quiet, thoughtful; a real home bird. No demons in her. Not even a whisker.

*

I thought he would want to hear more. But John Mark is somewhere else, his attention no longer with me. His head is bent, and he is writing rapidly on his tablet. Suddenly he looked up. "Why did he call you 'Mary'?"

"It was a name he gave me, after an incident with his mother. He shut her out once. I didn't like the name; it had bad associations for me, but he used it occasionally."

"Yes. Yes, of course; it all fits!" He made a note for himself then asked me to go through it all again. "Are you sure you have told me everything? Everything you can remember? Are you definitely sure it was Him? Even though you were confused at the beginning, even though you didn't touch him?"

"I know he was there. Clothed, and in something like the remains of his old body, but it didn't define him anymore. He held on to it—how shall I say—with difficulty. It wasn't just his old self brought back to life. He had changed inside. He had come to a point.

"If you had touched him you would have known for certain that he was there, that he wasn't just a vision or an apparition. Some of the men claimed that they…"

"That wasn't why he didn't want me to touch him!" How do I explain to this man about visions, explain that if you are as attuned to someone as I was to Yeshua, he only has to think of something for you to see it too? [cclxvii]

"Peter didn't want visions," he says. "For him, there was a lack of authenticity. He didn't want touching either."

"Because?"

"For some of the men, the older ones especially, there's a purity issue. They think it improper, for a woman to…"

"Women are not spiritual enough, I suppose?"

John Mark gives me a glance of shame.

"What I saw that day was not a vision, whether I touched him or not. He was there in his body, but he was…still injured, not quite free of it all. He was going from us; he was not coming back. It was only the message that mattered to him now. He was there as his own message, his own angel. He was there in his words. And it was I who was spirited away afterwards, not him."

"No, Magdalene, no! That's not how it was. You and I both disappeared for a while. We had to do it. We were the teacher's most closely guarded bank of secrets; the field in which he hid his treasure. We would have been captured. The temple guards would have come back. We would have been arrested. Interrogated, tortured. Pressure would have been put on us to tell the story they wanted to hear. We would all have been silenced."

Familiar arguments. I have heard all this before. My old worry surfaces again.

"When you are writing you gospel, will you and John say I was *not spiritual enough*?"

"No, Magdalene. Don't even think it! John will idealise you, almost as you say to the point of disappearance. He will do the same with me. He'll create an ideal family for us; tell a story in which we appear, but unrecognisable, not as we were in this life but according to the new model. You will be there as the perfect, obedient disciple, a quiet woman from a good family who listens to the Lord and whose love he returns; I as some ne'er do well, a heap of walking grave clothes who none the less comes up smelling of roses. He will perfume us both. A pair of etherealised beings, hardly a body between us!"

"An ideal family? But I thought this gospel was supposed to be truthful!"

"It's the mystery, Magdalene. Don't you see! Truth is a triangle. John's isn't a gospel like Luke's; it's not about the birth family. John's family is a model of the kingdom; it's a family of resurrected love. You and I, we'll both be there, Magdalene, there in John's Bethany, but not as we were in this life, complex and damaged and devoted, not as the ones he loved, first and last. John himself will take over that role. That's the deal we made, so that I could come and look for you at last. John will become the beloved one, just as he always wanted. He'll be the favourite, the one who always comes first in the race, the one who always gets there before Peter. He's an old man now and it means a lot to him.

"As for me, I'll be all but invisible, a man brought back from material death to re-enter the family of the Spirit. A version of the Baptist, from what you've told me; the one you pleaded for when you went back to Jericho! As for you, Magdalene, you'll be our mystery woman, the woman people guess at, the one whose grief made our Lord weep, while the Jews look on in astonishment at this family who can show the world what it means to love."

"And Judas?" I ask, that old anxiety still gnawing at my heart.

"Hanged on a tree, pockets turned inside out, coins all around the corpse like bits of broken pottery. An object lesson."

"Yes." A huge relief wells up inside me. He and John have taken my part.

"I wish I could hate him," I say. "The strange thing is, I can't."

John Mark thinks about this. "There was," he says, "something of the teacher in all of us. Even in Judas, for all he sold out to the authorities. He betrayed himself as well as the Lord and he knew he had done it. Another of the Lord's strange choices, hey! In the end, he took his place on the tree."

He raises his left eyebrow, suddenly comical.

"They went back to Galilee, you know."

"Who did?"

"Peter and John and the rest. You told them the Lord was going home to his father's house. So that's where they went. Back to Galilee! Literal to a fault, as ever! It wasn't until they went out fishing that they realised…"

"Realised—"

"That the fish that had caught them once before was fully cooked now; that it was a journey of understanding. John intends to use this as his ending, that journey back to the beginning. It will be his alpha and omega. A fine touch, I think!"

Another small scroll of memory unwinds in my mind. John Mark has already told me that Nathan met up with them again there. Back in the Galilee he had always despised. Nathan, my impossible bridegroom; from the family that died!"[cclxviii]

"And now," John Mark speaks quietly, "talking of returns, I must prepare myself to go back to Ephesus before John gets so old, he can't remember anything! I must go, Magdalene, though I do so reluctantly. I could stay here forever."

And with those words, our gripping acquaintance of two weeks start to loosen its hold; we will meet briefly just once more before we take our leave. Then like two startled birds our paths will separate, flying off in different directions.

*

2.11   The Jericho Road

Once more, the ending is a door that swings suddenly open. Memory, like a young girl, is there to answer it.

The Jericho Road.[cclxix] What is hidden behind that door comes forward slowly, timidly as if it needed some introduction. We had been back across the Jordan to the Baptist's old place by the river. Philosophers say that no one steps in the same river twice, but that was not true for us. We had gone back to our beginning: John, flapping his arms about like a great bird on the edge of the water, clearing the banks, shouting aloud his message of repentance.

"John recognised me there," Yeshua told me as we walked by the water. "He was the first one to recognise me. You were the next, the first person to whom I ever spoke of myself. By that well in Samaria, do you remember?" He sounded sad, low-spirited, nostalgic even.

James and John, Zebedee's sons, overheard some of our conversation. It didn't go down well with them. They had different ideas. Yeshua had chosen them recently to witness a special event[cclxx]; it made them conscious of their pre-eminence; keenly aware of their position.

The rich boy when he appeared, when he stepped forward out of the crowd in Jericho, immediately caused ripples. He was exceptionally beautiful, for a start, but his beauty was of a good order, fine features, well-bred and respectable. He appeared confident, sure of what he wanted but at the same time deferential in manner and sweetly spoken. What he wanted was to become a disciple. He wanted that ultimate luxury: salvation, the right to enter the Kingdom of Heaven.

There was an instant rapport between him and Yeshua, the rapport of those who have richness within them. There was an immediate frisson of jealousy among the disciples at the sight of this latecomer, a youth who had everything to offer: charm, wealth, education. And confidence too: it showed in his manner. The rich, those whose money could buy respect and bring about change, always created anxiety in the group.

"Give up everything you have," Yeshua said, looking him straight in the eye like a card player reading the hand of his opponent. "It will cost you not less than everything. You must give it all up."

There was a gasp from the crowd. In this exchange, the stakes were high. No one knew quite what was at issue.

Then Yeshua turned to those of us listening and said, "The Kingdom of Heaven, it is like dying. You must lose everything that makes you recognisable, everything that makes you who you are. To find salvation, you must go back to the beginning, to the time before you were. You have to shed everything, become nothing all over again."[cclxxi]

An irritated murmur swept through the crowd, then a hush of attention. Judas muttered something cryptic.

The youth looked nonplussed. "Surely, Master, there must be some other way. What you ask is…"

Yeshua stopped him with a glance. He touched his arm, seemed to be encouraging him somehow, egging him on to go further. Their eyes kept meeting in a dance of glances, as if it were some kind of game between them, seduction even, exciting and reckless.

James, John and Peter, they were annoyed at this, annoyed at the young man's persistence, annoyed at the attention he could command. They sensed some rapport in the interchange, something from which they themselves were excluded. Compared to the newcomer, what they had given up to be with Yeshua suddenly seemed of little account, something he could almost take for granted.

As for this rich, handsome boy, becoming a disciple was nothing more than a whim that he flirted with. Peter was rattled, hurt, as he so often was, a hurt he made no attempt to hide: "We have given up everything to be with you, Lord. We've all done this for you from the beginning. And now some newcomer…" A sudden quarrel sprang out of nowhere. Others joined in.

James and John were so put out, so jealous of their position, they even got their mother to speak up for them, to argue their claim. This annoyed Yeshua; crosscurrents of annoyance ran every way, the air was thick with it.

Eventually the young man himself took the hint, seemed to realise that he had lost the first round, become an object lesson in the futility of riches. Everyone breathed easily again. We thought we had seen the last of him. Then, a few days later, just as we were leaving the city, his sister appeared, an acquaintance of Joanna's, someone with court connections, well-dressed (I stifled the envy), with a tall, confident, pushy presence. She certainly pushed me aside and went down on one knee at the teacher's feet.

Her brother had been taken ill. He had a desperate fever, she said, and was now beyond ordinary help. Three nights ago his life had been despaired of, the following day he was lifeless, now they had taken him to the tomb. "If only,

Lord, you had been able to keep him with you. He loved you so much. You could have prevented this!"

The men all gathered round, angered again by the interruption, even more annoyed when Yeshua seemed inclined to listen. Suddenly she turned to me: "You tell him, lady," she said. "You know better than anyone what it is to have a love that has no limits. Help me with this, I beg you. Persuade him. Tell the Rabbi to come to us. I promise you; you will have your reward."

I, no more than he, could resist the direct appeal. I took him by the sleeve. "Remember the Baptist!" I said, the words coming from nowhere but charged with emotion. "Remember how you could have saved him. How you did nothing, just took over his ministry, took his people for your own. John could have saved himself. Herod would have bought him off, silenced him willingly. He chose not to. He became nothing instead. He gave up his life for you. You let him die."cclxxii

Yeshua's eyes seemed to shrink deep into his face. He turned away from me. I thought I had gone too far this time. Then I saw that he was weeping.

He was a man of great emotional depth; he often drew upon these depths in his healing, in his preaching. But I had never seen this before. I watched and wondered. Then I understood that he wanted the youth, wanted him for some special purpose. The more he wanted someone the higher he set the bar.

I turned to the disciples. "This young man who came to us; he was sincere, genuine, compelled in some way. Wealth doesn't save us from everything, the way poor people always think that it does. Money can't perform miracles the way Yeshua can, but it is not always our enemy. From those who have, more can be asked. And some of those who have, know how to pay their debts."

There was a lull as the men took this in. Money was getting shorter; expenses increasing all the time. No one could deny this. But still, I feared I had made an enemy, I just wasn't sure whom. Yeshua, who had turned away, walked over to us.

"The rich'" he said, "don't understand our currency. They are too blinkered by their own."

Judas and Peter nodded at each other. This made me speak.

I argued the need for money, the necessity of having it behind us: "In the life ahead, what will we do then? We are not lilies; we are not birds; what we build in your name we must pay for in the world's currency."

I don't know why I said this; I probably didn't say all of it. John Mark's story has already coloured my memory! I do know I stood astonished at myself, the prophetess, after all, of God's hidden wealth.

And then Yeshua was striding off with the woman, laughing as if he conceded a gracious, amusing defeat.

By the time he got to their house, he told me later, the youth was shrieking to get out. They could hear him from the top of the garden. He had spent three nights in the darkness of that little tomb and his nerve had gone. The stone had got stuck in its grove and he couldn't budge it from the inside. Yeshua pushed it away easily. The lad came out, exhausted and ashamed. The victory over death is not so easily won.

"That's the rich for you!" James said, exultant, when we talked over the episode afterwards. "When it comes to the point. No stamina."

"Nonetheless," said Yeshua, "an invaluable experience! A remarkable young man too."

"Seemed ordinary enough to me," said Peter.

Yeshua patted him on the shoulder. "Three nights in the tomb," he said evenly. "You have to hand it to the boy. He knew what he was doing; he made it through."

Later, a messenger bought me a note with 300 denarii inside. There was no signature. Judas, drawn instantly as always by the mere smell of money, watched me from a distance.

I took the coin without a word. Pocketed it. Spent it all on myself.

*

And then the miracle occurs. John Mark makes it happen. He knows I am sad; sorry he is leaving and still sick inside. I hide my illness well, but I still carry the past with me, a sickness from which I have never recovered.

He asks me that last day what it is I grieve for most. He listens as I tell him about Barabbas, the one who knew me in my youth, the one the crowd shouted for, the one they didn't crucify, the one they released instead of Yeshua. I stand there to be judged, my sinful past the sordid dress I have never taken off.

"He was there in all of us," John Mark says again. "Even in Barabbas. The crowd chose what they understood but the teacher was showing us something else, something not bound by the blind standards of the world. Where are they now, the powerful men who condemned him? Caiaphas is gone, Antipas has fallen.[cclxxiii] Jerusalem itself has gone. Only our Lord has risen."

"And only I have no place. He has gone from me and I still cannot find him. I will stand outside his tomb forever."

"You will find your place in time, Magdalene. Meanwhile, don't grieve anymore over your past. It was part of what interested him, what he loved, about you. What happened was not your fault. You were the hinge, the key that turned both ways, towards the world and away from it. Those two men, you bound them together. Though their aims and methods were different, they had something in common; they were both revolutionaries. One in the way of the world, and as the world understands it, doing in the end more harm than good, for it was Barabbas and his gang who destroyed Jerusalem. But our leader destroyed Jerusalem too, in a different way. He was a thorn in the world's side, a sign hung above time itself, a king of different conclusions.

"Don't grieve about this any longer. Barabbas was killed with Simon, the night the city fell: that was not your fault either. You are not all the guilty women in the world, for all you seem to think you are! I've told you this before. For the teacher you were always Sophia, wisdom herself, fallen from heaven and caught in the trammels of the world. You are what He came here to rescue. Think of it like that!

"You have taught me so much these last few days, Magdalene, changed the way I see what I must write about. I know He chose me to write His gospel, set me also impossible conditions I somehow had to meet. You too, I think, through all these years of sadness and solitude! While we began our work in the outside world; you have held a secret treasure for us here. You must see that for yourself now, as you saw it for me all those years ago on the Jericho road."

I bless him for saying that, though at first, I can't take in his meaning. I had spoken on impulse, told him something I could hardly bear to tell myself. He had listened; accepted, understood. Just as Yeshua used to listen! There was a judgment for our sins, but he showed us how to live with that, how to work with it, transform ourselves in the new light that it brought. Hearing John Mark's words of kindness and of wisdom, it eased a pain I thought would never heal. He has seen me the way that God looks at things, all of a piece, as if everything were already revealed in its own pattern, complete and acceptable. I could not do that for myself.

That little episode in Jericho had proved something of the rich boy's worth, something that even Peter came eventually to recognise, and to use. The rich have their own gifts. Mark's was the power to amaze us. To find one miracle after another, like a little goat in a circus, climbing determinedly upwards, one foot at a time, making its way up to the heights on human chairs and tables and stools.

And what he climbed on, he developed in himself.

*

Being recognised: I have lived in fear of that for so long. Now I find that recognition, having your own lost image restored to you, free of its faults at last, it is that which brings renewal of life.

"Is it possible," John Mark asks tentatively, putting away his notes, "it was not Him you met with that first morning? Is it possible it was…your own spirit?"

"Perfectly possible," I tell him, pleased for once to have the right answer. "He was my own spirit."

*

John Mark says some people found it hard to recognise Yeshua in that short period when he returned to us. He seemed changed, they said. I have thought about this. Now it seems to me it was not only he who had changed. The change we saw was the one taking place in our own understanding.

He had told us his spirit would be strong enough to carry him through death but, when it came to the point, we did not believe him. We were wrong.

Seeing him again as we did afterwards, it changed our understanding. We thought he looked different but the difference was there in ourselves, in what we had become. We had been through death with him; we had lost the one who mattered most to us. Suddenly, there he was again. After the violent trauma of his 'death', this sudden shock of light. His unfamiliar appearance, what was it but our dawning realisation of whom he really was?

*

2.12   The Other Mary

It is our last morning. I have taken John Mark to my secret place, the one point among the rocks at the top of the village where you can look out across the valley and up towards the mountain peak. There they are as always, the three peaks: the great majestic mountain in the middle, serene and ineffable; the two smaller ones to either side.

He sees at once what we are looking at: "You have kept the faith then, Magdalene?"

There is no need to answer this. Since I came here, I have been my own church: a church of solitude and tears and sunlight. I have kept the faith as best I could. I was healed back into an unconditional love and that was my unalterable fact, my own core miracle. The demons could not live with me again after that.

I am worthless, I told Yeshua all those years ago. *God would not spare me a single glance.*

Your name, he said, *is Magdiy'el. Mary Magdiy'el.*

But what does it mean?

It means: She who is precious to God.[cclxxiv]

He had harrowed the hell inside me. The demons had gone. The light came flooding in.

*

"I have one final question of my own," I tell John Mark, "that I want you to answer. It's about Mary. *The other Mary.* What happened to her?"

"By the 'other Mary', you mean his mother, I think, not Mary Salome, her daughter?

I nod.

The mother became our responsibility for a while, mine especially! I had no real family of my own; most of the men in the group had, by this time, and besides, she had taken a liking to me. She found me well-spoken; respectable. *A nice boy!* Mary left Judaea and travelled with us for a while. First, to Alexandria which she already knew a little. The family had lived there for a while, many years before.[cclxxv] We had one of our first communities there and she settled well. I spend a year working with the Naassenes, they had a base there, too and I learnt a lot from my time with them, though I could never be as unworldly as they are. Then Rome. Mary died there. Afterwards, after my disastrous travels with Paul, I came to Ephesus and started working with John.

222

"Like you, Mary needed time to recover, some peace away from the family. Mary Salome kept the younger children with her; she and Cleopas were good parents and the older Mary was not particularly fond of her youngest ones. There was a cult growing about her, you see! Then, towards the end of her life, we went back to Rome and she became the leader of our house church for a time. Quite the grand lady, in a restrained, formidable sort of way!

"Though she disapproved of their goddesses, Mary liked Rome, it suited her, gave her status. Her son was no longer a provincial rabbi, executed as a criminal; he had arrived now, was gaining cult even in the imperial city. She died there, peaceably enough, shortly after Peter's escape from prison."

Then he takes my breath away again: "Don't be too hard on Peter, Magdalene. He had his faults, God knows, but he was not a schemer. It was not he but she who influenced the others, she who made the arrangements for your departure. We thought her motives were good at the time; she spoke of 'protecting' you. But she had her own jealousies to deal with. I have come to the conclusion she never accepted you as her son's choice. She persuaded Luke of this. She persuaded Peter too, not that it was very difficult. John knows the truth though and he will tell it, I promise you. For him, you are the Mary who matters most, the one who gave birth to our Lord's risen life. You still have power to shed light on that life, if only you could see your way to it."

But I cannot deal with this. My heart stops when he tells me. I know immediately that what he has said is true. Mary. She was the one.

I need to be alone before I can think about this. I shovel her name up like a scorpion, something to deal with later. I call up white space to empty my mind, promise myself time to reflect on it when John Mark has gone.

We kneel together and say our prayers towards the mountain. There is sunlight across the slopes, every shade of green transforming the view again after the colourless shades of winter. A distant breeze commands a party of light clouds; they assemble and mass across the peak, gradually obscuring it from view. We see an eagle rise above them for a moment, then pass out of sight. Something has vanished from us. It is time to go.

"Goodbye, Magdalene. And I'll send word, when it is finished. Also, Paul's letters. I have left you some copies. I'll send more as and when I can." He kisses my fingers briefly. "I will never forget you, Mary Magdalene. I hope I will see you again."

I watch him start to walk away. Tears well up in my heart, my eyes blur. He has become a mirage, wavering in the watery air. As if I had called out, as if he had suddenly heard me cry, he stops, turns around, walks quickly towards me again.

"Bless me, Magdalene!" he says. "Put your arms round me and give me your blessing. Just once. Before I go."

I hug him. He kisses my face, my forehead, my hair. He kisses me over and over again. Our hands shake as our fingers join. It is as if our touching will never come to an end.

223

Now that he has gone, my visitor from the past, my solitude has changed. The silence seems emptier; it makes me feel restless and uneasy. I had stopped waiting and wanting. Now something stirs inside me again, some desire for life and action struggling to find form.

Now that I have nothing to distract me, my old illness troubles me again. I do not want to turn into one of those old pythonesses, bubbles frothing from her mouth, hot liquid pouring up from her lungs, dribbling helplessly through her lips. It was, as Felix would have said, very unsightly. And I do not want to be seen like that.

There were times when it could be hidden, times when it could not. I don't know how much John Mark saw. How much he guessed.

This wrong inside me: why can't I identify the cause, find some way of setting it to rights? There is a poison in my lungs: vestiges of some old demon perhaps that I cannot rid myself of. It keeps me quiet at least. Instead of words, this foaming flux of watery nothingness.

There are times when I think I have left it behind; then it repossesses me again.

When I hear that it was Mary who had sent me away, the poison stirs in me with a vengeance; I begin to cough. I cough all through that first night after John Mark's departure. Pons arrives, kind and curious, bringing lemons and nutmeg and thick, sweet local honey. I drink what he gives me; then surrender myself to the fever.

In my lucid intervals, I try to understand why she might have done what she did. What were her motives? Was it jealousy? The ordinary jealousy a mother feels towards a rival for her oldest son's affection? Was it the wish that she alone should determine his being? Did she consider me a blot on his reputation? Each suggestion agitates my mind unbearably. Anger and anguish wrestle inside me until dawn. I vomit out a thick yellow poison and lie with my face to the cold rock of the cave floor.

*

Despite this setback, I sleep for an hour or two, then wake and drag myself to the light. I have so much beside this illness to think over in what John Mark has told me. My mind is busy filling in the details, the gaps in what he did and didn't say. He knows almost too much of what happened in that extraordinary week when the death of our leader shifted the shape of our world and all our identities with it; but John Mark's memory is faithful to the movement. Unlike me, he is happier to tell the story, than to have his own story told. His loyalty is to Peter, Peter first, and then to John. What concerns him most is the quality of his writing.

John Mark's loyalty to Peter disturbs me. Although it is John's account he is writing now, his vision is multiple; he sees what he writes through at least two pairs of eyes, and one pair, I am sure, still belongs to Peter. Peter himself was direct and outspoken; he was never a writer. He would need someone else, a ghost, as they say, to give life to his memories.

I sit down, exhausted, an old woman again, unequal to such excitements. My tiredness this week, since Marcus left, is phenomenal. I try to understand it, as I try to understand everything these days. It is like losing a pair of wings. The rush of sensation, the intensity of my thoughts, has come to a stop; I drop to earth but still feel the flight path pulsing through my blood. I felt like this for days when I disembarked in Massalia, the motion of the boat still churning in my feet. Now it is the giddiness of the earth I feel, dropped down again into the seclusion of Mèthamis, on this foothill of the great mountain, where time is as solid as the rock face with the wind bouncing off it; leaden as an empty tomb.

And yet I have begun to dream again, to dream incessantly, great scripts of dream material, too much to process. I could write down my dreams, one at a time and store the parchments away in a jar somewhere. A *jarre*. A *jarriere,* the great pot they use to store food and oil over here. Peter has already written his story, and Matthew too: first, the important ones, and then this suave young doctor who travelled with Paul, the new convert they never entirely came to trust. Now, at last, before it is too late, John, John the survivor! As I put these pieces of information together, there is still something missing, always something I cannot quite comprehend. While they have been busy with their gospel-writing, I have been maundering over my lost love. I realise, that in doing this, I have failed him in some way, failed to understand what he wanted me to become.

I wonder what John and his scribe will make of the oral testimony I have given them; how they will set it down. I trust John Mark at least and am glad that they need me for something. I am grateful for that.

That there have been controversies, unresolvable oppositions in the group, that much is obvious. There is uncertainty about what happened, ambiguity in how it should be told. There is a square, I draw it on the ground with a stick, and inside that there is a circle. The square stays still but the circle keeps turning.

This ambiguity: am I to be its sign in these new gospels? A woman speaks, a woman gives her testimony and it is already, almost by virtue of who she is, a cause for suspicion. What she says will never be accepted as the truth; no rational man, no real judge of realities, will fully believe her. Am I to be what John Mark called me: *Mary Magdalene, his sweet Mistress of Perhaps!*

Is it, I ask myself through a wave of nausea, some kind of strange joke, like the virginity of Yeshua's mother, they are now starting to debate? Mary thought it best not to be too much with her other children, to keep in line with Matthew Levi's account and that of Luke too. Both of them emphasise Mary's role at the beginning, diminish mine at the end.[cclxxvi] John the Baptist and I, we had much in common; we both gave way to another!

If Mary is the virgin mother, what does that make me: the harlot death, perhaps? Death who has had so many men but cannot keep hold of the one she wants? Yeshua is too powerful to be held by either love or death. He escapes her grasp; he escapes the controlling influence of her love, of death's demand on his body. *Once free of the tomb, death cannot touch him again.*

Mistrust overtakes me, as if we were racing together, self-mistrust – my enemy self – suddenly in the lead. It tells me first of all that my story does not matter; then, that it will be made to matter in the wrong way.

The sickness deepens. I wake up one morning wondering from some place far outside my mind if I really am the sign of the Christ's resurrection: the woman known as Magdalene with her tall story, both of them a little larger than life. The sort of story that women love to tell, of things not strictly, not literally true, but shaped by emotion, over-inflated by imagination: *supernatural*. The texture of a woman's truth: still soft and liquid with internality.

I wrestle with this while the fever rages in me and I still can't get it straight. Peter was unhappy with John Mark's ending; he tore it up. Then John sends him to look for me again, to hear first-hand the details of my account. The two together will tell a very different story to the one he composed with Peter. And yet, he said, the two accounts must be harmonised. Peter will become the leader while John will become what he always wanted to be: the Loved One, the Lord's favourite disciple. Peter will become the outer man, the one who organises their growing movement; John, on the other hand, will become the holder of the mysteries, the one who holds the secret of his inner circle, his esoteric teachings.

"You are the door between them," John Mark said, "the solution to their rivalry, the door that looks both ways, inward to the secret mysteries of the spirit and outwards to the human story they will tell the world. Sent away by one, embraced by the other! A cup: dirty on the outside perhaps, but clean within.[cclxxvii] Or at the very least, in the process of being cleaned."

On and on I go, fever asking the darkest questions as I toss restlessly beneath my fleece.

There was no body in the tomb. Either I had mistaken the grave, or someone had removed the body during the night. Either there was a secret passageway at the back of the tomb, or he had come out into the light and left of his own accord, with a little help from his tomb servants. There was no body in the tomb. Whether he was still walking about in it or it was buried somewhere else, it was his final vanishing trick. He was no longer Yeshua, no longer "Jesus of Nazareth" as they call him now. He was homeless and bodiless; a solitary guest in the world, anyone who needed his light could invite him in.

The body I saw was his body; but it was a body like no other, a body he was growing out of and would leave behind. A body both injured and at the same time untroubled by its injuries; emptied of passion, anger, or the wish for revenge. When he walked out of the tomb, he walked free of all our earlier interpretations.

It was that which made him hard to recognise, created a new version of the man we thought we had known.

And yet I did know him!

These dark rememberings, they come from my fear than in speaking out, I have disobeyed him, broken his final command. *Tell no one of this!* I have reached out my hand: I have touched his presence.

I hope you are ready this time, I say to him, sobbing through my prayers. *I hope we both are!*

*

When we suffer for the sake of the truth, we shall be raised. It is the suffering itself that frees the soul from what it was trapped in; it is that freeing which enables us to rise above what we were before. Birth pangs, growing pains. Sometimes there is no other way.

*

Next morning, I wake, refreshed and cool and peaceful again. The agitation of the fever has left me. I reach below my bed and, without any fore thought, draw out what is hidden there. My jar of precious ointment, empty now, still cracked at the neck where Martha mended it for me but the very same jar. I thought I had lost it, but I have it with me still!

Whatever it signifies, my heart, my tears, my visionary ointment, even the well-earned money I bought it with, this is my gift to his church. I'm sorry it cost us all so much.

*

I stand tonight and watch the sunset over the great mountain, drinking in once more the three-peaked view that has been my only idea of his church.

Mulling again over my conversations with John Mark, I know that I have come to understand it all much better than I did. The great peak at the point of the triangle, the one that never varies; but the two smaller ones below it, they vary more. They change all the time. Sometimes I see the two thieves, sinful men suffering a punishment more terrible than their crimes. Sometimes I see Mother Mary standing there with John, her heart pierced with a sword. Sometimes I see John Mark and myself, our faces turned upwards to his own, trying to catch his spirit with our eyes.

Tonight I see another triangle; the one Yeshua told me of himself; in this, the Baptist takes the place of John Mark. I stand to the other side, holding my jar like a miniature well[cclxxviii] in both hands.

These are the triangles of love that carry his vision forward.

*

It is time to go back to the world now. I can't hide here any longer, a hermit soul lifted up by the angel light of this beautiful land. Perhaps it is simply my time to die. I have told my story. What else is there left for me to do?

*

Part 3
The Time of the Magdalene

Jesus replied, "Very truly I tell you, no one can see the kingdom of God unless they are born again."

"How can someone be born when they are old? Nicodemus asked. "Surely they cannot enter a second time into their mother's womb to be born!"

Jesus answered, "Very truly I tell you, no one can enter the kingdom of God unless they are born of water and the Spirit. Flesh gives birth to flesh, but the Spirit gives birth to spirit."

—John 3: 3-6

"Mary Magdalene…Mother of the Resurrection."
—St Peter Chrysologus, Sermons on the Resurrection, 33 -37

"Love heals us of the multitude of our wanderings. "[cclxxix]
—The Gospel of Philip

*

3.1   Finding Sarah

Sarah was a princess in her own land. Both of us agree about that. We found each other almost by chance though I like to believe that Joseph sent her to me, as a comforter and a companion. Someone as foreign as myself, a friend to talk to! A paraclete of my own.

Joseph, who was, I have learnt, responsible for so much. *My Joseph*, as I like to think of him now, back in that other life.

*

It is not just Sarah who has made me happy.

John Mark has kept his word. He has had Paul's letters copied for me. The strangest thing is, now I have read them, I can't remember what my thoughts were before I had. Paul's words have so entered my mind they seem to be the very stuff of it. It's like looking in a mirror, seeing a face I recognise as my own. I am no longer alone in a desert, but part of a habitable land. There are other people here.

And Paul is right! Resurrection is not given us for the sake of the dead; it is given for the sake of the living. The teacher said this to us once, though I can't remember when.[cclxxx]

John Mark has sent me two of Paul's letters and with them, one that he has written himself. Everyone, it seems, is writing and sending letters now, replacing our slip-shod memories with written words. He has written about our meetings, our long talks in hidden places looking out towards the mountain. I read his words over and over again. Hearing these things, that too is like coming alive again. I even feel there might be some improvement in my throat and lungs. Today, I caught myself singing. A piece of thick yellow phlegm suddenly swam up into my mouth. A piece of bad memory, perhaps, finally loosening its hold.

I think of what he told me about Peter and his description of female beauty, how it is not to be found in external features but in that gentle and quiet spirit he never found in me. It became almost a joke between us, when I started to talk too much, to get over-excited or upset: John Mark would remind me of this saying. It sums up the way Peter liked women to be. With Yeshua, it was different.

Yeshua liked the way we dared to speak out, that curious courage some women have. And he could hear our voices too, their pitch and lilt which most men can't, or pretend to be deaf to; he could see at once where we were coming from. Women challenged and trusted him just as I did; they felt they could speak their minds. He had what Peter himself lacked, a spirit that was centred, poised and alert, folded inwards but always ready to respond, his attention exact to the point.

Now I have read the letters, I remember things differently. I start to remember different things.

What is more, I have been on a journey, the longest journey I have made since I came here, nearly forty years ago. I have been to the place they call *Necromane, the place of sacred remains.*[cclxxxi] I caught the wagon that goes each week to Beaucaire, then went on across country by foot. I first heard of this place in the forum at Veisoun: I heard of it as place very ancient and very sacred. People of renown often wanted to be buried there; it is so high, so close to heaven. But that wasn't why I went; it was because Marcus mentioned someone who had worked with Paul, a Syrian called Trophimus, a man he met when he went to make contact with the small group of fellow believers who have their base there.

Trophimus is their leader and John Mark thinks highly of him. He has told me what I should look out for if, as he recommends, I go there myself. It is just off one of the coastal routes, quite a centre of activity and trade, and with the merchants come the tales, exotic, full of that magical exchange that is the core of their profession. There are cloth workers who make that journey too, people whose language I have always been familiar with.

It is time to go now, I thought as soon as I finished reading.

And so, I made the journey and it was both exciting and straightforward, as if another door had just swung open and I could step through it at last. There were no obstacles, no corpses on the threshold. I wanted to meet this man who knew all about Paul and how he had transformed the people he worked with in different lands, building a church in his footsteps. He fascinates me, this Paul, he writes at times like an angel; you can feel yourself drawn up towards heaven when you read. He writes of the End-time with the clarity of a great conviction.

"Freres, nous ne voulons pas vous laisser dans l'ignorance au sujet de ceux qui se sont endormis dans la mort; it ne faut pas que vous soyez abattus comme les autres, qui n'ont pas d'esperance. Jesus, nous le croyons, est mort et ressuscite...Au signal donne par la voix de l'archange, et par la trompette divine, le Seigneur lui-meme descendra du ciel, et ceux qui sont morts dans le Christ ressusciteront d'abord...Ainsi, nous serons pour toujours avec le Seigneur." cclxxxii

I find it hard to believe that Paul is dead; his writing has such vitality, such presence: his whole mind active and alive in the words.

John Mark found him difficult. Like Peter and John, he retains a certain distrust of Paul. He loved Barnabas though, sweet-tempered, a born follower, an embodiment of all the qualities that Paul writes about but did not possess himself: that gentle, unassertive wisdom that stays in the mind, especially after a quarrel when the anger starts to drain away and calm reflection settles in its place. I wonder if he is still alive and if we would still recognise each other?

I reflect endlessly on these names, these people and the oppositions between them: trying to form a picture of the new churches that are being set up and nurtured by the apostles. What wonderful work! Paul's experience of the risen Christ set him free from the darkness in his mind; it took him out into the world, to teach what he had learnt.

For me, it was the opposite. Experience thrust me back into myself, back into my guilt, the guilt of my first marriage especially. I could never entirely cleanse myself from that. The dirt stuck with me. It left me high and dry in these mountains, as far from the outer world as I could get.

Now that I have left that place, now that I have told my story, I am free to travel at last.

When I arrived at *Necromane*, I stayed there for a week, first of all just doing what the others there were doing, about forty of us in all. It took me several attempts to find the entrance to the place: it is hidden high in a steep wood and the walk is through a grove that rises all the time, the path turning this way and that.cclxxxiii When I finally got to the top, to the entrance gate, I was so unprepared I had to go back to the bottom again and decide what it was I wanted to say.

What I wanted most was to speak to Trophimus, that was my one idea: John Mark thought I could tell him the truth about who I was, but the thought of this made me anxious again. Mistrust is never far away. What if he were not the kind of man who would welcome me or want me in his fold? Would it not be better to look around and see if there was anyone else who might be more accessible? Someone I felt safe with?

And that is where I met Sarah. She was waiting there like a servant, helping with the visitors, looking after the group. I noticed her at once, her beautiful Egyptian profile, the great liquid eyes, her timid, nervous glance. She looked at everyone, uncertain, her gaze always dimming away to one side.

I had introduced myself as someone who had once known the lands they were speaking about; said I had been present occasionally, even been a witness to some of the miraculous events, but that I had lived a long time now in a land of strangers and had never spoken to anyone of what I had seen.

I had come, I said, because I had read some of Paul's letters and now wanted to speak; to share my thoughts, to listen and learn from someone who might understood more than I, and to hear more of what had been written since I left. I showed them the food and gifts I had brought, explained that I was not in want but was willing to help serve those who were. They took me in and showed me where I might sit and wait until the services were over. Where I might speak to Trophimus when his daily work was finished.

The place is a great house made of natural rock, a vast, decorated cave with many levels to it, always rising to the very top of the hill on which it stands. From there it looks across to another hill close by and then again out across a great passage of water that leads north to Avenia[cclxxxiv]. It can be seen for miles from the sea but is hidden in woodland from the north. The Romans know of it, of course, and once made it a shrine for travellers, dedicated to my old friend, the goddess of the moon; it still has her woods and water and sacred burial spots. Rightly or wrongly, I found this a comforting detail. The intimate, familiar talk of other women, even my sister on neutral days, had always been one of the things I missed most when I left my native land. The talk of other women is a nourishing thing, even if it contains a little venom at times.

I knew at once when I saw Sarah's hasty, half-anxious glance that she was looking for someone. At first it did not occur to me that this could be me. She came to where I sat, bringing water for the visitors and spoke haltingly in the language of the land. I replied in Aramaic, then added a few phrases in her own tongue.

"I have been here a very long time," she told me. "Though I come from far away."

"Me too. A very long time. But still, I miss the land I knew."

"I look for a lady," she said. "I look for her a very long time. But the lord, my teacher, tells me she will come. He will bring her here. I am to give her help. There is work we must do. When I find her."

"And the goddess?" I gesture across at the hilltop shrine opposite. We are standing on our own by this time, moving unconsciously up through the chambers of the cave and out into the eternal sunshine.

"She is like her, yes, but not the same. She takes the second place."

"Did you know your teacher well?"

"Once, as a very small child. He took me in his arms. I was child of a slave girl. But she had been a princess before that."

"She was freed?"

"She died. I look after the donkeys."

"And your name?"

"My name is Sarah now. My mother gave me a different name but I have forgotten it."

"How did you get here, Sarah?"

"I came in a boat."

"Yes, I came that way too. Did someone send you?"

"Yes, a wealthy man, a friend of my lord. He paid my passage. Said I must come here and find my lady. But then it is not easy. I have a child then."

She looks at me, curiously passive, waiting my judgment.

"A child?" I query. "And where is it now?"

"Freed," she says. "Now I work here. Wait 'til my lady comes."

I take hold of her hands.

I have been told Sarah is not just a maid but a nurse too. She works in their little hospital. She can heal people sometimes just by touching them, by the power of her smile. But only, it seems, if they are foreigners, people without a language to help them recover.

When I look at her again, I realise she is much older than I thought.

*

Trophimus arrives here on the third night. I decide I can speak to him; some of Sarah's faith has given me a new confidence.

"I knew the teacher. I knew Peter; I knew John and James and Philip and Andrew. And I knew Nathaniel too, until he left and went back to Lebanon for a while. I knew Barnabas too. And our Lord's mother! I have been a recluse but recently…" and then I tell him the story of John Mark's visit.

At once, he confirms what I already know. John Mark is more than a scribe, he is a writer; he has written an account, has had access to those closest to the events and collected their testimonies. Now he travels round the new churches; he even travelled with Paul on one of his journeys, until Paul decided to choose his own historian! Trophimus is a calm man, he has a narrow, fine-lined face and far-seeing eyes. He understands at once.

"For a woman," he says, "it is not always easy, to find the right path. You say your name is Sophia. Do you have the wisdom of that name? Can you read and write?"

"Both," I say, "and I have learnt a new wisdom too, one that can be silent, long-suffering; kind."

"So you have you read them?" he asks. "The famous letters?"

"A few," I say. "I want to read all of them, of course. That is partly why I have come."

"You know that he is dead now, the man who wrote them, that he was executed, at the order of that madman who was their emperor? Nero was an evil man, his soul damned to all eternity. Paul had the words of eternal life but still

233

he was murdered, martyred for the Lord. He shared his fate. There is danger for you too," he adds. "For anyone who is recognised."

"I know that. It is of no consequence."

He nods his head: "You have come for Sarah?" he says.

"Yes."

"You have left it late. But there is still much work to be done. If you agree, we will talk of this again, before you leave us. It is good that you came."

Later he tells me of a secret gathering, up in the hills a long way to the north of where I live. He asks if I will come, sounds even as if it is important that I do and that it matters to him to have me there. He will give me directions, details. If I agree, he will ask me something in return. The joy in my heart is sharp and sudden as a pain, emotions frozen to stone now summoned back into life. I can feel again. It is an act of extreme daring, like waking up in the wild. Being wanted, being included. And the power it gives, this small act of recognition. When I thought I had vanished forever, suddenly here I am.

"Sophia," he says with a slight smile. "It is a good name for you."

*

3.2 Good Things Come to Me

Having Sarah with me has made a great difference. She is to stay three months; then I have to send her back. She has work of her own now that she must accomplish. The more we talk together, the more I see the deep wisdom that lies inside her. She draws on it as if it were second nature, trusts her instincts more easily than I.

Before she came here, my world was a dialogue with dreams. Dreams that gripped and puzzled me as if they were asking something of me which I struggled to understand. I dreamt that as I lay sleeping Yeshua was there just beyond the wall, just outside the window. He had risen again but in a different form. He was there as someone who sang a song unlike any other; once as a vortex of living light, a whorl of spiritual energy that rose much higher than any human height, an immense spinning flame that made other people seem pale and insignificant in comparison. These dreams were like a summons I wanted to obey but hardly knew how. They spoke in a language of intensity I seemed to have forgotten as if I too had dwindled and become small and insignificant.

Now I have Sarah to talk to, though it must be said I take almost as much pleasure from simply watching her face, her grave, full, heavy lidded eyes, like a coloured carving. There is a bond between us that neither of us feels any need to question. We talk freely of our lives, as if trust, or mistrust, was simply not an issue between us. Our experience of loss is one of the things that binds us together but she does not live through her losses. She sees through them instead.

She talks of her child, her son, lost almost before he was born, dying as she struggled to give birth. Most of the money Joseph had given her had been stolen on the voyage and there was no one to help her. She blames herself for her own ignorance, her own carelessness, her self-abandonment on board that desperate ship. It was the way she had secured her passage, though she knew it had been the wrong way. She had become a Christian just a year before they set sail and she felt she had injured her faith, become unworthy of it, in doing what she did. The captain convinced her that she was a masthead and would bring good fortune to the voyage. She went into labour two months before term and the little still-born corpse was dropped overboard while she slept.

"I make the sign of the cross," she said," but it is not the same on the water. There the cross is like an anchor; it only stays at the very bottom of the sea."

Her story stirs memories and I tell her something of my own history; my struggle to learn some ways of controlling that process so blessed and so bitter for women; the herbs and drugs I experimented with in my youth, the one disastrous miscarriage that left me infertile.

Sarah nods as she listens. "Gifts," she says, thoughtful and judicious. "From the unborn. So generous, so full of love, they give themselves to us as gifts sometimes. Instead of life's troubles."

It had taken her a long time, she says, a very long time to come to terms with her loss but she had been helped by the certain knowledge that the soul of the child was not angry with her, it had forgiven her for not saving its life. For a long time, the child's spirit had been a presence with her: a kind of foresight, or foreknowing would take hold of her and she would know each evening as if it were already past what was to happen the following day. She could tell the future. Unborn, unnamed, the little spirit was still attached to her, filling her with terrible love and terrible anxiety and a strange gift of hearing and healing at a distance. Her thoughts had agency and active power. They came to her from his little lost spirit.

Though Sarah's own life had become a perilous journey, she knew there was something that looked out for her, though she feared at times that it might be a demonic being, and that her own soul would pay the price. We both knew this experience. But after she arrived at the sanctuary and found a place there, the spirit began to come to her in a different way, through the services they held; the Lord's Supper especially. When she attended that supper, the spirit would come to her with long silver-violet fingers and it would touch her and make a different kind of contact. It helped her with her healing, the touch of those long, cold, shining spirit hands, though they came less often now.

She had not told anyone this part of her story for fear they would judge her a murderess but she said I should not blame her or reject her because it was the child spirit that had brought her fully to the Christ. It was that which had secured her faith, and made it grow strong. Without it, she might have let go her newfound belief but now she knew that would never happen. Now that she had found me, she thought the little spirit was happier, though still not free to fully enter the holy realm.

"Does it have a name, your spirit child?"

"No name. I dare not give one."

I suggest she think of a name for it now and the one she chose was *Valentin, Valentin Esprit*. Perhaps the spirit liked the name because afterwards it seemed to vanish and Sarah said that must mean it would soon be time for her to find her own people at last. She had a complete and serene faith that life would direct her to this end: that all she need do was watch and obey. Such wise passivity I could only admire. She would travel with her people, she said, be as the captain had called her, a figurehead, only she hoped it would be for a horse and caravan this time and not for a ship. She disliked the sea. She wanted, she said, to belong to the gypsies, the people of the earth. She saw me as like them, a wise woman who had run away from her home, as old as time and as free as the wind, someone who belonged nowhere and had no welcome from other people.

*

3.3   Hair

But that too was changing. The way I thought about my past, the little anecdotes I confided in her, the sheer pleasure of intimate human company, all of this made me think of my past in a different, more vital way. Something good had come to live in the lonely absence that had been my life. The strange illness I had had for so long had shown me that something was damaged inside; I had lost the strength I used to be able to call upon when healing was needed. The damage was deep: I could neither cure myself nor find any other source of healing. Despite this, goodness had reached me again, like the sound of familiar voices, hearing one's own native tongue.

I want to be able to say this goodness had brought my health back too, but that was not the case. I was as sick as ever. Even Sarah could not help. I had learnt at best a way of managing the condition. I hid its unsightliness from others, the horrible frothing at my lips; the turbulence in my throat and my chest. I lived a life of incessant water; water not air was what I seemed to breathe. Over and over again, my lung would fill with liquid as if there were a sea storm inside me and then the liquid would gush out of my mouth, sometimes a burning liquid that ate at my mouth and left my lips red raw and bleeding, a rawness that spread across my chin like a horrible rash. Day by day the cycle repeated itself, the liquid rising and gathering in my chest then bubbling out of me in unsightly streams of froth and phlegm. For years I waited for death to be the result but still it continued, the turbulent liquid effusion whose daily rise and fall governed my life.

And then one morning of exceptional clarity, I studied the frothy liquid I spat out onto a stone basin and saw for the first time that there were tangled lengths of hair and coloured fibre mixed with the phlegm in the bubbling liquid that spilt from my mouth. For four years, this mysterious hair-like fibre continued to appear and with it a black substance I could not identify. To me it looked like evil itself.

Though I had no idea of how it had got inside me, the phantom hair was a kind of memory. I did not need reminding of how vain I had been about my own; that was something I had never forgotten. But this was not my own hair: it was different in texture, different in colour. This difference was the sign of horror, as if I had some ghost or demonic being trapped forever inside me. Some demon still unexorcised. How could this have happened?

Once I had learnt from John Mark that it was Mary who had been the cause of my leaving Judaea, I became uneasily preoccupied with the idea that the hair was in some mysterious way hers. The other Mary, the one who haunted me now: the thought of her filled me with a dread mixed with loathing. She too had beautiful hair, black hair much darker and thicker than mine, and she had the gift to wear it in proud and unusual ways that set her apart from other women, just as her dignity and self-possession had done. I came to realise there were other similarities between us too, things that half explained why I had become so close to her son.

Sarah had a touch of this too, a sexual wildness set against a degree of self-control that made it seem dangerous, a weapon she might use. Mary's past was ambiguous and unorthodox. Everybody knew the man she had lived with was not the only one she had belonged to. You would have called her a loose woman if you had dared but her hair made her regal, even when silver white she wore it as a kind of advocate in her own defence, a justification for anything she may have done. When it came to womanhood, Mary was a professional.

Yeshua equated that wealth of hair with extravagant love. I knew that early and, as women do, I knew how to do things with my own that would draw his eyes, perhaps even his heart. Though I had never greatly liked Mary, we had that in common, she and I. To my astonishment, Yeshua was entirely untroubled by my past; he made no judgment upon me and I may have had her example to thank for that. He understood that my life was how I was, just as I understood that about him. He was not, in any case, looking for a wife in the ordinary senses of the word. And perhaps it was useful, being associated with a woman like myself, to whom no assurance of an ordinary future needed be made. I was a reproach to his mother, perhaps; a reproach she in turn could never turn against me. He had the unanswerable response!

Despite this, I saw her as my opposite: cold, proud and ambitious. A woman who knew, right from the start, the sacrifice that would be demanded of her son, one that would nail him from birth to a great but terrible destiny. She was proud that she had been chosen for this: proud too that she outranked her cousin, Elizabeth, just as her own son would be infinitely greater than John.

I think of Judas, how each of us was chosen for a particular role, a set path or task. Mary always referred to me as 'the Magdalene', and I knew she was referring not to her son's name for me but to the Galilean town where my grandfather had one of his bakeries.[cclxxxv] There was a great synagogue there and, partly because of this, it had a bad reputation for loose women. Like Jerusalem, it was headed for disaster. Barabbas's mother lived there. I knew the place, had stayed there sometimes but it was never my home. It became my nickname, partly ironic just as Peter's was, and everybody called me by it.

I might have been proud once; I do not doubt that I was. Now this terrible nemesis has taken possession of me. Like my capacity for love and truth and deception, for angels and demons, the hair was all inside me, my lungs were full of it. No one could explain this to me and I could not explain it to myself, except by the obvious explanation, that the hair was the sign and consequence of my sinful past. Or was it perhaps an expiation for that, the slow cleansing of a dead demon? Was I responsible for my own illness? Or was it an accident, random and without meaning?

Sometimes I think it must have come from the sacking in the death cart that took me away from Judaea and into Ceasarea; the loose hair and clothing of some dead woman I was lying close to and had inhaled on that terrifying journey that brought me to Massalia. Sometimes, I think of Judas and how I spat at him like a serpent.

I'd love to say that I had cut off all my own hair as an act of penitence and mourning but I was not capable of that kind of heroism. I had it still, both outside and in! A poisonous irritation in my lungs that nothing seemed finally to expel; hair mixed with fibres from the beautiful fabrics that had always been my passion.

*

Only one thing helped me: the practice of silent prayer. I had always been able to find that silence within me, a place that belonged entirely to me, and served me in good stead once I had settled here. It served me in place of many other things I might have thought I needed but in actuality did not.

They say that the best place to meet God is in a cave and I have found this true.

Within my cave, I could go deeper still, deeper into the hidden, invisible places where another kind of life came into being. One of the first things I heard when I began to make that retreat was the sound of a woman's voice screaming, screaming in the night like an angry child crying to attract attention. To make someone come!

I did not believe the crying was my own but it could have been. The crying seemed to be that of some unhappy spirit, some other Mary perhaps. It disturbed me deeply. Like my dreams, this strange, haunting experience made a demand on me, seemed to ask me for something I did not know how to give. I wanted to respond and yet at the same time I did not altogether trust it, did not feel safe opening myself to its distress. Spirits of this sort are dangerous to deal with: I knew that for certain now.

Every day I would enter as deeply as I could into the darkness and silence in the depth of my cave. Sometimes I did not eat for days. Then one day, or one night it may have been, he came to me. He was there when I entered the cave and my heart gave a sudden start of fright. It was as if some rare and beautiful bird had entered my domain and any movement I made might scare it away.

I simply stood there and looked. He had come to me not as on that first occasion in his wounded, almost unrecognisable body but entirely healed as if he had recreated himself from some perfect prototype that had become his own. If I could paint I would have filled the walls of the cave with that vivid likeness so that I could see it always. It shone by its own light, radiating an intense glow I wanted to capture before it slowly faded away. It seemed to me the figure raised one hand and held it out to me in greeting, then faded away and vanished altogether.

*

I told no one, not even Sarah, about this, though she knew of my sickness and had done her best, *summoned her best angels*, she said, to try and heal me. I certainly did not tell John Mark. It is not just the light that figure conveyed but an instant emotional power. I fill with tears when I contemplate it and the outlines shimmer and dance in liquid light. I am goddess of a strange underworld when this happens, my cave a birth pool of water and the spirit!

After a while, I limed the walls with white lime and tried to shape some semblance of what I had seen. It came to me that if I could draw my own figure on these walls, there would be no absence at all any longer. The two images would always be together, a part of each other, in a marriage sweet and magical beyond telling. I remember how the prisoners in the quarry used to carve out likenesses of those they wanted to remember, their own likenesses too sometimes, to keep a vestige of their former selves alive.

Sometimes, recently I have begun to sit here and take bread and wine, as he told us to do, as a way of remembering him. It brings me sustenance, a brief shot of wellbeing and intoxication. Sarah and I take turns with the service.

There is a reason why I do this: I have been invited to a gathering. Trophimus has, as he promised, sent me a message, giving me directions to the large secret assembly that is being held in the wild hills to the north. Those who come will gather together in prayers and practice the same ritual of remembrance. The *Eucharist,* he calls it, the *thanksgiving.*

"Will I," he asks me, "be one who serves the cup?"

Sweetness floods my mind and heart. After being so long an exile and outcast, I have at last been invited, included, asked to participate. He wants me to hold the cup, hold forward the offering of the wine. The images on my cave wall shall be coloured wine-red to mark the event!

The thought of this is pure poetry: like a slow and beautiful bell tolling gently and distantly in the honeyed lemon sunshine. The chime has three notes, then four and finally five, each one fainter and gentler than the last, then the sequence begins all over again, five sweet notes that soften into the distance, delicate and precise, like a voice quietly speaking, quietly repeating the same few words, between each one a light, lingering pause. Something in my breathing starts to heal as I listen. I have told him I will come.

*

And then I remember something I have completely forgotten; forgotten so completely I can hardly believe it is still there. I remember the dress. Hidden

239

away at the back of my cave-house, never worn, never even looked at. My part of the sacrifice! Heart in mouth, almost sick with this strange recovery of lost time and worried the fabric will have rotted away in the dark and damp, I start to look for it.

The soft silvery green of the fabric, the colour of young wheat with tiny clusters of purple violets pricked out on the bodice and sleeve. I unfold it in astonishment, that after so many years of neglect and burial, the fabric is still intact.

I stroke the soft velvet of the dress; I shall wear it when I go. I wish there was someone I could leave it to when I die. Someone who would appreciate the beauty of the material, the delicacy of the design; but there is no one. I shall keep it as long as I stay here. Then I will leave it in a place I have chosen for some unknown woman to discover.

*

"You learn to love again," Sarah said, our last evening together. "We three women are same woman when our losses are counted. She gave her son to the cross and become a great lady after. I lose my son to the waters; I become black Madonna who knows the secrets. You lose everything and become world's invisible treasure. It is a great gift, my lady. So many little pieces to your heart! Each little piece we find, we make a new picture of you. But you must keep back for yourself a bit of this treasure.

"When your heart smile, He knows where to find you. He comes back in time for you then. You open the little door, here!" She points to the space between her eyebrows, the peak of the triangle. "After the Lord's supper, that is your time. He speak to you then. And we who did not know Him, you must teach us how. Then maybe He speak to us too."

*

3.4   The Chalice

It takes me days to get to the place and to my shame and annoyance I am ill again. I set off walking slowly for the horrible froth that keeps gathering in my mouth. But as I get closer to the wild remote land where the secret gathering is to be held, I feel so alive, so excited that the condition recedes. I could almost believe, though I know it is not true, that I am growing well again.

The place itself, so secret, so gathered into the inward curve of the landscape, is wonderful to discover. This is wild country, it's strange, inaccessible mountains a law unto themselves. In the end a long, winding, slowly descending track leads to an opening, where there are signs of cultivation, a couple of fields tended for corn, the low roof of a barn, a homestead and suddenly I see small bands of people all walking in the same direction. We have a sign, one I recognise from many years ago, with which we identify ourselves, reassure each other that we are part of the same invisible community.

Then we begin to climb upwards again until we find ourselves in a vast circle of rocks shaped exactly like a Roman amphitheatre, except that there are trees growing everywhere, small scrub oaks and the sweet chestnut trees, the *châtaigniers*, that grow in such profusion and feed the people here, shading the rows of rocky grass which provide natural aisles and steps and seats for the people who are gathering here. [cclxxxvi]

If you did not know of it, you would never find this place. It has a dream-like actuality as if art and nature had exchanged tools to create it. Summer too seems to reach its destination here: it stops and stays in a magic circle of warmth and sweetness among rocks from which there is no onward track. Tales of Paradise might be realised here; a taste of happiness among these strangers, an overpowering sense of journey's end.

Dreamlike too is the feeling of fellowship that circulates among the crowd; there must be several hundred of us here. Trophimus, when I eventually find him, is visibly surprised. *It spreads like water*, he says, *more than we thought*. The Word travels along the waterways, an invisible presence, and people are drawn as if by some summons they have been waiting to receive.

They are all sorts of people here, not just those whose land it is but strangers, foreigners with different eyes and hair and skin, different clothing too, speaking in voices that sound soft and incomprehensible though the same message has brought them together. There are Jews here, several families of them, groups of merchants displaying wares; even some Romans, not many but standing in discreet groups, household leaders with a small band of slaves; there are workmen and women; solitary holy men and, to my astonishment, a band of young children who stand and sing softly together when their leader instructs them.

Apart from these children at whom I stare hungrily for their sweet faces, so different from the dusty waifs of the quarry, I do not look long at the people; indeed I avoid looking. Recognition could create danger. It is the whole gathering that astonishes me, peaceable, largely silent, communicating only with glances, smiles and the smallest of gestures. Last night food was shared among us; those who could pay did so, others simply accepted their share. There may be traitors here, spies and enemies but I cannot believe it. Whatever purpose has brought people here, it welcomes them, and no one will offend against its laws.

After Trophimus and two others have delivered their teaching, I stand with my chalice where he has directed me and, after the singing and a short service of remembrance, offer a drink to those who queue silently to receive it. Sometimes as I say the words, I find myself looking into eyes of a shape and colour I have never seen before. One woman who looks both young and old at the same time is staring at me intently as I hand her the cup. I wonder for a moment if this is truly a dream and that I am meeting some fetch of myself from a different time and place. She does not resemble me, her eyes are a dark and piercing blue where mine are amber brown, but she stares at the dress I am wearing, almost as if she could read its history. Suddenly, she smiles, nods her head slightly, says, "Yes, yes, I understand. I know who you are!"

Our eyes meet and suddenly I see myself, vividly pictured in her glance. She sees a woman with long loops of silver brown hair, caught up from her shoulders in a loose clasp. She looks intently into my face, studies its shape, the outline of my mouth, the large dark eyes that have my own expression in them. She has seen me as I am. My image has not been lost.

Though it is I who hold the cup, I feel as if I have received something too. For there I am, pictured in her glance, a person in the world, entirely visible, not the shadowy woman preoccupied by her own thoughts who has been my usual self. I still exist; am not, after all, a ghost from times long passed.

Later, when the communion is over and I seek my own place near the top level of the rugged amphitheatre, I hear a voice that whispers along its row:

"Look! It's the Magdalene! She has come. She's really here!"

Somebody knows my secret. John Mark, it seems, is not the most discreet of men!

*

There is singing later. The children are leading us, and we pick up the notes of the simple tune, our voices lifting from theirs and swelling with each tier of sound. People are still arriving, some struggling to manage the upward climb through uneven rocks. An old man in a rough, ragged brown cloak stumbles just below me and I stand up to catch his crooked arm and steady him. He sits down beside me for a moment to catch his breath, his profile gaunt and deeply furrowed with wrinkles, a glance of his grey eye catching mine.

Suddenly, as if in thanks, I feel him take my hand, his fingers moving along my wrist until mine make contact with his palm. They pass over the taut skin and a shock goes through me. I trace there the contours of an unmistakable wound, as if – my first thought is – he carries the scar of a terrible snakebite, the trap of a python's fangs in his hand.

His palm is twisted, the ridged flesh indented round a deep cavity where the bones of the hand seem broken. A hiss of breath, a slight pressure of his fingers and he is on his feet again climbing upwards to the higher level. I help him rise. He does not look back as he passes me, but hours go by before my heart beats quietly again, my breath returns to normal and I can stand up and walk.

*

Normal, I say, but nothing is normal now. A great wave of activity has brought me news and with it so much excitement and energy I can hardly keep my hands or my thoughts steady. There is news of the new gospel: it is beginning to circulate, a friend of Trophimus has heard of it. I might even get to read parts of what has been written so far and see what John Mark has made of what I told him and what, if anything, he has said of me. Perhaps this shouldn't matter to me but, in truth, it does!

While I am dizzied with excitement, my own life has acquired strength, become something written; something that can be recognised, greeted and known. *This is how it was;* it will say*, this is what happened. This is how I remember it. This is who I am!*

Three days have gone past and I have had no symptoms. The turbulence in my lungs, the watery flooding seems finally about to subside. Though the symptoms reoccur, I am grateful for the respite and resume the burden with more heart.

"Too much love, too many enemies", Sarah had said when she tried her healing. *"When you cannot keep them out, they make ghost doll inside you. You must do exorcism. That doll bad image, not what you are."*

Though I make my way back to my mountain retreat, I know I am changed by what has occurred. I can no longer ignore what is happening in the world around me. Like Sarah, I have become convinced that events are slowly gathering and taking shape, pushing and pulling our destinies in a certain direction, even if I do not know yet what that will be.

For myself there are choices too. Do I stay here in Mèthamis, in my no longer secret hideaway, do I complete my own writing and then…but here a void opens. To whom can I entrust it if I do? Who would read it? What chance does it have of being accepted along with the all other things that men are writing in memory of him?

Self-doubt conceals a deeper fear: If I am there in the writing, what judgment will be passed on me? Will my life bear fruit? Will the figs be ripe on it?

Or will I be shaken to the core, scorched and shrivelled by his wrath?

The judgment of a life! To be seen clearly through and through, to face that scrutiny, the soul itself examined for its worth: will it be found acceptable, will there be cause for rejoicing? I have tried not to hide my sins; I have kept them with me like a flock of goats for whom I am always responsible. They are the ones my conscience condemns me for: I see my path as *a via dolorosa* of stepping stones across a turbulent water.

*

"Do you want physical love, Magdalene?"

That question! The one I always found so hard to answer. Yes, I wanted it; the want at least was always in me, from childhood on. With him I wanted it most, because I loved him beyond knowing. The difference was, I was free to want him because with him that wanting went beyond the body. Like love, it went forward like an arrow and though he was its target, it did not lodge there, it did not stop but travelled onwards bound forever to the course on which he was set. It went with him, forward into all eternity for all I knew. It would not be stayed, ever.

In the end, a wise man once said, all one wants is that the beloved should still be alive.[cclxxxvii]

That is the only thing that really matters. There among the sweet chestnuts, in that strange assembly of strangers who had made the journey, I felt that arrow had found its mark.

This is the happiest land![cclxxxviii] I rejoice that I have come here. It is greater than that other one, that place of tragedy. My happiness is greater too, greater even than Venus, with her eternal laughter!

*

Epilogue
The Final Journey

Should I go back now? Back to Judea, back to Galilee, back to Samaria? Do I need to return, to see again the people I once knew, if any of those I can remember are still alive? Outside our group, the only one I really cared for was Philip, Philip who went to Samaria, as John Mark told me: I love to think he chose that for reason of our friendship. He was a great reader, Philip, and the purest friend.[cclxxxix]

I do not want to hear that he is dead; I hope that he remembered me sometimes when he prayed near Mount Gerizim. But forty years is too great a distance to travel. I cannot go back. Everything that has happened since then has happened there without me and I do not know what bridge I could find that could span the distance. Such reunions might work between two people, an old intimacy might be revived, but for a group such as ours who have passed their lives without seeing each other, only the way of the stranger remains. It is only through that strangeness now that we can meet him again or remember our fellowship.

For those who live in thought, the mind travels its own distance and memory obliterates the tracks, allowing only a few markers to remind us of the way we have come. I have become my own inner journey and this writing I have made is my map. I hope it shows a way worth travelling, a way of rediscovery.

As for my outer journey, I have come to love the land of my exile. It has been all along the companion of my thoughts and I hear in the chime of its bells that I belong here. There are paths I have walked, streams I have followed, rivers I have dreamed of; mountains for which I have invented names.

When nothing else did, it spoke to me and now its language has become my own.

I think of John, of John Mark and their new gospel, one that picks up everything that Mark, when he wrote with Peter, had already laid down. I am like that too, I think. I have picked up the old garment of my life and made a new one out of it, the same materials are there, but the design is different. Between the old and the new, something intervened: a judgment was cast. All those who brought Yeshua down, Pilate, Herod, Caphiais the High Priest, Judas the accountant, David's Jerusalem, one by one they have felt the judgment. They fell, each one in turn. Only He has been raised by his fall. And he goes on rising. I cling to his feet, to the hem of his robe and know that between us it is still a seamless garment.

Now I am stronger, I revisit the mysteries he taught us, the spiritual states he encouraged us to practice with him, the inner energies of transformation we all carried within us, the pure spirit we could become, the mysterious kingdom of heaven that could open inside us, the golden way of that garden, the love we could bring safe through every catastrophe.

Then I think of all that has happened wrong, the hurt and betrayal, the pride and anger; the cynical indifference, the dismal dismissing that seemed at times the best panacea for pain: none of this outweighs for a moment the happiness that now lives inside me. The misery recedes; my spirit is fertile again.

*

And so, without more anxiety, I set off to join Trophimus for a while. I hear news of Sarah who has travelled with two companions to a small community on the great marshland where the white horses and the black cult bulls are bred. [ccxc]I read more of Paul's letters to the new churches that are now being copied and circulated from Necromane and come to understand how John and Marcus want to create a new and esoteric gospel of spiritual birth to set beside Paul's theology.

*

"Do you believe in the resurrection?" It is Trophimus who is asking that. It is the question he always asks the seekers and half believers who make their way to him, drawn by the fame of the apostles which has spread quietly and far.

"What does it mean, the resurrection? We aren't sure what to make of it."

When they ask him that, Trophimus replies:
"Sit with the Magdalene. She is the one who brought Him back to us; the one who conceived the idea. She wants you to understand that. She prays for the wisdom to teach you what she knows. Stay here with us until you begin to see for yourself what she is telling you."

He calls it *'the moment of the Magdalene'*, this sitting time we share. After the bread and the wine, after the Lord's Supper, they come and sit with me. We sit in silence at first. We have received his body and blood, yet ours remains for a moment the silence of the tomb. We sit here in the dark, alone. Then the bell chimes, the silence changes, the darkness thins away. It is almost light. We have come to look for him; we find he is already there.

In that space while others are waiting their turn at the table, he is waiting for us. He is his risen self. Stay still, stay calm, feel the peace. Speak with him or listen if you wish. Simply be there. For everyone present, this is the moment when each one of us comes equally into His presence.

*

"You have seen him? You have read it to the end?"

I greet this Greek traveller like a soul out of paradise. He brings such welcome news!

"I heard some of it read, my lady. It isn't finished, you understand, not completely but he has the structure in place. Now, while it circulates, there will be discussions, controversies; amendments. That's the way it usually goes, but what John has told people is something different. *'Read it from the outside but understand it from within.'* It's causing a sensation in some of the churches!"

I am so happy, I can scarcely bring myself to ask: "And...how does it end, this new gospel?"

The Greek sighs and shrugs:

"It ends, lady, with the death of John. I am sorry to bring you sad news, but he was an old man, his health fragile, his eyesight gone. His death was peaceful, his great visionary work brought almost to completion. For us, it is a wonderful thing, this new gospel. And for you too, I believe."

"Yes? Really? How so?" The words fly out of my mouth like escaped canaries. I can't stop them.

"Not too Jewish, you know what I mean? The work has a strong Samaritan angle. There, I thought that would please you! Some say our Lord himself had leanings that way."

"Ah, yes! Indeed! Well, I'm extremely pleased to hear that."

"I thought so, thought so! John's scribe told me himself he was sure you, at least, would approve of what has been written. Not that he or John either had an entirely free hand. There has to be agreement with the other leaders before anything is finalised. But our church community, if I might say it, we think it is the best one, the very best gospel by far."

"Poor John, I am sorry to hear of his death. And...err...did he say anything else, this scribe you mention? John Mark, was it?"

"Now you mention it, yes he did! When I told him I was coming here and hoped to meet you, he said you of all people would like what he had done with the ending. The way it tells of the death of our Lord. He hoped you would pay it particular attention. The Lord's final words from the cross, they were so very beautiful."

"Oh yes, I'm sure. – As one would expect! And...how did he phrase it?"

"Our Lord thought only of his mother."[ccxci]

"What?"

"Yes, and such a truly loving gesture, at such a time, in such agony, for our Lord to show concern for her welfare. A truly *Christian* death*!"*

"Sorry. I must have misheard you. He said what?"

"It brings tears to my eyes when I think of it. Such true filial piety! Every man can understand that!"

There are so many forms of silence. This silence and I confront each other, like a door banging open in a wide and drafty corridor. The corridor is empty on either side; the door is my heart.

He said what? His last thoughts, his last words were for Mary! That John should take her into his house?

But it is a cruel joke. It must be! John Mark knows this isn't true. As for John himself, he knew perfectly well Mary had five other children. She didn't need another home to go to.

To make matters worse, I've just read a passage in one of the new copies of Paul's letter, a passage I hadn't noticed in the original one, a passage about women, needing to learn[ccxcii]…Oh no! Surely not! I have learnt in silence for too long already.

A bad day altogether. I plunge back into my old despair.

*

I tell Trophimus I must leave my work for a while: there is something I must pray about, something I must do before I return. I am making my last journey.

"You will never stop travelling, Magdalene," he says. "You will never end your strange itinerary."

Despite what he says, I leave the sanctuary and travel slowly back towards my home in Mèthamis. I know I will never come here again. I will die down there in the south where the land meets the sea that brought me here.

This land has been my discovery. Since John Mark left and I began to feel alive again, I have found new places, surprised in myself a passion for exploration. The Romans have built fine roads here and curiosity has driven my steps. I have walked the waterways, followed the paths that run beside the rivers, climbed the hills, visited villages, even taught again. I have stood so long admiring the source of the beautiful emerald river, they call the Sorgues, I could happily have become a statue and never moved again. I have stood watching and waiting for the miracle it performs here, a miracle hidden beneath the great rockface that conceals an underground basin.[ccxciii]

The purest waters rise here from the deepest depths of an underwater cave. You can watch the river come back to life here. It is the living water that he promised me: the very source of my story.

I am sorry to return so sadly to this place, but I have a funeral of my own to perform. John is dead but it is not him that I must bury. I have two treasures of my own that I must part with now: and this is where I will leave them. In one hand I clutch a parcel with my beautiful green dress, worn only once, inside; in the other, the manuscript of my own writings. It is time to let go of both of them. To clear my lungs at last of the detritus still trapped inside of them. I cannot endure another memory, another betrayal.

I spend seven days in this lonely, beautiful valley closed in by the great hills. On the seventh, with the palest, finest new moon my only witness, I go down to the river's edge and I let the water take the words I have written, translating them back into its own soft and shapeless language, which only the fish who swim here can understand. I have wrapped the manuscript in my grey shawl and laid it in a little bark barge. I watch as it floats free along the soft eddies by the bank. I have finally let go of it all.

The dress must stay with me a little longer.

*

His mother? His last thought was for his mother!

There is a tiger in these words; I wake in the arena and they spring at me the moment I open my eyes. Not even my sadness or all my resolution can quench the anger. I have let Yeshua go; I have let all of them go…and yet…and yet I am not at peace at all. Instead of freedom, a hydra-headed anxiety is hissing at my heart: *You have done a terrible wrong!*

Dressing hastily, I head back to the river. I pull off my clothes again as soon as I reach the bank and, leaving my things behind, I wade deep into the water. It is still early and there is no one about. I search and search for what is lost but the words have vanished. It is too late. With cupped hands, I pour water frantically over my face and hair, seeking some absolution for this latest sin. As I climb out clean and dripping, I see my manuscript, still wrapped in its grey shawl, caught up on one of the flat stones by the bank, drying serenely in the sun.

The water has refused to take it; it has sent it back to me again. I pull the manuscript out, Pharaoh's daughter after all, still staring about me in unbelief, torn between my devouring anger and the enormity of what I've done.

How can John Mark have betrayed me like this? I trusted him. He won my trust!

Seizing my clothes, I stride along the valley path, eager to return to my community, eager to see Trophimus again. I will work, even if I don't believe in it any longer, I will suffer, I will mortify my flesh, I will even cut off my hair…At the very least, I will get it cut.

It hangs round my face and shoulders, still wet from the stream, falling down my back in long loose strands. I stop for a moment and sit on the long low branch of a tree by the river, twisting my hair in my hands to dry in some sort of order.

But still it flares in me. His last thought was…If there were boats to burn, my anger would set fire to them all.

In the distance, I suddenly catch sight of a party of young people out for an early morning stroll and clearly coming in my direction. I see myself through their eyes, an old woman with hair down her back, a shepherdess cut loose from her flock, and probably unhinged as well. I fear they will mock my ragged state as they pass but instead, they greet me pleasantly and with respect, as if they knew who I was. They are elegantly dressed and obviously wealthy, one of the girls remarkably beautiful. I see she is carrying my parcel, left behind on the bank. They say *Bonjour Maman!* and ask where I am staying.

I tell them my home is far away, that I am about to set out on my last journey.

"But Lady Mother, consider...are you well enough to travel?"

"What did you say? What did you call me? *Lady what?*"

Suddenly, I am hit by a shaft of sunlight so bright I seem to vanish into it. Old habits of thought fall from my mind. I lose consciousness for what seems like hours. When I open my eyes I am lying on the ground and there are people standing round me, some bending over, others looking concerned and anxious. I must have had a stroke, a *coup de foudre*. I see a beautiful white temple and realise at once that *I have died*.

"Where am I? Where is this place? Have I gone to—"

"This is Ephesus, Lady Mother."

"Ephesus," I say, looking round in astonishment. "What am I doing here?"

And then I catch sight of a face I know. He is pushing his way through the crowd. Joy sweeps me up to the skies at the sight of him.

He stretches out his hand.

*

Indicative Bibliography
Biblical Texts

Holy Bible, New International Version, Hodder and Stoughton, 1979, 2011
   The New Testament in Four Versions, incl King James, Revised Standard, Phillips Modern English and New English Bible, Collins, 1967

Scholarly Academic and Creative Texts

John Angelo, The Healing Wisdom of Mary Magdalene, Esoteric Secrets of the Fourth Gospel, Bear & Co, 2015
   Margaret Arnold, The Magdalene in the Reformation, The Belknap Press, Harvard University Press, 2018
   Jonathan Black, The Sacred History: How Angels, Mystics and Higher Intelligence Made our World, Quercus, 2013
   Tom Bissell, Apostle: Travels Among the Tombs of the Twelve, Faber and Faber,
   2016, 2017
   Cynthia Bourgeault, The Meaning of Mary Magdalene: Discovering the Woman at the Heart of Christianity, Shambala Publications Ltd, 2010
   Daniel Boyarin, Carnal Israel: Reading Sex in Talmudic Culture, University of California Press, 1993
   Ann Graham Brock, Mary Magdalene, The First Apostle: The Struggle for Authority, Harvard Theological Studies 51, 2003
   Dan Brown, The Da Vinci Code, Doubleday, 2003
   Raymond E. Brown, An Introduction to New Testament Christology, Paulist Press, 1994
   Rudolf Bultmann, Jesus Christ and Mythology, SCM Press Ltd, 1958, reprint, 1964
   Butler's Lives of the Saints, July, Burns and Oates and The Liturgical Press, 2000
   Maurice Casey, Jesus Of Nazareth, T&T Clark International: Continuum, 2010
   Bruce Chilton, Mary Magdalene: A Biography, Doubleday, 2005
   R.J.Coggins, Samaritans and Jews: The Origins of Samaritanism Reconsidered, Basil Blackwell and John Knox Press, 1975
   David Conway, Secret Wisdom, The Occult Universe Explored, Jonathan Cape, 1985

Kate Cooper, Band of Angels: The Forgotten Worlds of Early Christian Women, Atlantic Books, 2013

St Peter Crysologus, Selected Sermons, The Fathers of the Church, Vol 109, The Catholic University of America Press, 2004, Vol 2

Ignace de la Potterie, The Hour of Jesus: The Passion and the Resurrection of Jesus According to John, trans Dom Gregory Murray, St Paul Publications, 1989

C.H.Dodd, The Interpretation of the Fourth Gospel, Cambridge University Press, 1953

Michael Donley, St Mary Magdalene in Provence: The Coffin and the Cave, Gracewing, 2008

Lawrence Durrell, Caesar's Vast Ghost: Aspects of Provence, Faber and Faber, 1990

Ralph Ellis, Mary Magdalene, Princess of Orange, Edfu Books, 2011

Amos Elon, Jerusalem, City of Mirrors, Flamingo, HarperCollins, 1996

David Flusser, Jesus, The Hebrew University Magnes Press, 3rd edition, 2001

Mark H. Gaffney, Gnostic Secrets of the Naassenes: The Initiatory Teachings of the Last Supper, Inner Traditions, 2004

Max Gallo, Jesus l'homme qui etait Dieu, Pocket, 2010

C.M.C.Green, Roman Religion and the Cult of Diana at Aricia, Cambridge University Press, 2007

Martin Goodman, Rome and Jerusalem, The Clash of Ancient Civilizations, Allen Lane: Penguin, 2007

Michael Haag, The Quest for Mary Magdalene, History and Legend, Profile Book, 2017

Susan Haskins, Mary Magdalene, The Essential History, Pimlico, 1993

Graham Holderness, Re-Writing Jesus: Christ in 20thCentury Fiction and Film, Bloomsbury, 2015

J.H.Hunter, The Mystery of Mar Saba, Evangelical Publishers, 1940

Alan Jacobs (trans), The Gnostic Gospels, Sacred Texts, Watkins Publishing, 2005

Frederique Jourdaa and Olivier Corsan, Sur Les Pas de Marie Madelene, Editions Ouest-France, 2016

Robert Knapp, The Dawn of Christianity: People and Gods in a time of Magic and Miracles, Profile Books, 2018

Robin Lane Fox, Pagans and Christians, Penguin edition, 1988

Katherine Ludwig Jansen, The Meaning of the Magdalene: Preaching and Popular Devotion in the Late Middle Ages, Princeton University Press, 2000

Jean-Yves Leloup (trans), The Gospel of Philip, Jesus, Mary Magdalene, and the Gnosis of Sacred Union, Inner Traditions, 2003

Jean-Yves Leloup trans, The Gospel of Mary Magdalene, Inner Traditions, 2002

Thomas E. Levy, The Archaeology of Society in the Holy Land, Leicester University Press, 1995, 1998

Eli Lizorkin-Eyzenberg, The Jewish Gospel of John: Discovering Jesus, King of All Israel, Israel Study Centre, 2015

William John Lyons, Joseph of Arimathea: A Study in Reception History, Oxford University Press, 2014

James P. Mackey, Jesus, the Man and the Myth, a Contemporary Christology, SCM Press 1979

Martin Meyer (ed), The Nag Hammadi Scriptures, The Revised and Updated Translation of Sacred Gnostic Texts, The International Edition, HarperCollins and Harper One, 2007, 2008

Caitlin Matthews, Sophia, Goddess of Wisdom, Bride of God, Quest Books, 2001

Hyam Maccoby, Jesus the Pharisee, SCM Press, 2003

P.G. Maxwell-Stuart, Astrology from Ancient Babylon to the Present, Amberley Publishing, 2002

Jurgen Moltmann, The Crucified God, 40th Anniversary edition, Fortress Press, 2014

Frank Morison, Who Moved the Stone?, Faber and Faber 1983, Authentic Media Ltd, 2016

Edwin Mullins, Roman Provence, Signal Books, 2011

Jerome Murphy-O'Connor, The Holy Land, An Archaeological Guide from Earliest Times to 1700, 3rd Edition, Oxford University Press, 1992

Petrarch, Canzoniere, trans J.G. Nichols, Carcanet, 2002

Avraham Negrev and Shimon Gibson (ed), Archaeological Encyclopedia of the Holy Land, Continuum, 2001

Gerald O'Collins, SJ, Saint Augustine on the Resurrection of Christ: Teaching, Rhetoric and Reception, Oxford University Press, 2017

Elaine Pagels, The Gnostic Gospels, Phoenix, 1979

Lynne Picknett, Mary Magdalene, Christianity's Hidden Goddess, Constable and Robinson, 2003

Jean-Pierre Ravotti, Marie-Madeleine, Femme Evangelique, Salvator, 2010

John Redford, Bad, Mad or God? Proving the Divinity of Christ from St. John's Gospel, St Paul's Publishing, 2004

JohnRedford, Who Was John? St Paul's Publishing, 2008

Michele Roberts, The Secret Gospel of Mary Magdalene, Vintage, 2007

E.P.Sanders, The Historical Figure of Jesus, Penguin, 1993

Silvia Schroer, Wisdom Has Built Her House: Studies on the Figure of Sophia in the Bible, Michael Glazier, The Liturgical Press, 2000

Graeme Smith, Was the Tomb Empty? A Lawyer Weighs the Evidence for the Resurrection, Monarch Books, 2014

Morton Smith, Jesus the Magician, HarperCollins, 1978, Hampton Roads Press, 2014

Morton Smith, The Secret Gospel: The Discover and Interpretation of the Secret Gospel According to Mark, The Dawn Horse Press, 1982

C.K.Stead, My Names Was Judas, Vintage, 2007

Tacitus, The Annals, trans J.C. Yardley, Oxford World's Classics, OUP, 2008

Colm Toibin, The Testament of Mary, Penguin, 2013

J. Tyson, Jesus, Mary, Lazarus, and Child: The Great Secret of the Fourth Gospel, Tetra, 2013

Jean Vanier, The Gospel of John, The Gospel of Relationship, Darton. Longman and Todd, 2016

Geza Vermes, The Authentic Gospel of Jesus, Penguin, 2004

Geza Vermes, Christian Beginnings From Nazareth to Nicaea AD30-325, Penguin, 2013

Geza Vermes, The Resurrection, Penguin, 2008

Jacobus de Voragine, The Golden Legend: Selections, trans Christopher Stace, Penguin, 1998

Graham Ward and John Milbank, Radical Orthodoxy: A New Theology, Routledge, 1998

J.P. Williams, Seeking the God Beyond: A Beginners Guide to Christian Apophatic Spirituality, SCM Press, 2018

Rowan Williams, God with Us: The meaning of the Cross and resurrection. Then and Now, SPCK, 2017

Rowan Williams, Meeting God in Mark, SPCK, 2014

Rowan Williams, Resurrection: Interpreting the Easter Gospel, Dartman, Longman and Todd ltd, London, 1982, 2002, 2014

G.A. Williamson (ed), Josephus, The Jewish War, Penguin, 1959, 1970; (ed) E. Mary Smallwood, 1981

N.T.Wright, The Resurrection of the Son of God, SPCK, 2003, 2017

Films:
Denys Arcand, Jesus of Montreal, 1989
David Batty, The Gospel According to John, 2014
Garth Davis, Mary Magdalene, 2018
Terry Jones, The Life of Brian, 1979
Cyrus Nowrasteh, The Young Messiah, 2015
Kevin Reynolds, Risen, 2016
Martin Scorsese, The Last Temptation of Christ, 1988
Franco Zeffirelli, Jesus of Nazareth, 1977

*

Endnotes

[i] The Gospel of John, 20: 17, King James Version, 1611

[ii] *Sermons* (184-229Z), trans Edmund Hill, New Rochelle, NY: New City Press, 1993 p 297. See also Gerald O'Collins SJ, *St Augustine on the Resurrection of Christ: Teaching, Rhetoric and Reception,* OUP, p 36

[iii] The Gospel of Philip, trans Jean-Yves Leloup, Inner Traditions, 2004, p 55

[iv] There are many versions and transliterations of the Lord's Prayer in Aramaic. This one is taken from the Diocese of Bath and Wells Ministry for Mission Study Guide, Exploring Christianity, (2003,2010) p 12

[v] The Occitan Provencal text of the Lord's Prayer is also a reconstruction of which there are many variant versions.

[vi] Matthew 27: 45-55

[vii] As testament to her intelligence and interiority, Mary Magdalene is one of very few female saints traditionally depicted with a book in her hands.

[viii] According to Luke's Gospel, 8:1 Joanna was 'the wife of Chuza, the manager of Herod's household.' The women named were most likely the wealthy ones who helped to finance and resource the Jesus Movement.

[ix] See The Dialogue of the Saviour in Marvin Meyer (ed)The Nag Hammadi Scriptures, Harper Collins, 2007/8, p 303: "Mary said…where do my tears come from, where does my laughter come from?' The Master said, "[The body] weeps because of its works and what remains to be done. The mind laughs [because of the fruits of] the spirit."

[x] See the Dead Sea Scroll prophecy on the coming of the messiah, Robert Knapp, **The Dawn of Christianity**, Profile Books, Ltd, 2017, 2018, p 121

[xi] For MM as the lighthouse and the watch-tower of the Jesus group, see Michael Haag's summary of many discussions in **The Quest for Mary Magdalene: History and Legend**, Profile Books Ltd, (2017) p 17

[xii] For the new Eden, see Ezekiel 47:12; Revelations 22:1-2

[xiii] This is the impression given by the Nag Hammadi and other early Coptic gospels. These consistently show MM having to defend her place in Christ's inner circle against the jealousy and cynicism of ambitious male disciples such as Peter and Andrew.

[xiv] Luke 7:31-35

[xv] See Graham Ward's illuminating essay, 'Bodies: The displaced body of Jesus Christ' in **Radical Orthodoxy: A New Theology**, Routledge, 1998, pp 163-181.

[xvi] The kingdom of heaven like a mustard seed: Matthew 13: 31-32

[xvii] St Peter Chrysologus, **Selected Sermons**, Vol 2, in The Fathers of the Church, Catholic University of America Press, Vol 109, 2004, No. 34, p 147: "He turned and saw her: saw her with divine eyes, not with human ones: whomever God has seen is endowed with good things and lacks evil".

[xviii] For this important field image, see Alan Jacobs (trans), **The Gospel of Thomas**, logion 21 in **The Gnostic Gospels**, Watkins Publishing, 2005, and Cynthia

Bourgeault, **The Meaning of Mary Magdalene**, Shambala Publications, Inc, 2010 p 65

xix For the significance of dreams and astrology as potential channels for communication with the divine in the early years of Christianity, see P.G. Maxwell-Stuart, **Astrology from Ancient Babylon to the Present**, Amberley Publishing, 2012, pp 34-82

xx Matthew 25: 1-6

xxi Food and feasting is a recurrent and absorbing concern of Mark's Gospel

xxii The phrase is from Petrarch's poem addressed to the Magdalene written after his visit to the Dominican-run Magdalene cave-shrine at Sainte Baume in 1336.

xxiii James, the elder son of Zebedee and the brother of John, was, according to Acts 12:2, one of the first martyrs of the early Christian Church.

xxiv Mathew, Luke and John each have different accounts of these sightings and the difficulty the disciples had in recognising the figure as Jesus. See Rowan Williams, **Resurrection**, Dartman, Longman and Todd, 1982, 2014, pp 27-37 for a discussion of these 'bereavement apparitions' to use the current, secular term for these phenomena. In **God with Us**, SPCK, 2017, Williams comments, p 76: "what we have is a series of resurrection stories that are abrupt, confused, vivid and unpolished. I don't think one can overemphasise that oddity about the resurrection stories." Freud's famous formulation, "the demons of mourning can be very persistent", indicates the inner spiritual work which such apparitional sightings always ask us to undertake.

xxv Pentecost

xxvi Acts 2. Despite her prominence in all four accounts of the resurrection, there is no mention of Mary Magdalene's presence at Pentecost in Luke's account.

xxvii For commentators as diverse as Rowan Williams in **Resurrection** and Gaza Vermes, in **The Resurrection**, Penguin, 2008, it was this return of faith ("this Resurrection in the hearts of men", Vermes p 150) that constituted the most undeniable sign of the Christian resurrection.

xxviii For a succinct account of James' change of heart and subsequent leadership of the Jerusalem church see Frank Morison, **Who Moved the Stone?** OM, Faber and Faber, 1983, 2016, pp 141-149

xxix The origin of this dream seems to be Nebuchadnezzar in Daniel 4: 9-15

xxx Both Mark 3:20-34; 6:1-6 and John 7: 1-13 stress this initial family opposition.

xxxi According to the Jewish-Roman historian, Josephus, Jesus's brother, James, was condemned by the Sanhedrin and stoned to death in AD 62

xxxii The modern Marseilles retains its identification as the place where, according to legend, MM disembarked when she reached Provence.

xxxiii See the gnostic **Gospel of Mary** and Cynthia Bourgeault's interesting and persuasive discussion of it in **The Meaning of Mary Magdalene,** pp 43-73

xxxiv For *kenosis,* or self-emptying of this kind, see J.P. Williams' account of the *via negativa* in **Seeking the God Beyond**, SCM Press, 2018 pp 35-40

xxxv A Provencal reconstruction of *Give us this day our daily bread*

xxxvi The Aramaic name for Magdala on the shores of Lake Galilee. It was a Roman-style city with a strong Greek influence and its own synagogue. See Thomas E. Levy (ed), The Archaeological Encyclopedia of the Holy Land, Leicester University Press, 1995, p 307

[xxxvii] The story of Mary Magdalene as a merchant's daughter can be found in Cynthia Bourgeault: **The Meaning of Mary Magdalene**, p 113

[xxxviii] The Virtuous Woman: Psalms 31. 10-31 See Robert Knapp, The Dawn of Christianity, pp 29-31, for a balanced and informative account of women's skills and duties in 1st century Palestine.

[xxxix] Mark 12:16 'The stone the builders rejected has become the cornerstone'.

[xl] John 14:5-6

[xli] For this dimension of MM's name identity, see Haag, p 17

[xlii] For Mary Magdalene and the Wisdom tradition, see especially Caitlin Matthews, **Sophia, Goddess of Wisdom, Bride of God,** Quest Books, 2001 and Susan Haskins, **Mary Magdalene: The Essential History**, PImlico, 2005, pp 48-53

[xliii] For an analysis of Mark's background and possible identity, see Rowan Williams' **Meeting God in Mark**, SPCK, 2014, pp 9-19

[xliv] See the last two sayings of the gnostic **Gospel of Thomas**, p 52: "I'll guide her soul to that place which transcends the difference between the sexes, so she'll become a living spirit," and Haskins' discussion of this passage, p 43

[xlv] Homer, **The Iliad**, Bk 5, line 424

[xlvi] In the Gospels Nathan is one of the more mysterious disciples, named as "Nathanael from Cana" only in John's gospel (21:2) and introduced into the group by Philip (1:44-50). He is not mentioned again until he reappears in John 21 as one of the small group of disciples to see the risen Christ while fishing in Galilee, their miraculous catch on this occasion replicated in the calling of Peter, James and John in Luke 5. He is not listed in any of the other three gospels and not in Acts either. His link to MM is through John's distinct and peculiar dramatis personae in the 4th Gospel, and his emphasis on Christ as the bridegroom through his opening miracle of the wedding at Cana. For a different version of the marriage at Cana, this time between MM and John the Evangelist, see Margaret Arnold, The Magdalene in the Reformation, The Belknap Press, Harvard University Press, 2018, p 20

[xlvii] Lynn Picknett's strictures on the importance of Egyptian culture both in the ancient world and for early Christianity are important here. See her provocative study, **Mary Magdalene**, Constable and Robinson, 2003, p 159. According to Matthew, 2: 13-16 Jesus was partly brought up in Egypt. Scholars such as Morton Smith and early critics such as Celsus, categorise him as an Egyptian magician and trickster.

[xlviii] Simon, called "the Zealot" is named in all four gospels. 'Zealots' was the name given to a sect who believed in active resistance to Roman oppression. Their actions were largely responsible for the Roman retaliation that destroyed Jerusalem in 70 AD.

[xlix] John's gospel makes Christ's clearing of the temple courts and his prophecy of its destruction the opening scene of his Passion narrative. See also John 2:23 "He did not need any testimony about mankind, for he knew what was in each person".

[l] Christ's prophecy about the fall of Jerusalem and the destruction of its second temple is one climax of Mark's gospel (Mk :13) and the immediate cause of his

arrest. There is no reference to it in John. For an account of the Jerusalem massacre and the burning of the Temple, see Josephus, **The Jewish War**, Book vi, pp 337-373

[li] The modern town of Vaison-la-Romaine has extensive remains of the former Roman city.

[lii] Isaiah 62. 1-5

[liii] Mark 13; Mark 14: 55-65

[liv] For a justly renowned discussion of the "theological clash" between Christ and the righteousness of Judaic Law, see Jurgen Moltmann, **The Crucified God**, 40th Anniversary edition, Fortress Press, 2015, pp 186-195

[lv] See Rowan Williams' discussion in *God with Us* of the resurrection as heralding in "the new age" which defined for all time God's new relation with humanity, pp 61-71

[lvi] For the story of the man blind from birth, see John: 9

[lvii] See John 1:46 for Nathan's famous rhetorical question: "Nazareth! Can anything good come from there?"

[lviii] *Turning point*. For the cult of Artemis/Diana, see C.M.C. Green's brilliant and enthralling study **Roman Religion and the Cult of Diana at Aricia**, CUP, 2007

[lix] For hostilities between Jews and Samaritans, see R.J. Coggins, *Samaritans and Jews: The Origins of Samaritanism Reconsidered*, Basil Blackwell, 1975 (and John Knox Press) 1975, pp 138-148

[lx] According to the Mishnah, grain from around Sychar was used for this purpose, despite its being a Samarian city. See **Archaeological Encyclopedia of the Holy Land**, p 484

[lxi] for a discussion of John's phase in 4:9 see Coggins, p 1 and p 139

[lxii] See John 4 for Jesus's meeting with the Samaritan woman. For a discussion of the elusive figure of Nathan, only mentioned in John, see Bissell, *pp 39-52*

[lxiii] Coggins, p 139

[lxiv] Sebaste (Samaria) was reputedly the site for the murder of John the Baptist (Mark 6: 17-29) following Herod's infamous dinner party. See Picknett, p 209 for her outspoken but thought-provoking account of how Jesus benefitted from the murder of John.

[lxv] In John's gospel, Christ's meeting with the much-married Samaritan woman at the well in Sychor in Ch 4 is the first time that he openly proclaims his identity as the messiah. It is also the only extended conversation he has with a woman in any of the four gospels, but, in keeping with its Samaritan theme, John is the only one to describe this incident. For a different interpretation of Jewish-Samaritan relations, see Eli Lizorkin-Eyzenberg, **The Jewish Gospel of John: Recovering Jesus, King of all Israel.** This argues that Jesus had a political agenda aimed at re-unifying the Northern and Southern kingdoms of Israel and Judaea and was successful in reconciling some of the ancient enmities that existed between Jews and Samaritans. On the esoteric level, the well image continues the theme of the new birth, the transformation of water and the spirit. It points forward to Christ's heart-rending last words on the cross: "I thirst…It is finished."

^{lxvi} For Felix Antonius, sometimes named Procurator of Samaria, see Tacitus, **The Annals**, Book 12.54 p 261-2.

^{lxvii} The Vulgate's translation of John's famous rendering of Christ's speech to MM immediately after the resurrection, *Noli me tangere* is, in modern English editions, more usually translated as *Do not cling, or hold on to me.*

^{lxviii} See Luke, 7: 36-39 In Luke, the anointing of Christ is performed by an anonymous sinner woman, not as in John 12 by the respectable 'Mary of Bethany'. Luke's passage is largely responsible for MM's subsequent representation as a sinner and a prostitute. For a more literal translation of the Greek word, *hamartolos,* see Haskins, pp 18-19

^{lxix} For the classic discussion of Christ's suspension of the Law, his 'liberation from legalism', in favour of the grace of forgiveness, see Bultman, pp 189-211

^{lxx} The account of the woman taken in adultery at John 8: 1-11 is a late edition to the Gospel. It was also included in some manuscripts at Luke 21:38 to reinforce the connection between MM and the betrayal of Christ by Judas.

^{lxxi} The writing of John's Gospel has often been associated with the expulsion of Christians from the Jewish synagogues circa AD 85

^{lxxii} The Gospels do not have authors in the modern sense of that word. The names ascribed to them were added in the late 2nd century AD by Irenaeus of Lyon and are intended to trace the apostolic authority and oral source from which the particular material derived. The **Gospel of Mark**, Eusebius suggested, derives from material supplied by Peter. The writing itself was often undertaken by scribes working in the context of a particular church community with its own specific needs and perspectives. Composition often involved a compilation of different source materials as drafts of the synoptic gospels were circulated amongst them. Scribes not uncommonly interpolated details and alterations of their own.

^{lxxiii} For a detailed study of Joseph of Arimathea and the evolution of his legend, see William John Lyons, **Joseph of Arimathea: A Study in Reception History,** Oxford University Press, 2014

^{lxxiv} See Matthew's account of Jesus's message after the Last Supper 26:32 "But after I have risen, I will go ahead of you into Galilee".

^{lxxv} In John's Gospel, the recognition was John's. See 21:7 His gospel is the only one to include the fishing episode, though Matthew also sets the ascension in Galilee.

^{lxxvi} For one of the best accounts of the much discussed relationship between Peter and MM see Ann Graham Brock, **Mary Magdalenee, the First Apostle,** Harvard University Press, 2003 and also Katherine Ludwig Jansen's section on the Gnostic Gospels in **The Making of the Magdalene,** Princeton University Press, 2000, 2001, pp 24-32

^{lxxvii} John (19:39) is the only gospel to mention Nicodemus as present at the entombment. Nicodemus is an enigmatic but important esoteric figure in John's Gospel, a rich man who seeks a night-time initiation into the secret of Christ's kingdom. See John 3: 1-21. A similar initiation ritual is mentioned in Mark 4:10 and provides a central thesis in Morton Smith's controversial book, **The Secret Gospel: The Discovery and Interpretation of The Secret Gospel According of Mark,** Dawn Horse Press, 2005

lxxviii See also Bissell, p 212-213

lxxix St Roch with his life-saving dog remains a powerful local saint in the Vaucluse region of Provence.

lxxx For this detail of the medieval legend of MM, see Jacobus de Voragine, **The Golden Legend: Selections,** Penguin Classics, 1998 pp 165-74. This European bestseller was one of the first books published by Caxton's printing press.

lxxxi The sensational secret at the heart of Dan Brown's bestseller, **The Da Vinci Code**, makes a good story but it is based on a complete misreading of John's gospel.

lxxxii For MM's nickname as the watchtower, or *migdal*, see Michael Haag, The Quest for Mary Magdalene, p 16-17

lxxxiii For MM's relationship with Peter see Dialogue 4 in **The Gospel of Mary Magdalene** and Cynthia Bourgeault's illuminating discussion of it in **The Meaning of Mary Magdalene**, p 74-81

lxxxiv See The Gospel of Luke 11: 24-28

lxxxv For an interesting light on exorcism as practiced both by Mary Magdalene and Christ, see Bruce Chilton, **Mary Magdalene: A Biography**, Doubleday, 2005, pp 1-32

lxxxvi See C. M. C. Green, *Roman Religion and the Cult of Diana at Aricia*, p 114 - 125

lxxxvii There is a scholarly consensus regarding the chronological order of the canonical gospels, first the synoptic gospels, Mark, then Matthew, then Luke and finally, sometime after the others, the Gospel of John.

lxxxviii For the Jewish law on witnesses, see Rowan Williams, **Resurrection**, p 97

lxxxix For the healing of Jairus' daughter See Mark 5:21-43 and Luke 8: 40-56

xc See Acts 9: 19 and 2 Corinthians: 12; 1-4

xci See Acts 11: 26

xcii For a strong argument to this effect, see Hyam Maccoby, **Jesus the Pharisee,** SCM Press, 2003, pp 15-25

xciii Acts 9: 1-19

xciv See Acts 13: 1

xcv For further details of Manean and this conversion at the centre of Herod Antipas's court, see Haag, pp 70-72.

xcvi For Peter's miraculous escape from prison, see Acts 12, 1-18. This passage from Acts also contains, at 12:12, a powerful identification of "John, also called Mark" as one of those who was present on this occasion.

xcvii Paul's Letter to the Romans 7:4

xcviii For an introduction to the "factionalisation" of the gospel-writers, see Bissell p 64-69

xcix The author of Luke's Gospel is also the author of **The Acts of the Apostles**.

c See John 6:60-68 "Lord, to whom should we go Lord? You have the words of eternal life."

ci Paul's Letter to the Romans 8:11 "he who raised Christ from the dead will also give life to your mortal bodies because of his Spirit who lives in you."

cii This phrase, *What is it like?* the quest for the perfect analogy, is so frequently found in the gospels, both canonical and gnostic, that it suggests an actual usage among the disciples.

ciii See Acts 16: 13-15 for Lydia. See also Kate Cooper's ground-breaking study, **Band of Angels: The Forgotten World of Early Christian Women**, Atlantic Books Ltd, 2015, pp 15-20

civ See The Gospel of Philip, trans Jean-Yves Leloup, p 59 and 73 The Gnostic Gospels are full of images of robes and robing which depict the interplay of physical and spiritual levels of meaning. Translations vary considerably and can change both emphasis and meaning.

cv Sacred songs to aid meditation by invoking the presence of the divine associated with the daughters of Job in Ancient Jewish Literature. According to Chilton, Magdala was a centre for this practice, see **Mary Magdalene: A Biography**, p 61

cvi The unicorn is the symbol of Wisdom in The Way of the Chinese sage, Confucius.

cvii Bruce Chilton considers MM an adept at exorcism and sees her as the main oral source for the three exorcisms recorded in the gospels. See pp 33-46

cviii The reference here is to the "living water" which structures the discourse of John 4:10 -14. See the first meeting between Christ and MM, 1. 10 above.

cix Paul's Letter to the Romans 6:4-5

cx The eagle is the traditional emblem of John the Evangelist.

cxi For a variety of approaches and a range scholarly discussions about these distinctions surrounding the post-mortem Christ, see Rowan Williams, Resurrection, p 32-37; N. W. Wright pp 587-682; Graeme Smith, **Was The Tomb Empty**, Monarch Books, 2014, pp 166-180, Maurice Casey, **Jesus of Nazareth,** T&T Clark International, 2010, pp 455-498; Geza Vermes, **The Resurrection**, pp 143-152;

cxii For the importance of Egyptian and Jewish magic rituals and incantations to the ministry of Christ, see Morton Smith, **Jesus the Magician**. These discourses were familiar and available in First Century Palestine and a recognisable part of Christ's relation to the supernatural.

cxiii See Mark H. Gaffney, **Gnostic Secrets of the Naassenes: The Initiatory Teachings of the Last Supper**, Inner Traditions, 2004, for one account of what these rites might have included.

cxiv See Acts 12: 25 and Acts 13, 1-14

cxv See Acts 15: 37

cxvi This is a strong theme of Paul's writing. See Romans 8: 8-12; 15:17-19

cxvii The allusion here is to Nathan of Cana, see John 1:47

cxviii For an interesting gloss on John 2:13-23, see Chilton's suggestion that it was Caiaphas, the high priest at the time, who had replaced the ancient tradition of Israelites offering the work of their own hands at the temple with a new system of vendors and extensive trading, p 49

cxix For the Greeks, *agape* was the term for spiritual love, love of the divine and the cosmic love feast that was its sign.

cxx See Wright's account of John's handling of the Resurrection: "John's two Easter chapters rank with Romans 8, not to mention the key passages in the Corinthian correspondence, as among the most glorious pieces of writing on the resurrection.

John and Romans are of course utterly different in genre and style. Instead of the tight argument and dense phraseology of Paul, we have John's deceptively simple account of the Easter events, warm with deep and dramatic human characterisation, pregnant with new possibilities." P 662

[cxxi] See Wright, p 656

[cxxii] John 2:19

[cxxiii] See John 17: 13-19

[cxxiv] The earliest versions of the Gospel According to Mark end abruptly at 16:8. Verses 9-20 were a later addition.

[cxxv] See Chilton pp 82-85 for a thought-provoking suggestion to this effect. Like the transfiguration recorded in Mark 9:2-10, the empty tomb provides a threshold into the divine where intense visions frequently occur.

[cxxvi] See Matthew 28:17

[cxxvii] See Rowan Williams, pp 74-76

[cxxviii] There have been countless discussions over the past 2,000 years as to whether Mary Magdalene and Mary of Bethany are one and the same person or two entirely different women. John's gospel offers an ingenious solution to this conundrum of the Synoptics, which is largely the result of Luke's treatment of the anointing scene and his division of the two women into two opposing types.

[cxxix] See Luke 24.

[cxxx] See Bissel, p 198-9 for a graphic description of Revelations with its "barbarous" Greek idioms.

[cxxxi] John's gospel is the only one to include the doubter, Thomas Didymus, in its resurrection scenes.

[cxxxii] Unlike the Synoptic Gospels, John's Gospel makes no mention of the Eucharist at the last supper. It is referred to instead much earlier in Christ's ministry in John 6: 53-60 and it causes many to fall away from the fellowship.

[cxxxiii] See Bissell, p 206 for a hotter account of John's death.

[cxxxiv] See the first of The Last Supper Discourses in John 13:1-17

[cxxxv] Christ's washing of the disciples' feet at the Last Supper at 13:1-17 is a repetition of Mary's action when she anoints Christ's feet at 12:1-8

[cxxxvi] This is the pattern of Christian autobiography that St Augustine in his **Confessions** derived from Paul's writings and made the great *exemplum* of how to construct and interpret a Christ life.

[cxxxvii] For a painstaking examination of the effect of faith on the resurrection appearances, see Ignace de la Potterie S J, **The Hour of Jesus: The Passion and the Resurrection of Jesus According to John,** (trans Dom Gregory Murray), St Paul Publications, 1989, Ch 8, The Genesis of Easter Faith, pp 159-186

[cxxxviii] See John 13: 6-9

[cxxxix] The ending of John's Gospel emphasises this point. See John 21:15-25

[cxl] The river is the Rhone, the ancient settlement referred to here is currently known as Saint-Roman at Beaucaire.

[cxli] According to Luke 8:3, Mary Magdalene's companion, Joanna, was the wife of Herod's steward, Chuza.

cxlii See J.P. Williams on *paraconsistent* logic, p 164. "…if the fundamental nature of the universe is really such as it now appears to be, our definitions of truth and logic need to incorporate difference and contradiction."

cxliii Mount Gerizim in Samaria

cxliv Pompey the Great claimed Jerusalem for Rome in 47 BC. The administrative province was set up by Julius Caesar in 47 BCE

cxlv For a full account of this aspect of the incarnation, see Graham Ward's essay, *Bodies The displaced body of Jesus Christ*, in **Radical Orthodoxy**, pp 163-181

cxlvi The gospels of Mark and John's in particular capture this rapid, mercurial quality. See Mark 6:49 or John 9:12

cxlvii See Mark 1: 23-25

cxlviii See Morton Smith, **Jesus the Magician**, Harper Collins, 1979, Hampton Roads Press, 2014, Ch 7, pp 129-193

cxlix Pilate was removed from his post for corruption and incompetence shortly after the crucifixion, in AD 37. Caiaphas, the High Priest at the time of Christ's trial, suffered the same fate.

cl Mount Ebal stood opposite Mount Gerizim. The 12 tribes of Israel assembled here to hear the curses and blessings connected with the Law. See Deut. 27: 1-9)

cli Mont Ventoux, the giant of Provence.

clii Matthew 11: 29

cliii For an account of these populist insurrections, see Josephus, **The Jewish War**, p 147. The Egyptian was a false prophet who led an army of 30,000 to the Mount of Olives before attempting to force entry into Jerusalem. The insurrection was suppressed and the Egyptian fled with a few of his followers.

cliv See Mark 6: 56

clv Morton Smith in **Jesus the Magician** provides a fascinating account of the practice of magic and the magical discourses available at the time of Christ, an obvious cultural context within which his own work could be located and identified as providing a 'credible picture of a magician's career'. See especially pp 129-193.

clvi John 5: 1-15

clvii See Mark 10: 28-29

clviii See Rowan Williams, pp 77-81

clix Like Artemis herself, the medieval Mary Magdalene became the patron saint of fertility and childbirth.

clx For the Greek, then Roman, city of Marseilles, see Edwin Mullins, **Roman Provence,** Signal Books Ltd, 2011, pp 23-24

clxi The city of Nimes, where these miracles of hydro-culture are still visible.

clxii See C.M.C. Green, pp 222-231

clxiii Arles

clxiv The cult of Artemis was one of several mystery cults in the region that had close links with early Christianity. The cult of Mithras was another.

clxv Green, pp 32-54

clxvi See Green, pp 147-184

clxvii See the Gospel of Mary Magdalene, p 58

clxviii The Feast of Artemis/Diana was between 22-23rd July. In the Christian Calendar, MM's feast day is 22nd of July.

clxix For a different take on MM and exorcism, see Chilton, pp 25-32

clxx In the 1st Century AD, Christ was not infrequently conflated with and represented as the Sun God, Apollo, brother of the moon goddess who presided over his daily death and disappearance.

clxxi See the Gnostic gospel known as *The Dialogue of the Saviour* for this account of Judas and Mary Magdalene as the two disciples who wanted to learn, know and understand it all. See Marvin Meyer (ed), **The Nag Hammadi Scriptures**, HarperCollins 2007/8, pp 308-309

clxxii See Matthew 5:14

clxxiii See Christ's description of the Baptist and his prophetic mission in Matthew 11:7

clxxiv This fictional Felix bears more than a slight resemblance to the Antonius Felix referred to by Tacitus in **The Annals** as the procurator of Judea and the Governor of Samaria, see Book 12. 54.

clxxv For a fascinating discussion of Herod Antipas's show city, Tiberias, see Haag, pp 60-80

clxxvi See Matthew 12: 43-45

clxxvii For the Merkavah, see **The OT** *Book of Enoch*; and Chilton, pp 60-61 for its link to Mary Magdalene.

clxxviii For an account of John's birth, see Luke 1:5-80

clxxix The King's Highway, the *Tariq es-Sultani*, was the great road that ran due south across the Syrian desert from Damascus down to the Red Sea.

clxxx For an interesting and informed account of the play of these prophetic identities and their relevance to John the Baptist and Christ (Elisha), see Gaffney, **Gnostic Secrets of the Naassenes,** pp 20-4

clxxxi For details, see Picknett's thought-provoking discussion, pp 203 -211

clxxxii For the famous story of Elijah's experience of this alternative voice of prophecy, see 1 Kings 19:12.

clxxxiii See John 12:20-26

clxxxiv See **The Dialogue of the Saviour**: "Everything born of woman dies; everything born of the truth lives." The Nag Hammadi Scriptures, p 309

clxxxv See John 1:9-14 for the first reference to the new family of God developed through the Gospel of John. See also Luke 8: 19-21

clxxxvi The episode of the fig tree signals a chronological disharmonisation in the gospels. In Matthew (21:18) it occurs immediately after the cleansing of the temple, in Mark 11:12 it immediately precedes it. Neither Luke nor John mention it at all.

clxxxvii The raising of Lazarus is one of the most problematic incidents in John's Gospel. For provocative and insightful discussions of John the Baptist and Lazarus, see Picknett, pp 52-54 on whom I have drawn in this respect.

clxxxviii See Mark: 10: 1

clxxxix See Picknett, pp 209-10 7 pp 222-3

cxc See N.T.Wright's exhaustive study, **The Resurrection**, for the Jewish background to this subject and the Sadducees' position.

^{cxci} See Matthew 22:23-31

^{cxcii} See John 1: 48

^{cxciii} The festivals were those of Passover, Weeks, Tabernacles

^{cxciv} Miriam is the sister of Moses. For her triumphal dance see Exodus 15: 19-21

^{cxcv} Chilton makes the interesting suggestion that it was the High Priest, Caiaphas, who had authorised trading in the Temple in place of the traditional practice by which Israelites were to offer the work of their own hands there. See p 49

^{cxcvi} See Matthew 21 1-31

^{cxcvii} The reference here is to the execution of John the Baptist.

^{cxcviii} See the explorative insights of J. Tyson, **Jesus, Mary, Lazarus, and Child,** Tetra, 2013, pp 71-77 for a fresh eye on Martha's role in the Jesus movement.

^{cxcix} See Matthew 21: 18-22; Mark 11:12-26

^{cc} Matthew 23:33

^{cci} See Mark, 12:41-43

^{ccii} John's gospel uniquely places the cleansing of the Temple at the beginning of his narrative, see 2:13-23. It is followed in 3:22-36 by a reference to the decline of the Baptist's ministry. One of John's esoteric links connects John the Baptist with the final event of this part of the narrative, the raising of Lazarus. Both are associated with a place called Bethany, one near Jericho, one near Jerusalem. For a discussion of the two Bethanys, see Picknett, pp 47-57. John's story of the raising of Lazarus in Bethany evokes, and elides, the raising of John the Baptist also. In this account, the Baptist is present when Christ cleanses the temple in preparation for his own passion.

^{cciii} For significant variants on this most controversial moment of anointing see Mark14:1-10; Matthew 26: 6-13; Luke 7:36-50; John 12: 1-11. The symbolism of anointing is explored in detail by Bourgeault, pp 181-190

^{cciv} In all the Gospels except that of Luke, the anointing of Christ with expensive perfume is the given as the reason for Judas' betrayal.

^{ccv} Mark 14: 1-10; Matthew 26: 6-13; John 12:7-8

^{ccvi} See *The Gospel of Philip*, pp 84-85, Section 56

^{ccvii} For this image of the second birth, see John 16:21-23

^{ccviii} For the Essenes and the prohibition against oils, see Josephus, The Jewish War, Ch 7, p 133

^{ccix} The story of the woman taken in adultery does not appear in the earliest versions of John's gospel, the only gospel in which it occurs. It is a late addition to Chapter 8: 1-12. In Luke's gospel, a sinful woman anoints Christ at the end of chapter 7: 36-50. In the lateral reading of the Gospels, these two stories are therefore directly linked. Luke's chapter 8 opens with his first reference to Mary Magdalene, as a woman out of whom seven demons have been cast. See Luke 8:1-4

^{ccx} For angels and the power of Christ, see Jonathan Black, **The Sacred History**, Quercus, 2013, pp 170-184

^{ccxi} see Raymond E. Brown, **An Introduction to New Testament Christology**, Paulist Press, 1994, p 64 for a helpful discussion of this and other translations of dynamis/*dynameis*.

ccxii Matthew's Gospel begins with the patriarchal genealogy of Jesus the Messiah. There is a break in this patriarchal line at 1:16. Joseph is referred to only as the husband of Mary, not as the father of Jesus.

ccxiii For an intelligent and persuasive discussion of 'the Son of Man' as distinct from the concept of the Messiah, see Gaffney, pp 38-48

ccxiv See Mark 13: 32

ccxv For one of many interpretations of Christ's mission as an attempt to reunify the two kingdoms of the Jewish people, see Eli Lizorkin-Eyzenberg, **The Jewish Gospel of John: Discovering Jesus, King of All Israel**, Israel Study Centre Publication, 2015

ccxvi Luke, 1: 5-25

ccxvii Luke 1: 39

ccxviii Compare Matthew's short account of Mary's pregnancy "through the Holy Spirit" at 1: 18-24 with Luke's much longer one at 1:26-56

ccxix For the angels and human marriage, see Luke 20:27-37

ccxx For MM as an oral source for New Testament, see Chiltern's chapter on 'Mary's signature' p 33. Though I disagree with his thesis, his idea is an interesting one.

ccxxi See Luke 2:22-40

ccxxii Jesus as a figure in hiding is a recurrent motif in the gospel stories. See John 12: 35-36

ccxxiii See Luke 2: 41-52

ccxxiv See John 1:1 *In the beginning was the Word.*

ccxxv See Luke 2:22-38 for Simeon and Anna

ccxxvi For the Naassenes, see Gaffney, pp 32-38

ccxxvii For a discussion of the lazar house at Bethany, see Morrison, pp 84-94

ccxxviii Read, and read again, the enigmatic chapter 8 of Luke's Gospel for our first introduction to Mary Magdalene.

ccxxix For the story of Mary Magdalene's marriage to an elderly merchant, see Bourgeault, p 113

ccxxx For an equivalent to this story, see Simon Magus and Helen, who danced in chains as part of his magic show, in Picknett, pp 145-6. See also Black, **The Sacred History**, p 208

ccxxxi For an account of early Christian baptism, see J. P. Wiliams, **Seeking the God Beyond**, pp36-37

ccxxxii Psalm 37, verse 9

ccxxxiii Psalm 32: verse 5

ccxxxiv All four gospels are in agreement that Christ's baptism by John is the beginning of Christ's period of ministry, see John 1: 29-34, Luke 3:21-23, Mark 1: 9-12; Matthew 3:13-17

ccxxxv Samaria (*Shomron; Sebaste*) was the ancient capital of Israel and according to early Christian legend the burial place of the Baptist.

ccxxxvi Tiberias was the capital of Galilee until Nero gave it away in AD 61. It came under Roman in 100 AD, then became an important centre for Jewish learning in the 3rd century when the Mishna and the Talmud assumed their final form. For further details of Herod Antipas's city, see Avraham Negev and Shimon Gibson (ed) Archaeological Encyclopedia of the Holy Land, Continuum, 2001, pp 504-505

ccxxxvii For Lady Folly, the opposite of Wisdom, see Proverbs, Ch 8 and 9:13-18

ccxxxviii Luke's isolated reference to the casting out of seven demons from Mary Magdalene is an example of the many ways in which his gospel diminishes her stature and significance.

ccxxxix For Paul's conversion, see Acts 9:1-20

ccxl See Paul's Letter to the Romans, 6:5-14

ccxli See Elaine Pagels, **The Gnostic Gospels**, Phoenix, 1979, pp 37-38:
"Paul describes the resurrection as 'a mystery', the transformation from physical to spiritual existence.
If the New Testament accounts support a range of interpretations, why did orthodox Christians in the second century insist on a literal view of resurrection and reject all others as heretical?"
Pagels examines the political implications of this in relation to apostolic authority. A literal and physical account of the resurrection was considered to have primacy over one that was defined in spiritual or visionary terms.

ccxlii See Geza Vermes, **Christian Beginnings from Nazareth to Nicaea AD 30-325**, Penguin, 2012, p 128

ccxliii See Rowan Williams, **Meeting God in Mark**, pp 64-74

ccxliv This crucial episode of Christ's conversation with Nicodemus occurs very early in John's gospel, see 3: 1-21.

ccxlv *Paraclete* is Greek for *intercessor, advocate* or *helper*

ccxlvi For bereavement apparitions, see Maurice Casey, Jesus of Nazareth, Ch 12, pp 488-498

ccxlvii Matthew 28:18

ccxlviii For an extremely detailed and scholarly discussion of these alternatives see N.T. Wright, **The Resurrection** and Geza Vermes, **The Resurrection**

ccxlix For the golden serpent in the visionary tradition, see William Blake's illustration, *The Temptation of Eve.*

ccl It is only John's gospel, the last to be written, which includes this clinching detail of the spear wound, in case the validity of Christ's death was challenged, perhaps.

ccli For disparities in which of the women were present at the entombment see Mark 15:40 (MM, Mary the mother of James the younger and of Joseph, and Salome); Matthew 27:55 (MM, Mary the mother of James and Joseph, and the mother of Zebedee's sons), Luke names no one specifically amongst the group of women who "saw the tomb and how the body was laid in it" (23:55)

cclii Luke is alone in mentioning Joanna, the wife of Herod's steward, as present at the resurrection along with MM "and others". 24:10

ccliii See John 19:39 The extreme generosity of Nicodemus in providing thirty-five kilograms of myrrh and aloes for the entombment parallels the generous and 'extravagant' amount of perfume ("half a litre of pure nard") with which Mary anointed Christ at Bethany in 12:3. For hints that Nicodemus was actually the father of Mary Magdalene, see the discussion of the Talmud passage in Ralph Ellis, *Mary Magdalene, Princess of Orange*, Edfu Books, 2011, p 3 ccliv For the use of the Bethany house as a hideout for the disciples after the crucifixion, see Morison, pp 89-92 This also contains a well-thought out, alternative reconstruction of the events of Christ's passion and resurrection.

cclv For the dream of Pilate's wife and her connection with the equally prophetic dream of Julius Caesar's wife, see the excellent reconstruction of the trial of Christ in Morison, pp 41-61

cclvi For a discussion of Mark's gospel as a gospel of secrets, see Rowan Williams, Meeting God in Mark, Ch 2, 29-50

cclvii For the youth who fled without his loin cloth, see Mark 14:51 For John Mark and his possible contribution to this gospel, see Morison, p 157

cclviii see Mark 10:1

cclix For the rich young man, see Mark 10:17-27

cclx See Gaffney, pp 152-173 for an account of what these initiatory teachings might have been.

cclxi See John, 20: 3-10 for the inclusion of this detail in his account of the resurrection.

cclxii For John's Greek, see Bissell, 198-199

cclxiii The Book of Revelation 21: 1-8

cclxiv See Rowan Williams, **Meeting God in Mark**, pp 65-74 and his observation that 'Mark…is in many respects more like John than he is like Matthew or Luke". (p 71). See also Rowan Williams, **The Resurrection,** pp 37-41 for the repeated turning of MM at the entrance to the tomb. This is the essential movement of the key between esoteric and exoteric modes of understanding.

cclxv I am indebted to Tyson for this translation, see p 335

cclxvi See John 20 1-18

cclxvii The question of visions and where they come from is the starting point of the 'Gnostic' Gospel of Mary Magdalene. For the authority they were seen to confer, see Pagels, pp 39-43

cclxviii John's gospel (21) ends with this resurrection appearance in Galilee and with the reinstating as Peter as the lead apostle. Matthew's gospel (28:16-20) also concludes in Galilee but here with a mountain top appearance which "some doubted" instead of the fishing incident used by John. Luke also includes a mountain top ascension scene but sets his in Bethany, a gesture to the importance of this location.

cclxix For this incident of the return to Jericho and the rich boy rejected by Jesus, see both Mark 10:1-29, Matthew 19:1-30, Luke 18: 9-27. John does not include this encounter but has instead the story of the raising of Lazarus. The link between these episodes occurs in Luke 16:19-31 which offers a different version of the raising of Lazarus and the problem of wealth and spiritual salvation.

This vital connection between apparently disparate subjects is made even more explicit in **The Secret Gospel of Mark**, ostensibly the first draft of the canonical gospel. This contains a strange account of the story of the raising of Lazarus as told by John. See Morton Smith, **The Secret Gospel** for his account of his own discovery of this controversial passage authenticated by Clement of Alexander in the 2nd Century AD.

For a brief, succinct but very partisan discussion of this, see Pyknett, pp 51-54

cclxx The transfiguration. See Mark 9:2-13

cclxxi For the Way of Apophatic Christianity, see J.P. Williams.

cclxxii See John 10:40 for Christ's return across the Jordan to the place of his baptism by John. This reference immediately precedes the resurrection of Lazarus in John 11: 1-44 and in **The Secret Gospel of Mark**.

cclxxiii See Tyson, p 358 for this fall from power of the men most responsible for the crucifixion.

cclxxiv See Tyson, p 303

cclxxv For the escape to Egypt, see only Matthew 2:7-23. The importance for Christianity of Egyptian culture still needs considerable elucidation. According to Morton Smith, Christ was referred to in Jewish writing as "the Egyptian magician".

cclxxvi Matthew's gospel (1 and 2 introduces a supernatural account of the birth of Christ which is expanded by Luke (1 and 2). No reference to this is found in either Mark or John.

cclxxvii See Matthew 23:25-26

cclxxviii This is a reference back to the Samaritan woman of John 4 and to the Magdalene's alabaster jar, emblematic of the spiritual womb from which the new birth of human spirituality will emerge.

cclxxix The Gospel of Philip, p 141

cclxxx Matthew 22:31-32 "But about the resurrection of the dead – have you not heard what God said to you, "I am the God of Abraham, the God of Isaac, and the God of Jacob? He is not the God of the dead but of the living."

cclxxxi This remarkable ancient site is now known as St Romans and is still worth the long walk to get to it.

cclxxxii See 1 Thessalonians 4:13-18

cclxxxiv Avignon

cclxxxv For one of the best discussions of Magdala/Magadan/Migdal Tsebaya and its association with MM, see Haag, pp 8-19. See also Pyknett for a different, and Ethiopian, location for this town. P 146-147.

cclxxxvi The Cevennes location is at Mialet, a sacred site for French Protestants who hid here to avoid religious persecution. The *châtaignier* is the emblem of their survival.

cclxxxvii A wise man like Elias Canetti, see **The Human Province,** p 70 "The attempt at keeping memories of people alive in their stead is nevertheless the greatest thing that mankind has heretofore accomplished…Keeping people alive with words -isn't that almost the same as creating them with words?"

cclxxxviii A debt to Petrarch's **Canzoniere**, no 108

cclxxxix For Philip's mission to Samaria and beyond, see Acts: 8. It is the Gnostic *Gospel of Philip* that sets MM in the place of the Beloved Disciple.

ccxc The Camargue is one legendary home of the cult of the Black Madonna and of the three Mary's who, with Sarah as their servant, landed on the coast at the village known by their name.

ccxci John 19: 25-27

[ccxcii] 1 Timothy 2: 11 "Let the woman learn in silence with all subjection."

[ccxciii] The famous beauty spot of Fontaine de Vaucluse, mysterious underground source of the River Sorgues, still retains its legendary beauty, despite the crowds in summer.

CPSIA information can be obtained
at www.ICGtesting.com
Printed in the USA
LVHW081910020321
680379LV00007B/182